Illustrations

	facing page
The Merchants' Coffee House, Liverpool	116
Bristol Stock Exchange	117
Manchester Stock Exchange	132
The Council of Associated Stock Exchanges, Windermere, October 1913	133
Birmingham Stock Exchange	292
The Dealing Room of J. W. Nicholson & Sons, Sheffield, in the mid-1930s	293
Glasgow Stock Exchange	308
Glasgow Stock Exchange: the General Market in 1907	309
Glasgow Stock Exchange: the new floor	309

Acknowledgements

I am greatly indebted to the Trustees of the Houblon-Norman Fund for a grant during the period 1967–69, which enabled me to visit all the provincial stock exchanges in England, Wales, and Scotland to consult their records. Also, I am grateful to the University of Liverpool for earlier financial assistance. To the Committees of all the stock exchanges who kindly allowed me access to their records I wish to tender my sincere thanks, and equally, to their Secretaries for giving me every facility and assistance on my visits to their exchanges, occasionally when they were hard pressed by daily duties. In particular, Mr C. G. Smith (Manchester Stock Exchange), Mr H. Rudge (Birmingham Stock Exchange), Mr F. R. Parry (Liverpool Stock Exchange), and finally Mr Arthur Owen, O.B.E. (Secretary to the Liverpool Stock Exchange, 1947–65, and the Northern Stock Exchange, 1965–72) for opening many doors to me, smoothing my path through many a problem, for reading the whole manuscript thus saving me from several technical errors, and for his unfailing generosity in all matters, big and small.

My debts also extend to the academic world. My thanks are due to Mr J. R. Killick, University of Leeds, for several hours of rewarding discussion about the workings of the provincial markets in the nineteenth century, and for his collaboration in some earlier work on the subject. Dr J. R. Porter, University of Exeter, left me in his debt by allowing me to draw on his knowledge of the cotton mills of his native Oldham. Mr P. L. Cottrell, University of Liverpool, helped in more ways than I can mention here; I am particularly grateful for his willingness to read and comment on a large part of the manuscript. Finally, Professor E. Victor Morgan, University of Manchester, once again left me greatly in his debt by giving so readily of his time to read a large part of the work and for making helpful suggestions, all of which served to improve the end product. The errors of commission and omission that remain are all my own.

Liverpool, 1972   W. A. THOMAS

Introduction

This is merely a brief word about the purpose, the arrangement, and the main sources consulted for this book.

The provincial stock exchanges have long been an area of considerable neglect in the study of the history of finance and investment. In some ways this is rather perplexing. Admittedly, they have always been dwarfed by the London Stock Exchange, but at least from 1836 onwards it was not the *only* market in the country. Those who have traced the development of the English capital market have been careful to point to the importance of provincial capital in railway promotion, yet while the role of provincial capital was emphasized, the praises of the 'vehicle' which helped to mobilize such funds went unsaid. It is difficult to see how provincial investors would have been prepared to commit so much of their capital resources for such purposes without some assurance of being able to liquidate their holdings fairly speedily, since for most of them London was at some distance. What follows then is an attempt to fill a gap—to trace the origins of the provincial investment 'vehicle' and its progress to the present day.

Provincial markets sprang up to meet local needs for investment facilities at different periods in the nineteenth century. One possibility would have been to trace their separate histories, which would have produced some dozen and a half minor monographs, an endlessly repetitive and extremely tedious result. A little of this has crept into Chapter 3 but there it seemed somewhat inevitable, while the Oldham Stock Exchange and the Scottish Stock Exchanges have been given a corner to themselves. Overall, however, an attempt has been made to seek a unity of subject matter at the expense of geographical tidiness. Some markets figure more prominently than others but this is merely a reflection of their greater size and importance.

As to the main stock exchange records consulted, the following may briefly be said; the other sources used are detailed in the footnotes. Those wishing to trace stock exchange history may avail themselves of three sets of documents; if they have survived war, fire, flood, and frequent moves to new premises. They are the minute books of the committees governing the stock exchanges (and occasionally of sub-committees), rule books, and share lists – daily, weekly, or monthly. Unfortunately the minutes are not the great repository of information one would perhaps at first expect them to be. The completeness with which proceedings were reported varied a great deal, and the worst instances make for infuriating reading. The reporting of the larger exchanges is usually much fuller than that of the smaller brethren, but towards the end of the last century even the larger markets returned to their early reticence, a trait induced by fears that someday the minutes might be required in a court case. Sadly for economic historians no one sat down periodically to chronicle the significant changes which occurred in market practices, business transacted, etc.; the minutes are understandably mainly concerned with technicalities (some of which are of interest), not description. One could not write an account of their development without the minutes, but to rely on them entirely would produce a relatively incomplete picture.

The rule books, which are few and far between as separate publications, are valuable for tracing changes in the rules governing the conduct of the markets, but all too often it is not possible to ascertain why a particular rule was introduced, or why a particular change was made. Finally, there are the share price lists. Generally, these record the business done by members, but never all of it, while they also provide a list of closing quotations for the day's dealing. They provide an indication of price changes but they do not give any information as to the quantity of stock traded. What they do readily provide is an idea of the range of shares dealt in by the various markets. If all the lists had survived then it would be possible at some pains to calculate a provincial share price index, but it would be more likely to tell more about the compiler's stamina than reveal an unsuspected profundity.

PART ONE

England and Wales

1 The Origins of the Provincial Stock Exchanges

Liverpool and Manchester

The London Stock Exchange was not formally constituted until 1802, with some 550 subscribers and 100 clerks, but the beginnings of share dealing in London go back to more than a century earlier. By the mid 1690s share dealing was taking place in a highly developed form, with brokers and jobbers engaging in time and option bargains as well as staightforward buying and selling.[1] The shares and bonds dealt in were those issued by the early trading companies established by royal charters, such as the East India Company formed in 1600, the Hudson's Bay Company of 1668 and several other colonial companies. It was estimated by W. R. Scott that there were some 140 joint stock companies in 1695 with a total capital of £4.5 million.[2] The supply of shares to the market was given a substantial, but somewhat shortlived, boost from the large number of company formations during the period of the South Sea Bubble; about 190 new companies appeared between September 1719 and August 1720, involving a total nominal capital of £220 million, but the actual capital raised was probably much less than this.[3] From the stockbroking point of view the intense public interest in speculation attracted many new entrants into the trade, but the ending of the mania with the passing of the Bubble Act in 1720 caused some of them to abandon share dealing. The Bubble Act declared that companies formed without a royal charter or act of parliament were illegal and that transactions in their shares were null and void. It was not repealed until 1825, but it is doubtful whether it seriously impeded capital formation prior to this date since the capital requirements of many industrial enterprises was obtained by partnership, loan or mortgage.

The major activity which promoted the growth of stockbroking throughout the eighteenth century was the continued increase in the size of the national debt from a mere £5 million in 1698 to

£71 million in 1749, reaching £497 million by 1800. This large debt, in the form of easily negotiable securities, provided an ideal raw material for the developing market, while stockbrokers were involved in the issue procedure as well as acting as agents and jobbers in the Funds.[4] There were also plenty of opportunities for dealing since the debt was widely held, many holders having less than £1,000 each.[5] Dealing activity was centred around the city coffee houses, the Old Stock Exchange and also the Rotunda of the Bank of England where the stock registers were kept.

At the time of the opening of the Stock Exchange in 1802 the main business of the market centred around gilt edged. Such industrial shares as existed, for example, canals, waterworks and docks were not even listed in the daily list until 1811;[6] the entire trade in shares up to the beginning of the railway investment boom of the mid 1840s was handled by "four or five brokers and a comparatively small number of jobbers".[7]

While there were a large number of gilt edged holders towards the end of the nineteenth century, they were not widely scattered geographically, being mainly located in and around London. One contemporary observer, Joseph Low, stated that "in the provincial parts of Britain, public funds were comparatively little resorted to as a deposit for private property . . . because the inhabitants are little acquainted with the security conferred on property by public register and the power of transfer".[8] Not only were the facilities unfamiliar to provincial asset holders, but they were also at a considerable distance from them. Facilities for gilt edged transfer were centralized at the Bank of England, and the method used for transferring legal title to the stock involved either the presence of the individual, or the granting of power of attorney, a device liable to misuse.

However, the few provincial holders of the public funds, and those wanting to acquire them, were not entirely without access to the London market of the period. Dealing facilities were offered to them by London stockbrokers advertising in provincial newspapers. One such stockbroker, Richardson, Goodluck & Co. stated in advertisements in Liverpool and Manchester newspapers in 1792 that he had tickets for sale in the latest state lottery, and further that "Persons in the country, favouring these offices with their commands, may depend on the most punctual attention and fidelity in every legal department of the Lottery business and Public Funds. . . . Orders sent by different stage-coachmen, carriers, etc, particularly addressed to these offices, will be as honourably transacted as if the parties themselves were present." Country correspondents would then "have tickets or shares sent to them on remitting bills of short date, country bank bills, prizes in any former lottery, or cash by the stage coaches." Another London stockbroker, Hornsby & Co. offered investment "schemes gratis" and stated that "Bank, India and South Sea Stocks, with their several Annuities, India Bonds, Navy and Victualling Bills and all Kinds of Government securities, bought and sold by Commission." An advertisement inserted by Thomas Wilkie said that he employed provincial agents in Liverpool, Exeter and Norwich through whom lottery tickets could be purchased; all three were printers and booksellers.[9]

Company promotion before the advent of the railway booms did not create the necessary conditions for the existence of a well organized market with full-time specialists. The conditions required may be summarized briefly as being a large number of securities with dispersed ownership among a wealthy investor class, together with a developed legal and banking framework to assist the process of transfer. At the beginning of the nineteenth century part of the institutional framework existed in the provinces, but the company promoting activity of the canal mania of 1791–2, and the company booms of 1807 and 1825–6, did not fulfill the remaining conditions.

Large scale canal building in Britain began in 1761 with the construction by the Duke of Bridgewater of a canal from Worsley to Manchester, a distance of eleven miles. It proved a great success in reducing the cost of transporting coal to Manchester, and it was later extended to Runcorn. However, it was largely financed by the Duke of Bridgewater. Later canal promoters adopted the joint stock form and the success of each successive project, in cutting transport costs by as much as a third and paying out 20% dividends, encouraged increasingly ambitious schemes.[10] The culminating point was reached in 1791–94 when 81 acts of parliament were passed permitting canal construction. The capital raised varied from £20,000 to over £1 million for the Grand Junction Canal, this variety reflecting differences in length and engineering problems. In general, companies with small capital tended to pay out higher dividends.[11]

Successful promotion of a canal company frequently involved a considerable amount of local support. A promoter without adequate capital enlisted the interest of prominent local citizens, and with their backing set up an investigation fund. Subscriptions to such a fund sometimes only meant that it entitled the contributor to some shares, while in other cases the subscription constituted part of the deposit. Following a favourable decision an act of incorporation was obtained which set out the share capital and its division into a specified number of shares. The deposits on shares

B

was fixed and subscription books were then opened. Frequently subscriptions were collected in the main centres along the route of the proposed canal.[12] In most cases the lists were filled quickly, particularly during the speculative mania of 1792. The opening of the subscription books for the Ellesmere canal was followed by a frenzy of applications; nearly £1 million was offered for £300,000 capital by 1,234 would-be investors, 758 of these offering £1,000 each.[13]

The majority of shareholders in canal undertakings lived in the neighbourhood of the project. In the case of the Leeds and Liverpool canal 71% of the shareholders, holding over half of the original share issue, lived in the counties of Lancashire and Yorkshire.[14] With the passage of time the extent of local shareholding obviously diminished with migration and the disposal of shares through the London market. However, most proprietors of canal shares held very few of them. In the case of the Leeds and Liverpool canal 393 of the 469 original shareholders in 1789 held five shares or less.[15] This feature of canal share ownership stemmed in many instances from provisions in the statutes prohibiting a person from holding more than a certain number of shares. Subscribers to the Manchester, Bolton and Bury canal were not allowed to "subscribe for . . . more than Five shares". Such restrictive provisions made canal shares rather unpromising material from a stockbroking standpoint, since it discouraged speculative activity in large blocks of shares. Canal share turnover was also extremely low. An examination by G. H. Evans of the share registers of the Leeds and Liverpool canal for the years 1789, 1795 and 1800 revealed that during the six years separating the first two dates 60% of the shareholders still possessed their original shares, and that over the longer period from 1789 to 1800 at least 46% of the shareholders continued to hold the original shares.[16] This degree of stability was in marked contrast to the turnover in the shares of the East India Company on the London market; in 1692 the whole of the nominal capital of the company changed hands about once every two years.[17] If the majority of canal shareholders possessed the degree of loyalty shown by those of the Leeds and Liverpool it is not surprising that canal share dealing did not induce the appearance of full time brokers in the provinces.

There is very little evidence of the extent of the canal share market during the years 1791–93. It is generally agreed that speculation in shares was excessive and that as a result many fraudulent promotions appeared on the market. The transport historian W. T. Jackman pictured the market in a state of "wild speculation and a perfect ferment about canal shares", and was of the opinion that the success of the early canals and the willingness of the public to take up shares led to the appearance of "schemes of all kinds". Promoters "were anxious to cause the prices of the shares of their projected canals even before the work of construction had begun, to rise to an unduly high figure; and then they would unload their stocks upon unsuspecting purchasers so as to net a great profit."[18] In London such speculative activity was presumably centred on the Coffee Houses and the Old Stock Exchange. Some of this enthusiasm seems to have rubbed off on the provinces; the canal share market in Liverpool in 1792 was described by Thomas Baines in his *History of Liverpool* as resembling the railway share market in 1845. He cites an auction of canal shares, which was probably the main method of marketing used in the provinces at this date, which occurred in October 1792 at which the prices of shares in the Trent Navigation reached £183 15s each (issued at £50 in 1777). Those of the River Soar Navigation sold for £803 5s, while shares in the Erewash canal, issued at par, reached £674 2s.[19] However, the local press for the period contains little to support Baines' report.

It can be seen from the values quoted above that canal shares were rather large and sometimes of curious denominations. They ranged from £3 10s. 0d. to £250 in value at the time of issue, but most were £100 shares. In addition they displayed some very odd sums, such as the Loughborough canal shares issued at £142 7s. 6d, the Huddersfield canal at £57 6s. 8d, and the Birmingham canal issued at £79 5s.[20] Such odd values and large denominations were not particularly suitable for general sharedealing activity, and they were certainly unlikely to enlist the interest of those with modest savings. It would appear that as a result of the amount of capital involved, the ownership pattern and investment behaviour, and the nature of canal shares, that canal promotion did not provide a sufficient volume of share turnover to sustain provincial stockbroking activity. With the ending of the 1792 mania canal share dealing centred on London and up until 1831 there was a considerable volume of trading, but afterwards stock market interest switched to the growing railway market.[21]

The remaining activity in company promotion prior to the railway period did little to induce the appearance of country specialists. The first period of speculative company promotion was the short lived boom of 1807–8, when some 40 companies were set up, among them five insurance, seven brewery and four distillery companies. When two of these newly formed companies were prosecuted for claiming that shareholders liability was limited by trust deed, widespread alarm among promoters and investors resulted in most of them folding up.[22] The second period occurred in 1824–5 following upon low interest rates and general monetary ease, but the initial company promotion was mainly in foreign mines and foreign loans. Domestic company promotion followed on the sensational success achieved by Barry's and Rothschilds in floating the Alliance Insurance Co. Parliament was besieged by private bills, some 250 in the first quarter of 1824. A mere application for a bill tended to drive shares to a premium, and speculation was encouraged by the smallness of the initial instalments. The boom reached its peak in December 1824 and January 1825, and the government, unable to sort out the good from the bad companies, compromised by repealing the Bubble Act.[23] The repeal implied that there was no longer anything illegal about the formation of an unincorporated company, or in dealing in its shares.

The extent of the boom was accurately traced by an industrious and observant London stockbroker, Henry English, who found that 624 company prospectuses had appeared, involving a total capital of £372 million. Within this total, foreign investment companies accounted for £52 million, canal, railroads etc., £44 million, mining companies (mainly South American) £38 million, and insurance companies £35 million. However, after the 1825 crash which was induced by restrictive monetary measures, most of these enterprises folded up; only 127 of the companies projected in 1824–5 survived, and of their authorized capital of £102 million only £15 million was paid up, with a market value of £9 million. A further 118 companies were abandoned after £2.4 million had been advanced on their shares; the rest did not even get that far.[24] English's calculations were based on London company promotion and excluded "many provincial companies, and others founded in Scotland and Ireland."[25] Unfortunately, the provinces did not produce an equally meticulous observer.

In addition to his observations on 'boom' companies Henry English calculated that 124 companies had been formed prior to 1824 and were still in existence in 1827. They had a nominal capital of nearly £50 million, with £34 million paid up on 764,534 shares. The main groups within the total were 63 canals with £12 million paid up, 25 insurance companies with £6.5 million paid up out of £20.4 million nominal capital, 16 waterworks with £2.9 million paid up, and 27 gas companies with a paid up capital of £1.2 million.[26] He notes that these were formed because "individual capital could not be supposed to be adequate for the completion of the object for which the Company was formed".

As far as can be discerned from the fragmentary evidence available company promotion in the provinces between the canal and the railway periods centred mainly around waterworks and gas companies. During the early nineteenth century urban water supplies were provided by private companies, in contrast to the previous municipal monopolies. The changeover, sanctioned by parliament, was designed to improve the service and reduce water rates. By 1818 London's water supply was provided by several private water companies, with capitals ranging from £80,000 in the case of the Vauxhall Water Works, to £528,000 for the West Middlesex. They were sufficiently well organized to implement market sharing agreements in order to maintain profit levels, with the result that by the 1830s their shares had attained the status of debentures.[27] In Liverpool, water supply was undertaken by two companies, the Liverpool and Harrington Waterworks and the Bootle Waterworks, and their shares were certainly dealt in locally during the late 1820s. Manchester also had its own company, the Manchester and Salford, whose shares were widely held and quoted in London.[28] Numerous water companies were created throughout the country following rapid urbanization, but in most instances the capital involved was probably small.

The provision of gas lighting during this period was another amenity which required capital subscription from the public. The first London coal gas company obtained its act of incorporation in 1810, and after 1820 gas light companies sprang up throughout the country; the total capital investment involved by 1826 has been estimated at £3.1 million.[29] The Liverpool Coal Gas Light Company was formed in 1816 with a capital of 200 shares of £30 each and any "additions a general meeting may decide upon", but no individual was "to hold more than 20 shares", and its act of incorporation was obtained in 1818. Its rival, the Liverpool Oil Gas Company was formed a few years later with a capital of £30,000 in £100 shares and both companies were well supported by local subscribers.[30] The older company seems to have enjoyed greater success than its competitor, judging by the subsequent changes in market share values. From £380 in 1830 the Coal Gas Company's shares increased to £455 by 1833, while those of its rival fell £2 from the £124 of 1830. Rather surprisingly Manchester's Gas Works at this period was a municipal affair. The shares of the provincial gas companies were "but little known in the London market" of the period.[31]

Other local investment opportunities featured in the advertisements of share auctions which regularly appeared in the Liverpool newspapers after about 1827. At this time, it was quite usual to dispose of shares at general property auctions. At one such sale in Liverpool in 1829 two shares in the Liverpool Gas Company, two shares in the Londonderry Steam Packet Company, ten shares in the

Imperial Life Assurance Company (which was quoted in London), together with one share each in the Atheneaum, the Liverpool Library, the Royal Institution and the Botanic Garden, were offered, illustrating the equity element of the portfolio, and the social standing of the deceased.[32] Thomas Coglan, later a founder member of the Stock Exchange was probably one of the earliest Liverpool auctioneers to undertake auctions exclusively in shares. In 1827 he held "at the George Inn", a sale of Steam Packet Shares which included "one share in the Londonderry and one share in the George the Fourth Steam Packets; shares in the Dublin and London Steam Marine Company; . . . Shares in the . . . St George, the Lord Blagney, the St Patrick, the Edipol, the St David, the Lee and the Severn Steam Packets", and a remnant from his general auctioneering days, "a few shares in the Scotch Kirk".[33] At a subsequent sale in January 1828 he sold, in addition to steam packet shares, those of the West of Scotland Assurance Company, the Birmingham Waterworks, and also shares in several "well known Flintshire mines". At this time he described himself as a Commission Agent and Broker, but by the end of 1828 he claimed to be a full time "Sharebroker"; he stated in his advertisements that he was prepared to buy and sell "shares in the different Public Establishments" at his office in Exchange Street East. It seems therefore, that he made the transition from a one-way type of market to a more satisfactory two-way market, that is, acting as a dealer, in a short space of time, and before railway shares became popular in Liverpool.

Coglan was not alone in share dealing activities. One T. Winstanley & Son was also holding share auctions in 1829. Harmood Banner, an accountant, was another, while "Mr Percival Broker and Commission agent" stated in 1831 that he bought and sold shares "in all the Joint Stock Companies", and possibly in order to add a degree of sophistication through the use of time bargains he was prepared to lend "£15,000 in one or more sums on approved security."[34]

With the growing interest in railway companies after the successful opening of the Liverpool and Manchester line in 1830, the activities of the emerging stockbrokers centred increasingly on railway shares. Coglan by this time was advertising that he had "for sale on reasonable terms shares in the Liverpool and Manchester Railway, and in various other Railway Companies"; presumably Coglan had been stagging some of these shares. By 1831 Percival seems to have attracted an investing clientele since his advertisements indicate that he was looking for stock "at best Marketable Price", while some of his sales seem to be loss cutters, being done at "under the market price".[35]

The first detailed share list for the Liverpool market is to be found in the *Liverpool Mercury* of March 12 1830 and is headed "Prices of shares" with the following preamble; "As very inaccurate quotations respecting the Price of Railroad Shares, Canal Shares, etc., are frequently being published it is our intention to give weekly, such as can be implicitly depended upon". Presumably this list came from Thomas Coglan, although his name was not appended to it until later. It comprised the following stocks and prices.

Liverpool Coal Gas	£380	per share
Liverpool Oil Gas	124	" "
Liverpool and Harrington Water Works	410	" ".
Bootle Waterworks	260	" "
Liverpool and Manchester Railway	65	premium
Bolton and Leigh Railway	25	premium
Warrington and Newton Railway	12	10s "
Wigan Branch	15	"
Mersey and Irwell Canal	700	per share
Leeds and Liverpool Canal	450	" "
Rochdale Canal	85	" "

By 1833 the list had doubled in size, with the addition of seven railways and the shares of the Bank of Manchester, formed in 1829, and the Bank of Liverpool, formed in 1831.

From 1834 onwards, the pace of company promotion in general increased considerably throughout the whole country, culminating in the boom promotions of 1836. These were induced by the general improvement in trade after 1833, especially trade with the United States. In addition, the flow of capital in the direction of foreign speculations had been greatly reduced after the crash in 1835, which involved Spanish investments. This coupled with a downward movement in discount rates, which reached their low point in the spring of 1836, provided a strong financial incentive for participating in domestic company formation.[36] The main sphere of such activity was railways' although the formation of joint stock banks followed closely behind, together with a miscellaneous selection of other financial institutions. Parliament, of course, was quite accustomed to such rushes of company promotion, even in railways. During the 1825 boom it had sanctioned nineteen new lines most of which perished in the crisis. Thereafter, about five new railways received parliamentary sanction each year until 1836, when 29 were sanctioned with 17 in 1837. It has been calculated on the basis of 194 prospectuses issued in 1835 and which were listed by the Select Committee on Joint Stock Companies of 1844, that the nominal capital involved was £70 million for railways, £32 million for banks etc., £7 million for mines, and £26 million for other concerns.[37]

The excesses of the promotion boom were authoritatively described by Poullet Thomson, President of the Board of Trade, in the
following passage taken from his speech in the Budget debate of
May 6 1836.

"I felt it my duty, some time ago, to direct a register to be
kept, taking the names merely from the London and a few
country newspapers, of the different joint stock companies,
and of the nominal capital proposed to be embarked in them.
The nominal capital to be raised by subscriptions amounts to
nearly £200,000,000 and the number of companies is between
300 and 400. I am just now reminded of the speculation for
making beet-root sugar, but that is a sound speculation compared with some in my list. The first is the British Agricultural Loan Company, with a capital of £2,000,000. . . . Another
company is proposed for supplying pure spring water, capital
£300,000 . . . and, again, to show the way in which these
companies are starting up, for objects either of the most absurd
kind, or for objects such as private individuals are perfectly
able to accomplish. I find the Liverpool British and Foreign
Trading Company, capital £250,000. Now, it is perfectly well
known, that it is not at all an unusual thing for an individual
in Liverpool to embark £250,000 in foreign trade; and there
are many who have a great deal more engaged in that business.
I know that these companies have not their origin only in
London. In 1825, London was the great centre of speculation;
but I am afraid that these companies have now their origin
in other parts of the country. . . . I fear that the place I
represent (Manchester) can . . . furnish instances of schemes
for objects which can never be beneficial to anyone, and on
which the parties will be throwing away their money. The
fact is, that the greater part of these companies are got up
by speculators for the purpose of selling their shares. They
bring up their shares to a premium, and then sell them, leaving
the unfortunate purchasers, who are foolish enough to vest
their money in them, to shift for themselves."[38]

In Liverpool the boom was particularly evident; Sir Robert
Peel claimed in the same Budget debate that he could not pick up
some Liverpool newspapers "without witnessing a rage for the
formation of joint stock companies". He had seen prospectuses in
one Liverpool newspaper of schemes which completely astonished
him "proceeding as they did from a place so eminent in the commercial world, so noted for the astuteness of its inhabitants, especially that class who there carry on commercial affairs".[39] One

estimate of the number of companies formed in Liverpool between January and April 1836 put the total at 39 with a nominal capital of £5,387,500, but this level was quickly surpassed in the "mania" months of April to June.[40] In the columns of the *Liverpool Mercury*, presumably the paper referred to by Sir Robert Peel, some 60 prospectuses appeared between April 15 and June 1, involving a nominal capital of nearly £6.0 million in April, £15.0 million in May and £0.5 million in June.[41] Most of the companies were similar in nature to the speculative adventures condemned by Poullett Thomson.

The boom in joint stock banks deserves further comment. Up until the passing of the Banking Copartnership Act of 1826 (7 Geo. IV. c.46) country note issuing banks took the form of partnerships of up to six persons. The only corporation with note issuing powers was the Bank of England. Small banking partnerships however were liable to frequent failure and after the 1826 crisis, which emphasized their vulnerability, note issuing joint stock banks were allowed outside a radius of 65 miles from London. A declaratory clause in the Bank Charter Act of 1833 (3&4 William IV.c.98) indicated that joint stock banks were legal within the specified radius, but without note issuing facilities. However, the Act also indicated that the members of a banking company would not have limited liability, and this protection was not given until the Companies Act of 1879. Between 1826 and 1833 28 joint stock banks were set up, but after 1833 the pace quickened reaching a peak in the 1836 boom when 59 banks were promoted some of which were merely the customary bubble companies characteristic of such speculative periods. The record figure of promotions for 1836 was induced by the low rates of discount ruling at the time, by the quite good dividend records of the early joint stock banks (see Table p.16) and by the opportunity now afforded of challenging the established bankers, since capital resources became a function of numbers and not of individual wealth.

Even after the 1833 amendment, it was in the country that joint stock bank formation was most active, and particularly in Lancashire. London with its large population of private bankers was particularly hostile to the new banks, and the common cause they organized against them compelled the London and Westminster Bank to go to the provinces to obtain its £50,000 of paid up capital.[42] The joint stock banks were very much local banks with "a large proprietary who contributed capital adequate to the wants of the district in which the bank is located".[43] Certainly, the proprietary was large, for example, the Bank of Manchester had 600 proprietors, the Manchester and Liverpool District Bank (later

the District Bank) had over 1,000 shareholders, and the Bank of
Liverpool had 400 shareholders. The local origin of the capital is
indicated by the ownership of the Bank of Liverpool since half its
shares were held in Liverpool, about a third in Manchester, and
the rest elsewhere.[44]

The methods used to promote joint stock banks were similar
to those of other corporate ventures. A provisional committee was
formed, usually consisting of powerful local interests, and the
prospectus contained the usual invitation to apply for shares. In
some instances, applications were made directly to the temporary
offices of the new bank, but more commonly, they were received by
stockbrokers acting as agents for the company. In Liverpool,
Thomas Coglan, Richard Dawson, J. Bach and Samuel R. Healey
were active as agents, while the Manchester brokers Thomas
Cardwell, David Holt and E. H. Levyssohn displayed similar
industry. During the early years of bank promotion the share
allocation was done by a company official, but later this task was
sometimes left to the broker. This was a particularly vital aspect
of promotion since most banks deliberately allotted shares to
persons who would bring business to the banks by attracting new
depositors or persuading others to transfer accounts from established private banks. Some bank officials however did not display
equal zeal in the matter of getting shareholders to sign the Deed
of Settlement. This omission tended to lead to difficulties since such
shareholders could not be held responsible for liabilities, and neither
could they be compelled to meet calls for additional capital. Even
"respectable" persons were a little hesitant in meeting that particular commitment.

The accompanying table of the joint stock banks quoted on the
Liverpool Stock Exchange in 1836 illustrates the main features of
bank capital and share values for the period. The nominal capital
ranged from £400,000 to £5 million, but there was usually a large
margin of uncalled capital. For example, the Bank of Liverpool
called up 10% of £3 million, the Manchester and Liverpool District
Bank 15% of £5 million and the Bank of Manchester 25% of £2
million. A large reserve of uncalled capital was advocated by
leading joint stockbankers as a display of solidarity, but frequently
all it did was give a false impression of strength which resulted
in dangerous speculation in the shares of the bank.[45] A further
practice, even among respectable banks, was to reserve shares for
disposal by the directors, for example, 25,000 in the Bank of Liverpool were kept back for this purpose; it did of course support the
issue since a large block of shares were kept off the market. In
addition, it provided means of obtaining additional capital for bank

JOINT STOCK BANKS QUOTED ON THE LIVERPOOL STOCK EXCHANGE — AUGUST, 1836

	Date of Formation	Nominal Capital	Paid up Capital	Nominal Share value	Paid up value	Market Price	Dividend %
Bank of Liverpool	1831	3,000,000	300,000	100	10	25¼	8
Commercial Bank of Liverpool	1833	500,000	500,000	10	10	20¼	6½
Liverpool Union Bank	1835	600,000	300,000	20	10	17⅛	–
Royal Bank of Liverpool	1836	2,000,000	210,000	1,000	105	–	–
Northern and Central Bank	1834	711,860	711,860	10	10	15⅜	–
Liverpool Tradesman Bank	1836	–	–	–	5	5⅝	–
Liverpool United Trades Bank	1836	400,000	120,000	20	6	8⅜	–
North and South Wales Bank	1836	600,000	150,000	10	2½	2¼	7
Bank of Manchester	1829	2,000,000	500,000	100	25	–	–
Manchester and Liverpool District Bank	1829	5,000,000	750,000	100	15	22½	7½
South Lancashire Bank	1836	–	–	–	5	–	–
Liverpool Borough Bank	1836	–	–	–	5	13	–
Commercial Bank of England	1834	500,000	250,000	5	5	5½	6
Wilts and District Bank	1835	300,000	100,000	15	5	–	5
East of England Bank	1836	1,000,000	250,000	20	5	5	5

Sources: Liverpool Stock Exchange share lists, and C. Fenn, *A Compendium of the English and Foreign Funds*, (1838).

expansion, and frequently the shares were used by directors as bait for new clients who coveted such allocations when shares stood at high premiums in the market. Naturally, certain abuses appeared, such as trafficking in reserved shares for the sake of the premium, while the unloading of large blocks of shares lead to sharp fluctuations in prices. On the whole the best concerns tended to minimize such activity by placing restrictions on the sale of shares.[46]

The nominal values employed also tended to vary reflecting the diversity of contemporary opinion on this point. High nominal values, £1,000 in the case of the Royal Bank of Liverpool, were supposed to appeal to a more elevated clientele, but lower values certainly predominated in the boom period of 1836. Even where high nominal values were used, they were little more than prestige symbols since the paid up element was seldom over 10%. There were, of course, obvious dangers in holding such shares for speculative purposes. Shares of low nominal values certainly appealed to a larger investing public and provided an enlarged source of capital for bank expansion and the wider dispersal of ownership thereby induced greater share turnover.

Viewed from the stockbroking standpoint the promotion boom was far more favourable than any previous activity in share dealing. In the first place, the share denominations appearing on the market were much smaller and this increased the attraction for investors with small sums of money. Many large issues resorted to £50 shares, but those below £200,000 frequently issued £10 and £5 share units. Most of the railway companies incorporated in 1836 had share units of £50 and £20 falling to £10 in the 1840s, whereas prior to this the majority issued £100 shares. It was therefore fairly easy to deal in round marketable lots. In the second place, the deposit required on an application for shares was frequently only a small proportion of the nominal value. This undoubtedly helped to encourage many of the "Ladies and clergymen" class to engage in speculative activities. Unfortunately there are no details as to the composition of the new investor class, but contemporary commentators portray a greatly widened interest among the lower income groups. In all probability, the stockbroking trade would not have increased so rapidly without a large injection of new investors into the market, since the potential expansion from the traditional monied interest would have been inadequate to sustain the share boom.

The rising prices of railway shares between 1834 and 1836, together with the increase in turnover, attracted a growing number of persons into the stockbroking trade in Liverpool. On the evidence of *Gore's Directory* for 1834 there were about half a dozen full time dealers in shares, and they probably met for dealing on the

"Flags" of the Exchange Buildings or in local coffee houses. Over the next two years the numbers increased steadily, and when the railway share market was at its peak in April 1836, twenty-one sharebrokers met at the "Mersey Coffee House on April 8" and "formed themselves into a body to be called the Liverpool Sharebrokers' Association". Richard Dawson was elected chairman, and William Reynolds to the post of Honorary Secretary. Little else was done at this initial meeting except suggest that new members should be elected by ballot at monthly meetings, and that "one blackball in five shall exclude a candidate".[47]

The leading movers in the establishment of the Association were probably the nine sharebrokers given in the 1835 Liverpool Directory. Richard Dawson entered the stockbroking profession in 1827 having been a "gunpowder agent" and one time agent to the Norwich Union Fire and Life office. Thomas Barber, Thomas Harris and Thomas Read became brokers in 1834, John Fletcher in 1835, as also did Jonathon Flounders who gave up his previous profession of being a "Gentleman". Joseph King described as an accountant in 1825 took to sharedealing around 1827, as did William O'Kill, also an accountant. Thomas Coglan was certainly active in sharedealing in 1827 and was also the proprietor of the Floating Bath in the Mersey. In addition to the twenty-one at the first meeting, ten new members joined in April, and a further fifteen during the remaining months of 1836. They were attracted to the market from diverse activities, accountants and insurance agents being well represented along with general merchants, a few cotton brokers, shipbrokers and a few oddities such as "notary and translator", a customs and excise agent, an importer of Havanna cigars, and an attorney, Owen Tudor, later to become secretary of the Association.[48] Some of them probably did not entirely abandon their previous occupations on entering into share broking activity.

At subsequent meetings held at the Mersey Coffee House and "Mr King's office" the admission fee was fixed at 10gns and a Committee for General Purposes of five members, later increased to seven, was elected. It was instructed to "frame certain Rules and Regulations for the adoption of the Association" and these were submitted and approved on July 8. The early rules dealt with membership and admission, committee election and procedure, hours of opening, commission scales, quotation of prices, settlement of disputes and defaulters, and were signed by thirty-seven members.[49] (At the same date the Association moved into a suite of offices in Exchange Street West.)

The reasons underlying this move by the brokers to establish a formal market are not reported in the contemporary minutes, but several reasons suggest themselves. A centralized location certainly increased the ease and convenience of dealing and also of settlement, and it might have been thought desirable to protect the business of existing brokers by attempting to limit entry into the trade; although operating outside the formal market involved some minor handicaps it did not however restrict the growth of outside brokers. A more important reason perhaps is that the creation of a formal market with commission rules greatly limited the appearance on the market of individual investors aiming to avoid commission. They could only avoid payment of commission by becoming members, but conditional entry tended to discourage commission evasion on a large scale. It might be of course that they simply wished to emulate London.

During the years 1837 to 1841 the Association took in twenty-six new members, giving a total membership by 1841 of forty-one. However, the Association did not include all the brokers in Liverpool and a sizeable group remained outside it until 1844. It is possible that the origins of this outside group go back to 1836, since some two weeks after the Association was formed the proprietors of the Clarendon Rooms were prepared to provide a room for dealing between three and five each day, provided twenty "Gentlemen" came forward with a subscription of one guinea per annum. Whether or not this was successful is not known.[50] The reasons for their successful existence outside the Association are probably twofold. In the first place, although "None but Members of the Association shall, under any pretext whatsoever, be admitted into the Stock Exchange", strangers were continually found in the immediate vicinity of the market.[51] The rules however did not prevent members from supplying prices to outside brokers, the only restriction being that they should not supply prices to the newspapers, as this was done by the Secretary. It was therefore relatively easy to deal outside the market on the basis of up to date prices. In the second place, outside brokers objected to certain rules and procedures which the Association adopted. They disliked the use of a ballot vote for the election of new members, and preferred an open vote. Also, they disapproved of the creation of a permanent fund financed out of the entrance fee.[52] It is also possible that many of the newer entrants into the stockbroking trade found it difficult to comply with the new rule introduced by the Association in February 1841 whereby two sureties of £250 each, or a deposit of £500 in cash or securities, was required.[53]

On October 22 1842 the majority of outside brokers met at the office of Henry Davies & Co., "the approach of the Winter having induced the Share Brokers not members of the Sharebrokers'

Association to desire some alleviation of the inconvenience and discomfort arising from not having a place of meeting especially after the closing of the Exchange News Room at 4 o'clock". At this meeting Henry Davies & Co. offered a "commodious counting room" for the use of all the sharebrokers as temporary accommo- dation for a month's trial, and this was accepted. Business was to commence on October 24, with dealing taking place daily at half past ten, at 1 o'clock and 4 o'clock. At the end of the month they decided that the new market should be put on a permanent basis, and accordingly they set up a fund to meet necessary expenses with a subscription of two guineas, and in addition they obtained two rooms in the basement floor of the Royal Bank Buildings. Of the sixteen brokers present at the first meeting six were members of the rival organization. The membership increased to thirty-three by the end of 1843, and it is worth noting that only two of the members had been refused membership of the rival association.[54]

Applications for membership were submitted to the newly elected Chairman, John Hall, along with "two letters of recommendation", and the matter was then put before a general meeting of the sub- scribers. The members do not seem to have been in complete agreement as to whether they should deal on a cash or account basis. In January 1843 about a third of the membership decided in favour of adopting "the principle of dealing for the account and having two settling days in every month at intervals of 14 or 15 days".[55] Accordingly, rules were drawn up governing account dealings, and those using the system were required to sign them. It was not until June 1843 that the subscribers issued general rules and regulations for what they called the "Liverpool New Stock Exchange". The preamble stated that "This Association shall con- sist of Brokers of, and Jobbers and Dealers in, stocks of the Govern- ment of the United Kingdom of Great Britain and Ireland, Foreign Stock, stock of Public Companies, and Shares in Public Companies and Undertakings; but no person shall be a member of this Asso- ciation, whose place of business is not in Liverpool". In terms of content and coverage their rules were very similar to those used by the rival organization, while the New Stock Exchange opened at the same dealing times and used the same scale of commissions.[56] Unfortunately, there is no means of assessing the volume of business done on the New Stock Exchange, or whether it constituted a serious threat to the other market. They appeared to deal on a scale sufficient to warrant an account system, but it is doubtful if the volume of business done was detrimental to the other associ- ation since the railway share market was rapidly expanding during this period.

By 1843 they were sufficiently confident to discuss building a permanent stock exchange, but the response merely "extended to the letting of a shed in Sweeting Street". Instead, they rented two rooms (from the Royal Bank) on the east side of Sweeting Street at an annual rental of £60 p.a. However, by the autumn of 1843 there appeared to be a considerable divergence of opinion among the forty-seven subscribers as to the appropriate procedure for electing new members. One faction wanted to abolish election formalities since they constituted a slavish imitation of the procedures used by the other association, and out of the dispute there arose a proposal "that the existence of Two Share Broking Associations is a disadvantage to our individual Interests and that it would be desirable to unite the two bodies".[57] A few days later the old Stock Exchange passed a similar resolution which proposed that "the rules regulating the admission of members by Ballot be suspended for one month, in order to allow the admission of all Brokers, who are at present Members of the New Association or who may be elected at their next monthly meeting".[58] A deputation of three members from each exchange met later in the year to discuss the obstacles to amalgamation. The delegates from the New Stock Exchange felt that there were still rules operating in the Old Room to which "their Body cannot accede". The other side held that they had already made large concessions, but they were prepared to ask the Old Room to look again at some of the rules. At a subsequent meeting the points of disagreement were reduced to those of voting procedures and the retention of the permanent fund. The matter was put to a vote at a joint meeting of the two Associations at the Royal Bank Buildings in January 1844, when it was resolved that an open vote would be used, except for the election of new members and the Committee, and it was also decided to retain the fund. To govern the enlarged association a Committee for General Purposes of ten members was elected with John Hall, from the New Stock Exchange, as chairman, and Owen Tudor as Secretary.[59]

In addition to the nineteen brokers who joined from the New Stock Exchange, there were thirty-two other new entrants in 1844, which resulted in a doubling of the size of the Exchange. With increasing activity in railway promotion, and rising share prices, the intake of new members increased to eighty-four in 1845, thirty-five of whom joined in March, and a further intake of thirty-four in 1846. Of the one hundred and fifty members admitted during the period 1844–46 only seventy-six had previous occupations listed in *Gore's Liverpool Directory*. Of these, thirty-six were general merchants, three were book-keepers, four were already stockbrokers operating outside the Stock Exchange, and five were classified as

"Gentlemen". The remainder had rather varied occupations; a member of the famous Brown family, George Alexander Brown who joined the Stock Exchange in February 1845, noted in his diary, "the Share business was one I embraced from necessity and followed with disgust, the parties you associated with being mostly broken down Tradesmen or reckless gamblers . . . there are however honourable exceptions". Thus by the end of 1846 the membership of the Stock Exchange reached two hundred and twenty. However, many of these joined not in order to act as agents to the public, or indeed as market dealers, but simply to conduct their own share speculations on a commission-free basis

Many of the new entrants did not stay for long. This was partly because they joined without means or experience, and partly because the fall of market prices from the peak of July 1845 removed all prospects of quick capital gains. During 1849–50, twenty-seven members resigned from the Stock Exchange, five of them because they had not even bothered, or could not, pay the annual subscription. Most of them were people who had come into the Stock Exchange during the speculative years of 1845–6, and no doubt many others who had joined with highly inflated expectations, ended up doing very little trading.[60]

In Manchester, the beginning of specialist brokers dates from the same period as in Liverpool. In 1827 one Thomas Langston, an agent of the Guardian Assurance office and later a founder member of the Stock Exchange, regularly advertised in the local press to the effect that he was prepared to buy and sell canal shares on a considerable scale. The contents of the advertisements indicate that he had already assumed the role of a dealer, and was not merely an auctioneer of shares.[61] Later his buying and selling lists lengthened to take in the increasing number of railway shares appearing on the market. He seems to have been a person of considerable means with "£40,000 to advance on approved security". Other people soon followed him into stockbroking. In 1828 William Gibson became a "canal and sharebroker" in addition to his other occupations of "Accountant . . . agent to the Eagle, Colonial and Birmingham Assurance offices, and to the Savings Banks, and Commissioner for taking special bail in all the Courts". Four years later Charles James Julott and Thomas Leeds and Son appear as sharebrokers in the Manchester Directory.

By 1836 the number of sharebrokers listed in the Directory increased to twenty-three. Of those who entered the trade after 1832 four were insurance office agents, while the remainder were accountants, general agents, a collector of rates, cotton dealer, brewer, merchant, and quite a few of them had no record of any commercial

C

experience whatsoever. Dealing in shares during the early months of 1836 was probably conducted in the vicinity of the Exchange buildings. The precise location is a little uncertain; one account states that they met in a "hostelry" adjacent to the then existing Cotton Exchange, while another puts it around St Anne's Church. Brokers also widened their market by placing frequent advertisements in the local press indicating their willingness to buy and sell various shares. Railways shares dominated the market, along with bank shares, and canal shares occasionally appeared in the lists. In addition shares in a few local companies were also dealt in, for example, Manchester Assurance, Ashton Water Works, Oldham Gas Works, Rusholme Burial Ground, Manchester Public Baths, the Manchester Necropolis, and the Manchester and Salford Waterworks, also quoted on the London Stock Exchange. A large number of local companies had also been formed during the boom in company promotion in 1835–6, and one estimate put the number of Manchester companies at twenty-three, with a total nominal capital of £4.6 million; no doubt the paid up capital was much less than this. Also in terms of share turnover these companies were of negligible importance when compared with the rapidly expanding railway share market, which was the real basis of the increase in the number of sharedealers.[62]

On May 12 1836, when railway share prices were at their highest levels, seven Manchester stockbrokers met at the offices of J. Railton & Son and resolved "that it is desirable that an Association of Brokers be forthwith, and is hereby established". Such a move would ensure "the better and more efficient conduct and management of the business of Stock and Share brokers and Share dealers within Manchester". A sub-committee was set up consisting of J. Railton, Thomas Langston and Edward H. Levyssohn to "consider and report upon the arrangements necessary to be made . . . and to make enquiries for a suitable room, in the neighbourhood of the Exchange". A subsequent meeting was arranged and thirteen other brokers were invited to attend.[63] However, in August, the sub-committee was still searching for suitable premises, but eventually rooms were offered by the Committee of the Exchange buildings at a weekly rental of 30s. and the Stock Exchange was opened on Monday November 7.[64]

The sub-committee was also authorized to draw up rules for the "government of this association" which were adopted in October 1836. A Committee for General Purposes was duly elected, consisting of Cardwell, Langston, Duncroft, John Railton as Chairman, and Levyssohn as secretary. Between November 1836 and March 1839 sixteen new members were elected, paying a subscription of 3 gns, each applicant being proposed by two members. By 1839, therefore, the Stock Exchange had a total membership of twenty-three.

At a general meeting of the Association held on November 4 1839, with only fifteen present, it was decided to dissolve the Association. Later on the same day another meeting took place and a ballot was held to elect a provisional committee of four who were empowered to receive applications for admission to a new association. At a subsequent meeting two days later, the provisional Committee "resigned their powers into the hands" of five members they had themselves admitted, and this new committee proceeded to admit a further ten members. During the next four years some thirty members were elected to the Association. By 1846 the total membership was eighty-nine, but dropped to eighty within three years, a fall which was presumably associated with the decline of the railway share market.

Unfortunately, the minutes of the Committee for General Purposes for this period are very brief and incomplete. The sudden dissolution and re-formation of the Association, and the election of a new committee which differed somewhat in composition from the previous one, suggests that there was some dissension between various groups within the Exchange. It is only possible to speculate as to the causes; whether it was a difference of outlook as to the government of the Exchange, or merely a clash of personalities, the minutes provide no clues. But it is interesting to note that Thomas Langston, who had been a founder member in 1836, did not seek readmission until June 1840, while Charles James Julott, who had been a sharebroker since 1832, did not enter the Stock Exchange until April 1842. Presumably, they found that dealing facilities outside the Stock Exchange suited their needs.

Outside brokers in Manchester, of whom there were about fifty in 1845, were not so well organized as their Liverpool counterparts. Even so their existence and operations caused sufficient concern to the Committee of the Stock Exchange for it to pass a rule in August 1845 restricting members of the Association "from doing business at any time on the Commercial Exchange at Manchester, with each other, or with Brokers who are not members of the Stock Exchange".[65] In 1846, a number of the outside brokers sought admission to the Stock Exchange and successfully "underwent the ordeal of the Ballot". A few, however, were not so lucky. A hard core of brokers remained outside the Stock Exchange and their continued existence caused some concern to the organized market. In 1848 members complained to the Committee that certain parties within the Stock Exchange were buying and selling shares for outside brokers at rates below those fixed by the Committee.[66]

The continued depression of the share market in 1849, and the persistence of outside competition, induced a large majority of members to submit a memorial to the Committee directing attention "to the practice of buying and selling shares in the Electric Telegraph Company Room with Brokers not members of the Association, as one which is likely to interfere seriously with its business". The Committee responded by requiring all members to sign a declaration stating that they would not do business with non-members except on a regular half commission basis. Frequent evasions of the rule however undermined its effectiveness and a year later it was rescinded following a petition from a majority of the members.

No doubt members of the Stock Exchange found it difficult after the ending of boom conditions to ignore persistent outside competition, but they were possibly a little too nervous about it. With the large jump in its membership in 1846 the Stock Exchange was by far the largest share market in terms of membership, and probably of turnover. Some members of course might have been tempted to deal outside by a better price, or possibly because it was a cash market. Another factor reducing the degree of competition was that with depressed share markets in the late 1840s many brokers retired from that activity. By 1850 the Stock Exchange was certainly the most important market, and ample testimony to its status was the fact that in October of that year a deputation consisting of Mr Warner and Mr Armitage from the Cash Stock Exchange requested the Committee to consider an amalgamation in order to achieve "a concentration of the business of both institutions". The Committee resolved to suspend its ballot procedures and invited members of the Cash Stock Exchange to seek admission.[67]

NOTES

1 E. V. Morgan and W. A. Thomas, *The Stock Exchange: Its History and Functions* (1962), pp. 20-21. Separation of functions between jobber and broker was only beginning to appear at this time.
2 W. R. Scott, *The Constitution of English, Scottish and Irish Joint Stock Companies to 1720* (1912), Vol. I., pp. 335-36.
3 Scott, op. cit., Vol. III., pp. 445-58.
4 Morgan and Thomas, op. cit., p. 46.
5 Ibid., p. 52.
6 Ibid., p. 102.
7 E. T. Powell, *The Evolution of the Money Market 1385-1915* (1915), p. 535.
8 Quoted by A. D. Gayer, W. W. Rostow, and A. J. Schwarz, *The Growth and Fluctuation of the British Economy 1790-1850* (1953), Vol. I. pp. 376, 409-10. Lancashire interest in gilt-edged was comparatively small

towards the end of the eighteenth century. During this period what savings were available for investment usually went into mortgages; See B. L. Anderson, "The Financial Revolution in the Provinces", *Business History*, 1969, pp. 21-22.

9 *Williamson's Liverpool Advertiser*, October 10, 31, November 7, 1791, January 16, June 30, October 1, 1792, *Manchester Mercury*, January 10, 24, February 14, November 6, 1792. Other brokers who advertised were J. Wenham, and Hazard, Burne & Co.

10 W. T. Jackman, *The Development of Transportation in Modern England* (1916), p. 394, note 2.

11 J. H. Clapham, *An Economic History of Modern Britain*, Vol. I. (1926), pp. 81-2.

12 G. H. Evans, *British Corporation Finance 1775-1850* (1936), pp. 13-14.

13 L. S. Pressnell, *Country Banking in the Industrial Revolution* (1956) p. 273.

14 Evans, op. cit., p. 31.

15 Ibid, .p. 28.

16 Ibid, p. 33.

17 Ibid, p. 35. At this date the capital of the East India Company was £756,000; the number of shareholders in 1681 was 556.

18 Jackman, op cit., pp. 394-5.

19 T. Baines, *History of the Commerce and Town of Liverpool* (1852), p. 488. An examination of Liverpool and Manchester papers for this period did not reveal any evidence of an active market in canal shares. There were no price lists or advertisements of auctions.

20 C. Fenn, *A Compendium of the English and Foreign Funds* (1838), pp. 128-135.

21 Gayer, Rostow and Schwarz, op. cit., p. 417.

22 B. C. Hunt, "The Joint Stock Company in England 1800-1825", *Journal of Political Economy*, 1935, pp. 6-8.

23 Ibid., pp. 18-24.

24 H. English, *A Complete view of the Joint Stock Companies formed during the years 1824 and 1825* (1827), pp. 10, 16.

25 Ibid., p. 31.

26 Ibid., p. 31. Fenn lists 20 insurance companies as being formed before 1824, but confines his list to London, and makes no mention of provincial insurance companies. No insurance companies appear in Liverpool share lists until 1833 when the Liverpool Marine Assurance Co. is given; a £25 paid share quoted at £30.

27 Gayer, Rostow and Schwarz, op. cit., pp. 426-8. For example, in the early 1820s the shares of the Chelsea Waterworks were held by Drummonds Bank as part of their investment portfolio; see H. Boliths and D. Peel, *The Drummonds of Charing Cross* (1967), p. 215.

28 Ibid., p. 426.

29 M. E. Falkus, "The British Gas Industry before 1850", *Economic History Review*, 1967, p. 504.

30 S. A. Harris, *The Development of Gas Supply on North Merseyside 1815-1945* (1956), pp. 29-31, 233-39. See also Baines, op. cit., pp. 677-78. An example of the method of transfer used for shares by unincorporated companies at this period is provided by the rules of the Liverpool Gas Light Co., passed at the Commercial Inn, March 1, 1816. The shares were entered in a book and numbered with a certificate to be assignable in writing. The transfer was to be registered in the transfer book of the company before the assignee was considered to be a pro-

prietor or entitled to any vote or dividend, "and in order to facilitate such transfer, a letter in the handwriting of the holder addressed to the Secretary, directing such transfers to be made, shall be sufficient". Any shares forfeited due to unpaid calls were sold off by the Committee at "Public Auctions".

31   Fenn, op. cit., p. 137.
32   *Liverpool Mercury*, March 13, 1829. The Royal Institution, for example, had a fund of £22,000 in shares of £100; H. A. Omerod, *The Liverpool Royal Institution* (1953), pp. 10-11.
33   *Liverpool Commercial Chronicle*, March 24, 1827. According to Clapham (op. cit., Vol. III. p. 206), ships had been owned in fractions of "sixty fourths since time out of mind".
34   *Liverpool Mercury*, January 31, March 20, 1829, August 11, 1830, June 10, 17. August 12, 1831.
35   *Liverpool Mercury*, September 3, 1830, August 12, 1831.
36   R. C. O. Matthews, *A Study in Trade Cycle History 1833-42* (1954), p. 160.
37   Ibid., pp. 160-1. 91 prospectuses were issued during April – July 1836.
38   *Hansard*, May 6, 1836.
39   *Hansard*, May 6, 1836.
40   *Manchester Guardian*, April 30, 1836.
41   At the height of the boom in April 1836 the *Liverpool Mercury* were content with saying that the "great advantages derivable from Joint Stock Companies are so well known and highly appreciated as to render all comment unnecessary"; April 22, 1836.
42   Powell, op. cit., pp. 304-5.
43   S. Evelyn Thomas, *The Rise and Growth of Joint Stock Banking*, Vol. I (1934), p. 98.
44   G. Chandler, *Four Centuries of Banking* (1964), p. 255. There were no directors from Manchester on the Board. The Manchester and Liverpool District Banking Co. allocated shares to places where they were going to open branches; T. S. Ashton, "Centenary of the District Bank", *Manchester Guardian*, June 19, 1935.
45   Thomas, op.cit., p. 222.
46   Ibid., p. 225.
47   Liverpool Sharebrokers' Association, Minutes of the General Meeting April 8, 1836. Lists of sharebrokers in the various commercial directories cited are drawn up on the basis of broking firms. In this study the number of firms is taken as a reasonable guide to the number of brokers; there were some partnerships, but these cannot be relied upon to include two or more active brokers.
48   *Gore's Liverpool Directories*, 1834-5.
49   Liverpool Sharebrokers' Association; Rules and Regulations 1836.
50   *Liverpool Mercury*, April 20, 1836.
51   Liverpool Sharebrokers' Association: Rules and Regulations 1836, Rule 9.
52   Liverpool Sharebrokers' Association, Minutes of Monthly General Meetings, January 11, 1844.
53   Ibid., February 23, 1841.
54   Minutes of the Liverpool New Stock Exchange, October 22, November 18, 1842.
55   Ibid., January 13, 18, 1843.
56   Ibid., January 13, 1843.
57   Ibid., November 10, 1843.

58 Liverpool Sharebrokers' Association, Minutes of Monthly General Meetings, November 13, 1843.
59 Minutes of the Liverpool New Stock Exchange, January 8, 1844.
60 Liverpool Stock Exchange, List of the Past and Present Members; also Minutes of the Committee for General Purposes, 1849-50.
61 *Manchester Guardian,* January 20, 1827, and on several subsequent dates.
62 *Manchester Guardian,* April 30, 1836. Company capitals ranged from £10,000 to £1 million.
63 Manchester Stock Exchange, Minutes of the Committee for General Purposes, May 12, 1836. The minutes do not record whether the meeting was held.
64 Ibid., August 10, 1836, November 3, 1837.
65 Ibid., August 4, 1845. In 1847 some 110 subscribers to the Commercial Exchange were listed as Stock and Sharebrokers; *Manchester Exchange Directory,* 1847.
66 Ibid., July 19, 1848.
67 Ibid., October 23, November 5, 1850. No minutes appear to have survived from the Cash Stock Exchange. Presumably this was the title given to the outside market on the Commercial Exchange by virtue of doing only cash bargains. The minutes of the Stock Exchange for October 1850 also mention having previously admitted "members of a different association", but earlier minutes throw no light on this mysterious fusion. It is possible that these were members of an Association of Sworn Brokers (every member swore to act only as a broker and not as a jobber or dealer) formed in July 1845; *Hull Advertiser,* August 1, 1845.

2 The Railway Share Market in the Provinces

The first railway promotion boom of 1836 led to the formation of stock exchanges at Liverpool and Manchester. The second and much larger railway mania of the mid-eighteen forties resulted in the setting up of similar institutions in most of the large cities and industrial towns of England, Wales, and Scotland. The City correspondent of *The Times* in November 1845, held that "these marts for trafficking in stocks and shares were not at all called for, as real business could be transacted through any local banker with little delay and on as good terms and in London". He further alleged that they had been "principally instrumental in fomenting all over the country the fatal passion for speculating in railways".[1] His complacency as to the facilities of the early London railway share market is understandable but the sweeping condemnation of provincial markets, and the provincial investor, betray an ignorance of the significant contribution which provincial capital made to railway development, and also the importance which reasonably sophisticated provincial investors attached to having easy access not only to speculative but also to investment facilities.

Railway promotion in Britain in the eighteen twenties was characterized by some serious schemes which appeared alongside others of a highly speculative nature, such as those floated during the 1824 – 25 boom. Some of the former were eventually successful after overcoming formidable opposition, while most of the latter, which were premium getting promotions, quickly disappeared in the 1825 collapse. It was not until the successful completion of the Liverpool and Manchester Railway in 1830 that investors came to realise the potential profitability of railway investment. The next five years accordingly witnessed the projection of the major railway links between some of the main cities, for example, the London to Birmingham line, the Grand Junction Railway, and the Great Western Railway. However, the objectivity which marked the approach of both promoters and investors to these particular projects was replaced by wild optimism in the 1836–37 boom when some £46.0 million of capital was authorized for railway construction.[2]

The 1836 boom was generated by the prosperous state of trade during preceding years and by the falling level of interest rates following upon easy conditions in the money market. As Sir John Clapham put it, "Blind capital, seeking its 5 per cent, a totally different thing from the clear-eyed capital of the Quaker businessman from the Midlands and the North, had accumulated for the raiders'.[3] Many of the promotions were based on extremely optimistic forecasts and cited the profit and dividend record of the Liverpool and Manchester Railway as supporting evidence. Inflated expectations and an unprecedented readiness to part with money among the public provided the promoters with easy pickings. Some of them never intended to undertake construction, they were only interested in getting as much as possible out of the shareholders; others who actually intended to build lines did so merely to guarantee their own personal takings regardless of the profitability of the project.[4]

By the end of 1836 the boom was tailing off following more stringent conditions in the money market arising from an adverse balance of payments. In 1837 railway promotion, along with other joint stock company formation, virtually came to a standstill and remained at this low level until the 1844–46 upsurge.

The next promotion boom had to wait upon improvements in the general state of trade. The revival of trade and the long period of cheap money in the early eighteen forties had laid the foundations of the boom which began in 1844 when 48 railway acts were passed. The figure increased to 120 in 1845, and culminated with 272 in 1846. The total nominal capital for these three years amounted to £214.6 million. Many more, of course, never got that far, and no less than 1,398 railway companies were registered during the first ten months of 1845, to say nothing of those formed without registration.[5] Railway promotion slackened off in 1847 when 190 acts were passed involving a nominal capital of £40 million, while the figure for 1848 was down to a mere £4.5 million. The construction peak, however, occurred during 1847–49 with the opening of some 2,700 miles of track. As in the 1836 boom much of the promotional activity was of a speculative nature and of the 9,000 miles authorized between 1845 and 1852 only 5,000 were actually built.[6] This large mileage was for a time operated by a multitude of companies but the amalgamation of lines, particularly after 1845, produced by 1850 a more rational main railway network, a development which had been considerably motivated by the search for managerial and operational economies.

The procedure for the formation of a railway was very similar to that used in canal promotion, especially so, in the case of those promoted outside the hectic boom periods. Railway promoters were generally drawn from the ranks of local mearchants and manufacturers, and they would arrange for the survey of the route while at the same time enlisting local support for the project. For this purpose local meetings were held along the proposed route and subscriptions were received by local agents. *The Circular to Bankers* claimed that the role of the agent was very important in ensuring a full subscription list, and that in the promotion of the Southampton Railway "brokers of character having extensive connections" were used to sell shares; it was alleged that they deliberately impeded the sale of other railway shares thereby improving the market for their own shares.[7] Members of the public who applied for shares then received letters of allotment and these were later exchanged for scrip (partly paid shares) when the deposit was paid. Scrip holders then proceeded to sign the subscription contract and armed with this and other requirements the promoters applied for an act of incorporation. In order to ensure the bona fide of such submissions parliament required a deposit of 10% of the authorized capital to be placed with the Bank of England. In 1844 the deposit was reduced to 5%, but raised to 10% in the following year.

Most of the railway companies formed between the opening of the Liverpool and Manchester Railway and the 1836 boom raised their capital at a time when the market was not particularly enthusiastic about this new investment outlet. Not only did promoters contend with lack of response, but they were also confronted with problems arising from the sheer size of the issues which were larger than anything the private sector of the market had hitherto experienced. For example, the London-Birmingham line had a capital of £2.5 million, the Grand Junction a capital of £1.0 million. In the absence of an underwriting network, or indeed the sort of contractor system used at one time by the Government in loan operations, the only answer was to engage in wide-spread publicity, particularly along the projected route. This meant of course that the bulk of the capital for a line would come from local sources.

The financing of the Liverpool and Manchester line was certainly heavily dependant on local support. Of the 2,904 shares allotted in 1826, 1,979 were held by 172 Liverpool people (Richard Dawson, later a member of the Liverpool Stock Exchange had a relatively large holding of 47 shares), while 15 Manchester people held 124 shares. The other main source of funds was the London area with 96 shareholders possessing 844 shares, but these holdings were less stable than those of northerners.[8] Manchester's reluctance to support the project possibly arose from the depressed state of the cotton trade, while a correspondent of *The Liverpool Mercury* attributed their unwillingness to the losses sustained by Manchester investors in the canal boom some fifty years earlier; the former was probably the weightier influence.[9] One interesting feature, but not from a stockbrokers viewpoint, of the local participation was that sixty of the original Liverpool shareholders were still holding the shares in 1845.[10] Other major lines projected at this time also enjoyed considerable local support, for example, the Grand Junction was supported in Birmingham by a large and enthusiastic group of merchants and manufacturers. Naturally their motives were commercially angled as against purely investment considerations. Again, in the case of the Manchester and Leeds line some 90% of the capital was subscribed by locally interested people in Lancashire and Yorkshire.[11] Less significant lines also displayed the same feature. Towards the Taff Vale Railway, completed in 1841, local shareholders contributed £171,200 out of the total subscription of £226,200.[12] There were, however, some notable exceptions to this pattern. The transport historian W. T. Jackman states that local support for the Great Western Railway was only built up very slowly and after a great deal of persuasion. The investors of Lancashire and Birmingham, anxious to secure good returns, subscribed for the shares but the wealthy classes of Bristol remained rather indifferent to the opportunity afforded them, presumably because attitudes had not yet adjusted to the new investment media; northern investors knew railways from local experience and their geographical investment horizon was certainly wider than that of southerners.[13]

Railway companies in practice kept the allocation of shares firmly in their own control and they showed a distinct preference for local investors. There were several reasons for this. They wanted to ensure that shareholders could meet their commitments on shares and here brokers were useful since they usually possessed some knowledge of the financial resources of shareholders. Frequent sales of forfeited shares would reflect badly on a company's standing and depress share prices. An interested local participant was also far more likely to be a long term holder. A further important consideration was that a locally supported line was more likely to obtain parliamentary approval. In order to encourage local participation many railway companies publicly advertised the fact that they had "ample reserves of shares for any parties likely to be affected by the projected railroad".[14]

An exceedingly prominent part was played by Lancashire capital, particularly by a group of wealthy merchants known as the 'Liverpool Party', in the financing of lines in other parts of the country.[15] *The Circular to Bankers* in 1838 claimed "that more than $\frac{2}{3}$ of some of the most costly lines are held in shares by the people of Lancashire, and the manufacturing and commercial interests which centralizes in Manchester and Liverpool".[16] Lancashire people held two-thirds of the Manchester-Leeds, about seven-eighths of the London-Birmingham, and they also figured prominently in the Southern Railway, the Great Western, the London-Southampton, and the Eastern Counties.[17] In the case of the South Eastern Railway a quarter of the £100,000 received from bankers on account of instalments of shares remitted through them came from Lancashire bankers.[18] The surplus capital of the 'Liverpool Party', which included Croppers, Rathbones, Horsefall's, Booth's, Sanders, Moss' and Lawrences, was no doubt seeking higher returns than available from alternative investments, particularly gilt edged. Accustomed to taking commercial risks they were prepared to accept the additional liability present in the new railway schemes. They had of course some reassurance from the profits already earned by the Liverpool and Manchester Railway. According to *The Circular to Bankers* this surplus capital came from the large profits which "all manufacturers and merchants in Lancashire acquired in 1834–35"; very little of it came from the newly established joint stock banks.[19] Given the size of share holdings and the extensive commercial experience of Liverpool and Manchester investors it is not surprising that their activities provided the growing ranks of brokers with adequate commission incomes.

The dominant role played by provincial sources of finance was described in the famous passage in Henry Burgess's *Circular to Bankers* of November 6 1835:

"It is a remarkable fact that the Railway system advanced and became established in the public confidence almost wholly without the assistance of the [London] Stock Exchange. The support accorded to it was derived almost exclusively from the capitalists, and men of thrift and opulence, in the mining and manufacturing districts of the North of England. We will venture to assert that taking into account all the Railways now in operation in the counties of Northumberland, Cumberland, Durham, Yorkshire, and Lancashire, not one twentieth part of the capital expended upon them was provided by members of the Stock Exchange or Stockbrokers. When the Birmingham and London Railway (incorporated in 1833) was brought out they participated more largely in this enterprise, as they did to a lesser degree in the Grand Junction (incorporated 1833), which unites that with the Liverpool and Manchester Railway. The commencement of these two great lines may be stated as the first occasion when the Stock Exchange people began to take any interest in this description of property".

Burgess was possibly a little hard on London's contribution.[20] As already noted Londoners held a sizeable portion of the shares of the Liverpool and Manchester Railway, although they were not long term holders. London brokers acted along with provincial brokers and solicitors as agents for receiving share applications, while London bankers were involved in railway promotion and direction from the late eighteen twenties onwards.[21]

Dependence on local sources and active local promotion were not however features of the bulk of railway financing. Most railway companies appeared during the two railway booms when "it was sufficient for a company to place an advertisement in a railway journal to be flooded with applications". For example, the New Gravesend Railway received 80,000 applications for 30,000 shares in 1835, the Great North of Scotland was oversubscribed three times in 1845, while the Great Western Railway received 1,400,000 applications for 120,000 shares.[22] Although the railway companies kept the allocation of shares within their control they made extensive use of agents to obtain subscriptions to shares during boom periods, as indeed they had done in more normal times. Provincial brokers, along with London brokers, solicitors, and banks, played a prominent role in this activity. The names of Liverpool and Manchester brokers figured prominently on the prospectuses of some of the early lines, while during the 1844–46 boom prospectuses frequently carried the names of a dozen or so provincial brokers drawn from large and small towns. Very few railways, however, were handled exclusively by provincial brokers. Out of a sample of sixty prospectuses in *Bradshaw's Railway Gazette* for 1845 only four relied solely on provincial brokers.

The large increase in the number of Liverpool and Manchester stockbrokers during the boom periods has already been indicated, and similar developments in other provincial centres are dealt with in chapter three. Their stock in trade, railway shares, also displayed an equally dramatic increase and is summarized in the following table for the main provincial markets, and for London. It gives the number of railway companies listed at the end of the year where available in the lists of exchanges, or where such lists are not available in the lists published in the local press.

	1835	1836	1844	1845	1846
Liverpool	11	38	100	305	233
Manchester	–	38	29	166	105
Leeds	–	13	51	77	69
Bristol	–	12	23	72	29
Birmingham	–	–	45	88	21
Sheffield	–	11	41	105	36
London	19	33	37	204	147

During the 1836 boom the inclusion of new railway companies in the share lists of the Liverpool and Manchester Stock Exchanges did not require the assent of the Committees. Indeed, they were fully occupied formulating procedural rules and even more so, settling disputes between brokers involved in 'difference' claims.[23] Liverpool took no measures relating to new issues until 1841 when it was resolved that sales and purchases were to be subject to the fixing of a special settlement by the Committee. The procedure was for seven brokers to requisition the Committee requesting a special settlement. Presumably the fact that so many brokers made the request indicated that sufficient market interest existed to justify fixing a settlement.[24] During the peak of the 1845 boom this procedure proved too slow and was discontinued. The object of a special settlement of course was to minimize the period during which buyers and sellers had to wait for cash or stock. At the height of the boom members were even requesting the Committee for a "partial settlement" in order to expedite bargains in new shares.[25] Where possible the Liverpool Committee tended to fix the same special settlement days as London, and in 1845 they reached an agreement with Manchester to adopt the same dates for special settlements.[26] After 1846, however, settlements in new shares were included in the ordinary twice monthly account and governed by the same rules.

As to quotation requirements the exchanges were not very demanding. The only requirement in 1841 for inclusion in the Liverpool list was that the new stock should have been sanctioned by the proprietors of the company at a general meeting.[27] Later, the Committee added that they wanted to see the scrip, although this was not necessary if the company had an act of parliament. The Birmingham Stock Exchange was not prepared to quote transactions in shares of new railways which had not issued the scrip, and this provision was also adopted by Bristol and Leeds. Both these exchanges stated quite categorically that such transactions should not be done in the market. After the July-August 1845 crisis in Leeds following the 'bear' selling of the Huddersfield, Halifax and Bradford Union, the Leeds Committee withdrew from their share list all lines the scrip of which had not been issued.[28]

Dealing in the share markets was not of course confined to scrip shares or fully paid shares. Many provincial markets dealt extensively in shares for which no letters of allotment, deposit receipts or scrip had been sent out. Contracts in shares "to an enormous extent" were made as soon as advertisements appeared and these transactions had an immediate appeal for those with the "appetite but not the means for gambling". *The Bankers' Magazine* made the seemingly exaggerated claim in 1845 that "multitudes of men and women, who, with no earthly means of any kind would buy and sell with the greatest coolness for 'delivery on scrip' (that is, whenever scrip might be issued) hundreds and thousands of shares in almost any company that might be proposed to them".[29] More real claims to shares also enjoyed a speculative market. On the London Stock Exchange letters of allotment were very popular and they were equally so in the provinces since they had the attraction of a premium without the need for a deposit.[30] In the 1836 boom deposit receipts were actively traded. This arose largely because many companies took a long time to issue scrip after the payment of a deposit, and therefore the deposit receipt was used as a transferable claim to the shares. For example, on the sale of new shares the selling broker would send around to the buying broker for cash settlement and deliver the receipt. In some cases the deposit receipt was for more shares than had actually been dealt in, in which case the broker held the receipt, giving an undertaking for the shares in lieu of a receipt. Later when the scrip or share certificate arrived this would be handed over.[31]

The movement of railway share prices from 1830 to 1850 is given on the chart below. Prices climbed slowly from 1830, culminating in the 1836 boom; in January 1836, the index stood at 96 and reached its highest point in May, standing at 129, then it fell back to 98 in December. Prices continued to fall into the first quarter of 1837, but they were still comfortably above pre-boom levels. The recovery of prices and the climb to the peak of the 1845 boom was interrupted by two minor setbacks in 1839 and 1841. From 1842 onwards, however, the index rises steadily reaching its highest point (168) in July, 1845. This of course is a general picture of price movements based on a small sample of shares. It does not portray the full extent of the movements in more speculative shares, particularly the scrip speculation which occurred at the height of the boom. Some idea of the range of price movements is given by the following figures; in the case of fourteen railway shares the difference between the highest and the lowest price for 1845 exceeded £40, the difference for the Great North of England was £117, while two other lines approached £100. After the collapse of the market in the autumn share prices fell continuously and by 1850 the share index stood at seventy.

Although the share prices used by Gayer, Rostow and Schwarz to calculate their index were taken from Wetenhall's Lists it is very likely that the movements indicated also portrays the general experience of provincial markets over the same period. A survey of the railway share prices in *The Economist's Railway Monitor* for the latter half of 1845 for London, Liverpool, Manchester, and Leeds markets indicated that for the majority of shares common to these

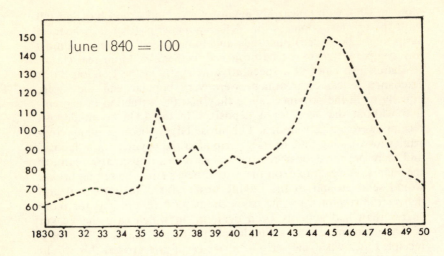

RAILWAY SHARE PRICE INDEX.
Source: Gayer, Rostow and Schwarz, Vol. I, op. cit., p. 437.
The index is based on 14 railway shares quoted in London.

markets prices were well within one per cent of each other. Occasionally larger differences appeared, attributable no doubt to changes
in local conditions. Prices, however, were unlikely to diverge greatly
because even if London prices were not known before the close of
a provincial market they would certainly be known for the following
morning call over, the most important of the daily dealing sessions.
Also country brokers had correspondents in all the important centres
from whom information on market prices was easily obtainable.
For example, George Eadon of Sheffield received price lists from
some of the principal brokers in London, Manchester Liverpool
and Leeds. There was also a large degree of uniformity with respect
to the spread of prices, and on the leading provincial markets, as on
London, this was about two per cent for most stocks.[32]

With regard to the size of provincial railway share markets there
is some evidence to indicate that they were not completely out-
stripped by London in the 1845 boom. On the basis of 280 shares
listed in *The Railway Monitor of The Economist* during the period
October to December, London made prices in approximately 180
shares on four days out of six trading days per week. The figure
for Liverpool was 190, with Manchester 175, and Leeds 80.[33] On
this basis the two largest northern markets certainly rivalled London, but the important question of turnover is ignored.[34] Unfortu-

nately no figures are available on this matter. An idea of the rapid increase and decrease in the volume of business on the Liverpool market for 1845 can be obtained from the share lists. A rough count of the number of prices 'marked' gave the following figures, expressed as daily averages: 97, end of January account period; 134, end of March; 160, end of June; 208, end of September; 32 end of December.[35] These figures are undoubtedly gross underestimates since all bargains were not marked particularly so in hectic dealing periods, and also because marks merely recorded price changes and not the number of bargains done.

Although there are no detailed accounts of the local markets during the 1836 boom, the 1845 boom is however more adequately covered. *The Economist* carried in addition to its London intelligence, reports on the main provincial markets. The Leeds report came from R. B. Watson & Co., a firm established in 1836, while the Liverpool report came from E. S. Boult & Co., a member of the Stock Exchange since 1836. Manchester activity was reported by John Railton & Son, a founder member of the Manchester Stock Exchange. Occasional reports also appeared from Newcastle, Belfast and Edinburgh. It is evident from them that active dealings on the smaller markets centred largely on local lines, while transactions in the national lines ("old" railway shares) were usually transmitted to the larger markets, whose activity encompassed the entire range of railway shares.

During the early stages of the 1845 boom speculation centred mainly on "investment stocks" (presumably dividend paying stocks), which tended to increase when the Board of Trade indicated that some projected lines would not be approved.[36] The provincial correspondents to *The Railway Monitor* were all highly critical of the need to seek Board of Trade approval since frequent leakages of information gave rise to "an immense amount of gambling and speculation". By April the speculative mania for new lines had really got underway with hectic dealing and very large and sharp price movements. Speculators tended to concentrate on the small stocks, scrip shares (the "light" stocks), while the "old and dividend paying stocks are nearly neglected, or if thought of it is only to be sold that the scrip shares may be bought, and prices are given for scrip shares which nothing but a ten per cent dividend could warrant". In September, J. Brancker of Liverpool saw no prospect of an end to the appearance of new schemes, "nor will there be so long as solicitors and engineers can get a premium in the market".[37] People of "the highest rank" borrowed money on the security of railway shares at rates varying from 10 to 40% in order to speculate in such schemes.[38]

D

The 1836 share boom had widened the ranks of the sharedealing and shareholding public. Before this shareholding was the preserve of the monied classes but rapid rises in share prices coupled with promises of large dividends enticed smaller savers into the market from the ranks of "Ladies and Clergymen".[39] The 1845 episode saw an even greater participation in the capital market. In the prevailing casino atmosphere the great attraction for new investors was quick capital gains. Opportunities were plentiful since scrip shares could be bought with small sums and quickly realized at a premium, perhaps, before further calls were due. *The Economist* commented in June, 1845, "Everybody is in the Stocks now. Needy clerks, poor tradesmen's apprentices, discarded serving men and bankrupts – all have entered the ranks of the great monied interest[40]." A more sober assessment of the new clientele came from E. S. Boult who stressed the need for caution when dealing with the new rush of principals. He claimed that "a large proportion of present purchases are by people of small means, from whom should the differences (which in this instance means losses) be great there would be small chance of recovery".[41] This was the view of a well established broker but it is doubtful if many of the newer entrants to the profession were equally restrained in their pursuit of commission income.

Some interesting particulars about subscribers to railway shares were given in a Parliamentary Return of June 1845 which listed all parties who had signed subscription contracts during the session for sums of £2,000 and upwards.[42] In the £100,000 plus range there were several Liverpool and Manchester names. From Liverpool, James Macgregor (banker) and Robert Browne (merchant) subscribed for sums approaching £600,000 each (probably trustee holdings), Joseph Hornby and Robert Gladstone (both merchants) subscribed for £220,000 and £140,000 respectively, while John Moss (banker) subscribed for nearly £158,000. David Hodgson Esq., had £114,000 against his name, and the merchant banker Edward Cropper had £118,000. Four Manchester merchants, Thomas Broadbent, John Smith, J. Hargraves, and Henry Holdsworth signed for sums ranging from £120,000 to £150,000. David Waddington (gentleman – a term calculated to impress contemporaries and mislead investigators) signed for nearly £130,000; Samuel Brooks (banker) for £154,000 and Leo Schuster (merchant banker) for nearly £170,000. Subscription contracts of course were merely promises of support, but even so any of these gentlemen would have been valuable clients to any stockbroker.

Liverpool brokers could not have been short of clients judging by the following list which gives the professions of Liverpool parties who had subscribed for sums ranging from £5,000 to £100,000.

Professions	No.	Subscribed For.
Merchants	73	£1,327,300
Gentlemen	31	777,480
Sharebrokers	15	194,120
Bankers	8	221,200
Brokers (other)	7	66,120
Solicitors	4	76,090
Merchant Bankers	3	119,200
Goldsmiths	3	38,000
Miscellaneous	10	157,200
Total	154	2,976,880

It is apparent that the merchants and gentlemen class dominated the ranks of Liverpool investors, with far less participation from other professional classes. Sharebrokers signed for a large total of stock but only one of them, Matthew Wotherspoon, subscribed for a large sum, nearly £50,000. Whatever profession or social class the smaller investor may have been drawn from, the large scale operators seem to have come predominantly from merchant circles. It does not necessarily follow that the large shareholders were the main stock market operators but it is very difficult to suggest why this should not be so.

As in London the feverish boom activity caused various strains to appear in the organization of the markets. As early as 1842 Liverpool was complaining to the Edinburgh and Glasgow Railway Co., that if the old scrip was to be returned prior to the issue of new scrip very great difficulties would arise in "the settlement of bargains in the market, where the amount of shares held and the number of transactions are large".[43] By 1845 the pressure of business was such that the Liverpool Committee considered means "for the better conduct of the business of the open market", and also took steps to prevent "the crowd of persons assembling at the head of the stairs, to the great inconvenience of members passing in and out".[44] The pressure of speculation during July and August led members to petition the Committee to close the Stock Exchange, whereupon they decided that "it is expedient that there be some cessation from business by means of a holiday". It was also resolved that dealing facilities should be curtailed during the ensuing weeks, with the market closing after the making up of the morning price boards.[45] London's difficulties in completing accounts was also experienced in Liverpool. The heavy settlements of July and August led the Committee to postpone the rendering of balance sheets because it was impossible to get all the tickets signed.[46]

Similar delaying tactics were also used on some of the other provincial markets. Bristol brokers agreed in July that the Exchange should be closed for a week in order to abate the speculative fever.[47]

In Leeds the Committee closed the Exchange during the first week in August, a move induced by the massive bear operations which had been conducted in the scrip of the newly formed Halifax, Huddersfield and Bradford Railway Co. It was estimated that five times the number of shares in existence had been sold and as a result bargains could not be enforced.[48]

The inevitable collapse came in the autumn of 1845. For some time conditions in the money market had been increasingly tight following the immobilization of large sums of capital, persistent railway calls, and seasonal pressures on funds. The Bank of England, however, did not raise Bank Rate until October 16th, when it put the rate up by half per cent to three per cent. This, and the prospect of further withdrawal of funds for parliamentary deposits caused prices to slip backwards. With the reversal of expectations sellers appeared taking their profits, and once the downward trend was evident loss cutting by speculators merely accelerated the decline. The Liverpool market correspondent of *The Economist* claimed that the change in Bank Rate had "alarmed all speculators so much that we have had the market overwhelmed with stock, and prices have consequently fallen tremendously in all scrip shares". By November the Liverpool market "had given up the ghost" except in old stocks and these were only dealt in for cash.[49] In Leeds most of the new schemes were standing at purely nominal quotations as a result of the tide of speculation turning away from scrip shares, and the Committee recommended that until further notice all business would be for cash.[50]

The decline in railway share prices during 1845 to 1850 had several important repercussions. One was the change in allotment practices of new companies when discounts replaced premiums on scrip shares. At the height of the boom when share issues were greatly oversubscribed railway directors frequently only allotted a small proportion of the issue to the public thus driving up premiums even further, much to the annoyance of unlucky applicants. In many instances this practice was merely an attempt to support an issue in its early stages; it was however also used by directors of fraudulent companies to rig the market to their own advantage.[51] Companies allotting shares at the collapse of the boom, and holding out little hope for a recovery, took full advantage of large subscriptions and sent out letters of allotment to "unsuspecting applicants in the most liberal manner".[52] The companies proceeded to demand deposits, which were not forthcoming, and the shares consequently moved to even lower levels.

The construction peak for the railways projected during 1845–46 was reached in 1847, involving in that year an estimated expenditure of around £70 million. In order to obtain funds railway companies made further calls on their shares. Some shareholders anticipated the calls and disposed of their scrip shares. Many sold holdings of shares in established lines to meet such calls, while others sold gilt edged.[53] Such reactions by investors were extremely depressing from a market standpoint and the provincial markets reacted somewhat differently to the situation.

Liverpool's concern is reflected in their action of setting up a sub-committee in March 1846 to examine the best means of reducing the number of bills coming before parliament. Despite a good deal of campaigning, petitioning, and consulting with other markets, little was achieved in practical terms.[54] The Leeds Stock Exchange presented a petition to parliament on such lines, through the hands of Mr George Hudson, which pointed out the possible adverse effect on the money market if a considerable portion of the pending bills were passed, and also noting that many local shareholders in such projected lines were anxious to withdraw applications to parliament and dissolve the company so that deposits could be repaid.[55] The continuing depressed state of share prices in 1847 induced the Liverpool Committee to send a deputation to meet the directors of the Manchester-Leeds, Manchester-Sheffield, and Lincoln lines "to impress upon them the necessity of suspending as far as practicable, during the present pressure, all unproductive work, and to withhold making all calls that can possibly be avoided – and to urge that a public announcement to this effect would give considerable relief". Little came of this move either, and by September the members were extremely anxious about the lack of business. Accordingly, they held a special general meeting and urged the Committee "to take immediate steps to bring about if possible some amelioration of the pressure now felt by the shareholders and the public generally in consequence of the heavy calls and applications for loans by the different Railway Companies". In effect the Committee could do little except write to the railway companies suggesting a "cordial union" of railway interests to discuss the matter.[56]

Some of the other exchanges displayed equal concern for the depressed state of the railway market, but not all were prepared to move in the matter. From Hull came the radical suggestion, which received no support, that the Treasury should provide finance for companies in difficulty.[57] Birmingham, while agreeing with the general assessment of the situation, argued that it was not the province of brokers to intervene and that any such moves by them would merely help speculators.[58] Characteristically, Manchester took an equally independant view and held that active measures should be left to railway directors and proprietors.

From the point of view of the exchanges the depression in share prices during the late forties and early fifties meant loss of turnover, income, and in many instances of members.[59] For the railway companies it implied reduced availability of capital and a rise in its cost. To help surmount these difficulties railways resorted to alternative methods of borrowing, some of which involved the stock exchanges. The most important development from their viewpoint was the increasing use of preference shares which succeeded in attracting capital by promising preferential dividend treatment. Sometimes additional privileges were attached in order to increase their attractiveness, such as cumulative dividends, participation in profits, the right to subscribe to new issues, and voting rights. Given the state of the market, low dividends, and restrictions on borrowing, many railways experienced great difficulty in raising funds for the completion of projects by means of share issues. In these circumstances they resorted increasingly to preference issues. Companies in more favourable financial positions also made extensive use of preference issues to finance extensions and undertake consolidations.[60]

The growth of preference capital was particularly rapid, as a percentage of all share issues authorized by parliament it increased from 4% in 1845, to 11% in 1846, and reached 66% in 1849.[61] More often than not they were offered to existing shareholders provided they had paid previous calls on shares. In general they were well received by the market and they occupied a prominent position in the lists of the provincial exchanges. In the Liverpool daily list the preference section took up about a third of the space with quotations for over 70 preference shares in the eighteen fifties, while the Manchester and Birmingham lists were similarly weighted with "preferentials".

Additional finance was also obtained by selling shares at a discount, a device used by "highly respectable railway companies". Usually the shares were offered as a bonus to the proprietors. It was an extremely costly form of finance and prior to the passing of the Company Clauses Consolidation Act of 1845 it had the additional disadvantage that the issue of shares at a discount required parliamentary authorization. An extension of the practice was the issue of half and quarter shares carrying benefits equal to those on fully paid shares. They were issued by many of the leading railway companies and the provincial exchanges witnessed frequent dealings in them.

The share lists of several exchanges included a number of Irish lines. Their presence reflected not only the general interest in railways but also the strong trading ties of Lancashire with Ireland which induced many Liverpool and Manchester businessmen to take up Irish shares. In the 1836 boom Lancashire dominated English investment in Irish railways. For example, Lancashire provided £120,000 of the original capital of the Ulster Line compared with £20,000 from London, while all but £4,500 of the £25,000 of English money in the Dublin and Drogheda Line came from Lancashire.[62] However, by 1844 London assumed the dominant role in the provision of capital but the provincial flow certainly had not ceased; Manchester investors were guided into the shares of the Great Southern and Western by a local stockbroker, George Carr, whose father was a director of the railway.[63] At the height of the 1845 boom the Liverpool list carried quotations in nearly forty Irish lines, while the Manchester list had about half this number. Provincial stock market interest in Irish lines reflected the fact that half the £8.7 million of private capital invested in them by 1850 came from England.[64]

Investors of the period were also actively interested in continental railway development, especially in French projects. French development was quite similar to the British experience, beginning with a few local lines and the real starting point coming with the financial success of a short line outside Paris in 1837. Following this success three lines of first rate importance were projected, the Paris-Rouen, Paris-Orléans, and the Strasbourg-Basle lines.[65] The railway law of 1842, by which the government hoped to nationalize railway development, fixed the size and pattern of the network with the important lines naturally radiating from Paris. Under the law the state provided the land, the local authorities the railway infrastructure, and the successful company provided the line and the rolling stock. In practice the company which got the concession ended up providing everything, and all that remained of the 1842 law was the right of the state to buy up the railways.[66]

British participation in terms of promotion, capital provision, and actual construction was indeed extensive. In 1840 Edward Blount, an Irishman, secured on behalf of the directors of the London and Southampton Railway a concession to build the Paris to Rouen line, and two years later a further concession to extend the line to Havre. As was the case with many other continental lines English interests were well represented on the board of directors. Among the Paris-Rouen board were Sir John Easthope, a London stockbroker, and also two leading Liverpool bankers, John Moss and Charles Lawrence.[67] The success of the Paris-Rouen railway coupled with the publication of Stephenson's survey on French railway prospects drew other promoters in search of concessions. One of the most active was J. D. Barry, who had been sent over by a group of capitalists to open a Paris office, survey routes and obtain local connections. In 1843 he succeeded in getting the Orléans-Tours concession and on the basis of this success a large financial group was set up consisting of several influential provincial bankers, and which proceeded to construct several important lines in western France. At about the same time another London based promoting group led by John Masterman secured concessions for the Nord, the Paris-Lyons, the Orléans-Vierzon, and the Dutch-Rhenish, which for many years was the only important Dutch railway. With the intensification of railway building towards 1845 a vast number of less reliable promoters appeared on the scene projecting various ill-fated bubble schemes.

J. D. Barry was a Manchester stockbroker. He joined the Stock Exchange when it was reconstituted in 1839 and it is probable that he took to sharebroking in 1836 when he gave up the editorship of *The Chester Chronicle*. Whether or not he used his Manchester connections to dispose of French railway shares is not known, but it seems unlikely that such an outlet would have been entirely neglected. When the French railway boom subsided Barry turned his attention to Portugal and organized in 1852–53 the Central Peninsular Railway Co., with a capital of 20 million francs, to build a line from Lisbon to Santarem. The line was not finished and in 1858 the Portuguese government revoked the concession. Barry was also a director of the Paris-Orléans Railway.[68]

Capital raising by share issues for continental railways was done on very much the same basis as that used for British lines. Usually the company opened a London office from which shares could be obtained, while in the provinces brokers acted as agents for share applications. Frequently about a dozen or so brokers acted as agents for a company, and among them were such leading firms as Ridsdale of Leeds, Cardwell of Manchester, Sohmes and Tripp of Bristol, and H. Davies & Co. of Liverpool. The important lines also used a provincial banker in addition to a London one, reflecting the significance attached to provincial interest in continental share issues. Usually shares carried nominal values of £20, with an initial deposit of 10%. This was quite safe since the director could not proceed to any expenditures until the concession was obtained. An attractive feature for English investors was that transfers in foreign shares required no stamp tax, while interest was payable from the very start. Further, shares could be traded in with equal facility in Paris, London, and the provincial stock exchanges.

The large scale purchases of continental railway shares were of course motivated by expectations of getting relatively high dividends, which were in fact realized, and of obtaining capital gains on relatively small outlays. The resulting participation of English capital is reflected in the following figures; half of the 1,750 original subscribers to the Amiens-Boulogne line were English, drawn from all parts of the country; in the case of one company seeking the Nord concession London interests applied for 400,000 shares, while only 150,00 was offered for sale.[69] L. H. Jenks estimated that about £80 million of English capital was promised for the fifty or so French railways in 1845. The actual amount was naturally far less than this; it has been reckoned that for the French lines started before 1847 that half the privately supplied capital, about £25 million, of which about half was called up, came from England.[70]

The first French line quoted on the Liverpool Stock Exchange was the Paris-Rouen, listed in 1840. The members however seem to have been a little suspicious of dealing in the shares and passed a rule allowing them to "demand and reject the names of principals".[71] By 1844 the number of foreign lines had increased to six with the addition of the Paris-Orléans (fully paid up), the Paris-Lyons (10% paid up), the Rouen-Havre (30% paid up), the Strasbourg-Basle, and the Paris-Strasbourg (both 10% paid up). With the 1845 boom the number increased from thirteen in January to forty-four in September. The interest of provincial investors in the speculative concession hunting companies is indicated by the quotation of four of the companies competing for the Paris-Lyon route, namely Lafittes, French, Gannerous, and Callous, with a considerable number of transactions being marked for all four.[72] Similarly, the Northern of France, with quotations of the English, French, Lebeuf's, Rossamels, and Pepin le Halleur groups. All these were scrip shares of low value, usually 10% of the nominal, with prices fluctuating according to the prospects of getting the concession. Most of the foreign shares quoted in Liverpool were of low value, only two were fully paid, and only two others were 50% or more paid up.

As far as dealing in foreign shares is concerned the most active period, judged by the markings in the Liverpool lists, was from March to April, 1845, with activity being evenly spread over the list. New shares of course attracted considerable speculative interest, and dealings in these later dominated the foreign railway section. For example, when the scrip of the Dutch-Rhenish appeared on the market in mid-July 1845, the number of bargains marked reached about twenty per day, a volume greatly exceeding that of existing lines. The price of the £3 scrip rose from this level to £10 within a few days, and sufficient bargains were made to merit the fixing of a special settlement fairly promptly. On the Bristol Stock Exchange the capital of the Dutch-Rhenish is supposed to have been turned over no less than six times during an account.[73]

Within a few years the foreign railway list contracted rapidly. By the end of 1846 only twenty French lines were quoted in Liverpool, and by 1858, the figure was down to fifteen. Several reasons can be suggested for this relatively rapid decline of interest and participation in foreign lines. As with English lines the persistent railway calls helped to depress the market and induce selling.[74] Large sales of shares, estimated at about £6 million, were made in 1847 to help finance an adverse balance of payments and assist recovery from depression.[75] A year later the political turmoil in France led to further sales on an already depressed market. With these events the flow of English capital to European railways came to a temporary but abrupt pause.

NOTES

1 *The Times,* November 14 1845; quoted by B. C. Hunt, *The Developement of the Business Corporation in England, 1800-1867* (1936), p. 108. In Scotland the stock exchanges at Glasgow and Edinburgh were formed in 1844, while Aberdeen followed in 1845.

2 For full details of the early history of railway promotion see W. T. Jackman, *The Development of Transportation in Modern England* (1916), Clapham, Vol 1, op. cit., and H. G. Lewin, *Early British Railways, A Short History of their Origins and Development 1801-1844* (1925).

3 Clapham, Vol. 1, op. cit., p. 388.

4 R. C. O. Matthews, *A Study in Trade Cycle History 1833-1842* (1954), p. 111.

5 C. Duguid, *A History of the Stock Exchange* (1902), p. 17.

6 H. G. Lewin, *The Railway Mania and Its Aftermath* (1936), p. 473.

7 *Circular to Bankers,* June 13 1834, p. 379.

8 H. Pollins "The Finances of the Liverpool and Manchester Railways", *Economic History Review,* 1952-3, pp. 92-3. Some 50 shareholders forfeited their shares through non-payment of calls, and a public auction was then held to dispose of their shares.

9 Ibid., p. 91; *Liverpool Mercury,* September 31, 1830.

10 Ibid., p. 83.

11 S. A. Broadbridge, "The Early Capital Market; the Lancashire and Yorkshire Railway", *Economic History Review,* 1955-56, pp. 203-4.

12 C. R. Fay, *Round About Industrial Britain 1830-1860* (1952), p. 83.

13 Jackman, op. cit., p. 562. Sanders, Secretary to the G. W. R. stated to the Select Committee on Railways of 1844 that the bulk of the original subscriptions came from the West of England (Q. 4954/5).

14 H. Pollins, "The Marketing of Railway Shares in the First Half of the Nineteenth Century." *Economic History Review,* 1954-55, p. 238. *Liverpool Mercury,* November 2. 18. October 30, 1830.

15 Clapham, Vol. 1, op. cit., p. 387; see also S. A. Broadbridge's contribution to M. C. Reed (ed.), *Railways in the Victorian Economy* (1969), pp. 207-8.

16 *Circular to Bankers,* April 13, 1838.

17 *Circular to Bankers,* April 13, 1838; T. Tooke, *History of Prices,* Vol 2, (1838), p. 275; Matthews, op. cit., p. 110.

18 M. C. Reed, "Railways and the Growth of the Capital Market", in M. C. Reed (ed.), op. cit., pp. 175-6; Jones, Lloyd & Co. of Manchester sent £9,600, and Barned & Co. and Moss & Co. of Liverpool sent £5,300 and £12,750 respectively.

19 *Circular to Bankers,* March 10, 1837, pp. 373-4.

20 Dealing in Railway shares on the London Stock Exchange increased from the middle of 1833 when the principal railways serving London where authorized; M. C. Reed, "Railways and the Growth of the Capital Market', op. cit., p. 169.

21 H. Pollins, "The Marketing of Railway Shares in the First Half of the Nineteenth Century", op. cit., p. 232, note 4.

22 Ibid., p. 233.

23 The Stock Exchange committees spent hours adjudicating on very long lists of difference claims; at many meetings they did nothing else.

24 Liverpool Stock Exchange. Minutes of the Committee for General Purposes, January 29, 1841, May 8, 1844.

25 Liverpool Stock Exchange; Minutes of Monthly General Meeting, June, 1845.

26 The London Stock Exchange introduced special settlement requirements in October, 1845, which were designed to ensure a reasonable market in the shares of a company. "The Committee will entertain no application for fixing a Settling Day in the shares of any new company unless the member applying for the same attend the Committee in person – with a Certificate from the Secretary of such company that the Subscription List is full (with the exception of such shares as may be reserved for special purposes); that not less than $\frac{2}{3}$ of the scrip have been paid upon and are ready to be issued; that the period publicly advertised for signing the Deed has expired and that there is therefore no impediment to the Settlement of the Account". Minutes of the London Stock Exchange Committee for General Purposes, October 20, 1845.

27 Liverpool Stock Exchange; Minutes, February 23, 1841.

28 Birmingham Stock Exchange: Minutes, October 15, 1845; Bristol Stock Exchange; Minutes, August 27, 1845; Leeds Stock Exchange; Minutes, August 4, 1845; also *Leeds Intelligencer,* August 6, 1845. The number of shares sold was put at 80,000, but only 7,500 was available through allotment, and prices rose from 30s to £15 per share. The Leeds Stock Exchange Committee at a special meeting on August 7, adopted a resolution to the effect that no buyers of shares "in any projected railway where the scrip was not issued at the date of the Contract shall be allowed to purchase in such shares against the seller". Neighbouring Stock Exchanges took a dim view of this action, particularly Sheffield, where brokers had been buying for local clients; *Sheffield and Rotherham Independent,* August 9, 1845.

29 *Banker's Magazine,* 1845, "A Railway Panic Lesson – The Yorkshire Share Markets and the Halifax and Bradford Union Railway Co.'s Scrip", p. 143. It was not uncommon to buy shares under guarantee where the seller bound himself to deliver scrip, in which case the guaranteed shares stood at a higher price than mere chances for shares; *Leeds Mercury,* December 7, 1844.

30 Provincial markets do not appear to have thrown up special dealers in letters of allotment, known as "alley men" on the London market.

31 *Liverpool Mercury,* August 26, 1836.

32 It is probable that there were bigger differences in prices between markets in the 1836 boom since communications were less developed, and the correspondent or agent network was only just being set up.

33 This is not to say that there was a broad market in every share for which a price was given. L. H. Jenks in his admirable book *The Migration of British Capital to 1875* (1927), p. 131, states that Leeds "for a few months outclassed London as a centre for transactions in railway securities". The source for this claim is not given, and although Leeds had three share markets (one report claims four!) it seems unlikely that this superiority ranged over the entire list of railway shares. Undoubtedly it possessed a superior market in local shares, as indeed did the other exchanges — this was an important reason for their existence.

34 A contemporary observer, D. M. Evans, the author of *The City, or The Physiology of London Business* (1845), p. 61, noted that in provincial towns where markets had been established that "as much, if not more, business was transacted than in London".

35 Liverpool Stock Exchange, 1845 Share List. Most of the accounts were of eleven days duration. A Leeds sharebroker informed *The Economist* in July 1845 that the "transactions in shares (principally in scrip) in that town account on the average to £500,000 a day". *Economist*, July 19, 1845, p. 686. In the first week of September 2,812 sales were reputedly effected on the three Leeds Exchanges; *Leeds Intelligencer*, September 6, 1845.

36 *Economist*, January 18, 25, 1845; pp. 60, 81.

37 *Economist*, September 13, 1845, p. 875. The peak of activity in terms of dealing and prices of scrip was undoubtedly in the autumn; the high point of prices for the 'old' stocks occurred earlier in the year.

38 M. C. Reed, "Railways and the Growth of the Capital Market", op. cit., p. 178.

39 Matthews, op. cit., p. 111. Hugh Hornby, a director of the Bank of Liverpool, provides a good example of the Liverpool brand of wealthy investor. From 1830 to 1835 he bought shares in the main railway companies, holding £8,500 in 1835. His profit from share operations in 1836 amounted to £8,700, but he fared badly in 1837 making a loss of £3,700. Nevertheless, he reckoned that his railway holdings were worth £25,800 in 1838, out of total assets of £76,000. His performance in the 1845 boom was even more impressive, and in the period 1844-46 he made a profit on share transactions of £21,600; in the next two years he made a loss of £16,200. His operations ranged from the established lines to the newer ones and were conducted in lots ranging from a few shares to lots of 50 or 60 shares standing at nearly £200 each: Diary of Hugh Hornby, Picton Library, Liverpool.

40 *Economist*, June 28, 1845, p. 601.

41 *Economist*, February 15, 1845, p. 153.

42 *Liverpool Mercury*, Supplement, July 4, 1845, gave a list of Liverpool "Railway Speculators", and also a list of subscribers for over £100,000. Of the capital promised in subscription lists in the Spring of 1845, more than £21 million involved sums below £2,000, promised by some 20,000 people, and many sums were around the £100 level; quoted by L. H. Jenks, op. cit., p. 374, note 13.

43 Liverpool Stock Exchange, Minutes, January 3, 1842.

44 Ibid., April 14, 1845.

45 Ibid., August 11, 1845.

46 Ibid., Minutes of Monthly General Meetings, August 1, 15, 1845.
47 Bristol Stock Exchange; Minutes, July 11, 1845.
48 *Bankers' Magazine*, 1845, pp. 134-5.
49 *Economist*, October 25, November 15, 1845.
50 Leeds Stock Exchange, Minutes, November 26, 1845.
51 D. M. Evans, *The Commercial Crisis 1847-8* (1848), pp. 39-40.
52 Ibid., p. 28.
53 It has been estimated that for 1846-48 railway calls involved over £100 million; C. N. Ward-Perkins, "The Commercial Crisis of 1847", *Oxford Economic Papers* (1950), p. 86. The effect on the gilt edged market of meeting such calls lead to only moderate price falls since the Government broker was taking in stock; most of the new investor class had no alternative assets to dispose of anyway: *Economist*, February 1, 1845; see also E. V. Morgan, *Theory and Practice of Central Banking* (1943), pp. 153-4.
54 Liverpool Stock Exchange, Railway Legislation Committee Minutes, March 27 – April 17, 1845. Within these weeks the Committee conducted an intensive campaign, corresponding with other markets and the provisional committees of railways with bills before Parliament, and it also drew up a comprehensive petition for Parliament. Among its suggestions was that calls should be delayed until two years after the sanctioning of a bill, which they hoped would leave more funds in the market.
55 Leeds Stock Exchange, Minutes, April 8, 1846.
56 Liverpool Stock Exchange, Minutes, May 20, September 10, 11, 1847.
57 Ibid., April 18, 1848.
58 Birmingham Stock Exchange, Minutes, October 6, 1847; Manchester Stock Exchange, Minutes, September 18, 1847.
59 See Chapters 1 and 3 for details of the various stock exchanges.
60 G. H. Evans, *British Corporation Finance 1775-1850* (1936), pp. 90-93.
61 Ibid., p. 84.
62 J. Lee, "The Provision of Capital for Early Irish Railways, 1830-1853", *Irish Historical Studies*, March 1968, p. 42. The first Liverpool Stock Exchange share list, August 1836, carried quotations of the Ulster, Dublin Drogheda, and the Dublin and Kilkenny railways.
63 Ibid., p. 43.
64 Ibid., p. 41.
65 Rondo E. Cameron, *France and the Economic Development of Europe* (1961), pp. 205-7.
66 J. H. Clapham, *Economic Development of France and Germany* (1921), pp. 146-7.
67 Jenks, op. cit., pp. 141-2.
68 Cameron, op. cit., p. 314.
69 Jenks, op. cit., p. 147.
70 Ibid., pp. 146, 148.
71 Liverpool Stock Exchange, Minutes, June 10, 1840.
72 As many as eight to a dozen companies competed for the main routes to Strasbourg, Lyons, and Lille; Jenks, op. cit., p. 145.
73 *Financial News*, July 29, 1903.
74 Morgan, op. cit., p. 152. The total of foreign railway calls in 1847 was £5.8 million, and £2.7 million in the first ten months of 1848.
75 Jenks, op. cit., p. 380, note 67.

3 The Formation of the Remaining Stock Exchanges

In the course of the twelve months from October 1844 to October 1845 a great number and variety of stock exchanges were formed in twelve towns and cities in England, from Bristol in the south to Newcastle-upon-Tyne in the north, with Yorkshire claiming the greatest number. They ranged from reasonably formally constituted stock exchanges to the "marts for trafficking in stocks and shares" so roundly condemned by one contemporary observer. Only five exchanges survived the collapse of share prices in the autumn of 1845 to become permanent institutions; the markets in seven centres disappeared although in four of them stock exchanges were formed at the end of the century.

The first of these boom markets appeared in Sheffield in October 1844. However, the beginning of sharebroking in Sheffield dates from 1836 when the business was shared by T. N. Bardwell and John Field. Bardwell did most of his share dealing through the medium of weekly share auctions, and he even continued with them after the formation of the Stock Exchange. Two others, Edward Binney and John Gascoigne appeared briefly on the scene but soon reverted to the accountancy profession. More permanent additions who appeared shortly after this were Ebenezer Smith and Richard Muncaster, the former an accountant and the latter a draper. From six brokers in 1839 the numbers increased greatly with the onset of the second railway boom reaching twenty-eight by 1845. A few of these were drawn from the ranks of the accountancy and legal profession, one left his trade as a cutlery dealer, but the previous professions of most of the recruits were not recorded in the local trade directories.

The main business of the brokers undoubtedly centred on railway shares but the dominance of railways was not really asserted until 1845. The first share list put out by Richard Muncaster in the local press in March 1844 included only fifteen railways, along with nine banks, five canals, and eight miscellaneous local companies.[1] By July 1845 Muncaster's list ran to 60 railways, along with six French lines. The only surviving early Stock Exchange list, for January 2, 1846, contained 105 railways, half of them new lines.

Unfortunately the early records of the Stock Exchange have not survived successive moves to new premises but it is possible to indicate the course of events from fragments of evidence in the local press. The Sheffield Stock Exchange was formed on October 4 1844 but while the local papers at the close of 1844 frequently referred to share dealings in the town no direct mention was made of the new local Stock Exchange, only to the 'knowing men of the Liverpool and Manchester Stock Exchanges".[2] The twenty-eight brokers in the town, however, seem to have been very divided in their views as to how best to organize themselves. Nine brokers, the older fraternity, formed the Sheffield Stock Exchange, but another group of ten brokers formed a rival association called the Sheffield and Hallamshire Stock Exchange, with a further nine broking firms remaining outside both organizations.[3] As to the reasons for this division it is only possible to hazard a few guesses. It is possible that the rival association permitted membership from a wider geographical area, but it seems more likely, on the basis of developments in other towns, that the main reason for the appearance of a rival body was that entrants to the trade disliked the rules and formal procedures favoured by the established brokers. The rival association was shortlived and none of its members later joined the Stock Exchange, indicating perhaps, that they were very much part time 'gentlemen'. A few of the brokers outside both associations later joined the Stock Exchange.

The Stock Exchange seems to have lapsed a little after the collapse of the 1845 boom and was reorganized in 1848 when there were twenty-two broking firms listed in the local directory.[4] Of the firms composing the re-constituted market only four survived into the twentieth century, namely John Watson & Co., Frank Wever & Son, F. E. & S. Smith, and J. B. & R. Roberts.

J. H. Ridsdale was certainly one of the first stockbrokers in Leeds and was listed in the Leeds Directory for 1830–31 as a 'Canal and Railroad Sharebroker'; his main business at that time probably centred on canal shares. Also listed was one George Marsh, agent and sharebroker, but his name does not appear for subsequent years. The 1836 railway boom witnessed no sprouting of share brokers in the city so that share dealing was shared between Ridsdale and R. B. Watson & Co. Both were active in the receipt of share applications for new railway companies, while a price list of some thirty "Iron Railways" published by Ridsdale in the local press in the summer of 1836 indicates a considerable local interest in railway promotion. The picture changed a great deal with the 1845 railway boom.

R.B. Watson writing to *The Economist* in 1845 stated, "What a contrast do the present times present to those which prevailed in the share market in Leeds about nine years ago, when the writer first broke the ice of the market, having then only one competitor. There are now upwards of one hundred, with the prospect of an increasing number."[5] The growth of the share market between 1836 and 1845 was not in any way gradual. The number of brokers increased rapidly following the resurgence of railway promotion in 1843–44; in 1841 only four were listed in Leeds, by 1843 the number rose to eleven, and to twenty-six by 1844, with the big upsurge occurring in 1845.[6]

The business background of these entrants into the broking profession in Leeds is very similar to that found in other share markets. Among the older brokers William Sampson was an accountant and commission agent, while John Potter was an insurance agent. The previous professions of the twenty or so entrants into the market in 1844–45 which can be traced are too numerous to detail here, but among them were two bankers, a flax spinner, a wool merchant, a gentleman, a brewer, and one who gloried in being "a Sheriff's Officer, appraiser, and deputy to the bailiff of the Honour of Pontefract". The background of about 60 brokers could not be established which suggests a large entry from the non-professional class.

The nucleus of a 'Leeds Share Market' existed as early as 1843 but unfortunately there is no evidence available as to its precise location. At that time numerous brokers advertised 'wanted and on offer' lists in the local press, while others engaged in share auctions alongside informal market trading. By the autumn of 1844 many of the established brokers were anxious to obtain a formal and efficient organization. Accordingly, in December, arrangements were completed for the formation of the Leeds Stock Exchange Association, and the market was opened for business on January 13 1845. After accommodation in temporary rooms the market moved to the local Music Hall in October, and shortly afterwards to the new exchange building.[7] According to R. B. Watson "the opening of our Stock Exchange is expected to give that standing to our share market, which the business done here fully entitles it to take."[8] The local press was, pardonably perhaps, a little more euphoric. *The Leeds Intelligencer* commented, "There can be no doubt that this establishment will tend to increase the importance of Leeds Share business, by facilitating transactions, and thus centering in Leeds that portion of the share trade which the opulence and situation of the town have a right to claim, but which has hitherto (for want of an Exchange in Leeds) been transacted in other marts".[9] The members themselves celebrated the event with a dinner, the first of many, at the White Horse Inn, and elected J. H. Ridsdale, the moving spirit in the formation of the Stock Exchange, to the office of chairman which he held until his death in 1875. As chairman he urged his fellow brokers to conduct their business honourably at a time when stockbroking in the town was expanding very rapidly; while he was doing well himself he was not jealous of others who might be doing better! The other committee members were R. B. Watson, William Walker, Richard Binney, H. Beardshaw, John Rhodes and Richard Bowlby. At the date of formation there were eighteen members, mostly established brokers, a further eleven were admitted in 1845 and twelve in 1846.[10]

Many brokers remained outside the Stock Exchange, and in February thirty-seven of them formed a rival organization, the Leeds Sharebrokers' Association. Presumably their main stimulus arose from disapproval of certain entry requirements in the rules of the Stock Exchange. For example, candidates for admission were required to have been in business "as a sharebroker in Leeds for at least six months", they needed sureties to the sum of £600, and they were not allowed to engage in any other business. In most other respects the rules of the Sharebrokers' Association were very similar to those of the Stock Exchange.[11] The Association was controlled by a committee of management, admission was by ballot, and every partner in a firm had to be a member. Their commission scale was similar to that of the Stock Exchange, with half-commission on bargains with other brokers. Fortnightly settlements were arranged and the published list gave details not only of the Association's dealings but also bargains done with members of the Stock Exchange. The Association's rules prohibited a member from "buying or selling shares, stock or scrip on his own account".

A further twenty or so brokers remained outside both organizations and held a third market on the Leeds Commercial Exchange, presumably a convenient meeting place. This market had no formal constitution or rules. When dealing was extremely active in the summer of 1845 the volume in the first week of September reached "2,812 sales . . . on the three Exchanges, which is a good stroke of business".[12] Business was such that the magistrates called in the police "to keep the footpaths clear in the streets where the Stock Exchanges are situated (in the area of Albion Street and Commercial Street), so great is the crowd of speculators attending there during the hours of business". At the Leeds Post Office such was the "crowd of applicants for letters every morning that policemen are obliged to be employed to keep them in order", while according to one observer "shares have actually been sold at the Parish Church. This is really too bad".[13] There is no means of telling which market

E

had the largest turnover or the greatest influence on prices; the Sharebrokers' Association had the largest membership but the old brokers probably had the richest though not necessarily the most speculative clients.

With the fall in share prices, and most of the new scrip shares standing at merely nominal quotations, many of the newer entrants left the sharebroking trade. Within a few months negotiations were in hand between the Stock Exchange and the brokers of the "Leeds Exchange" with a view to admitting the latter to membership of the Stock Exchange.[14] The outside brokers disapproved of some Stock Exchange rules but the committee was not prepared to grant unconditional entry. Indeed, some members were strongly opposed to admitting outside brokers but their motion to introduce a rule prohibiting members from dealing with outside brokers "belonging to another Association in Leeds" was defeated. In October 1846 however the Stock Exchange decided to suspend their entrance requirements in favour of all parties who were candidates for admission, provided they had six months stockbroking experience.[15] Very few outside brokers applied for admission which suggests that most of those who entered the trade in 1845 left as abruptly as they had entered, and the rival associations disappeared. By 1850 the membership of the Stock Exchange settled at around 50, and remained at this level for many years thereafter.

Up until the 1836 railway boom Bristol had but one sharebroker, an accountant, L. Beck, of Bank Court, who entered the trade about 1830. At the time of the boom he was joined by another full time broker, G. Edwards & Son, previously a commercial agent, and by a flood of speculators. Beck and Edwards probably did most of their business through press advertisements, while during the boom itself they also went to the established and well patronized Bristol Commercial Rooms. At the height of the boom in the spring of 1836 some 25 tradesmen "who had hitherto never supported the establishment" became subscribers, but judging from contemporary newspaper accounts they were mainly interested in their own speculations, entering into a considerable volume of time bargains.[16] They dealt in about a dozen or so railway lines, mostly those associated with the south west. With the ensuing fall in share prices business declined abruptly and dealing activity in turn reverted to the 'old' brokers. During the years between the two booms very few people entered the stockbroking trade, reflecting the general apathy of investors in the south west to this new investment channel. In 1840 there were four brokers in Bristol, Luke Arnold and Robert Goss having joined the two pioneers of 1836. In 1841

S. Johnson entered stockbroking, while J. S. Tripp did so two years later. The quickening pace of railway promotion in 1844 brought S. Morgan, W. Wreford and Sohems & Co. into the trade. These nine brokers constituted the nucleus of the 'old' brokers and they played a central role in the eventual formation of the Bristol Stock Exchange.

The initiative for setting up a stock exchange did not however come from the ranks of the established brokers. On March 11 1845 one of the newly emerged brokers, Bradley Barnard of Albion Chambers, sent an invitation to eight people, all new brokers, to attend a meeting so as to form a provisional committee which was "to make arrangements for the public meeting" already called by Bradley Barnard. Invitations to this meeting had been sent to the old brokers and to a very large number of interested commercial parties, over sixty people in all. The reason for calling it was that "Several Gentlemen having experienced great inconvenience from the want of an establishment in this City similar to those of Liverpool and Manchester for the conducting of share business have determined on holding a meeting . . . for the purpose of forming an Association to be called 'The Bristol Stock Exchange', and to nominate a Committee to frame the rules for the Government of the same". At the "numerous and highly respectable meeting held at the offices of Bradley Barnard & Co.", with twenty-five people present and R. H. Webb in the chair, it was resolved that an "Association be formed of Brokers and Dealers in Stocks and Shares for more effectively conducting Stock and Share business in this City and that the same be called 'The Bristol Stock Exchange Association' ". Entrants joining before the end of March paid a subscription of five gns, but later ones were required to pay an entrance fee of twenty gns, a subscription of five gns, and go through the ordeal of the ballot. It was also decided to appoint an outsider as President, who along with the Vice President and nine other members, formed the Committee of Management. The President acted as treasurer of the Association and was made an honorary member; Mr (afterwards Sir) John Kerle Haberfield, the Mayor of Bristol, was approached and he willingly accepted the office.[17]

It is difficult to see what major advantages the proposed stock exchange possessed over the existing Commercial Exchange since the provisional committee thought in terms of an open stock exchange and indulged in a large scale publicity campaign to get likely persons to join as members. A circular from the President reminded prospective members "of the importance of such an Association, not only for the protection of individuals making investments, but on account of the facilities it will afford by the Establishment of a market for the purchase of stocks and shares".[18] These were flowery and ambitious claims in view of the rather heterogeneous membership of the new stock exchange.

Progress with consolidating the new organization was soon disrupted by the resignation of William Wreford and his partners. At the time several of the old brokers, including Wreford "had combined themselves together to form a society to consist solely of brokers, and to do all they could to set aside the proposed 'Bristol Stock Exchange'". Attempts to persuade them to join came to nothing and they continued to "use every exertion to oppose it." Despite outside disapproval the Association proceeded to formulate its rules which included a provision to the effect that "any Member of this House found doing business with or for any individual carrying on the business of a Stock or Share broker in this City, but not a Member of this House, shall be reprimanded by the Committee for the first offence, and if repeated shall be subjected to be expelled from the House". A large number of members voiced strong opposition against this proposal to coerce the old brokers. They complained of the retrospective aspect of the proposed rule and urged that the Association should exercise "patience with the prejudices of certain parties and await the issue of time and circumstances to convince them of their error, rather than prescribe them with a view to destroy their business, and annihilate them as Brokers unless they become Members of the Stock Exchange". The prospect of more or less total evasion of the rule led to the addition of a rider which made it inapplicable to brokers who had been in business prior to March 31 1845.[19]

In the face of hostility from outside the Association went ahead with plans to obtain an exchange of share lists with other markets, and even to obtaining very flamboyant livery for the porter who was bedecked in a "Blue Coat, turned up with red, Gold-striped dark Oxford trousers, Buttons with City Arms, . . . and plain Hat with Gold Braid". The Exchange itself, presumably on Bradley Barnard's premises, was opened with due form on April 16 1845. However, it soon ran into difficulties. About half the membership favoured the dissolution of the Association but this move was temporarily frustrated. After considerable debate it was decided "that all members not recognized Brokers previous to the 31 March 1845 do retire having their subscriptions returned in full." Sir John Haberfield remained as honorary President. It was generally "allowed on all sides that the machinery did not work well"; the merchants and manufacturers were altogether out of place on the Stock Exchange.[20] Presumably difficulties had arisen with the enforcement of bargains, and also as a result of the fact that most of the so-called jobbers were no more than speculators anxious to avoid the payment of commission to the brokers. The jobbers retired and their interests were taken over by the remaining "professed brokers". Following these developments and the remodelling of the Association the "old standard brokers" consented to become members, and Edwards, Arnold and Goss were immediately elected to the committee on the resignation of three of the members. Some of the old brokers were admitted merely on the payment of the entrance fee, while the remainder were given a concession in that sureties could be found outside the House.[21]

Following the withdrawal of the non-professional element the membership of the Exchange dwindled from over 40 to 18 by April 1846. With the contraction of share business in that year the Stock Exchange was compelled to reduce its expenditures because of lack of finance. The post of salaried secretary was discontinued and alternative accommodation sought. By 1850 the membership had fallen to 15 and it remained at this level for several decades. On the evidence of the local directories there would seem to have been very few brokers operating outside the Association, but even the few that did were regarded as a nuisance, sufficiently so for a rule to be adopted stating that the Stock Exchange would not recognize them and would expel any member who repeatedly did business with them.[22]

The doyen of Hull sharebrokers was Charles Wilkinson who entered the trade in 1833.[23] Other early sharebrokers were T. & W. Collinson (general agent, ship insurance brokers and warehouse keepers) who probably came into sharedealing in the early 1840s.[24] These few firms appear to have catered for the local sharedealing needs until the 1845 boom when they were joined by a large and very miscellaneous group of new brokers, making a total of nearly 50 firms in 1845. It is not possible to trace the previous occupations of most of them, but the few that can be identified pursued occupations closely linked with the town's port; Blyth and Wright, shipping brokers; Richard Cattley, wine merchant; Henry Staniforth, foreign and commercial agent; John Day, warehouseman; Thomas Binney, corn factor. Two merchants who took to sharebroking were Woodhouse, Ramsey & Co., and James Bowden, who ran his business from the delightful address of 8, Land of Green Ginger.[25]

This mushrooming of sharebrokers was of course exclusively connected with the railway share boom; there were very few local industrial and commercial undertakings listed alongside the 31 railways given in the share list of Collinson & Flint for January 1845.[26] By March there was sufficient business, and brokers, to merit the setting up of a stock exchange and it is probable that Charles Wilkinson was the leading figure in this move. On March 10 1845 at a meeting held at Wilkinson's office in Scale Lane attended by William Collinson, James Bowden, J. Alsop, F. Stamp, G. Bowlby, J. Schofield, Henry Staniforth, and Charles Johnson, it was decided that "the Parties now present form themselves into a 'Stock and Sharebrokers' Association'", with an entrance fee of £25, an annual subscription of £5, and all "members admitted afterwards to pay £50". A sub-committee consisting of Collinson, Alsop, Stamp, and Schofield was appointed to "prepare rules, negotiate for a Clerk, Place of Meeting for business, and other measures necessary for carrying out the objects of the Association".[27] Charles Wilkinson was elected chairman and Charles Johnson temporary secretary. By the end of March the Stock Exchange had 12 member firms. It held two business meetings daily, with one call over at 12.00 – 12.30 and the other from 2.30 – 3.00. The exact location of the Stock Exchange is not known but in all probability it was held in one of the broker's offices; in October the Stock Exchange was anxious to participate in the promotion of the Hull Exchange and Commercial Building Co. which was a venture to build a commodious Commercial Exchange and News Room where they hoped to get suitable accommodation. However, by 1851 the number of members had fallen off sharply and the remainder were content with a less grandiose, but certainly quaint, address at 8, Land of Green Ginger.[28]

Many brokers remained outside the newly formed Stock Exchange, deterred by the entrance fee and rules. In April 1845 a small group of them, half a dozen firms, decided to form a rival exchange, the Hull New Stock Exchange, with Thomas Sibary as chairman and S. Bennett as secretary. It had the attraction of a low entrance fee and was open to brokers "not having a place of business in Hull". No doubt a considerable attraction of the competing institution was the provision in its rules that the members would "charge but ONE Commission for the re-purchase or Sale of Shares within the same account".[29]

Brokers within and outside the stock exchanges engaged in frequent advertising but it is interesting to note that it did not extend to using "wanted and on-offer" lists commonly used by brokers elsewhere. By October 1845, the height of the boom, the Hull share list included 93 railway companies while a considerable volume of business was done in the town, not all of which met with local approval. *The Hull Advertizer* in a leading article in November accused some brokers of creating alarm by the imprudent conduct of their business, referring particularly to the "infamous system of repudiations, which we regret to hear spoken of in Hull". As to the subsequent history of sharebroking in the town there is little to tell; by 1872 there were only five firms, including Wilkinson and Flint, nine firms are listed for 1882, with the same number in 1914 of which only T. W. Flint & Co. provided a link with the hectic boom of 1845.[30]

The Newcastle Stock Exchange was probably unique in that its first meeting place following its formation on April 29 1845 was at a tea dealer's shop, which was not altogether inappropriate since two of the leading brokers were drawn from the retail trade. John Drewry was a grocer, tea dealer and sharebroker, while J. J. Kimpster was a wholesaler, retail grocer, tea dealer and general sharebroker. Along with W. T. Fordyce, printer and bookseller, and Jones & Gibson & Co., commission and property agents, they probably entered stockbroking during the 1836 boom. Following the increase in railway promotions the number of brokers increased to nine by 1841, remaining at this number until 1844, and increasing to about 20 in 1845.[31] Prior to the 1845 boom share dealings were largely confined to local issues; a share list of 1844 gives nine banks, eleven railways, six shipping companies, and twelve miscellaneous companies among them a cemetery, the Theatre Royal and the gas and water undertakings, all with a paid up capital of about £390,000, over half of which was attributable to four companies.

The Association consisted of brokers of "stocks and shares in public companies, but no person whose place of business and residence is not in Newcastle or Gateshead, or immediate neighbourhood and who has not been engaged . . . as a Sharebroker for at least six months shall be eligible to be proposed a Member", while members were not allowed to engage in any other business. It held daily business meetings, issued a weekly list, insisted that all members should be individually responsible for the due fulfilment of contracts, and did cash transactions.[32] By the autumn of 1845, presumably due to the decline in turnover, the members decided to hold "for the accommodation of parties desirous of purchasing or disposing of shares, a public sale by Auction". Shares were entered for sale through the brokers who took the usual commission laid down in the rules. The auction was conducted by a professional auctioneer at the offices of the Stock Exchange, situated in Grey Street opposite the Exchange News Room. The advertisement for the auction pointed to "the Advantages of the above arrangement to persons engaged in Share Business, as they will thus be enabled to exercise a rigid Superintendence over every Transaction and to know with certainty the actual amount realised in every case without the secret Intervention of irresponsible speculators", in other

words the jobbing fraternity who came in for a good deal of criticism in the provincial press of the period.[33]

Sharebroking at York goes back to 1835 when James Grayston,
auctioneer, appraiser, law stationer and agent to the London Assurance Association, added it to his already impressive list of pursuits.
By 1838 he had been joined by Thomas Gatliffe and Ralph Todd
but by 1843 both had disappeared from the share dealing scene, to
be replaced by W. H. Cowling and (?) Beattie, two accountants. With
the 1845 share boom the number of broking firms shot up to thirty-
six.[34] The previous occupations of half the new entrants to the
trade can be traced from local directories and the main feature
which emerges is the great diversity of their background. Among
them are a jeweller, watchmaker, bookseller, tailor, engraver and
printer, grocer, builder, attorney, tobacco and snuff manufacturer,
proprietory of a repository for fancy goods, and a clog and
patten manufacturer. The main dealing activity centred on railway
shares, but a distinctive feature of a share list for January 1845 put
out by Grayston and Earle was a section of twenty-one banks.

As for so many of the smaller centres there is very little by the
way of accessible information on the formation of the local stock
exchange. On the evidence of a broker's advertisement in the local
press it would appear that there existed a "York Stock Exchange"
by March 1845; a more positive piece of evidence is a York Share
List given in *The York Herald* from April onwards which states
that it was published "under the authority of the Committee of the
Stock Exchange".[35] Evidently not all the brokers in the city joined
the Stock Exchange since at the time there was a move afoot to set
up a less formal market. The Merchants Hall Co. opened their
Ancient Hall as a 'Railway Exchange Room' for the "convenience
of sharebrokers and railway speculators", with a 10s. subscription.
Meetings were held daily at 11.0 – 12.0 and 3.0 – 4.0 for the transaction of business, presided over by Mr Sheriff Bellerby, President
of the York Mercantile Association, who "takes notes of all proceedings at the meetings, he sitting at the head of the table, and all
commercial engagements being openly transacted". Thus it was
claimed "will Brokers and speculators – Buyers and Sellers – meet
and mingle together, as in the olden time, for the general advantage
of the enterprising multitude". By September it had a membership
of nearly two hundred.[36] Very few brokers however continued in the
business after the collapse of the share boom; by 1855 there were
only seven, and by 1872 the number had fallen to five.

The history of the Huddersfield share market falls into two distinct phases. The first is associated with the 1845 railway mania, the
second with a far less spectacular event, the passing of the 1899

Finance Act. To turn first to the former event. By the early months of 1845 five brokers had appeared in the town, among them, James Bulchart, John Hawxby, a broker since 1837–38, and Moore & Gatliffe. By the autumn the railway mania was "raging furiously in Huddersfield and 'applications', 'scrip' and 'repudiation' form about one half of the conversation of the inhabitants," all of which resulted in a rapid increase in the number of stockbrokers.[37] In the middle of June "a tolerably numerous meeting of sharebrokers and other gentlemen was held persuant to public notice in a large room in Chancery Lane, for the purpose of desiring the best means of instituting a Stock Exchange for this town. Such an institution would be of infinite advantage to all persons connected with the funds of the country, and to none more than to the numerous stockbrokers who have lately established themselves here in that particular line." A few weeks later the first meeting of the "Huddersfield Association of sharebrokers took place . . . for the transaction of business". The Association "which now numbers 20 members have a commodious exchange in preparation, where their business will shortly be conducted and on the same principles as at the Exchanges at Manchester, and Leeds, or other important towns".[38]

Dealings took place daily between 11.30 – 12.30, and a list of closing prices was published, most of which was taken up with railways "pending a decision next session". Only seven of the brokers came from traceable occupations, and of these two were chemists and druggists. With the decline of share turnover after 1845 the number of brokers decreased, reaching 13 in 1848 and only 2 in 1858. No doubt, the Stock Exchange closed down within a few years of the end of the share boom.

The re-establishment of a stock exchange in Huddersfield in 1899 was a direct consequence of the provisions of section 13 of the Finance Act of that year. Six brokers, W. Moore, the only link with the 1845 era, T. K. Mellor, W. Wimpenny, R. Ramsden, W. Lakewood, and F. W. Bentley sent a memorial to their local Member of Parliament protesting against the injustice of the new act. Under the provisions of the 1891 Stamp Act contract notes between brokers were exempt from duty, but an amendment in the 1899 Finance Act restricted the exemption to brokers who were members of a stock exchange in the United Kingdom.[39] This meant, however, that brokers outside a stock exchange were liable to double duty on one transaction, and this prospect prompted the Huddersfield brokers to form a Stock Exchange in July 1899. At the first meeting held in the offices of Mellor and Wimpenny, William Moore was elected chairman, rules were drawn up, and it was decided to obtain rooms in the Huddersfield Exchange. Initially the Association was open to brokers throughout the West Riding but this was later changed when the five mile radius provision was generally adopted.

The founders of the Association were determined not to lose any of their previous 'rights, usages and priveleges', and to this end provisions were inserted in the rules. In particular, they could continue to "advertise for business purposes", and also send out circulars, share lists and prospectuses to other than their own principals.[40] These highly individualistic rules were abandoned when the Huddersfield Stock Exchange obtained admission to the Council of Associated Stock Exchanges in 1913.

The present Nottingham Stock Exchange was established in 1909 but its predecessor was formed during the 1845 boom. The first brokers in the town were Charles Spencer and John Wildey, both listed as such in the Nottingham Directory for 1840; there is no evidence of any sharebrokers appearing there in the 1836 boom. By 1845 the number had increased to fifteen with the new entrants drawn from a variety of occupations ranging from George Spencer, boat builder, W. P. Talham, grocer and tea dealer, to F. Wakefield, Jun., gentleman. The market was dominated by railway shares, the list being about equally divided between completed and new lines. There were a few local companies; local banks, gas works and canals. One broker, however, Peet & Son, seemed to specialize in bank and canal shares and his press advertisements in 1843 suggest that he was an active dealer in them, as well as in railway shares.

With rapidly rising share prices in the middle of July;

"The increase of business in the world of speculation, produced by the railway schemes which have so abundantly started into life, has even in our town, been so great as to cause the origination of a project of some influence and note. This is no other than the establishment of a Stock Exchange, where the prices of shares may be obtained correctly – where sharebrokers can assemble to converse over their affairs and consult with each other – and where merchants may congregate for their various purposes they may have in view. The stock and sharebrokers of this town have had a meeting, to consider the propriety of establishing such a mart of intercourse and traffic and not only have they decided among themselves to do so, but have also invited the stock and sharebrokers of the neighbouring towns, or from any distant part, who may not have a place of business in Nottingham, to co-operate with them. The convenience of an exchange of this description cannot but be the most salutary, as the nearest town where such a mart can be obtained is Leeds, distance upwards of fifty miles. Weekly share lists are to be

published, and daily gatherings take place from half past
twelve to one, and from quarter to five to a quarter past five
daily, while from the number of respectable names of stock
and sharebrokers, of this town, attached to . . . [it] . . . we
have little doubt of its being finally most complete in its prosperity".[41]

Eight broking firms were involved in the new Stock Exchange and
they met for their daily call over at the offices of Raworth &
Shepperly in Long Row. The only surviving record of this early market
is the list published by "Authority of the Committee of the Nottingham and Midland Stock Exchange" which gave quotations for
seventy-eight railways and six local companies. It ceased to appear
in November 1845. A few brokers did not join the Stock Exchange
on its formation, but may of course have done so later.

The Stock Exchange probably folded up with the onset of the
depressed markets in 1846, while by 1848 the number of brokers
had fallen to five. During the remainder of the century Nottingham
maintained a link with the stockbroking trade, albeit, a tenuous one.
Throughout the 1850s Pearson Peet provided quotations to the press
of local stocks, while James Cater & Son did so in the 1860s. W. F.
Bromley put out a share list throughout the 1880s and 1890s, a
period during which the local miscellaneous section grew rapidly
in size with local breweries, tramways and cycle companies being
well represented. E. M. Kidd & Son took over in 1900 and his list
reflects the predominance of cycle interests with forty cycle, ten
tube and ten tyre companies.

The increase in the number of brokers after the turn of the century was no doubt associated with the much expanded industrial
share market. In December 1909 thirteen local brokers decided that
it would be desirable to establish a Stock Exchange, and accordingly
rooms were obtained at Queen's Chambers in King Street, F.
Beeby was appointed honorary secretary, and W. F. Bromley chairman. The first meeting of the market was held on May 10 1910. A
daily call over was held and a monthly list put out. Facilities were
also provided for advertising 'wanted and on-offer' lists of unlisted
securities, while members were requested to adhere to the minimum
scale of commission laid down in the rules "in respect of all local
securities".[42] Not all brokers in the town were anxious to join at
the outset being deterred by the advertising and commission
requirements. However, by 1926 the membership had risen to 20,
mostly single partner firms.

According to local trade directories sharebroking began in Halifax in the early 1840s; the 1842 directory gives three brokers,

Richard H. Hartley, Joseph Cockin Hoatsin and James Hervey, whose share list appeared in the local press of the period.[43] A further two brokers appeared in 1844, while the 1845–46 directory lists eleven brokers, drawn from a diverse range of occupations. *The Halifax Guardian* commented, "the extent to which speculation in railway and other shares has attained in Halifax may be gathered from the fact that there are now no less than 9 sharebrokers in the town. A year or two ago there were only three . . . ; we suppose the next move will be the erection of a Stock Exchange".[44] It is almost certain that no such Stock Exchange was ever erected; by 1848 the number of brokers was down to seven, and a decade later to four.

The re-establishment of a local stock exchange at the end of the century occurred in 1896, presumably under the impetus of the company boom of the period. There was no legislative change to induce it. The only surviving document, the rule book, outlines the objects of the Association of Stockbrokers as "the provision of facilities for local dealing, the joint quotation of Local Prices, the issue of Lists, the regulation of Brokerage, and generally the maintenance of the interests of Members".[45]

A similar pattern of events occurred in Bradford. The first brokers appeared during the 1836 share boom, namely Thomas Holmes and W. F. Heyland, and they held the floor until the year 1844 when four new brokers entered the trade, and the 1845 boom brought the total for the town up to sixteen.[46] Unfortunately there is no means of dating the formation of the Stock Exchange but it can be surmized that it was probably formed in the summer of 1845; certainly the autumn reports on the share market of the local press speak of "our" market when there were rules for "prompt delivery and payment of scrip".[47] The decline in turnover with the collapse of the boom probably saw the dissolution of the Stock Exchange, and certainly a reduction in the number of brokers. By 1870 there were only five in the town, only one of which had a link with the railway mania period. The second Bradford Stock Exchange was opened on August 4 1899, with nineteen members for the same reason as at nearby Huddersfield; a desire to avoid the provisions of the Finance Act, and in addition for "the better and more efficient conduct and management of the business of stock and share brokers within Bradford".[48]

Leicester boasts a particularly early association with share dealing since it was a leading provincial centre of canal enthusiasm. Dealings in canal shares in the 1790s boom took place by private negotiation, public auction, or in 'Navigation Share Offices'. A leading Leicester broker of this period was one John Wilkinson who did a considerable amount of advertising for business and who also had an office in Market Place "for the accommodation of the Public, who want to Purchase or Sell, in any of the present or intended canals".[49] Local interest in canal investment persisted into the 1840s since a local share list for 1844 is dominated by canal shares, thirty-two in all, as against only nineteen railways. A particularly interesting feature of the share list is the marked contrast in share denominations since nearly all the canal shares displayed paid up values of over £100 and some stood at very high prices e.g. the Loughborough canal quoted at £1,140 (by August 1845 it had fallen to £850).[50]

Although Leicester's outburst of share speculation occurs well on in the 1845 railway mania its leading brokers date from earlier years. John Windram & Son was established in 1829, and George Eaglesfield added sharebroking to his auctioneering acivities in the early 1830s. By 1840 they were joined by two more, John Bailey and Joseph Berrington. The 1845 speculation brought several additions to their ranks making eleven firms at the beginning of 1846, most of them entering the trade in the summer of 1845 "when the high fever of railway business was raging in this town".[51] In September 1845, in consequence of the "increasing business and importance of the town", and the "high fever", the sharebrokers "on Friday se'n night (September 5) resolved that a Stock Exchange should be established". Each member paid a subscription of £30, and gave security of £200 "to ensure the respectability of the proposed Stock Exchange . . . and the prompt settlement of all engagements". Transactions were for cash on delivery of scrip or transfer. The "Saloon at the Theatre" was hired for the purpose of holding the daily business meetings and the market opened on October 20, 1845.[52] But the days of the high premium had already departed and "utter stagnation" prevailed on the Stock Exchange for the ensuing months. While the Stock Exchange seems to have continued into 1846, it survived no further; by 1850 the number of brokers in Leicester had fallen to eight, and to half that number by 1863.

The emergence of sharebrokers in Birmingham between the early 1830s and the advent of the 1845 share boom was certainly a very gradual process. As far as can be judged from local directories one of the first brokers was James Harrison who was conducting sharebroking operations in 1830–31, along with his other activities of auctioneer, appraiser, and agent to the Phoenix Fire Office; he seems to have abandoned share-dealing shortly afterwards. More permanent entrants to the profession appeared in 1832–33, namely, James Scott, John Wade, and John Wrighton. The 1836 boom induced a few more brokers into the trade, and in addition some ephemeral dealers whose names never got into the local directories. Dealings in Birmingham prior to the railway share boom of mid 1836 centred largely on local bank and canal shares, but these were relegated to a secondary position once the boom got under way.[53]

With the gradual increase in the number of railway lines reaching the market a few additional entrants appear in the early 1840s, including in 1842 Nathaniel Lea, a leading figure in the formation of the Stock Exchange. By that year thirteen sharebrokers were listed in the local directories. Once again the previous professions of the new entrants were very similar to that found in other markets, with a good sprinkling of professional men such as auctioneers, accountants, and agents. Four of the brokers listed in 1842 in fact left the profession before 1845. By 1844–45 the number of brokers had increased to nineteen and by 1847 there were twenty-five. Among those who entered the trade during the boom were James Pearson, formerly manager of the Bank of Birmingham, the first chairman of the Stock Exchange, and John Smith, founder of the firm of Smith, Keen and Barnett.[54]

There seems to have been a sufficient number of brokers in the town by 1840 for them to meet informally and make a market in railway shares. A list headed the "Birmingham Share Market" appeared in the local press in October 1840 giving quotations for sixteen shares, including local banks, canals, and the main railway lines.[55] By 1844 the list had expanded greatly, with quotations for 56 shares, all except eleven of which were railways; in September 1845 the list ran to 106 shares. It would appear that several of the brokers decided as early as 1843–44 to form a Sharebrokers' Association and that John Wade, John Wrighton, Edward Wilson, Nathaniel Lea, James Robertson Lane, and James Pearson were members of this early market. Since it was probably loosely constituted it soon fell into abeyance. The growing volume of share business in the summer of 1845 brought to the fore a need for a formally organized market, and accordingly the established brokers decided that it was "expedient to revive the Birmingham Sharebrokers' Association, being convinced that the establishment of a Stock Exchange at Birmingham is absolutely necessary for the due and proper execution of the orders entrusted to them by their friends and the Public, have, therefore formed themselves into an Association for the purpose of establishing such an Exchange." It was opened for business on October 22, 1845.

The first meeting of the Association was held on September 24, 1845 at the Royal Hotel, Temple Row, attended by ten brokers with James Pearson in the chair. The purpose of the meeting was to consider the "Rules by which the Association shall in future be regulated, to appoint a Secretary, to frame a Share list, to engage suitable premises, and to take such other steps as may be necessary for the establishment of a Stock Exchange and for making the same known to the public".[56] James Pearson was duly elected chairman of the Stock Exchange, an office he held until 1852, and the Birmingham Banking Co. were appointed treasurers to the Association.[57] Premises were obtained at 2 Temple Row. During these early meetings several measures were passed which were designed to attain for the Exchange the organization necessary for the proper execution of orders given to members. The duties of the secretary were meticulously listed, and they included collecting information on railway calls, dividends, scrip, new issues, and to mark the prices of the daily transactions 'on-change', but not those between 'brokers off-change'. The share list was compiled by a sub-committee consisting of Lea, Wade and Smith, and included for the most part railways under the headings "Railways made, Railways making, Projected Railways, Foreign Railways, Canals and Miscellaneous". The call-over was held twice a day, settlements were fortnightly, and rates of brokerage were the same as those charged in London. Buying in or selling out was done by the Chairman or his deputy, while any income thereon went to the general fund. If they could not execute such a transaction in Birmingham, the Chairman could put the order through the London or Liverpool markets. All new issues were subject to the fixing of a special settlement by the Committee of the Exchange.

New entrants to the market had to pay an entrance fee of £40, and be recommended by two members, with a surety requirement of £600. The rules stipulated that as soon as the membership reached twenty no person was allowed to apply for membership unless he had been a sharebroker for at least six months. This provision remained inoperative since the membership never attained the designated ceiling. Of particular interest was the view of the Committee "that the business of a Broker and that of a Jobber or Dealer are in their nature and object entirely distinct, and they cannot both be carried on by the same person or the same firm consistently with the views of this Association". The fact that only sharebroking was allowed left the market highly dependent on London and the major provincial centres of dealing at Liverpool and Manchester. It might account for the fact that some brokers of long standing did not join the Stock Exchange.

The annual reports of the Committee to the General Meetings in 1846 and 1847 contain a certain amount of self congratulation. The total membership by 1847 had reached nineteen, including five firms. Despite the "extreme depression to which all share property has been reduced" no member of the Exchange had defaulted, a not very surprising fact given the restraint on dealing opportunities and the smallness of the market. Even if no one defaulted the market shrank rapidly in size and by 1851 the membership was down to ten.[58]

Three markets remain to be noted, but they fall well outside the railway era, those at Cardiff, Swansea, and Newport.[59] Sharedealing in Cardiff can be traced back to the 1870s, the first local share list being put out by Thackeray & Sayce in February 1874. It contained mostly local rails, along with twenty-four local miscellaneous companies, including Ebbw Vale and Llynvi, Tondu & Ogmore companies, both Chadwick promotions.[60] The only other Cardiff broking concern of this period was Roberts & Lyddon. By 1884 there were four brokers operating in Cardiff, increasing to nine five years later, and among these was Tregerthen, Dunn & Co., specialists in steamship shares (possibly one ship companies) who did their business by advertising and monthly auctions of shares. Despite the gradual increase in the number of local industrial and commercial companies by 1890 railways were still "the backbone of the market and when these don't prosper little else moves".[61] The conversion of numerous colliery enterprises into limited companies, especially during 1889–90, changed the picture and by 1895 the local list was dominated by coal and iron companies, with local docks also occupying a prominent place. The Stock Exchange itself was formed in 1892, shortly after the conversion boom in coal companies, and it had a membership of about a dozen brokers.[62] One of the main reasons for the formation of a formal market was that the "quotations of the London Stock Exchange are of very little value to investors in local stocks and shares. In most cases a very wide margin is allowed between buyer and seller and any alteration that is necessary is so tardily made that it becomes valueless".[63] As elsewhere a handful of brokers remained outside the Stock Exchange, doing quite a substantial amount of business.[64]

Sharebroking in Swansea also dates from the mid 1870s when a lengthy local list, mainly rails and small companies, was published in the local press by Sayce and Rake. By the early 1880s the number of brokers in the town had increased to four, with a further two added to their ranks by 1900. At this date they dealt in the familiar list of rails and somewhat less well known local companies, with breweries, gas companies, docks, and banks being well represented.[65] The Swansea Stock Exchange was formed in 1903, probably to afford more satisfactory dealing facilities, with nine member firms. H. Day O. Wills was chairman, and William M. Davies, the doyen of the local broking circle, was secretary. They met daily for the call over, and a weekly list was published.[66] Judging by the weekly list of 1905 the market specialized in coal and iron companies, but perhaps the most distinctive feature of the list was the relatively small capitalizations of many of the companies, under £20,000, which made for pretty narrow markets in such shares.

While the Newport Stock Exchange was not formed until a much later date the earliest broker in the town, F. P. Robjent started business in 1876. By 1890 he had been joined by three others, H. R. Evans, Betton, Sayce, Vaughan & Co., and P. Powell. When the Stock Exchange was formed in 1916, with recognized hours and a central location, there were still only four firms in the town, Robjent being the only survivor of the earlier period.[67] His new colleagues were W. F. Freeguard, Harold Griffiths, and Henry J. Pillinger & Co., whose advertisement gives a fair indication of the sort of business undertaken in the local market; he offered to make "close market prices for all Welsh Railway Stocks . . . all colliery shares and all miscellaneous securities, whether quoted or not. We are prepared to assist in the promotion of sound Limited Liability Companies, and to act as brokers to same for South Wales".[68]

NOTES

1 *Sheffield and Rotherham Independent,* March 23, 1844. The banks were local joint-stock banks, and among the local companies were the Sheffield Cemetery, Waterworks, Fire Office, and United Gas Co. Most of the leading brokers acted as agents for share applications, e.g., R. Muncaster, Ebenezer Smith, T. Bardwell, and George Eadon.
2 Date of formation given in an article in the *Financial News,* July 31, 1933; *Sheffield and Rotherham Independent,* September 14, 1844.
3 *Sheffield Directory,* 1845.
4 *Financial News,* July 31, 1933.
5 *Economist,* July 12, 1845, p. 663.
6 Leeds Directories. The 1847 Directory lists 97 broking firms, the figures probably refer to 1846. Local directory entries are not always comprehensive.
7 Leeds Stock Exchange, Minutes, October 2, 1845.
8 *Economist,* January 18, 1845, p. 60.
9 *Leeds Intelligencer,* January 18, 1845.
10 Leeds Stock Exchange, Rule Book, 1844.
11 Rules of the Leeds Sharebrokers' Association.
12 *Leeds Intelligencer,* September 6, 1845.
13 *Leeds Mercury,* August 9, 1845; *Bradford Observer,* October 25, 1845; *Halifax Guardian,* July 19, 1845.
14 Leeds Stock Exchange, Minutes, July 23, 1846.
15 Ibid., August 3, 1846. October 13, 1846.
16 **Bristol Gazette and Public Advertiser, March 10, 1836.**
17 Bristol Stock Exchange, Minutes, March 11, 1845.
18 Ibid., March 18, 1845.

F

19 Ibid., April 9, 1845; *Constitution, Laws and Regulations of the Bristol Stock Exchange*, Rule V.
20 *Bristol Times*, May 24, 1845.
21 Bristol Stock Exchange, Minutes, May 21, June 9, 1845.
22 Ibid., May 22, 1846.
23 *Hull Advertiser*, May 9, 1845. The Hull Directory for 1838 incorrectly lists him as a merchant.
24 T. & W. Collinson later became Collinson & Flint; they supplied the Hull Share List to the local press in 1845.
25 Hull Directories, 1842, 1846.
26 Four local companies were given, Hull Docks Co., Hull Flax & Cotton Mills, Hull Gas Co., and the Hull Banking Co.
27 *Hull Advertiser*, March 14, 1845
28 *Hull Advertiser*, October 10, 1845; Hull Directory, 1851.
29 *Hull Advertiser*, July 11, 1845.
30 An unsuccessful attempt was made in 1925 to re-establish a Stock Exchange in Hull; Council of Associated Stock Exchanges, Minutes, October 16, 1925.
31 *Williams' Commercial Directory of Newcastle-upon-Tyne, 1844*: I am greatly indebted to Sir Anthony Wagner, K.C.V.O., D.Litt., Garter Principal King of Arms, for the details from this Directory.
32 Rules of the Newcastle-upon-Tyne Stock and Sharebrokers' Association 1845.
33 *Newcastle Journal*, November 8, 1845.
34 *General Directory of Kingston-upon-Hull and the City of York, 1846*.
35 *York Herald*, April 5, 1845.
36 *York Herald*, April 26, June 14, September 20, 1845.
37 *Leeds Mercury*, October 4, 1845.
38 *Bradford Observer*, June 28, July 12, 1845.
39 Stamp Act 1891, 54 & 55 Vict. ch. 39 s.52(i); Finance Act 1899, 62 & 63 Vict. ch. 9 s.13. The object of the amendment was to prevent loss of revenue from foreign purchases.
40 Since the members issued their own lists there was no official Huddersfield list until the first world war.
41 *Nottingham Review*, July 25, 1845.
42 Nottingham Stock Exchange, Minutes, December 20, 1909, to September 21, 1910.
43 J. Hervey's list in the *Halifax Guardian* for January 1845 contained 41 railways, the July list 71, and 95 by the end of the year.
44 *Halifax Guardian*, April 19, 1845.
45 Halifax Stock Exchange, Rules, 1902.
46 *Bradford Directory*, 1845.
47 *Bradford Observer*, October 16, 1845.
48 Bradford Stock Exchange Rules.
49 *Leicester Herald*, November 10, 1792; L. S. Pressnell, op. cit., pp. 39, 274.
50 *Leicester Journal*, August 2 1844, August 29, 1845.
51 *Leicester Chronicle*, November 8, 1845.
52 *Leicester Chronicle*, September 6, October 11, 18, November 8, December 13, 1845.
53 Lists issued by Abraham Lambley in *Aris's Birmingham Gazette*, May 30, June 6, 1836.
54 Birmingham Directories, 1833, 1835, 1839, 1842, 1845.

55 *Aris's Gazette,* October 3, 1840.
56 Birmingham Stock Exchange, Minutes, September 24, 1845.
57 This bank absorbed the Bank of Birmingham in 1838. The latter was founded in 1832 but despite its rapid growth, reaching a note issue of £30,000, it soon found competition from its rivals too strong "particularly as the manager (James Pearson) although of recognized integrity, was by no means popular." It survived the 1836 boom but the failure of a large debtor in 1836 delivered the fatal blow, and it amalgamated with the Birmingham Banking Co. W. F. Crick and J. E. Wadsworth, *One Hundred Years of Joint Stock Banking* (1936), pp. 54-5.
58 Birmingham Stock Exchange, Minutes, September 24, 1845 – November 1851. There were very few outside brokers in Birmingham, and certainly none of the speculative excesses characteristic of some northern centres.
59 Reference should perhaps be made to two other Stock Exchanges, at Southport and Bournemouth, but these seem to have been no more than a desirable label.
60 *Western Mail,* February 3, 1874.
61 *Western Mail,* February 3, 1889.
62 Unfortunately none of the early records of the Exchange have survived.
63 *Western Mail,* March 23, 1892.
64 *Western Mail,* November 18, 1895.
65 The Swansea Directory for 1899 lists 33 purely local joint stock companies, among them, Weaver & Co., Graigola Merthyr Co. Ltd., Villiers Spelter Co. Ltd., Swansea Steam Trawling and Pure Ice and Cold Storage Co. Ltd.
66 During the early years they met in a broker's office, but in later years they moved to more amenable surroundings, the back bar of the famous Metropole Hotel.
67 *South Wales Argus,* November 6, 1916.
68 *Newport Directory,* 1916.

4 The Organization of the Provincial Stock Exchanges in the Nineteenth Century

As has already been noted in the preceding chapters the membership of the provincial stock exchanges of England increased rapidly during the railway boom period, reaching a figure of well over 500 members in 1846. By 1850, however, the total membership of the surviving exchanges fell to just over 400.[1] This reduction in membership over a comparatively short period was associated with the depressed state of the railway share market when a large number of "self commission men" retreated from the market, while a few members were also lost through being declared defaulters. By 1914 the total membership of the exchanges in England and Wales had increased to just over 550, but the increase occurred mainly at the end of the century, being associated with the boom in company promotion in the mid-1890s and the accompanying increase in share turnover. These changes were not uniform between markets. During this period Liverpool experienced a fall in membership, while Manchester increased from 76 in 1890 to 107 in 1901. Between 1890 and 1914 Birmingham trebled its membership, a development linked with the cycle boom of the mid-nineties and later the rise of the motor car industries. Sheffield doubled its membership over the same period. The middle years of the century were in comparison very unexciting probably because provincial markets did not participate to any considerable extent in the upsurge in foreign borrowing. The provinces got extra agency business and developed a few specialist lines in overseas stocks but the main markets in foreign loans centred on the London Stock Exchange. Provincial expansion occurred with the increase in company formation at local level during the last quarter of the century and the pre-war period. Thus they attained by 1914 a record membership of 559 and for most exchanges this was their high point; the only major exception was Birmingham which subsequently doubled its membership, a growth associated with the development of the newer industries of the Midlands in the inter-war years.

The membership of the provincial markets was not divided into distinct groups of jobbers and brokers. Country markets had their specialisms by way of broking, jobbing and shunting, but without any functional distinction among the membership. Although information as to the precise nature of individual operations is virtually nonexistent, what fragments as appear in surviving records indicate that within the smaller markets, with a membership of thirty or so, there was no local jobbing or shunting, that it was purely an agency business, while the larger markets, such as Liverpool and Manchester contained dual capacity firms acting as brokers, jobbers and/or shunters; it was not until 1908 that London took the decisive step to end dual capacity. As to the numbers involved acting as jobbers or shunters in the provinces there is no information available, but there is certainly no evidence of any acting solely as jobbing concerns. Of course, the dealing mechanism employed did not necessitate a body of principals in the market since prices were made by public auction rather than private dealing; anyway the turnover on individual markets was insufficient to sustain a full time jobbing mechanism of the London pattern.

Some members certainly ran private books alongside their broking business especially during active markets. On the Liverpool Stock Exchange in the autumn of 1845 a large number of brokers were reported as running large jobbing positions on their own account in railway scrip; the number of internal speculators increased apace with those outside the stock exchanges.[2] Certainly the Liverpool Committee when admitting new members in 1848 allowed them to act as "brokers and jobbers both". At the end of the century some Liverpool brokers operated jobbing accounts, keeping them separate from their other business, and were known in the market to be jobbers in various lines of stock.[3] Manchester on the other hand at the time of the 1878 *Royal Commission* had no "jobbers, so called" on the market.[4] Birmingham, however, during its early years provided an exception to the general practice of allowing members to act in dual capacities and the Committee were of the view that "the business of a broker and that of a jobber or dealer are in their nature and objects entirely distinct and they cannot both be carried on by the same person, or the same firm consistently with the views of this Association".[5] In view of the small membership and the moderate activity it was unlikely that any members would have elected to carry on only a jobbing business.

Limited country jobbing was supplemented later in the century, with the development of the telegraph by the emergence of what were termed "speculators acting in lieu of jobbers", that is, shunters specializing in arbitrage business between markets and distinguishable from jobbers by the fact that they were purely 'daylight' traders. The place of shunting activity in provincial markets will be discussed further below.

Provincial markets were basically auction markets with prices and bargains being done by public bargaining. Broker dealt with broker, the intermediary between them being the market auction rather than as in London, the services of a jobbing mechanism. The widespread use in the provinces of the call market system probably sprang from the early share auctions, or conceivably it could have been copied from the United States where it was used on the New York Stock Exchange; there is no record of conscious adoption from the U.S.A., or that any members had considerable experience of overseas practices. In the event it was the most suitable system since given the smallness of most provincial markets the volume of trading could not have supported a specialist group of dealers acting solely as principals.

The formal call market system operated along the following lines. If members had an interest in dealing they gathered in the market at times laid down in the rules. During its early years Liverpool opened "every week day from 11 to 11.30 in the forenoon and from 3 to 3.30 in the afternoon" and was then closed punctually at those times with the ringing of a bell. The growth in business during the railway boom of 1845 led the Committee to test the list more frequently, with three call overs daily. Gradually most of the larger markets by 1846 resorted to remaining open from 11 to 4 o'clock, with the call over taking place at fixed times. Manchester was particularly keen on prompt closure and insisted that "no gentlemen should remain in the room two minutes longer", and transgressors were subject to a five shilling fine.[6] Smaller markets such as Leeds found that two formal dealing periods were adequate, and with the decline in business in 1846 reverted to one call over. Bristol also had two business periods 11 to 12.0, "when members shall be rung out", and from 2 to 2.30 "when the House shall close". In fact the Bristol Committee for General Purposes would "take no cognizance of any bargain nor of any complaint thereon if not done between these hours".[7] There was nothing to prevent members from dealing outside these official times, but such bargains were not officially marked, which might cause difficulties in the event of a dispute between members.

During the official call over members usually sat in a semi-circle around the Chairman or the Secretary, who in most exchanges occupied an elevated position in front of the price "boards". At Birmingham, however, the members appear to have formed themselves into a circle, and the Committee refused to recognize marks of business done by members not in the circle, a stricture calculated to maintain orderliness. The Chairman took the chair, and the Secretary proceeded to ask for a quotation and the stocks listed were then gone through one by one. Richard Withers, Chairman of the Liverpool Stock Exchange, gave the following description of "making a market" with a call over system to the 1878 *Royal Commission:-*

"At 11 o'clock we commence. The share list is read from A to Z. We dwell a short time on each stock, and in that time the market is made for the stock by the brokers as buyers and sellers. They fight out the price amongst themselves. They call out the price, for instance, London and North-Western stock 145 to $145\frac{1}{2}$, at which it may be quoted the evening before in the list. That is tested in this way. The secretary calls out the price of London and North-Western and those who want to deal in London and North-Western stock declare themselves and make the market. If a man wants to buy and cannot buy at 45, he says he will give $45\frac{1}{4}$. That is made then the nominal buying price, say $45\frac{1}{4}$ to $\frac{3}{4}$, instead of 45 to $45\frac{1}{2}$. On the contrary, if sellers prevail and the market is lower, the reverse action takes place. They make an offer to sell at 45, the buying price the night before, and then that becomes the selling price, that is to say, the market is put down or put up according to the law of supply and demand at the moment, and that supply and demand is ascertained openly in the market by operations amongst the brokers, not by going to dealers to make a price. In London a dealer no doubt gives great facilities, because in a large market like that they could not make it in the way that we do *viva voce*".[8]

The price of a security was thus fixed until the next call, and those who wanted to deal between calls approached others who had shown an interest during the call and negotiated a price using the bid and offer prices established at the call as guides. There was no compulsion to use these prices, but they were at least arrived at under competitive conditions.

Nominally they went over the whole list, but those which were not current stocks were passed over. Any member present could mention other stocks and make a quotation in it. It normally took about twenty minutes to get through the Liverpool list during the morning call over. The bulk of the business was generally done at this session since in pre-telegraph days most orders and other news arrived by the morning mails. Business in the afternoon was generally not very active and there would only be "a less formal quoting of very current stocks" with the list being then closed for the day.[9] With the advent of improved communications more attention was given to the afternoon calling than during the early years; Birmingham in 1879 resolved that the full list should be called over at all the meetings, in the hope that this would benefit members.[10] It was held that too long an interval between dealing times was to the detriment of members and "beneficial to the shunters".[11]

An advantage of the call market system was that brokers collected orders for execution at the time when the stock was reached on the list during the call. The price arrived at was the result of the maximum number of bids and offers available at the time, when the market in that particular security had its greatest turnover. Prices reflected demand and supply pressures, while the technical problems of small share turnover were alleviated by concentrating dealing into fixed periods. This practice was particularly suited to local stocks which lacked the attributes of national stocks such as large share capital, turnover and number of shareholders. In such circumstances a price fixed at the call over was likely to be within narrower margins than that arrived at by attempting to deal by negotiation outside the call, while "turns" quoted by London jobbers on local stocks were regarded as extremely exhorbitant by provincial brokers.

But the call-over method also had some serious disadvantages, some of which were particularly apparent in the formative years of the provincial markets. It was certainly not as capacious as the London jobbing system during periods of speculative dealing activity. The deficiencies of the call-over were humorously described by T. W. Powell, who was a member of the Leeds Stock Exchange in 1845, to the 1878 *Royal Commission*. The membership of the Leeds Stock Exchange at the time was around 40 members, of whom some 25 sat around a long table, the rest standing behind. In accordance with traditional call procedures the Chairman then went through the list. However, when the business was at all lively: -

"and a good deal of speculation was going on, the immediate result of the calling over of any stock in which there was much business was a terrible babel, a terrible noise and confusion; and my own experience was that the men with the tallest persons, and the most audacious manner, and the biggest voices, almost concentrated to themselves the power of dealing during the continuance of that babel, the quieter men were not in a position to be able to carry on business during the busiest part of it; and it has frequently been my own experience that on account of the confusion, and the bigger voices, and so on, of tall persons, and possibly by their having a larger business at the moment, I was entirely unable to execute my business, although I saw other people transacting business at the prices at which I had desired to do business . . . those who were physically best qualified had a great advantage over those who were not so strong".[12]

The Leeds Committee attempted to quell matters by appointing "Monitors" from the Committee members to suppress unnecessary noise during business hours. Further, in 1846, the Committee ruled that no business was to be transacted with members who were not seated, and that only one representative from "each house shall make bargains on the Exchange at one time". Exchange officials also complained that frequently members did not confine themselves to dealing in the stock currently called, and the Committee responded in June 1845 by ruling that dealing should only take place "one line at once". Even greater disruption was caused when members requested the Chairman to "go back on the list".[13] These problems were common to most exchanges, and even at the end of the century the noise on the Manchester floor made it difficult to proceed with the list, while the Liverpool Chairman of the period pleaded with members to restrain their "natural exhuberance in doing business".[14]

During normal times the system operated more satisfactorily, but depressed markets brought further difficulties in the form of lack of attendance of members in the market. Absenteeism during the call over increased after the widespread adoption of the telegraph, but even in 1857 the Manchester Committee urged members to ensure a "more complete attendance in the Room" in order to reduce the thinness of markets.[15] Earlier in 1853 Leeds encountered the same problem since "the majority of members do not generally attend".[16] Later in the century Liverpool experienced the same sort of difficulty, when the jobbers in the market were reluctant to leave their telephones to participate in the call-over. However by this time the significance of the price fixing at the call had been considerably eroded.

One of the main disadvantages of the call system was the lack of continuity in market facilities. This particular deficiency was rectified in the late 1860s and 1870s by the development of shunting activity giving closer and speedier links with other markets, but more significantly, providing a price service from the London market. With the introduction and growth of this service the significance of the price fixing greatly diminished, except for purely local stocks, and even here limited jobbing in the larger markets provided a supplement to the call. Gradually, then, by the 1890s the call market proper had moved towards a continuous action market and the call over became more of a formality, merely fixing an official price, as against the main and most advantageous time of executing deals in the market.

In order to facilitate dealing procedures it was laid down in the rules of most markets that the share lots offered or asked for should be in easily marketable quantities. In Liverpool it was specified that "an offer to buy or sell, naming a certain number of shares, and also a price, is binding on the party making such an offer or to any part thereof, provided such part and the balance be both marketable quantities"; also "an offer to buy or sell any shares merely naming a price is binding on the party naming such a price, for at least a marketable quantity".[17] A marketable quantity usually consisted of 10 shares when the consideration was under £20, 5 shares when it was £20–£40, and one of £100 and upwards, or stock to the value of £100. Throughout the century most markets kept to the same amounts as marketable quantities, although in 1909 Birmingham members complained vigorously to their Committee that whereas all other markets had round lots of 10 or 20, Birmingham used 25 or 50, which caused great inconvenience as far as inter-market dealing was concerned since in Liverpool, Manchester or Sheffield "it was practically impossible to deal in 25 or 75 shares". In fact, Birmingham experienced a long dispute between members as to what constituted a convenient marketable quantity of shares, opposing sides citing the advantages of tens and twenty-fives. It is possible that the large increase in small shares during the bicycle boom in the mid-1890s accounts for this exception.[18] Where bargains in odd lots were done, frequently at a slight discount, these were specially marked as such on the price boards.

The price boards were a major feature of the market floors and were "large boards upon which in large chalk writing the name of every stock is given" and the price of the previous call was recorded. The main boards listed the officially quoted stocks, while alongside there were supplementary boards giving the prices of 'unlisted' stocks, and sometimes there was also a small board for deals in occasional stocks. During the call over the Secretary would mark prices up or down, while members could put 'marks' on the boards of prices done outside the call. Practices, however, varied between markets. Liverpool brokers were allowed to mark prices outside the call from very early days, provided they verified it with their signature.[19] In Birmingham it was not until 1886 that members were allowed to mark business done during the 'off change' period, that is, "transactions done otherwise than between the calling of the Stock in Question and the rising of the Chairman".[20] Also, it was not until 1885 that Birmingham members were allowed to mark business done in other markets. With the growth of intermarket dealing during this period it became necessary to allow the boards to carry such 'marks', otherwise the list would not reflect the prices at which a large volume of business had been done. The order of the stocks listed on the boards was changed to accord with current market interest, for example, in 1887 Manchester began the call over with foreign stocks followed by the remainder of the list. Stocks in which dealings had become infrequent were taken off the boards, particularly those on the unofficial boards, an action which in Liverpool at least brought a strong protest from dealers in these 'outside stocks'. They complained of "great loss and hardship" following the Committee's decision in April 1886 that no quotation on the unofficial boards would be granted to a stock unless it had a London quotation, or it had obtained a special settlement in Liverpool.[21]

From the closing prices of the day (also referred to as official or nominal prices) given on the boards the price list was made up, and details were also included of the business done during the day. During the early years these were "furnished by the Porter or Clerk under the authority of the Committee to the various newspapers." In 1836 the rules of the Liverpool Stock Exchange further stipulated that no individual member or members should sign any quotations for the "public prints"; the Committee found it very difficult in the late thirties however to check such practices by well established members, particularly John Coglan. By 1843 Manchester had set up a sub-committee to deal with the reporting of the Association's prices to the local newspapers.[22] The larger exchanges had sufficient business by way of securities dealt in and price changes to merit a daily list, but many of the smaller markets were content with less complete coverage. Sheffield, for example, up to the 1870s issued a list twice weekly, supplemented by a monthly list; from the mid-1870s a daily list appeared. Bristol, Newcastle, and Birmingham issued weekly lists, again supplemented by monthly lists which carried additional details of company capital and so on.

By the mid-1850s the share lists of the Exchanges had become reduced in coverage. Even as early as 1846 Manchester members complained that their list was very meagre, and as a remedy advocated prolonging the time of making up the list. Later in 1862 a more far reaching step was suggested, and adopted by the Committee, when a number of local and other miscellaneous stocks in which members were anxious to deal were quoted. The lists were relied upon by members to attract business to their exchange and this need alone accounted for the enlargement of lists in the 1870s and 1880s. Manchester members in 1873 complained bitterly to their Committee that transactions "were daily taking place in other markets and which for wont of quotations in our lists could not be affected here".[23]

Accordingly a sub-committee was set up to see how the list could be remodelled to meet changing market requirements and which subsequently instituted quarterly revisions. During the same year Liverpool enlarged their list simply by inserting "on the application of a Member to the Committee" the shares or stock of any company marked in the official list of London or any other provincial Stock Exchange.[24] Ten years later this expansionist policy was modified when the Committee declared their reluctance to grant a quotation for a company share or stock if it meant that Liverpool was to be dependent on London for a price, and thereafter they decided only to add to the list "business of importance". Later, if three firms applied for the listing of a London stock consent was given, and in 1891 a permanent List Sub-Committee was set up to keep the list up to date. This meant that if a stock ceased to be active it was then taken out of the list. Birmingham at the turn of the century followed a policy of retaining such shares on the list, but not "to mark prices until reliable ones had been obtained".[25] It was this criteria of being able to "almost daily follow the course of the market" which the Bristol Committee adopted in 1906 for permitting additional quotations in order to attract business.[26]

The share list gave details of the closing prices and also prices at which some sales were done. These 'marks' however gave no indication of the number of deals at that price, or the amount of stock involved; the object of the list was to record price movements not the volume of business done through the market. As early as the 1850s a lot of business missed the lists since brokers were increasingly marrying bargains in their offices, and "deals were increasingly done with outsiders".[27] The rules of the Birmingham Stock Exchange excluded such business from being marked, while in 1840 Liverpool adopted a rule that no "quotation be recorded where one broker only is employed"; the Birmingham rule on this point was not revoked until 1885. Naturally business done outside the call would not get marked unless the parties themselves did so.

When a bargain was done between members in the market they merely noted it in their own books. Later the same day written contract notes were exchanged; in Leeds the principal or a responsible clerk from each office attended at the Exchange after business to exchange contracts for that day.[28] This practice was general until 1871 when London, Glasgow and Liverpool Stock Exchanges agreed to do without written stamped contract notes and introduce market books instead; the Stamp Act of 1870 introduced a penny stamp on contract notes between brokers. Manchester, on legal advice, adhered to stamped contracts until the passing of the Customs and Inland Revenue Act of 1878 which removed the need to pay duty on brokers' contracts. Other markets stamped the contract notes sent to clients, but Manchester regarded this as an advice note since the actual contracts were between the brokers.[29] Birmingham also stopped using written contracts in 1878.

During the early years of the operation of both Liverpool and Manchester Stock Exchanges bargains were made on the basis of cash settlements. The volume of business at the time was probably insufficient to merit the introduction of account periods, while Liverpool members regarded such procedures as a "very speculative mode of dealing, and would lead to trouble".[30] Whether or not all bargains were actually done on a cash basis is open to doubt. At the peak of the 1836 railway share speculation what was disapprovingly described by *The Times* as a "new system of jobbing" was in operation in Bristol, Birmingham, Liverpool and Manchester. The practice was to sell shares when they reached a high premium and to take instead of money the "acceptances of the purchaser payable at distant periods". "The purchaser on his side when a further rise occurred, or, when it suited him to sell, did the same thing, and thus the same transaction, passing from hand to hand has created and brought into circulation bills to 10 or 20 times its amount". The total was estimated at several millions of pounds, and bills were discounted in the new joint stock banks, especially as most of them were "eager to get out paper and not overscrupulous about the means".[31] Liverpool brokers sent a prompt and angry reply to *The Times,* signed by 29 of them, firmly denying that they used such speculative devices and asserting that all bargains in railway and other stock were settled by cash payments; that still left quite a few brokers to pursue questionable practices.

With the increasing size of the railway share market and the return of speculative interest in the early 1840s the disadvantages attendant upon reliance on cash settlements became very apparent. As business increased the number of parties to every transaction grew and settlement between first buyer and ultimate seller could not be made without involving a number of persons, so that "in getting stock delivered and paid for, there were perhaps 20 clerks concerned in it, each of whom had contributed something out of the differences".[32] The first demand for reform in Liverpool came in 1841, and in response to this the Committee set up a sub-committee "to take into consideration the propriety of establishing settling days as on the London Stock Exchange for the better regulation of the business of the Liverpool Stock Exchange". A leading proponent of settling days, Benjamin Coleman, appeared before the Committee and made an eloquent plea for their adoption, claiming that the fourteen day account system, "would secure that regularity in our market which has been so much wanted and create a class of respectable men as Jobbers or Dealers . . . it would secure a mass of country business which is at present lost [to London] from our inability in the majority of instances to effect the orders of our Correspondents . . . it would obviate the complaints of Brokers who attribute their irregularity to the scarcity of Dealers or Speculators who in turn allege the same against the Brokers . . . it would do away with the obnoxious notices of selling out or buying in as now practiced which in some cases cannot be acted upon . . . it would establish differences to be settled by the Committee on the settling days without the necessity of rendering shares or money and that such practice would not interfere with legitimate business".[33]

The Committee rejected this plea to increase the importance and respectability of the Liverpool market and the matter was allowed to rest until 1844 when a sub-committee reported that the "present mode of settlement is very inconvenient", and recommended the adoption of a twice monthly settlement, coupled with the setting up of a Clearing House supervised by an Inspector of Clearing. Both measures were implemented in November 1844.[34]

The adoption of account periods thus meant that at the end of the account the buyer issued a ticket to the seller indicating to whom the stock was to be delivered, and on the following day, "pay day", stock and cash changed hands. If the seller did not receive a ticket he could have the stock "sold out" by the Secretary of the Stock Exchange, with any loss charged to the buyer; if the buyer did not get his stock he could have it "bought in" by the Secretary, with any additional cost charged to the seller. Due to delays in communication a period of grace was allowed in the preparation of transfer documents, three days for scrip and bearer stock, and 14 days for registered stock. By 1878 this lengthy period was reduced following discussions with the London Stock Exchange to 11 days, a reduction reflecting speedier communications and because the 14 days tended to overlap and complicate settlement in the ensuing account. The buyer of stock was expected to have cash at the ready.[35]

In addition to adopting settling days Liverpool in 1844 also instituted a clearing system for the more efficient payment of differences. The object was to eliminate the previous practice whereby sometimes about 20 people would be involved in receiving or paying differences in the process of getting stock delivered from first seller to ultimate buyer. On "account day" a ticket was passed from buyer to seller, which could if many members had bought and sold the stock, then pass from hand to hand by endorsement which stated the price and the difference paid or received by each successive party. Then on "pay day" each member sent into the Inspector of Clearing a balance sheet "in which shall be inserted the number of difference tickets and total amount of the same issued by him to each and every member, and also the number of Tickets, and the total amount of the same received by him from each and every member, the former in a column on the left hand, and the latter in a column on the right hand of the said Balance sheet".[36] If the differences due exceeded those payable by a member he received the balance from the Inspector, while in the converse case he paid a balance to the Inspector. Differences rendered to the Inspector of Clearing were done in cash until the turn of the century; a suggestion for the adoption of cheque payments for the clearing was rejected by members as late as 1903, with a "certain degree of frivolity and levity," but within a few years they were introduced, thus bringing Liverpool in line with Manchester, who had introduced them in 1899.[37]

With the "vast increase in share operations, local as well as from all parts of the Kingdom" the Liverpool Committee felt that the introduction of settling days was fully justified, and that it had greatly augmented the business of the share market. The Inspector of Clearing was certainly fully worked and in return for the onerous duties performed when "differences on each settling day have exceeded £7,000" the Committee in April 1845 raised his salary. Following the success of the Liverpool adoption Manchester introduced settling days in the following year, using the same days as Liverpool, which, because of communication problems were two days behind the London account days.

The Leeds Stock Exchange during its first months operated cash settlements, but later established settling days for all stocks except scrip shares which remained for immediate delivery. In 1846 suggestions were strongly canvassed for the introduction of a Clearing House but eventually the Committee decided against the idea. This was not because of its "being inappropriate to violent and trying fluctuations in prices", but because a new set of rules would be required, and more specifically, because of the increased liability imposed on a member since for the "carrying out of the [Clearing House] effectively he would have to be always ready to the day with cash, or security for his liabilities".[38] The Committee felt however that local clearings would be expedited if all members confine "Banking operations to one Bank", but it is doubtful if this partial move towards the elements of a Clearing House got very far. The Bristol Stock Exchange a year later, following dissatisfaction with their account arrangements, contemplated introducing tickets which would be negotiated among members in settlement of differences for the amounts they represented, such differences being payable on account days. The scheme was not proceeded with, possibly because of the decline in dealing activity, but more probably because of the difficulties of getting members to negotiate the tickets at the stated values.[39]

Virtually from its formation the Birmingham Stock Exchange operated a system of stock clearance whose object was "to simplify business by making the delivery of stock and shares as direct, private and inexpensive as possible". "Every buyer and seller enters the clearance by handing in a statement . . . of stock, or shares bought and sold, or the balance thereof and thereby gives his consent to abide by the arrangements of the Committee in respect of such stock and shares." On "name day" the Committee fixed making-up prices for each stock, usually the market price of that day, and then it put "the selling and buying Brokers together in the most convenient form for direct delivery of stock and shares upon which the original con-tracting parties are released from each other (except as to dif-ferences) and the parties thus put together by the Committee stand henceforth engaged to each other in every respect as tho' they had actually dealt together". On the settling day every buyer or seller paid or received the difference between the making-up price and the contract price, and in due course all deliveries of securities included in the clearing took place between the parties put together at the making-up price.[40] At the time of the cycle boom in the mid-1890s the Birmingham Committee contracted the clearing to one J. W. Barrett, who was assisted by one clerk; it was not always accom-plished smoothly, mainly because of late and faulty returns which required tedious investigation and correction.[41]

For those wishing to carry-over bargains to the next account the rules of most exchanges specified certain days for such transactions. All bargains had to be closed at the end of an account, so that, for example, a buyer wanting to postpone taking up stock would sell for cash and buy back for the next account. This would be done at the making-up price, which was usually fixed by the Secretary of the Exchange. The Manchester Committee experienced considerable difficulty in confining carry over activities to the account days. As early as 1858 they were forced to rule that carry-over transactions completed before the prescribed day would not be officially recog-nized. Similar problems prevailed in Liverpool, and following con-sultations the two Exchanges agreed to restrict carry-overs to one day, as against the previous two; evasion was probably frequent since in 1881 Manchester members made an "honourable agree-ment" to confine it to one day.[42] One problem which arose from carry over transactions done before the official day was the rate of "contango" to charge. In Liverpool "a widespread of rates" was the result of private arrangements arrived at before the overall market position for carry-overs was known, and accordingly the Committee in 1880 decided to make all such rates officially quoted. A further problem was that early carry-over tended to interfere with ordinary business.[43] As late as 1911 the carry over arrangements still had not been satisfactorily resolved. Liverpool members continued to be reluctant to abide by the fixed times because of the fear of losing business to other markets not so restricted and finally a compromise was reached by allowing a private carry-over before a fixed date. This did not involve public challenging beween members, but rather going "quietly" to give instruction to a dealer or "contango merchant".[44]

A matter which greatly occupied the time of all Stock Exchange authorities was that of commission levels. During their early years most exchanges introduced what amounted to recommended scales of commissions. The rules of the Liverpool Stock Exchange in 1836 set out a scale ranging from 2/6d. per share under £10, up to £1 on £100–£200 shares, and $\frac{1}{2}\%$ on £200 upwards.[45] This was a maximum scale, but competitive forces brought the actual rates paid below prescribed levels. Certainly, in Manchester, the established scale of commissions was evaded in the 1840s to a "very considerable extent".[46] Despite competition, commission rates on shares prior to the widespread adoption of limited liability tended to be above the $\frac{1}{2}\%$ range since brokers were involved in greater dealing risks. They were guaranteeing their clients bargains, and this left them extremely exposed to liability for large differences if share prices fluctuated violently, as they sometimes did in periods of panic or when a call was made on a share with only a low paid up value.[47] The newer markets of the 1845 boom tended to adopt London rates, although Leeds in 1846 brought their rates in line with those of Liverpool.[48] Birmingham urged its members to follow the recommended scale, based on London rates, and to display it prominently but found that evasion was extremely common, particularly as regard transactions with London.

The general picture in the provinces by the 1880s was that most brokers tended to charge under the maximum or recommended rate of $\frac{1}{2}\%$ and somewhere above $\frac{1}{4}\%$, charging as "well as they are able to". As early as the late 1850s dissatisfaction with this "haggling and disputing" method of fixing commissions had led to abortive attempts to get a minimum scale based on London rates generally adopted. In this Birmingham was the main provincial instigator. In 1857 the Birmingham Committee was of the opinion "that

G

a uniform scale of brokerage throughout the share market is most desirable, and that the same to be effective should emanate from London and be agreed to by Liverpool and Manchester".[49] This assertion that the main initiative should come from London was to be repeated by many provincial exchanges at the end of the century when they were again urged to adopt minimum commission scales. At the time Manchester and Liverpool felt unable to support Birmingham's overtures, although they were themselves conscious of the "existing anomalous state of this question". This was because they realized that such a scale would be very difficult to enforce, and also because the London movers in the matter were not recognized by the Committee for General Purposes of the London Stock Exchange.[50]

Most of the provincial exchanges were agreed on the desirability of greater uniformity in commission rates, but no action was really possible without full co-operation from London, which was not forthcoming until the end of the century. Richard Withers, in his evidence to the 1878 *Royal Commission*, voiced provincial feelings on the matter when he stated that they would like to have a minimum scale of commissions fixed through the medium of the "Commission or any other good tribunal".[51] The existing commission levels were "notoriously obsolete" and evaded in dealings with clients and agents. Competition was extremely keen, leading to widespread undercutting of rates, while the growth of dealing in the telegraphic markets, done at net prices (price inclusive of commission), scarcely admitted of the usefulness of a recommended scale of commissions. The rallying cry from the Birmingham Committee "to keep up our scale and our dignity" went largely unheard, and it is more than likely that some brokers resorted to speculation on their own account so as to compensate for low commission income.[52]

Despite the antipathy of London and lack of co-operation from provincial colleagues Birmingham went ahead in 1876 and adopted a minimum scale, enforceable by a system of fines. The new rules also prescribed the level of rebates to agents. The custom in the country was to allow half commission to agents, but the Birmingham Committee argued that such a level "has for some time pressed unfairly on the Members of this Exchange in as much as office and Exchange expenses absorb about $\frac{1}{3}$ of every commission". Accordingly, the rebate was reduced to $\frac{1}{3}$, "and as $\frac{1}{3}$ is really $\frac{1}{2}$ of the profit it will commend itself as fair to all parties concerned". This was later modified to allow half commission to correspondents in other markets.[53] Downward adjustments were made to the lower end of the scale in 1886 following the rapid increase in business in shares of small denominations.[54]

This early attempt to impose a minimum scale came to grief in 1889 when in August the Committee recommended to the members that the "scale of brokerage will cease to be a minimum scale", and that the substitute recommended scale would be lower. The pressure for abandoning the minimum scale came from outside the Stock Exchange, from "certain influential gentlemen in the City of Birmingham" who had informed the Chairman of their intention of getting a "reduction of charges made in Birmingham upon Stock Exchange Business". The response of members to this threat of losing business was to institute a "reasonable reduction of charges on ordinary business" and to charge less than the recommended scale "where the nature of the business demands it", presumably for large deals and in response to competitive conditions. The weakness of Birmingham's position lay in the fact that no other market had a minimum scale, leaving it shorn of bargaining power and very sensitive to fears of loss of business to neighbouring markets. The new found freedom was, however, interpreted as aiming to attract "legitimate business which at present [Birmingham] did not get". Under the new rules "members shall in all cases charge upon their contract notes the commission authorized by the scale and that in making any allowance by way of rebate at the time of settlement members shall not be actuated by a desire to compete with their fellow members, but shall have in view simply the object of retaining in or attracting to this market legitimate business which but for the allowance made would go to other markets".[55]

The Manchester Stock Exchange adopted a minimum commission scale in 1905, with the additional stiff requirement that "any division or rebate of commission be forbidden". In practice the scale proved too low to be effective and modifications were made in 1906, with rebates for banks, solicitors and accountants, but even this concession was revoked in December and thereafter members "were not allowed to rebate commission to anyone".[56] This hard line on rebates continued until the first world war and featured as Manchester's hardy annual resolution at the Council of Associated Stock Exchanges' meetings. Unlike Manchester, Liverpool did not adopt a minimum scale until London had done so in 1912, claiming that there was little point in fixing a scale until London's was known since an adverse differential would have the "effect of diverting business to London".[57]

A broker receiving an order from a client could not always execute it in his own market if it was for shares whose main dealings took place in another provincial market, or if it was in national shares with dealings centred on London. For the purpose of dealing in other markets brokers upon entering the trade established links with brokers in all the main markets and put orders through these agents if by so doing they could deal to the clients best advantage. In the late 1870s some London brokers had themselves sought new agency links with the provinces to procure additional business. The transactions of a country broker with a London agent for an account period were then lumped together, and the former simply received or paid the balance on the whole of the fortnight's business. The country broker was treated by the London agent as a principal and the latter took no cognizance of the parties to the original transactions.[58] It was, of course, a two way link in that orders came from agents in other provincial towns and from the London agent. The agency business, which up to the 1870s was the main link between markets, was conducted on a commission basis but without any rigorous convention as to the rebate given to the market agents. This free trade basis continued until the introduction of minimum commission rules in 1912 by the London Stock Exchange. The agent performed other services by way of supervizing delivery of stock and providing information as to market prices. The London agent also occupied quite a prominent position in the matter of lobbying the London Committee on behalf of provincial interests, as was certainly the case in the long drawn out commission debate of 1908–12.

Around the late 1870s the agency link with other markets was supplemented by the growth of shunting activity. The shunters were also described as "speculators who act in lieu of jobbers" on provincial floors. Generally they did little brokerage business but concentrated on dealing activity. If, for example, a shunter found that there was a demand for a share in Liverpool and knew that prices were sufficiently lower in another market to allow him a profit on the transaction, he would then buy up shares in the other market and sell in Liverpool. Alternatively he could sell shares in one market and pick them up more cheaply elsewhere. The successful operation of arbitrage business based on intermarket price differentials depended on very rapid communications and was made possible by the introduction of telegraphic communication in the mid-1870s. Shunters were in the habit of receiving a telegram every few minutes in the day and accordingly were well informed on prices ruling throughout the country. Good communications were indeed essential since "to procure even $1\frac{1}{2}$d. a share requires the essences of speed and ready knowledge of where and how to deal". They, of course, depended on price differentials, but their arbitrage operations meant that thereafter prices over many scattered markets were kept within fairly narrow margins. It was the home railway share markets which afforded the chief field for shunting activity.[59]

Shunting activity differed from London jobbing activity in several important respects. Shunters were not wholesalers of shares but usually matched buying and selling orders closely. Jobbers operated so as to balance their books at the end of an account, while the shunters bought and sold by telegraph throughout the day, closing their positions at the end of dealings and not carrying over open positions to the next day. Frequently they managed to close their books without going to London, but in the case of large deals London was usually the market of "last resort": there was little time to shop around the provinces. In normal shunting operations they took what business was going and did not seek out orders, and they did not restrict their business to a particular group of shares.

The shunter provided his own market with an important price service covering shares in other provincial centres and national stocks on the London market. In addition he placed at the disposal of the provincial client the considerable services of the London jobbing system, for example, the competitive facility and the "breadth and depth" of the main markets. Shunters also appeared on the London market which meant that country stocks and prices were placed at the disposal of London brokers. As a result outside brokers were able to deal in country stocks in London. When shunting activity reached its largest proportions at the end of the century a great deal of it was done on the basis of joint books. "The provincial broker, being kept advised of the state of the market in London by his allied jobber, bought and sold in Liverpool, or wherever else he might be established, and covered his bargains in London, dividing the profits or losses with the jobber".[60] Shunting activity on the basis of joint books had come to an end by 1909.

The essential point about this arbitrage network was that since the 1870s country brokers enjoyed direct access to the London jobber, and were thus able to deal at net prices. Country brokers also preferred the direct connection because London jobbers were prepared to guarantee transactions, a security which London brokers were not so willing to provide.[61] As a result of shunting activity the provinces had an up-to-date price service, and the call-over was greatly supplemented by the activities of local jobbers and shunters, while, on London, a great deal of business was possible in country stocks because of the overall shunting network. The main stream of business, however, certainly ran in London's favour and an estimate by Edward Rae in 1909 put the volume of business sent to London at twenty times that coming in return.[62] From the standpoint of London market turnover this was a beneficial exchange, and provincial brokers were always ready to point out that arbitrage business increased London's "size and freedom", rather than the reverse, However, at the turn of the century some London brokers formed a "dead set with a view of getting back the old style brokerage business of many years ago". Their intention was to channel all business through the broker, and cut the jobbers link with the provincial broker. Provincial onlookers interpreted the suggestion of not allowing free access to the jobber as an attempt to "make one market only in England, that is, London". At this stage in the dispute Liverpool observers painted an excessively gloomy picture of the future, claiming that if "the scheme is carried out it will be absolute death to our market, in as much as the public could get no facilities for dealing at close prices, and would further, after paying the Liverpool and Manchester brokers' commission and the jobbers' turn . . . absolutely debar business". In the opinion of the provinces this attempt to drive business back into the main market was the consequence of London's "incautious policy of admitting Members to an unwealdy extent".[63]

New London rules on the matter were not introduced until 1908 and as a result members were required to opt for either broking or jobbing activity. But of more significance to the provinces was the statement that "Shunting is to be abolished". This was the corollary of the decision to keep the two classes of broker and jobber quite separate, so that if a broker could not carry on the business of a dealer, then a dealer could not deal with a non-member. The new rules did not immediately cut off provincial ties with the jobbers since it was possible for a time to conduct remunerative shunting deals by passing the bargain through a broker at nominal commission rates. The 1912 minimum commission rules, introduced after much controversy, ended this loophole. The provinces agreed with London about the need for a minimum scale to the public, and were prepared to co-operate to ensure the success of this move. However, London also introduced a minimum scale for intermarket dealing which was aimed at cutting out shunting activity. Certain concessions were eventually obtained from London by the Council of Associated Stock Exchanges for country business, but nevertheless the brokers' scale remained as a compulsory minimum charge.[64]

The effect of the new London rules was to curtail intermarket shunting activity based on London. The costs of dealing through London had been put up and an accompanying widening of dealing prices in the provinces led richer clients to go straight to London rather than put the business through their provincial broker. Other clients reacted by dealing less frequently.[65] The restrictions also curtailed the range of technical facilities open to the country shunter. Since they closed their books on a daily basis, London was frequently the only market with sufficient turnover to permit this to be done with any certainty, especially in large deals. By taking away the "last resort" market the country shunter was forced to limit his business to shunting between provincial markets on a reduced scale and in a smaller range of securities. London jobbers dealing in country stocks were also adversely affected. It was now more difficult for them to undo business in the country, and they reacted by reducing the range of country stocks in which they were prepared to make prices. Some of the leading London dealers claimed that they were not consulted on the proposals to levy minimum scales for country brokers, and they were of the opinion that on balance the loss to the London market was greater than the gains likely from the new rules.[66]

Although many provincial brokers felt that they should continue to press for free trade they were not very hopeful as to the outcome. They claimed that the majority of London members felt "that the provinces had been making more out of the business than they had". In practice it was found that an increasing amount of business was done between the provincial exchanges; William Bell of Manchester said in 1912 that as far as Manchester was concerned that business with London had been severely restricted, but that people had taken "more pains to try all other markets", and had met with considerable success. It was pointed out that there were some 400 outside brokers who could be attracted to provincial markets, but opinion seemed to be more in favour of a central agency for keeping provincial business away from London. To this end an experiment was tried in 1911 in sending out buying and selling lists in London stocks, but it was both expensive and cumbersome. A more ambitious project in 1913 to keep business in London stocks in the provinces, the Central Enquiry Bureau at Preston, shared a similar fate and was closed down in 1914 due to lack of financial support.[67]

Provincial markets did a considerable amount of business with outside brokers. During most of the nineteenth century they were regarded by the stock exchanges as legitimate feeders of business, and were given commission rebates for business introduced. Some outside brokers also acted as dealers in local stocks and in such instances the stock exchanges offered them the same degree of freedom to deal at net prices as granted to dealers on provincial markets. Birmingham, in 1846, for example, recognized the dealer status of such outside brokers and their entitlement to certain concessions. However, outside brokers operating in towns where Stock Exchanges were situated, were not always treated so favourably. In Liverpool outside brokers were allowed to come into the "vestibule" to transact business, but Manchester on the other hand tended to regard them as undesirable competitors. In 1849 the members of the Stock

Exchange memorialized the Committee claiming that the volume of business done by outsiders on the premises interfered seriously with their business. Accordingly outside brokers were charged half commission, but the restrictive effect of this measure soon induced members to rescind the minimum charge.[68]

This fairly tolerant and accommodating attitude towards outside brokers, particularly those located in centres where there was a stock exchange, persisted until the end of the century.[69] The main reason for the change of treatment was probably the enlarged membership of many exchanges, and their increasing nervousness about competition. Stock exchange members became increasingly anxious to protect their commission income from what they regarded as the privileged position of outside brokers who did not bear the burdens and responsibilities of membership of a market. Further, they claimed that many outsiders were little more than "bucket shop" operators engaging in such professional activity as widespread advertising and conducting various other financial activities. Therefore between 1904–14 determined, but not altogether successful, efforts were made by some of the members of the Council of Associated Stock Exchanges to limit the access granted to outside brokers to provincial markets, and to provide reciprocal arrangements for protected areas, that is, that an exchange would not allow a member to deal with an outside broker operating within a five mile radius of an Associated Stock Exchange. The object was to curtail dealing facilities available to outsiders in the hope that they would either join the local stock exchange, or else, be driven out of business.

NOTES

1 These figures are estimated. Few exchange records convey details as to the annual membership, particularly during these early years.
2 *Bradford Observer*, November 15, 1845.
3 Liverpool Stock Exchange. Minutes, November 19, 1895, June 16, 1909, May 23, 1907. In June 1908 the minutes mention "Jobbers in American shares" taking their prices from London.
4 Statement by J. Edwards, Secretary of the Manchester Stock Exchange to the *Royal Commission on the London Stock Exchange*, Minutes of Evidence, B.P.P. 1878, XIX, Q. 8026.
5 Birmingham Stock Exchange, Minutes, September 24, 1845.
6 Manchester Stock Exchange, Minutes, November 6, 1843. The Manchester Committee of this period seem to have had an obsession on fining members for lack of punctuality in many aspects of the Stock Exchange's work.
7 Bristol Stock Exchange, Rules and Regulations 1846. Rule XVIII.

8   1878, *Royal Commission,* op. cit., Q. 7891-2.
9   Ibid., Q. 7898-7900.
10 Birmingham Stock Exchange, Minutes, September 9, 1879.
11 Bristol Stock Exchange, Minutes, June 19, 1911.
12 1878, *Royal Commission,* op. cit., Q. 5159-60.
13 Leeds Stock Exchange, Minutes, March 3, 1845, June 2, 4, 1845, August 19, 1846.
14 Manchester Stock Exchange, Minutes, June 3, 1900; Liverpool Stock Exchange, Minutes, November 1904.
15 Manchester Stock Exchange, Minutes, December 28, 1857.
16 Leeds Stock Exchange, Minutes, April 16, 1853.
17 Liverpool Stock Exchange, Rules and Regulations. Rule XL. This particular rule was adopted around 1840.
18 Birmingham Stock Exchange, Minutes, February 25, 1896; April 19, 1909.
19 Liverpool Stock Exchange, Minutes, June 23, 1849.
20 Birmingham Stock Exchange, Minutes, March 3, 1886.
21 Liverpool Stock Exchange, Minutes, April 12, 1886.
22 Manchester Stock Exchange, Minutes, November 6, 1843.
23 Ibid., August 31, 1873.
24 Liverpool Stock Exchange, Minutes, February 4, 1873.
25 Birmingham Stock Exchange, Minutes, June 20, 1903.
26 Bristol Stock Exchange, Minutes, December 5, 1906.
27 Birmingham Stock Exchange, Minutes, July 29, 1859.
28 Leeds Stock Exchange, Minutes, April 14, 1845.
29 Manchester Stock Exchange, Minutes, July 25, 1871, June 5, 1878; see also the 1878 *Royal Commission,* op. cit., Q. 8041-49.
30 1878, *Royal Commission* op. cit., Q. 7912.
31 *The Times,* June 22, 1836; E. Thomas, *The Rise and Growth of Joint Stock Banking,* Vol. 1, (1934), p. 204, notes the existence of "accommodation paper issued by customers and others in order to raise funds for speculative purposes".
32 1878, *Royal Commission,* op. cit., Q. 7912.
33 Liverpool Stock Exchange, Minutes, January 25, 1841.
34 Ibid., November 27, 1844.
35 1878, *Royal Commission,* op. cit., Q. 7913-7921.
36 Liverpool Stock Exchange; Minutes of the "Committee to take into Consideration the necessity of establishing Settling Days in this Market", 1844.
37 Manchester Stock Exchange, Minutes, January 4, March 22, 1899; Liverpool Stock Exchange, Minutes, June 1903. Manchester members during the railway period occasionally settled differences by means of I.O.U.'s, a practice not altogether favoured by the Committee; Minutes, March 10, 1848.
38 Leeds Stock Exchange, Minutes, March 2, 1846.
39 Bristol Stock Exchange, Minutes, August 26, 1847.
40 Birmingham Stock Exchange, Minutes, August 6, 1856.
41 Ibid., June 10, 1896.
42 Manchester Stock Exchange, Minutes, October 15, 1858, March 26, 1881.
43 Liverpool Stock Exchange, Minutes, September 23, 1880, March 1883.
44 Ibid., May 5, 1911.
45 Liverpool Stock Exchange, Rules and Regulations, 1836.
46 Manchester Stock Exchange, Minutes, August 14, 1849.
47 1878, *Royal Commission,* op. cit., Q. 7901-2.

48 Leeds Stock Exchange, Minutes, May 2, 1846. Leeds adopted a minimum scale in 1851, but it is doubtful if it was ever effective, allowing for the general practice of free competition. Leeds members however seem to have been very conscious of competition from local banks since in 1845 a rule was passed requiring that a full commission be charged. Sheffield also took a similarly rigid line at the time, but allowed a concession to "non-resident" banks in 1868; Sheffield Stock Exchange, Minutes, November 23, 1868.

49 Birmingham Stock Exchange, Minutes, June 3, 1857.

50 Liverpool Stock Exchange, Minutes, May 3, 1860.

51 1878, *Royal Commission*, op. cit., Q. 7903.

52 Birmingham Stock Exchange, Minutes, May 9, 1860.

53 Ibid., October 4, 1876, January 6, 1886; see also 1878, *Royal Commission*, op. cit., Q. 4634-38.

54 Ibid., October 27, 1886. During the cycle boom in the mid – 1890s Nathaniel Lea pleaded for a reduction in commissions, arguing that the novel position of the market would attract additional business from other centres.

55 Ibid., August 7, 1889. Later Birmingham rules in 1901 reaffirmed this concession but also introduced a "protected list" for local stocks, which prohibited members from rebating when dealing in locally quoted stocks; Minutes, December 4, 1901.

56 Manchester Stock Exchange, Minutes, November 1905, May 3, December 6, 1906.

57 Liverpool Stock Exchange, Minutes, November 8, 1910, May 7, 1912. Full details of the long and often bitter controversy with London over commissions are given in Chapter 9.

58 This was the "custom" of the London Stock Exchange, although it was not upheld by the courts in 1893 when a Halifax stockbroker failed; see *Economist*, February 18, 1893, p. 188.

59 1878, *Royal Commission*, op. cit., Q. 7952-54; *Economist*, February 18, 1893, p. 188, January 18, 1908, p. 114.

60 Hartley Withers. *The English Banking System*, U.S. Monetary Commission, 61st Congress, 2nd Session Senate Document, No. 492, Washington 1910, p. 118.

61 Liverpool Stock Exchange, Minutes, January 8, 1901. In the case of failures in the West Australian market at this time some London brokers asserted that in dealing with provincial brokers they were merely acting as agents, not as principals, an interpretation which the provinces regarded as a denial of a very long standing custom.

62 Ibid., October 20, 1909.

63 Ibid., December 2, 1902, February 17, 1903. A large number of clerks obtained admission in order to evade proposed changes in the membership rules.

64 Full details of this controversy are given in Chapter 9.

65 Liverpool Stock Exchange, Minutes, June 25, 1908.

66 Ibid., February 18, 1912.

67 Further details on the Preston Bureau are given in Chapter 9.

68 Manchester Stock Exchange, Minutes, February 28, 1849.

69 In 1899 the Sheffield Stock Exchange, Committee instructed members not to give any information as to prices or business done to any outside brokers in Sheffield, on penalty of expulsion; Minutes, April 26, 1896. Leeds Stock Exchange adopted a similar rule in December 1903.

5 Some Domestic Matters

The early entrants to the Liverpool and Manchester Stock Exchanges were able to gain admission by writing to the secretary and provided the applicant was recommended by two members, a ballot was then arranged. If they were successful in the ballot applicants paid an entrance fee and signed the rules and regulations. All applicants were not however admitted immediately since the ballot might go against them, and Liverpool in 1841 specified that "any candidate who shall be henceforth blackballed shall not be eligible for Ballot within four months after such rejection".[1] Also, in 1841, Liverpool required new members to "enter into a Bond with Two Sureties (being members of the Association) to the Trustees, or deposit security to abide by the rules". The security to be given was as follows: "In the case of a single member the sureties shall be Two members of the Association, in the sum of £250 each: or he shall deposit the sum of £500 in cash, or approved Railway or other stock in the hands and in the names of the Trustees: and in the case of a firm the sureties shall be three members, in the sum of £1,000 in equal proportion, or such firm shall deposit the sum of £1,000 in cash or stock. The Bond shall continue in full force, or the security continue deposited with the Trustees for three years".[2] The most likely reason for its introduction was a desire to protect existing members against defaulters among the ranks of the many inexperienced newer entrants to the profession. Up to that date neither Liverpool nor Manchester had experienced any substantial failures. Manchester however did not introduce somewhat similar surety requirements until 1845.[3]

The provincial markets set up in 1844 and after followed suit with regard to surety requirements. Birmingham in 1846 required two sureties of £150 for a period of two years, but they also had the novel provision that if the loss from the default of a member was in excess of £300 a further maximum of £300 could be raised by a rateable contribution on the other members.[4] Bristol from 1845 required two sureties of £300 for two years, while Leeds fixed the sum at £600 for two years from the mover and the seconder of the applicant, but it only covered the member's "transactions on the

Exchange" and a firm was required to give surety to the sum of £1,000.[5] Many of the smaller exchanges did not impose any surety requirement and usually contented themselves with the verbal assurances of an applicant's recommenders.

The amount and duration of the surety requirement was changed many times in later years. When membership fell off after the collapse of the railway boom the tendency was towards a reduction in the amount required, although some leading brokers were against this since it would let in "men of very small means". By the end of the century the surety for the larger exchanges varied from £1,000 to £2,000, while the duration ranged between Birmingham's five years and Liverpool's three years "from the time members started dealing". New applicants also incurred certain financial costs. An entrance fee was payable, which ranged from about £100 during the railway boom to some £200 at the end of the century, with concessions for sons of members and experienced clerks.

Other requirements were aimed at confining the liabilities of members to the share dealing business. Virtually from their formation most markets disapproved of members entering any other business except acting as agents for insurance companies. Neither were members allowed to join another exchange, and they were usually required either to reside in the town or at least keep an office there. Leeds also required its new entrants to have been in the sharebroking business for at least six months.[6] Members were also prohibited from entering into partnerships with outsiders since it would impair their sole liability to the stock exchange. In order to ascertain the connections and intentions of applicants some exchanges adopted the London practice of requesting them to appear before the Committee to answer a list of questions.[7]

The increased membership of some of the larger exchanges at the turn of the century gave rise to additional conditions being imposed upon prospective entrants. Birmingham, for example, in 1897 required new entrants to have had six months broking experience, and later in 1903 in response to demands from members to curtail the "precocious manner of granting new membership" entry was made conditional upon a new member bringing additional business into the market and the existing membership were very vigilant as to the enforcement of this provision.[8]

From their earliest beginnings most stock exchanges allowed members to introduce clerks to the market and they were able to deal provided they had the members' consent. Up until the 1860s each member had one clerk, but subsequently two clerks or more became quite general and provided an easy means of expanding staff to cope with additional business. Clerks were frequently used to handle the shunting side of the business. The larger exchanges maintained a distinction between unauthorized and authorized or accredited clerks, and on the Manchester Stock Exchange they had to serve one year as ordinary clerks in a broker's office before being introduced to the market as authorized clerks.[9] Towards the end of the century the number of clerks employed on the stock exchanges increased much more rapidly than the membership. Liverpool in 1902 had 88 clerks, Manchester 97. In Liverpool clerks were allowed to bring "orders to the Room, able to attend, watch the execution of the order and receive half commission". Such a facility was regarded by some Liverpool members as an important reason for the decline in applications for membership between the years 1892–97 and accordingly in 1905 the Committee resolved that clerks interested solely in "soliciting and receiving orders from outside clients" could not continue in such a position for more than one year. In practice about half the Liverpool clerks were interested in commission, and also drew a salary, while very few were solely dependent on commission business. No such restrictions operated at Manchester, although in 1914 a limit of four clerks per firm was imposed, and two years earlier Birmingham had imposed a limit of three clerks per firm.

Within a short time of their formation the membership of a stock exchange set about electing a Committee for General Purposes "upon whom shall devolve the management of the affairs of the Association." However, certain powers were frequently retained by the general meeting of members. For example, in Liverpol up to 1845 the approval of a general meeting was necessary to introduce new rules. With the growth of membership during the railway boom such approval was found to be inconvenient, time consuming, and frequently resulting in unsound precedents and hasty and undigested decisions; "the body has become too numerous to govern itself".[10]

The duties of such committees were seldom laid down in detail but they usually involved managing the affairs of the association, formulating rules on the conduct of members, and adjudicating in disputes between members. In this matter members accepted the decisions of the Committee where cases were referred to them on questions of "liability, default of payment, commission, or any other matter relative to or arising out of the bargains for the purchase or sale of stock".[11] They were also prepared to adjudicate on disputes between brokers and their principals if both gave an undertaking to accept the Committee's ruling. The larger markets tended to operate a system of sub-committees who dealt with such technical areas as formulating new rules, applications for quotations, and applications for admissions.

In the running of the stock exchanges two posts were particularly important, that of the chairman and secretary. The former was elected annually, but in most cases re-election was customary and outstanding personalities were re-elected to the office for long periods. The main administrative burdens fell upon the secretary and from the start most exchanges had full-time posts with an office "adequately equipped to assist members". The post of secretary to a large provincial market seems to have been a much coveted occupation particularly during the railway mania. When the Liverpool secretaryship fell vacant in 1845 the Committee received almost two hundred applications for the job. They appointed Harry Scrivenor, sometime manager of the British Iron Works at Ruabon. Scrivenor was the author of two important works which are still of considerable interest and value to economic historians. In 1841 he published *A Comprehensive History of the Iron Trade throughout the World*, followed in 1849 by *The Railways of the United Kingdom Statistically Considered in relation to their Extent, Capital, Amalgamation, etc.* As he states in his preface to the second edition of the *History of the Iron Trade*, published in 1854, other engagements "had withdrawn his attention from the iron trade", but these were not solely confined to the responsible but relatively unremunerative work of Secretary of the Stock Exchange. In 1851 he decided to take up stockbroking and accordingly became a member of the Liverpool Stock Exchange. Unfortunately for Scrivenor his talents did not extend in that direction and after a year's trading he was declared a defaulter. His failure arose from his inability to select solid clients. He dealt mainly for three principals, one of which ran a very large speculative position and who had been for some time notoriously insolvent. By allowing this client to carry over stock several times Scrivenor also had become insolvent into the bargain; he would have been declared a defaulter within the year were it not for his fellow brokers continuing to deal with him in the hope of getting paid.[12]

Liverpool and Birmingham appointed permanent secretaries from the start, but Manchester depended upon the services of an honorary secretary until 1848. The Lancashire markets also resorted to appointing inspectors of clearing during periods of heavy dealing, but Liverpool dispensed with a separate office for this in 1856. Bristol appointed a salaried secretary in 1845 at a sum of £100 p.a., and he was required to provide surety of £250, but this requirement was dropped in 1857. Shortly afterwards the secretaryship lapsed and the Association's affairs were handled by a member firm. A permanent secretary was not appointed until 1903.[13] Again some lengthy service was rendered by some of the secretaries. Joshua Cooke served the Leeds Stock Exchange for fifty years from 1847 as secretary and in various other offices. Owen Tudor was secretary at Liverpool for up to thirty years prior to his retirement in 1873, and John Phillips from 1878 to 1912. More recently Percy Rudge was secretary at Birmingham from 1916 to 1961 and Horace Richmond was secretary at Manchester from 1924–67, while two of his predecessors John Edwards and John N. Cain held office from 1849 to 1873 and 1884 to 1915 respectively.

The range of administrative services and the accumulation of reserve funds depended largely on the revenue from annual subscriptions and particularly on the entrance fees paid by new members. During the early years a dearth of new entrants meant reduced income and measures to curtail expenditure, a feature which occurred on most exchanges round about 1850. Some reduced their administrative staffs, while Manchester offered lower salaries to its officials and called for duties "to be more effectively performed". In 1848 the Committee of the Bristol Stock Exchange resolved to keep the expenses of the establishment as low as possible consistently with the comfort of the members.[14] Other economy measures took the form of reduced library facilities through the provision of newspapers, financial periodicals, and share lists.

From their earliest days the setting aside of reserve funds for various purposes occupied a prominent place in the finances of most markets. Liverpool set up a Guaranteed Fund as early as 1845 when four-fifths of the Association's existing funds and four-fifths of all the "Brokerage on the buying in and selling out of stocks or shares by the Secretary or his assistant" were allocated for that purpose. The fund was used to cover claims against defaulters to the extent of 5 sh. in the £1 but was not available automatically.[15] At the outbreak of the first world war Liverpool's General Fund stood at £10,000 while that of Manchester amounted to £40,000, a "useful reserve to meet unforseen claims on the Association".[16]

The stock exchanges exhibited a remarkable degree of mobility with regard to the premises they occupied and it was not until the end of the century that most of them obtained their own, designed to meet their specific needs. Before this they leased or rented accommodation which for the most part was cramped and unsuitable. Shortly after its formation in 1836 the Liverpool Stock Exchange occupied rooms in Exchange Street West, but these were soon found to be "inconvenient for the purposes wanted". Accordingly for a short while in 1843 the Association moved to rooms in the East Side of Sweeting Street. This was followed by a stay from 1844 to 1852 in rooms over the Royal Bank, but within two years of moving in a sub-committee was busy looking for an alternative and

more suitable "place of business for the future occupation of the Association." In 1852 they received notice to quit the Royal Bank Buildings, apparently because of the boisterous conduct of the younger members of the Stock Exchange which was not in consonance with the dignity of a mid-Victorian banking establishment. The Association then opened a new Stock Exchange on the West side of the Exchange Buildings, but in 1862 came yet another notice to quit and from 1864 to 1869 the brokers found themselves in a temporary building on the Exchange Flags, nicknamed "Noah's Ark", a location which was as uncomfortable as it was undignified. In May 1869, they moved to rooms on the East side of the Exchange Buildings. Finally in 1874 the Association decided upon a place of its own and bought land in Dale Street for £29,500 and by March 1879 the premises were sufficiently advanced for them to move in after an expenditure of £22,000. At the outset the funds were raised by mortgage but in 1882 it was decided to form the Liverpool Stock Exchange Building Co. with a nominal capital of £100,000 in £100 shares, £60 paid up, with 942 shares issued to the 157 members. Each member subsequently was required to hold qualification shares, the precise number being varied from time to time. The premises were enlarged in 1899 and this provided the accommodation of the Stock Exchange until 1971 when it moved to Tithebarn Street.[17]

Manchester enjoyed an equally roving existence. From 1836 to 1868 it occupied rooms in the Royal Exchange Buildings but relations between the Association and the landlord were not as cordial as their long stay would suggest. The latter disapproved of the use of the central arcade for dealing purposes, and persistent complaints from other tenants prompted the Committee in 1848 to set up a sub-committee to consider, and little else, the erection of a "building at some future time for use as a Stock Exchange". Notice to quit came in 1864 but they did not actually leave the Exchange Buildings until 1868 when they moved to the Commercial Buildings in Cross Street. A break in the lease in 1903 gave them an opportunity to look for more ample accommodation and it was decided to build a new exchange. At a cost of £86,000 the present premises were constructed, with up to two-fifths of it available for letting, and opened in 1906. The operation was financed through the formation of a Building Company with £65,000 of debt and £35,000 ordinary capital, of which £21,000 was called up. The accommodation provided was designed to provide room for expansion and to meet the understandable desire that "the Manchester Stock Exchange should have premises of its own".[18]

The first home of the Birmingham Stock Exchange was at 2

Temple Row West, which they occupied until 1856 when a move was made to 34 Bennetts Hill. They remained there until 1861 when they moved a small distance to rooms in Wellington Passage. With the growth of membership towards the end of the century the premises became increasingly "inconvenient and incommodius" (the primitive open stove did not help) and in 1901 premises were acquired in nearby Newhall Street financed by setting up a Building Company.[19] Between then and 1921 the membership increased from 41 to 77 and the number of clerks from 25 to 53, which made the existing premises somewhat cramped. Accordingly in 1926 it was decided to put up their own building in Margaret Street and it was occupied in 1928.

Bristol was no more fortunate with its early location than any other provincial market, but it ended up in 1903 with the ideal solution to such problems. The Stock Exchange began its life in 1845 in rooms in Albion Chambers, Small Street. Because of the "comfortless state" of the accommodation the market moved in 1846 to Bush Chambers in Commercial Street and stayed there until 1866. The next move was to rooms in the Royal Insurance Buildings at a rental of £50 p.a., but in 1875 they moved to less expensive accommodation in Small Street. Four years later they moved to the north side of Albion Chambers, and again in 1882 into premises previously occupied by the Bristol Chamber of Commerce. The need for more suitable premises towards the end of the century led to an offer from Mr (afterwards Sir) George White to provide the necessary accommodation provided he was given a free hand. He then presented the newly built Stock Exchange to the Association. Situated in Nicholas Street, it is an imposing building with granite columns and richly carved Corinthian capitals, while the Exchange room and the Committee room are elaborately furnished with polished walnut panelling.[20]

Leeds Stock Exchange was a little more status conscious than its provincial counterparts. Initially they occupied rooms in the Music Hall, but relatively soon afterwards they moved to their own building which had been erected on the site of the Reservoir in Albion Street. It was financed from the surplus funds of the Association and from members' contributions. By 1876 however it was too large for the slowly decreasing membership and they moved to rooms leased from the Bank of Leeds.[21] The early location of the Sheffield Stock Exchange is not known but in the 1860s meetings were held in rooms in George Street, and in 1873 they moved to premises over a music shop in High Street where they stayed, apart from two short spells in Davy's Buildings and the Cutlers Hall, until 1885 when rooms were obtained over the Union of London and Smith's Bank in High

Street. In 1910 they bought the Old Post Office in Commercial Street and the new market was opened with due ceremony in 1911.[22] Newcastle's early meetings were in a tea dealer's shop, but from 1857 to 1892 they met at Mrs Kennedy's, 113 Pilgrim Street. They then moved to the offices of the Incorporated Law Society and in 1898 to the library of the Institute of Chartered Accountants. Finally in 1912 they acquired premises in Moor Buildings where they remained until the 1950s.

One of the most profound influences on the growth and pattern of provincial stockbroking were the improvements in communications during the second half of the nineteenth century. Railway links had considerably reduced the time factor between London and provincial cities, and between provincial centres. However, as far as the provincial stock exchanges were concerned it was the telegraph system which brought the biggest changes in that it greatly facilitated inter-market business with rapid transmission of prices and orders. Shunting activity was the outcome of such an innovation.

The first recorded use of the telegraph for transmission of prices to the provincial exchanges is during the late 1840s. In 1848 Manchester received the London mid-day and closing prices from the Electric Telegraph Company, and in 1849 Liverpool obtained the prices of the funds and principal railway stocks from the same company. Shortly afterwards the Electric Telegraph Company was offering extended facilities in the form of the prices of the leading provincial markets of Liverpool, Manchester, Birmingham, and Leeds, in addition to the usual London intelligence, all provided at a fixed annual rental.[23] The service provided however was not particularly satisfactory and in 1851 Liverpool ended its contract with the company because of "the great irregularity and late arrival of both noon and closing prices of shares". Shortly afterwards Liverpool renewed the contract, but finally in 1854 it took out a new contract with a rival company, the Magnetic Telegraph Company for "all share and general information". Manchester also at the same time switched to the Magnetic Telegraph Company for the same reasons.[24] Continued dissatisfaction with the service led the Liverpool Committee to play one company off against another, but it proved of little use since the telegraph companies had an agreement as to their respective spheres of operation.[25] Liverpool's immediate response to the combination was to cease supplying its own prices to the telegraph companies but strong complaints from members led to a resumption of providing prices since the stoppage of Liverpool prices prevented "the small share markets of the provinces from getting them". Some of the small share markets themselves experienced similar problems with the telegraph service provided by the new companies.

Leeds in 1850 complained bitterly of the "entire cessation of the receipt of the quotations from the Liverpool and Manchester share markets". In 1852 Bristol installed "telegraphic communication with London" for a trial period but found the service very unreliable.

Despite the frequent complaints from the various exchanges as to the great irregularity of the service it was nevertheless extensively used by the 1870s. Prices were transmitted and agents were given orders to deal, etc. Most communications were dealt with speedily and delays of more than fifteen minutes were regarded as "prejudicial to business". The main links were between provincial markets and London although the others were not unimportant. Richard Withers stated to the 1878 *Royal Commission* that "one fourth of the whole telegraphic receipts in the town are from the Liverpool Stock Exchange. In fact such is the enlargement of the business with Manchester, Glasgow and London from Liverpool by telegraph, that the Post Office have given us a special department, special wires, and special clerks to carry on our business".[26] Sheffield in 1879 were anxious to participate in the system and pleaded with the local postmaster that a telegraphic apparatus would "greatly increase and facilitate the transaction of business with the other Stock Exchanges".[27] Certainly Leeds made considerable use of it and in 1886 it was estimated that some 67,000 messages had been sent.[28]

By no means all the exchanges approved of this development. The Dublin Stock Exchange stated in 1888 that it did not want increased communication with other markets because the "effect was to take business away from Dublin". Manchester put the same argument to the Exchange Telegraph Company in 1886 when the company asked for facilities nearer to the Stock Exchange to provide an effective "dissemination of prices".[29] The same fear of loss of business accounts for the reluctant approach to the introduction of the telephone, and even more so later, to the use of tape machines.

As well as having a direct link with London most markets by the mid-1880s were linked together on a direct stock wire. The possibility of setting up a network connecting all the stock exchanges, which might have lessened the flow of provincial business to London, was stifled in 1887 by the attitude and actions of the telegraph authorities. This involved a decision on the part of the London Post Office authorities "to discontinue direct communications between all provincial offices that have not a *direct* wire to the London Stock Exchange". Glasgow, Leeds, Liverpool, Manchester and Dublin had direct stock wires to London. Birmingham, Sheffield, Halifax, Huddersfield and Bradford had no such wire and their messages to the London Stock Exchange went to the central London office and then by tube to the Stock Exchange. Apparently the Post Office felt, without any prompting from the London Stock Exchange, that the provinces had some advantage over London and they indicated that the only remedy was for those without a direct link with London to seek one and they would then retain their previous privileges.[30] However, there was great difficulty in obtaining a direct stock wire to London. From 1876 onwards Birmingham tried to improve communications with London and even got up a weighty petition in 1884 signed by the members, local inhabitants, fifty-two London members and supported by Joseph Chamberlain, "in favour of a new telegraph station adjoining this Exchange with a stock wire to London". The Post Office replied that the volume of business did not justify it. After the cycle boom the Postmaster General relented and they obtained a direct stock wire in 1898 after a fifteen year struggle, but it was conditional on 400 messages a day.[31] Similarly, Sheffield got a direct wire to London in 1904 after a great deal of "hammering away" at the Post Office.

By this time another improvement in communications was slowly making its way into stock exchange operations, but to a rather cool reception. This was not solely provincial since an American observer had noted the same attitude on the London Stock Exchange where "telephones and private lines are but sparingly used". Neither did the protective concern of the Post Office for its telegraph monopoly help to foster the full exploitation of the new device. The first use of the telephone by provincial broking circles occurred in Manchester in 1879 when a member connected his office with the market, and within a few years the rest of the market followed suit. It would appear that the use of the telephone remained mainly local for many years after its introduction to the exchanges. In 1882 the Lancashire and Cheshire Telephone Exchange Company installed boxes in the Liverpool Stock Exchange but in 1896 the company was instructed to take out the trunk line boxes as "they were not such a vital matter to the Stock Exchange generally . . . seeing that it was only a question which affected comparatively few members".[32] In the same year the Bristol Committee could not feel justified in going to the expense of getting telephone communications in the market. Earlier in 1891 Birmingham indicated to the local telephone manager that "no advantage would be gained" from improving telephone links between Birmingham and London.[33]

After the turn of the century however the telephone began to replace the stock wire as the most important inter-market link. Technical improvements in the service, continued frustration with the delays to telegrams, and the fact that wire facilities did not correspond with the volume of business were all contributory factors in this development. By 1907 Manchester had ten boxes, with some

15,000 calls per year, two thirds of them trunk calls. Increasingly provincial brokers obtained direct lines to their London agents and by 1908 all the shunting business was done on private wires. War economies virtually put an end to the telegraph as a channel of business, and after the war the stock exchanges concentrated on developing telephone communications.

One change which followed on the increased use of the phone was the method of payment adopted by the stock exchanges. Initially, the expense was borne by the Committees out of subscription charges but after 1908 charges were transferred directly to the members since the burden on the committee had become excessive. By 1921 telephone charges were an important element in business costs and even small increases in trunk rates brought strong protests from the stock exchanges. Concern about cost however was soon dwarfed by concern about access to trunk line facilities and the possible opportunities for outsiders to take advantage of direct access to market floors. Prior to 1926 Birmingham did not allow members to have trunk lines with outsiders, but the rule was dropped since no other exchange pursued such a policy. Later, growing concern about loss of business through telephone links with outsiders led to various restrictions, agreed to by the Council of Associated Stock Exchanges and the London Stock Exchange, on the use of telephone facilities.[34] Equal concern about providing a free price service to outsiders led to delays in adopting tape machines. Both Manchester and Liverpool rejected offers by the Exchange Telegraph Company in 1923 to send prices between markets since it was feared that outside dealers might benefit from this.[35]

The initial membership of the stock exchanges was drawn from a wide variety of professions and other activities, and this pattern continued during the century. There was in addition a category drawn from amongst the sons of members and clerks, who frequently entered on preferential terms. The big surges of new entrants however came from strangers particularly during periods of active trading. Some of the applicants were rather extraordinary but this certainly did not debar them from entry. Liverpool in 1848 admitted a "medical man", while in 1864 a "brassfounder" was also admitted. Most of the strangers admitted to the Liverpool Stock Exchange during the twenty years after 1845 seem to have had some previous experience of sharedealing, although a few were honest enough to admit that it had not all been fortunate. There is very little evidence of movement of members between various exchanges, and in the case of Liverpool only three members were admitted from other markets in the years 1845 to 1865. No doubt this absence of mobility was associated with their dependence on an established local clientele who set great store on personal contact.

On the evidence of the financial accounts of a small number of broking firms it would appear that they needed little capital in order to commence business. In the case of ten Liverpool firms which were declared defaulters in 1870 the starting capital ranged from nil to £3,000. Half of them started with less than £500, a few with less than £800.[36] This sum was of course entirely separate from surety money. Manchester, during the nineteenth century, seems to have been the only market to require some minimum starting capital. From 1855 onwards candidates were required "to possess a clean and bona fide amount of not less than £1,000 of available capital".

Lack of capital was not however a serious disadvantage to budding brokers. Their main capital requirement involved meeting cheques at the settlement, which if they had to cover for a client could generally be done with the help of their banker. It was also the general practice in most markets that new members only engaged in commission business until their period of surety had expired. No doubt the sureties themselves were anxious to see this convention followed, and Manchester had a distinct rule on the subject requiring entrants to "confine themselves to commission business until capital was increased and the expiration of two years surety". In addition, the operating expenses of broking activity were really quite low. In the case of the ten Liverpool firms who defaulted in 1870 their annual office expenses ranged between £300 to £400 a year. One firm had a figure of £600, but £400 of this was for telegraphic expenses associated with shunting activity and inter-market dealing. There were of course exceptions, such as the Bristol firm which in 1845 "had its offices in the large building in Small Street, and used to keep an open house for clients, with champagne and cigars running all day, while the members of the firm drove to the office in a four in hand coach".[37]

As to the rewards of the profession even less is known. The commission income of the ten Liverpool firms already cited ranged from a rather low £660 to £4,700, with most of them around £2,000 per year.[38] This figure may of course be a little on the high side given the large market turnover of that period. The income from broking activity depended on individual turnover and commission levels, and the profit depended on the level of operating expenses against this. What is absolutely unknown is the return to the jobbing activities of members which could be very large, but which led to the undoing of some.

Again, as to the scale of their operations very little is known. The ten Liverpool firms of 1870 must once more provide the examples. It is apparent that some considerable positions were taken up ranging from £30,000 to £120,000, the bulk of which was on behalf of clients. The transactions were usually done on several markets with the largest positions being taken up on the London market for obvious reasons. The open positions in stocks were financed from several sources. Firstly, from capital sources which were usually small in relation to turnover. Secondly, the stock could be carried over in the market by other brokers. Thirdly, it was possible to borrow money from outside parties on margin against the security of shares or stock; for example, the Liverpool brokers, Irwin and Aspinall, and the Manchester firm of Johnson, Bradley and Walter borrowed on this basis from the Manchester merchant John Owens both for their own and clients needs.[39] Fourthly, speculative positions could always be financed with bank loans. The general practice was to use stock as security for the loan which was taken out by the broker, with a separate loan for each account. Generally rates paid were Bank Rate plus half per cent for loans which usually ran for three months or so. Rich clients were prepared to pay their broker an eighth per cent for the use of his name and the benefit of anonymity. Some provincial firms however refused to have more than a single loan outstanding at any one time.[40] Fifthly, a speculative position could be operated on the basis of a joint account, which was widely used, with equal division of profits and no commission charges for the participating parties. Successful speculators seldom kept stock open for long but contented themselves with small jobbing turns. If a transaction was slow in showing gains it could always be carried over to the next account.

Occasionally firms ran into difficulties, self inflicted or else beyond their immediate control. When the committee of an exchange was informed that a member could not meet his differences the member was suspended so that no further business should be transacted and he was generally allowed a little time to clear himself. In Manchester a broker was given until the next account for this and if he failed he was declared a defaulter. The practice was then to appoint a small committee of Inspectors; Liverpool appointed three, representing the interests of the Committee, the defaulter, and the creditors, and frequently one of them was a qualified accountant. They undertook "to wind up a man's affairs . . . report to the committee, and divide his assets, giving the outdoor creditors full participation in those assets". If surety was still outstanding this was divided solely among the members and not regarded as part of the general estate. Up until 1870 Manchester did not divide any part of the estate with outside creditors but thereafter changed their practice when they realised the illegality of the previous method.[41]

Readmission of a defaulter depended on the payment of a dividend out of the estate and his conduct before the default. Liverpool laid particular stress on the latter point, as Richard Withers noted to the 1878 *Royal Commission*, "the dividends receivable from a defaulter are not large as a percentage. We do not look so much to that as to his conduct, and to the amount of account originally opened, compared with his means when he opened it, and all the circumstances under which he has carried on business". Manchester, on the other hand, took a far less flexible attitude and would not readmit a member until he had paid "out of his own resources, at least 6s. 8d. in the pound".[42] Bristol, in 1846, would only readmit a member if he undertook not to do any business on his own account.

During their early years it was not always possible for stock exchange committees to establish that a person or firm was actually in default. It was sometimes the practice for brokers to whom differences were owed to allow their debtors to go on dealing in the market in the hope of clearing themselves, ultimately "at the expense of their brother brokers". However, an attempt by the Liverpool Committee to get powers to investigate alleged defaulters met with strong opposition from members.[43] Another problem during this period was that members sometimes reached a compromise with a defaulter by arranging the settlement of claims in lieu of a bona fide money payment. The Leeds Committee in 1852 threatened expulsion to any members who received or agreed to receive without the knowledge of the Committee a composition of less than 20s. in cash or otherwise in discharge of any debt due to him.[44] Even when a member had been declared a defaulter it was sometimes difficult to settle matters quickly, especially in the railway era, since some brokers did not keep any records. As Thomas Evans put it to the Bristol Committee in 1846, that "since all my bargains have been for cash with respectable clients I have never kept any books". Later in the century a Birmingham broker wrote to the Committee after his suspension, "We should not like an accountant to examine our books, never having had one to do so, and much preferring privacy". Such eccentricities had disappeared by the twentieth century, although one leading broker was reputed to keep his market bargains on his starched shirt cuffs; he too defaulted.

A broker found himself suspended and declared a defaulter either because of his own actions, or more commonly the action of his principals. The most common cause of default, where responsibility lay solely with the broker, was associated with speculation carried on with inadequate capital resources. Sometimes this involved stock acquired in dealing (jobbing) but left open when it could not be closed at a profit. Also difficulties arose where firms "adopted the accounts of defaulting principals" in the hope of redeeming the position. Lack of capital resources, inexperience and over-confidence were at the root of such failures which were much more numerous during the railway mania. They are characterized by the broker who wrote to his Committee, "I am strangled with unmarketable securities which are crushing me down to earth"; little wonder when he had a large open position in nearly forty stocks. The main problems arose however because of large defaults by principals, particularly where a firm ran speculative accounts for a few or even one client. One broker invited trouble by undertaking speculative accounts while charging commission in the event of any profits being made.

Provincial concern with the thorny subject of advertising rivalled that experienced by their London counterparts. At the outset of provincial sharedealing and indeed for a while after the setting up of the stock exchanges, individual brokers engaged in extensive advertising in the local, and more distant press, by ways of lists of shares with buying and selling limits. As dependence upon such outside orders diminished and the convention gradually emerged against invading other peoples territory, the stock exchanges moved towards adopting rules designed to limit the practice. Surprisingly Bristol was first off the mark as early as 1847 when the members agreed that they would not advertise in the local press, and the Committee in 1856 assumed responsibility for issuing all local press advertisements. Other markets did not adopt formal rules until London gave the lead in 1885 but by 1890 most of them adopted laws designed to prevent advertising, and similar provisions were incorporated in the Code Laws of the Council of Associated Stock Exchanges. Most of them ran along the lines of the Birmingham rule passed in 1887 that "members of the Stock Exchange are not allowed to advertise for business purposes or to issue circulars to persons other than their own principals". To compensate members for their inability to retaliate against outside brokers the stock exchanges engaged in collective advertising of a suitably staid tone. There were exceptions in some markets as late as the 1920s which took the form of advertisements aimed at widening the rather restrictive markets in shares of a purely local nature.

Some provincial stockbroking concerns have a long history and can trace their origins back to the earliest years of their respective exchanges. The Liverpool broking firm of Tilney & Company can trace its origins back to one of the earliest sharebrokers in the city. The link is to be found in the firm of Sing, White and Company, which merged with Tilney, Parr & Rae in 1966. Sing, White and Company was formed in 1825 by Joseph King, one of the first brokers in Liverpool, and Chairman of the Stock Exchange from 1840–44. In 1877 the business was continued by his nephew Alexander Millington Synge, and since then a member of the family has held a connection with the firm. Another important firm which was incorporated with Tilney's in 1958 was that of Parr & Rae. Henry Bingham Parr, son of the founder of Parr's Bank, joined the Stock Exchange in 1866, and in 1870 took in as a partner another broker with strong banking links. This was Edward Rae, second son of George Rae who was a director of the North and South Wales Bank and the author of the famous classic, *The Country Banker*. Born in 1847 Edward Rae had a varied and remarkable career even before he entered the Stock Exchange. At the age of eighteen he spent some time on the Continent surveying French and Italian docks and followed this interest in ships and engineering by going to Egypt to superintend the construction of vessels for the provisional traffic on the Suez Canal. It was this experience which led him to advocate dredging the Mersey Bar. During these years he also developed a keen and informed interest in primitive races and their languages which led to his travels in Lapland, Iceland, Palmyra and the Barbary. In 1874 he was elected a Fellow the Royal Geographic Society. He published his journals of these visits in three travel books, *Land of the West Wind* (1875), *The Country of the Moors* (1877), and *The White Sea Peninsula* (1888). His work in the Stock Exchange was equally varied and gifted. Following the Barton Frauds he initiated the successful movement which procured the passing of the Forged Transfers Act in 1891, and then energetically persuaded the leading railway companies to adopt its provisions. He was also instrumental in setting up in 1890 the Council of Associated Stock Exchanges, and in securing the adoption of the Code Law. He was President of the Council on four occasions, and was practically a permanent delegate from Liverpool. In 1890 he was elected vice-chairman of the Liverpool Stock Exchange, and to the chairmanship in 1894, an office he held until 1915. He died in 1923[45].

Three other Liverpool firms can trace their history back to the early years of the Stock Exchange. The name Neilson can be traced back to Daniel Neilson, a founder member of the Stock Exchange, and a Chairman from 1845–54. His nephew Henry Cottingham Neilson joined the Exchange in 1889, forming the firm of Neilson and Graves in 1890. Following amalgamations in 1936 and 1966 the firm became Neilson, Hornby, Crichton & Co.[46] Ashton Tod

McLaren has its origins in the partnership between Archibald Tod and Charles Ellis Ashton, both of whom joined the Stock Exchange in 1841. In 1855 they were joined by Henry Heywood Noble and the firm became Ashton Tod & Noble. The firm of Case, Leach & Company can be traced back through Case Ridehalgh to Robert Case who joined the Stock Exchange in 1844. In 1864 he left Liverpool to join the London Stock Exchange, and his brother James Case followed him in 1868. Henry Ridehalgh then took over the business. In 1966 Case Ridehalgh amalgamated with Harold Leach and Son, a firm formed in 1892.[47] One firm, which went out of business in 1936, Thomas Tinley and Company, was also among the earliest being founded by Thomas Tinley and George Adams Tinley in 1836. Thomas Tinley, the son of a Tyneside shipowner, lost an arm following an attack by highwaymen on his journey from the Tyne to Liverpool[48].

Two Manchester firms have connections dating back to the first railway boom. John Railton and Son entered sharebroking in 1836 and in 1850 he was joined by one Mr Leedham, and the name Railton Sons and Leedham remained unchanged until 1946. During this period J. R. Ward and E. H. Ward joined Mr Leedham in the 1880s and in 1929 W. H. Ireland became a partner, having joined the firm in 1901. In 1946 W. M. Musgrove Hoyle joined and the name changed to Hoyle Railton & Company. In 1956 W. H. Ireland, after over fifty years' association with the name Railton set up business on his own as W. H. Ireland and Company[49].

A number of Birmingham firms also boast a long history. The firm of Margetts and Addenbrooke was founded by James Pearson in 1843 and he was succeeded by his son ten years later. In 1875 H. Margetts joined the firm and in 1884 Jervis Addenbrooke became a partner[50]. An equally well established firm is that of N. Lea Barham and Brooks which was founded by Nathaniel Lea, a founder member of the Stock Exchange. Another founder member, John Smith, founded the present firm of Smith, Keen, Barnett and Company.

Two other provincial firms deserve mention in this context. The Bristol firm of brokers B. S. Stock, Son & Company derives from the early activities of Benjamin Spry Stock who established the firm in 1844. On B. S. Stock's death his son, Spry Stock, succeeded him in the business but died shortly afterwards in 1895. The business was then carried on by his partner Harold Merrett Stock (1871–1954), who was joined by his sons, K. C. M. Stock and G. E. M. Stock in the early twenties and whose sons have since joined the firm[51]. The Newcastle firm of J. H. and T. Richardson, which recently amalgamated with Boys-Stones, Simpson and Spencer, had a direct line of descent from J. Richardson who founded the firm in 1844.

NOTES

1 Liverpool Stock Exchange, Minutes, March 3, 1837.
2 Ibid., February 23, 1841. The London Stock Exchange introduced a surety requirement in 1821.
3 Manchester Stock Exchange, Minutes, August 4, October 15, 1845.
4 Birmingham Stock Exchange, Minutes, January 24, 1846, December 1, 1847.
5 Bristol Stock Exchange, Minutes, June 9, 1845; Leeds Stock Exchange, Minutes, June 2, 1845.
6 Leeds Stock Exchange, Minutes, March 3, 1845.
7 Among such questions were "What experience do you possess of stock-broking and where gained? Do you keep proper records? Is your business speculative or otherwise in character? Have you maintained a definite scale of brokerage and what was it?" Birmingham Stock Exchange, Minutes, May 29, 1899.
8 Birmingham Stock Exchange, Minutes, December 2, 1903.
9 Manchester Stock Exchange, Minutes, June 23, 1880.
10 Liverpool Stock Exchange, Minutes, April 7, 1845.
11 Liverpool Stock Exchange, Minutes, September 11, 1838.
12 Ibid., August 18, October 11, 1852.
13 Bristol Stock Exchange, Minutes, October 1845, February 5, 1857.
14 Manchester Stock Exchange, Minutes, August 14, 1848; Bristol Stock Exchange, Minutes, March 29, 1848.
15 Liverpool Stock Exchange, Minutes, September 10, 1845.
16 Ibid., April 7, 1915.
17 Ibid., July 6, 1847; List of Past and Present Members; January 19, 1874, December 10, 1877; March 30, 1878, March 13, 1879.
18 Manchester Stock Exchange, Minutes, July 14, 1848, January 9, 1900.
19 Birmingham Stock Exchange, Minutes, February 18, 1901.
20 Bristol Stock Exchange, Minutes, May 29, 1903.
21 Leeds Stock Exchange, Minutes, April 29, November 3, 5, 1845; October 1874.
22 Sheffield Stock Exchange, Minutes, December 1, 1910, November 6, 1911.
23 Liverpool Stock Exchange, Minutes, January 11, 1849. The Electric Telegraph Company was formed in 1846 and up until 1850 it had a complete monopoly of telegraphic communications; Clapham, Vol. 1, op. cit., p. 396.
24 Liverpool Stock Exchange, Minutes, June 30, 1851; Manchester Stock Exchange, Minutes, April 24, 1854.
25 Liverpool Stock Exchange, Minutes, January 4, 1865. The telegraph companies also had an agreed tariff which was fixed in 1865 after an attempt by the United Kingdom Telegraph Company to charge a uniform rate of 1 sh. irrespective of distance. The tarriff was as follows: up to 100 miles 1 sh; 100-200 miles 1s. 6d; beyond 200 miles 2 sh. J. C. Hemmeon, *The History of the British Post Office* (1912), pp. 202-3.

26 *1878 Royal Commission,* op. cit., Q. 7907. The telegraph system was taken over by the Post Office in 1870.
27 Sheffield Stock Exchange, Minutes, November 17, 1879.
28 Leeds Stock Exchange, Minutes, January 2, 1895. Leeds had its own stock wire from 1871 to 1895. By 1893 the number of messages sent had fallen to 42,000 and the Post Office reduced facilities to the market following "the worst period of depression this generation has known".
29 Manchester Stock Exchange, January 1886.
30 Ibid., June 13, 1887.
31 Birmingham Stock Exchange, Minutes, October 24, 1884, July 5, 1889.
32 Liverpool Stock Exchange, Minutes, March 17, 1896.
33 Birmingham Stock Exchange, Minutes, February 3, 1891.
34 See Chapter 10.
35 Liverpool Stock Exchange, Minutes, March 13, 1923; Manchester Stock Exchange, Minutes, March 12, 1923.
36 Taken from the accounts of defaulters. The year 1870 witnessed a crop of defaulters on the Liverpool Stock Exchange, associated with a sharp fall in share prices. Principals had difficulty in closing contracts due to the "state of panic on the Stock Exchange".
37 *Financial News,* July 29, 1903.
38 An estimate for the period 1846-52 put the average income of brokers on the Leeds Stock Exchange at £1,200 for 1846, falling to £300 in 1848, and rising to £700 in 1852; J. R. Killick and W. A. Thomas, "The Provincial Stock Exchanges, 1830-1870", *Economic History Review,* April 1970, p. 106.
39 B. W. Clapp, *John Owens, Manchester Merchant* (1965), pp. 146-152. Owens lent large sums between 1840-45 on railway shares usually on a 25% margin and at rates well above market levels, obtaining as much as 24% on occasions.
40 Liverpool Stock Exchange, Minutes, September 3, 1907.
41 *1878 Royal Commission,* op. cit., Q. 7935, 8065.
42 Ibid., Q. 7942, 8071.
43 Liverpool Stock Exchange, Minutes, January 5, 1849.
44 Leeds Stock Exchange, Minutes, February 2, 1852.
45 Liverpool Stock Exchange, Minutes; B. G. Orchard, *Liverpool Legion of Honour,* 1893.
46 I am indebted to Mr. F. J. Hennessy of Neilson, Hornby, Crichton & Company for supplying me with this information.
47 This information was kindly supplied by Mr N. C. Williams of Case, Leach and Company.
48 *Thomas Tinley & Sons. 1836-1936:* Commemorative Booklet.
49 I am indebted to Mr Jack Ireland of W. H. Ireland and Company for this information.
50 *Margetts and Addenbrooke. 1843-1946.*
51 I am indebted to Mr G. E. M. Stock of B. S. Stock Son and Company for this information.

6 Industrial Shares in the Provinces to 1914

The number of industrial, commercial and financial companies quoted on the London Stock Exchange in 1853 was just over two hundred with a nominal capital of £125 million.[1] By the outbreak of the first world war the number had increased to many thousands with a huge nominal capital of £1,500 million. Unfortunately it is not possible to quantify the development of the home industrial share market of the provincial stock exchanges in the same way but some indication of the changes for the period can be given. At the height of the 1845 railway boom most of the larger exchanges carried quotations in a miscellaneous range of purely local companies numbering well over a hundred, but relative to London companies their capital would have been much smaller. Following the passing of the joint stock acts of 1844, 1855, 1856 and the 1862 codifying act incorporated companies increased greatly in number, a development reflected in the share lists of the provincial markets. Acceptance by investors of shares in these companies depended upon, among other things, a market and a stock exchange quotation. The value of a limited liability share was largely based on its marketability, while a local quotation provided shareholders with the security and comfort they desired. The growth of company promotions in the eighteen seventies and eighties brought increased pressures for market facilities and in the case of 'home' industrials this was largely met by the provinces. *Phillips' Investors Manual* of 1885, one of the many of its kind, was of the opinion "that the provincial exchanges were of almost greater importance in relation to home securities than London."[2] This claim could not be equally asserted after the turn of the century, but as each major industry was converted onto a joint stock footing the local stock exchanges developed their own particular speciality so that by 1914, while they did not possess the vast range of the London markets, the main provincial centres dealt in a special range of shares with quotations dependant mainly on local information as to industrial conditions, "they do not vary, as gilt-edged securities and debentures do, with monetary and political conditions, nor do they take their tone from London".[3]

Excluding railways and canals, which obtained the privileges of incorporation by royal charter or act of parliament, joint stock companies in industrial and commercial activities were relatively insignificant prior to the eighteen fifties and were confined to gas, water, housing, public baths, and banking, where capital needs were beyond the resources of the partnership form of organization. This restricted use of the joint stock form was due to economic and legal factors. For most forms of enterprise a small sum of fixed capital sufficed and it was frequently well within the resources of an individual, his associates, or obtainable by mortgage. Also there was the "geographic accident" that most capital needs occurred at a distance from the largest but not the only financial centre in the country.[4] The legal impediments arose from the state of company law. Following the passing of the Bubble Act in 1720 it was illegal to act as a corporation and to issue transferable stock without obtaining an act of parliament or a royal charter. Both these procedures for securing the privileges of incorporation were exceedingly cumbrous and expensive, and were only granted reluctantly where parliament saw an overwhelming need which could not be met by private means. Many companies however proceeded without incorporation and by 1825 they had become so numerous, with an estimated capital of between £160-£200 million, that the Bubble Act was repealed since it threw grave doubt as to their legality and unincorporated companies were left to the common law.[5] Most of the companies listed in the provinces in the eighteen thirties and early eighteen forties were of this kind.

Some of the benefits of incorporation were extended to companies by the Trading Companies Act of 1834, and the Chartered Companies Act of 1837.[6] Under the former the Board of Trade could grant companies the right to sue and be sued in the name of their officers but it was conditional on the list of shareholders being available for inspection and on the liability of shareholders continuing for three years after the disposal of their shares. Following the 1836 boom promotions, of which Liverpool and Manchester had a fair share (see Chapter 1), the 1837 act granted by Letters Patent certain corporate rights to unincorporated companies, among them the right to sue and the regulation of the liability of individual members "to such extent only per share as shall be declared and limited", but liability ceased on transfer.[7] Very few companies obtained such privileges and they were usually restricted to mines, railways, insurance, and literary societies. The only home manufacturing company to obtain them was the British Plate Glass Company in 1841.[8]

Most of the companies formed in the early eighteen forties were of a highly speculative and decidedly hazardous nature. The only ones which lasted were those involved in navigation, gas, and insurance, the rest shared the fate described by William Parkes, a witness before a Select Committee in 1843, who said that there had been "an entire loss upon every joint stock company formed for the purpose of what we call trading" in Birmingham for the "manufacture of different metals, putting £30,000, £40,000 or £50,000 of deposit together in the nature of joint stock capital, everyone of them failed. I do not know that there is one of ten years' standing in existence now".[9]

As a result of the recommendations of the Select Committee set up in 1841, and which reported in 1844, to look at company law "with a view to the prevention of fraud" the Companies Act and the Winding-up Act (7 & 8 Vict c 110, 111) were passed in 1844. A joint stock company was defined as a commercial partnership with more than twenty five members and a capital divided into freely transferable shares, but with unlimited liability.[10] The office of Registrar of Companies was created to provide for the registration of all new companies. Incorporation under the Act involved a double procedure; a provisional stage which legalized the company for promotion purposes and the second ('complete') incorporated the company for carrying on business. This was conditional on the signing of the deed of settlement by at least a quarter of the subscribers both by number and capital. The Act also prohibited dealings in shares before registration was completed, but the provisions were totally ineffective.

In September 1844 there were 947 English companies in existence (excluding banking companies), of which there were 108 railways, 224 gas and water, 172 insurance, and the remainder spread over a diverse range of activities. In the ensuing years, from 1844 to 1856, just over 950 unlimited companies were formed in England and Wales, with two activities occupying a dominant position, insurance with 219 companies, and gas and water with 211. The other large sections were markets and public halls with eighty-five, and coastal shipping with forty-one.[11] All these were completed companies; over the same period nearly 4,000 companies entered the provisional stage, and half of them got no further which reflected a lack of seriousness on the part of promoters and a certain coolness on the part of investors.[12] Many promotions were killed off by scrip jobbing and premium hunting activities, while some companies were specially set up for this purpose.

The main omission from the 1844 registration Act was the granting of limited liability with incorporation. The subject came in for a good deal of debate in the eighteen forties and fifties; opponents pleaded the dangers of speculation, over-trading, and fraud; the

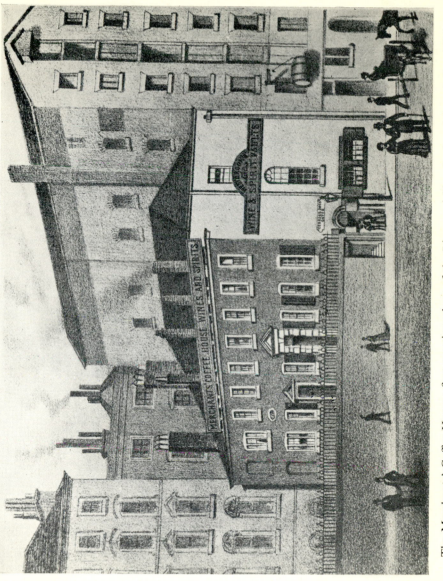

The Merchants' Coffee House; first meeting place of the Liverpool Sharebrokers' Association 1836.

Bristol Stock Exchange.

proponents countered with illustrations of success abroad and the fact that is was readily accepted in Britain for railways. Moreover, supporters pointed to the many anomalies created by the existing law. The wider view of the requirements of business emerged victorious and in 1855 an Act was passed (18 & 19 Vict. c.33) granting limited liability by registering under the provisions of the 1844 Act, provided the company had 25 shareholders, that 75% of the capital was subscribed and at least 15% paid up.[13] There were 283 provisional registrations under the Act but only forty-six completed ones.[14] The deficiencies of the registration procedure which were outlined by the Committee on Insurance Associations, led to the repeal of the 1855 Act and the introduction of a much more sweeping and permissive piece of legislation, the Joint Stock Companies Act of 1856 (19 & 20 Vict. c.4) by which any seven or more persons could obtain limited liability by placing with the Registrar of Companies a memorandum of Association stating the name and objects of the company and the fact that it was limited; gone were the two stage registration procedures, the deed of settlement, the capital requirements, registration of prospectuses and the sanctioning of the Registrar. All that remained was a "measure of publicity".[15] The 1862 Act merely codified existing company law and had more legal than economic significance.

Between July 1856 and December 1865, 4,859 companies limited by shares were registered in London. A large number were abortive, while many were exceedingly small companies; the Act had "enabled small capitalists to do what large capitalists could do before". Together these two types represented 36% of the total registrations for the decade.[16] The "abortive" companies reflected the rapid increase in the promotion of fraudulent companies after the passing of the 1856 Act, companies which were got up for premium hunting and little else, while some were formed and wound up with legal charges as a first claim on the assets.[17] High on the list of failure rates were the financial and banking concerns, while insurance and ocean shipping also had a 50% failure rate. The most successful companies were those in the coal, iron, and general engineering groups with only a fifth of the formations proving ineffective.[18] No doubt this was attributable to their local origin and acceptance.

Effective limited liability was however delayed until after the Overend, Gurney crisis of 1866. Up until then company nominal capital had remained greatly in excess of paid up capital. This was associated with the practice of converting partnerships at high and inaccurate valuations and also with the need to use uncalled capital as security for fixed interest borrowing. The danger was that shareholders tended to ignore the unpaid liability when making share

I

applications, as many found to their cost with the 1866 failure; Overend, Gurney shareholders had received the traditional, but in the event useless, promoters' assurance that only a small percentage would be called up. Share denominations for the period 1863–65 remained high with only 7% of companies issuing £1 shares, while two-thirds of all companies formed offered shares of £10 or above.[19]

The outburst of joint stocking had an impact upon the provincial stock exchanges. Rising from fifty-six new companies "brought forward" in 1861 to over 200 a year for the period 1863–66, those which managed to "raise their capital" were anxious to obtain a quotation on the recognized markets.[20] The Committee of the Manchester Stock Exchange in 1862 accepted lists from members of local and other miscellaneous companies whose shares they were particularly anxious to introduce. Provincial markets were keen to secure a market for shares which were locally held; "business would naturally gravitate to the market where a price was made and transactions recorded".[21] For example, Manchester members were anxious to quote the shares of the Patent Nut and Bolt Co. of Birmingham since most of the shareholders lived in Manchester.[22] Provincial stock exchange committees however were quite aware of the speculative nature of some of the new issues. The period saw the conversion or sale of old private partnerships to public limited companies formed to take them over. In 1864 the Manchester Committee expressed concern about new schemes of conversions "into Joint Stock Limited Liability Companies without any information being given in the Prospectus or otherwise of the nature of the transaction or amount of purchase money before the shares are subscribed or applied for". They decided therefore to withhold a special settlement unless the terms of the transfer were divulged. Approaches on the subject were made to London and Liverpool and the latter agreed to adopt similar measures to check "the great evils which may be expected to flow from the further extension of a practice now becoming so prevalent."[23] A large portion of the companies projected during this period did not succeed in "raising their capital", let alone requesting a quotation. Of the 287 new companies listed in *The Economists' Commercial History and Review* of 1865 only thirty-six had a market price at the end of the year. The long term impact of this surge of new issues on the share lists of the provincial stock exchanges was therefore small, except for certain key sections in the larger markets.

The formation of insurance companies certainly figured prominently in the annual new issues after the passing of the 1844 Act but of this crop of marine insurance companies only "one had so long a life as three years".[24] In the early eighteen fifties "something little short of an Insurance Mania had prevailed" and the formation of new offices persisted into the sixties.[25] During the period 1863–66 thirty-three insurance companies with an offered capital of £15 million were brought out.[26] There was already in existence a small group of joint stock companies in London and Liverpool which had survived from the eighteen twenties and thirties. As early as 1836 the Liverpool list included four local insurance companies, but only the Manchester Assurance Co. (formed in 1824) survived by the 1850s. The two large Liverpool fire and life companies, the Liverpool and London and Globe Insurance Co., established by act of parliament in 1836, and the Royal Insurance Co., formed in 1845, grew rapidly and by the mid-1860s the former was the most progressive and the largest provincial company.[27] Among the companies which appeared in Liverpool, with head offices there, at this period were the Queen Insurance Co. (Registered 1858, paid up capital in 1890 of £180,000), the London and Lancashire Fire Insurance Co. (1862, £185,200), the British and Foreign Marine Insurance Co. Ltd. (1863, £200,000), the Maritime Insurance Co. Ltd. (1864, £100,000) the Union Marine Insurance Co. Ltd. (1863, £142,240), the Standard Marine Insurance Co. Ltd. (1871, £100,000), the Sea Insurance Co. Ltd. (1875, £100,000), the International Marine Insurance Co. Ltd. (1879, £100,000), the Reliance Marine Insurance Co. Ltd. (1881, £100,000).[28] All of them quickly developed American connections.

The active markets in insurance shares were located in the provinces. *The London Financier* quoted by *The Economist* in 1871 commented, "the London Market is undoubtedly but an indifferent one for dealings in insurance property" with only the marine business being represented in the Official List. But for fire and life business reference had to be made to the

> "quotations of companies in *provincial markets,* these being amongst the few classes of investment that are systematically neglected by the London Stock Exchange. We have to do this, not because the fluctuations have occurred in companies little known in the Metropolis, but because, the required facilities not being offered here, the business has been driven elsewhere. For instance, there are few insurers who have not heard of the "Royal", the "Standard Life", the "Northern Assurance", the "Lancaster", and the "Liverpool and London and Globe"; and yet while we often do not find a transaction officially recorded in London, from one year's end to another, the dealings in the provinces are generally of daily occurrence. We point this more strongly because London brokers and dealers lose a share in what is really a very profitable business, just in the same way as

they have lost sight of carriage and wagon companies, of iron and steel companies, and the like."[29]

Liverpool's specialization in insurance shares continued through the century. In 1878 some twenty insurance companies were listed there which took "their rise there and their business is done there as a rule."[30] Later, in 1884, *The Economist* in a survey of provincial markets noted that London continued to be "a very lifeless market for insurance companies, while Liverpool, on the contrary, deals a good deal both in marine, fire and life companies".[31] Manchester at this time also listed some twenty insurance companies, mostly local, but they were smaller with less share turnover than their Liverpool counterparts. By the end of the century Manchester's insurance quotations occupied a less prominent part in their share list.

Shipping was among the first important industries in the 1860s to adopt joint stock company organization. There was already some degree of incorporation present in the form of the large charter companies, for example, the Peninsular and Oriental Steam Navigation Co. (incorporated 1840), the Royal Mail Steam Packet Co. (1839), and the Liverpool firm, the Pacific Steam Navigation Co. Ltd. (1840) which had a paid up capital in 1884 of £1.4 million. The advent of iron ships and steam propulsion in the 1850s, coupled with the need to operate whole fleets, increased the capital requirements of the industry which was met by resorting to joint stock organization and the capital market. The Charter companies were thus joined by a crop of new limited companies. By 1885 there were nineteen of them with a total capital of £15 million and representing a fifth of all steam tonnage.[32] Among them were several large Liverpool based companies; the West India and Pacific Steam Ship Co. Ltd. (formed 1863, with paid up capital in 1884 of £320,000), the British Shipowners' Co. Ltd. (1864, £532,400), the National Steam-Ship Co. Ltd. (1867, £992,690), and the Misissippi and Dominion Steam-Ship Co. Ltd. (1872, £428,510).[33] The Cunard Steam-Ship Co. Ltd. belongs to a slightly later period being formed in 1878 to take over two other companies with a capital of £1.6 million; a public issue of shares was made in 1880 but three fifths of the capital remained in the hands of three families.[34] These and several other local shipping companies, including the Liverpool Steam Tug Co., a survivor of the 1836 boom, were quoted at Liverpool where they were in the words of *The Economist,* "freely dealt in".[35] In 1890 only four of the Liverpool companies were quoted in London, but as Thomas Skinner notes in his *Stock Exchange Year Book,* "the principal dealings are in Liverpool".[36]

Provincial joint stock banks also figured in the early adoption of the corporate form of business organization. The early burst of joint stock banking in Lancashire in the 1830s (see Chapter One) did not continue into the immediately following decades, indeed between 1846 and 1860 only one new joint stock bank was formed.[37] This arose from the elaborate law for the regulation of joint stock banks sponsored by Sir Robert Peel in 1844 (7 & 8 Vict. c. 113) by which banks could only be registered if their capital exceeded £100,000 in shares of £100 or over.[38] Banks were excluded from the provisions of the Companies Acts of 1855 and 1856 and it was not until after the 1857 crisis with "some shocking cases of bank failures with unlimited liability", among them the Borough Bank of Liverpool, that new banks could be formed with limited liability and existing banks registered as limited.[39] The Codifying Act of 1862 covered banks as well as other associations of seven men. The only ones which took immediate advantage of these provisions were small or overseas banks. The tradition of unlimited liability remained practically unassailable until the City of Glasgow Bank crash in 1878 which brought the era of unlimited banks to a sudden end; every £100 shareholder in the Bank had to pay out £2,700.[40] By 1883 all but nine of the provincial joint stock banks were registered as limited. One of the advantages claimed for unlimited liability, the provision of security for customers deposits, was after legislation in 1879 provided by permitting banks to set aside a portion of their subscribed capital as a "Reserve" to be called only in the event of liquidation.

The banking system of England and Wales in the 1880s contained about 120 joint stock banks, the bulk of them provincial concerns. None rivalled the London joint stock banks in terms of size, even the largest, the Manchester and Liverpool District Bank with £11 million deposits was less than half the size of the National Provincial with £30 million deposits, the London and County with £26 million, and the London and Westminster with £24 million.[41] The leading provincial banks of the 1880s had deposits in the neighbourhood of £5–6 million and included several ambitious and extremely active banks who by amalgamations extended their coverage to London, for example, the Birmingham and Midland Bank, and Lloyds Bank. The shares of the provincial banks were not listed in London but quotations and dealings in nearly fifty were found in provincial markets. The following table summarizes the position for 1883.

The eighteen-nineties saw rapid movement towards the "big five" which emerged finally in 1918. The leading provincial banks however, especially those in Lancashire and Yorkshire, displayed a considerable degree of local pride and greatly valued their independence

Stock Exchange	No. of Banks	Paid up Capital £m.	Total Deposits £m.
Liverpool	7	2.6	16.1
Manchester	9	3.8	30.5
Birmingham	11	2.4	19.7
Leeds	13	3.8	19.5
Sheffield	5	1.0	6.1
Bristol	3	0.5	5.0
Total	48	14.1	96.9

Source: *Burdett's Official Intelligence* 1884, pp. 1182-95.

and their ties with the two main local industries, cotton and wool. They also strongly disapproved of such London practices as paying interest on current deposits and refusing to give "overdrafts on personal security". The main Lancashire and Yorkshire banks retained their independence up until the First War and included such strong banks as Parrs of Warrington, the Manchester and Liverpool District Bank (Manchester opposition ended an attempted merger with Lloyds in 1904), the Manchester and County Bank, the Lancashire and Yorkshire Bank, and the Bank of Liverpool (which joined with Martins in 1908).[42] These were all quoted and actively dealt in at Manchester and Liverpool alongside quotations of the big national banks which were listed on all provincial exchanges but which "took their rise" from London.

The iron industry was another key industrial sector which took early advantage of the joint stock form with limited liability. Up to the 1850s the ownership of the industry was dominated by partnerships but within a short space of time it was soon replaced by the company form. Established concerns were converted to a joint stock basis and some newer ones started up. The new steel making processes required additional capital while more working capital was also needed for the importing of foreign ores. For this purpose the joint stock form could tap outside sources of capital which was directed towards the industry by numerous financial agents of differing reputations. Businesses were also converted to avoid bankruptcy, while others did so in order to permit the partners to retire with their fortunes and maintaining only a limited responsibility in the firm.[43] The conversions of 1856–1863 were mostly companies with modest capitals of under £100,000, while those of 1864 and after were considerably larger. Charles Cammell & Co. Ltd. and John Brown & Co. Ltd., both formed in 1864, had nominal capitals of £1 million, the Staveley Coal and Iron Co. Ltd. of 1863 had £1.3 million, Bolckow, Vaughan & Co. Ltd. of 1864 had £2.5 million, while Ebbw Vale Steel, Iron & Coal Co. Ltd., also formed in 1864, had a nominal capital of £4.0 million.

Many of the larger iron and steel companies were promoted by the Manchester firm of accountants and financial agents, Chadwick, Adamson, McKenna & Co., which was headed by David Chadwick, sometime Town Clerk of Salford, and a prominent figure in the financing of the industry.[44] His most famous promotion, Bolckow, Vaughan & Co. Ltd. was formed in 1864 to acquire the iron and coal works of Messrs Bolckow & Vaughan. It had a nominal capital of £2.5 million of which £813,737 had been called up by 1867. A considerable amount of this sum was Manchester capital, with cotton merchants and spinners figuring amongst the directorate and large shareholders; of the ninety shareholders holding more than fifty shares or more, fifty-six came from Manchester.[45] In the case of the Ebbw Vale Company, another Chadwick promotion, a group of Manchester shareholders held over a tenth of the shares.[46] The attractions of investing in iron and coal shares must have been considerable for Lancashire capitalists and their optimism made Chadwick's task relatively easy. His formidable list of 5,000 clients probably consisted mostly of eminent local connections and the shares were offered to them "by private circular or prospectus . . . and they subscribe". While Chadwick's firm had "no connection with the Stock Exchange, no jobbing and very seldom any advertising", both his clients and the vendors, who usually took a part of the consideration in shares, were keenly interested in the existence of an active market in iron and coal shares.[47] Such dealings took place in Manchester from the early 1860s and the large local shareholding established Manchester as the leading centre in iron and steel shares, in companies which were mostly situated far away. *The Economist* in its first survey of the "Stock Markets of the United Kingdom" in 1884 said, "London attempts to quote sundry Yorkshire, Durham, and other iron and coal companies; but who would think of dealing here? Manchester, on the other hand, is a very good market in these securities, and the seventy or more members of the Manchester Exchange and the outside brokers carry on an important business".[48]

The other centre of iron company shares, Sheffield, "grew suddenly in notoriety in 1872–3 when dozens of Yorkshire iron masters seeing their opportunity, converted into public companies", for example, William Cooke & Co. Ltd., William Corbitt & Co. Ltd., and later in 1875 William Jessop & Co. Ltd.[49] These conversions were made at a time of rapidly rising share prices (see graph) permitting "sales of private concerns at inflated prices".[50] The twenty-five companies formed in Sheffield in 1872–73, with a total called up capital of £1.4 million were in addition to the twenty-five much larger concerns formed during 1863–71, whose total called up capital amounted to £5.3 million and which included such companies as

Charles Cammell & Co. Ltd., and John Brown & Co. Ltd.[51] By the mid 1880s Sheffield, along with Oldham, was "one of the two most important centres of joint stock in the country, with 44 companies, with a paid up capital of £12 million"[52] As early as the mid 1870s the Sheffield list had quoted all the leading coal and iron companies and in addition over thirty local companies described in the list as "Manufacturing", but which were mainly concerned with steel and engineering products. By the middle of the eighties, however, activity on the Sheffield market had declined but it is interesting to note that while *Burdett's* for 1890 lists many leading Sheffield companies the prices given were those marked at Sheffield, and not London quotations. Iron and Steel shares continued as the main speciality of the Sheffield market down to the war, when national interest centred on many local companies involved in the armaments industry particularly so on John Brown & Co. Ltd. and Vickers, Sons & Co. Ltd.

In the 1890s Newcastle also had an active market in a "number of important local stocks", among them many of the large north eastern iron, steel and shipbuilding companies. The following companies were actively dealt in; Sir W. G. Armstrong Mitchell & Co. Ltd. (Registered 1882), Consett Iron Co. Ltd. (Registered 1864), Dorman, Long & Co. Ltd. (Registered, 1889), and Palmer's Shipbuilding & Son Co. Ltd., promoted by David Chadwick in 1865.[53]

Among the earliest companies to adopt limited liability were railway carriage and wagon works.[54] They were neither very large or numerous but they displayed some interesting financial features. Arising from their close association with railways they employed somewhat complex financial practices compared to many other contemporary companies. They were among the first to use preference shares to raise additional funds, usually issued to shareholders, while they also used debentures to increase their capital gearing. They usually used low share denominations of £20, the majority of companies having £10 called up. *Burdett's* for 1884 lists 24 wagon companies with a total paid up capital of some £4.5 million. The main markets for these companies were at Birmingham, Sheffield, and Bristol.[55] Birmingham was the market for the larger companies, among them the Birmingham Railway Carriage Works Co. Ltd., with a capital of £450,00, and the Metropolitan Railway Carriage and Wagon Co. Ltd., paid up capital of nearly £250,000. Sheffield quoted nine companies, while Bristol dealt in a few local wagon companies of which the Gloucester Wagon Co. Ltd., capital over £500,000, was by far the most important.

One area of joint stock company formation in which the stock exchanges had a direct interest was that of telegraph and telephone

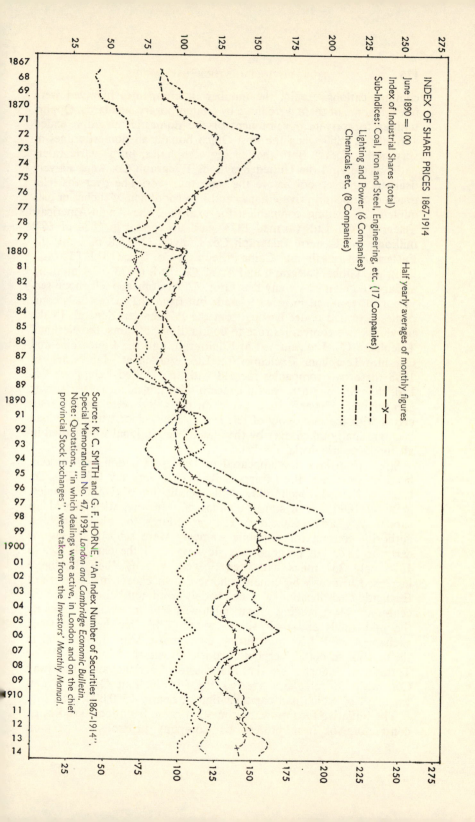

INDEX OF SHARE PRICES 1867-1914

June 1890 = 100

Sub-Indices: Coal, Iron and Steel, Engineering, etc. (17 Companies)
Lighting and Power (6 Companies)
Chemicals, etc. (8 Companies)

Index of Industrial Shares (total)

Half yearly averages of monthly figures

Source: K. C. SMITH and G. F. HORNE, "An Index Number of Securities 1867-1914",
Special Memorandum No. 47, 1934, London and Cambridge Economic Bulletin.
Note: Quotations, "in which dealings were active, in London and on the chief
provincial Stock Exchanges", were taken from the Investors' Monthly Manual.

communications. Again, the number of companies involved were few but some of them were large by contemporary standards. Opportunities for private development of the domestic telegraph ended abruptly in 1869 when the Post Office bought all domestic lines at very high prices.[56] Both the leading companies, the Electric International Co. and the United Kingdom Telegraph Co. were actively dealt in at Liverpool before the state takeover. The overseas telegraph remained in private hands and Liverpool and Manchester lists quoted the leading companies, for example, the Anglo-American Telegraph Co. Ltd. (formed 1873, paid up capital in 1884 of £6.8 million), the Eastern Telegraph Co. Ltd. (1872, £5.8 million), the Eastern Australasia and China Telegraph Co. Ltd. (1873, £3.5 million), the Globe Telegraph and Trust Co. Ltd. (1873, £2.4 million), all large companies by any standards.[57] The domestic telephone service also remained in private hands but from the early 1880s companies operated under licence from the Postmaster General. In the provinces two companies rose to dominating positions, the National Telephone Co. Ltd., quoted at Edinburgh, and the Lancashire and Cheshire Telephone Exchange Co. Ltd., quoted at Manchester. In 1888 these two companies merged with the United Telephone Co. Ltd. thus forming a powerful concern with considerable bargaining and financial power.[58] Its activities in the 1890s were mainly associated with the monopoly of telephone offices since trunk lines had been gradually taken over by the State. The National was quoted in all the large provincial markets.

Street tramways first appeared in 1859 in London and Birkenhead. A year later the Liverpool Road and Railway Omnibus Co. Ltd. was formed, which following the acquisition of rival companies, grew by 1890 to run some 60 miles of tramway, with a paid up capital of nearly £500,000.[59] The procedures for obtaining local authority consent for a public tramway were set out by law as early as 1870 but progress was slow up until the early 1880s. In 1878 only 237 miles had been opened, but by 1886 the figure increased to nearly 800, mainly horse-drawn except in the north of England; electrification was not widely used until the turn of the century.[60] Most leading provincial towns had tramway systems by the mid 1880s and their shares were quoted on the local stock exchanges, with Liverpool listing many more than those found in the neighbourhood. Liverpool of course quoted the Liverpool United Tramways, Manchester, the Manchester Carriage and Tramway Co., while Birmingham sported the Birmingham Central Tramways, all of which had capitalization of nearly £500,000 each.[61]

The initiative for tramway promotion came from local syndicates, contractors, or from professional company promoters. The most colourful of these was undoubtedly H. O. O'Hagan whose provincial promotions included companies in Birmingham, Manchester, Rotherham, Rochdale and Oldham. He went to considerable lengths to persuade local authorities of the desirability of local steam tramways and in one instance in 1880 gave a champagne luncheon to the corporation of a Lancashire town (Bury) so as to obtain their consent.[62] A less flamboyant promoter was a leading member of the Bristol Stock Exchange. Sir George White, Bristol's "tramway King", became secretary to the Bristol Tramways Co. at the tender age of twenty, and followed this with secretaryships to tramway companies in Gloucester and Bath. He later extended his promotions to other cities and pioneered in the mid-nineties, largely through the agency of the Imperial Tramways Co., the introduction of electric trams.[63]

The appearance of brewery shares in the lists of the provincial exchanges was concentrated into a relatively short period from 1888 to 1890. The successful 'limitation' of the famous Guiness concern in 1886, with a public issue of £6 million, attracted other prominent brewers to the market, and the preliminary canter became a flood in the last years of the decade.[64] By November 1890 the number had reached 200, while a further surge of 'limitation' in the mid-nineties increased the number to some three hundred by 1901. The public had quickly developed a ready appetite for brewery securities and there was little trouble in raising capital. Rising share prices (see graph), a yield of $6\frac{1}{2}\%$ on shares and from $4\frac{1}{2}$ to 6% on preference debentures in 1890 were increasingly attractive to the growing ranks of discerning investors. One estimate put the amount of capital raised by 1901 at £175 million.[65] The main market for these shares centred on London where it had been well established by the financial interests behind the early promotions. Provincial markets were left with some 30 or so local breweries and in addition they all quoted the large companies with London quotations, such as Guinness, Bristol Brewery, Bentley's Yorkshire Breweries, Bents, Allsopp, and Threlfalls. The total paid up capital of the "provincial only" breweries in 1897 was £11.7 million, almost equally divided between the three main categories of securities.[66] The main provincial markets in brewery shares were found at Manchester, Birmingham, Bristol, and Leeds, where they were "dealt in rather freely".[67]

Although one of the largest companies in the coal industry, Powell Duffryn, dated from 1864 the majority of the leading companies were not formed until the 1890s. Prior to that period coal production was largely undertaken by a great number of small concerns, few of which warranted corporate form. However, growing demand for domestic and export coal resulted in a series of public conversions in 1889–91. Among the South Wales companies were Main Colliery Co. (registered 1889, capital in 1897 of £120,000), North's Navigation Colleries (1889, £495,000), D. Davies & Sons (1890, £550,000), Great Western Colliery Co. (1890, £300,000), Penrhiwceiber Navigation Colliery Co. (1890, £350,000) and Albion Steam Coal Co. (1891, £275,000). The largest, Cambrian Collieries, was formed in 1895 by D. A. Thomas with a capital of £600,000, equally divided amongst three categories of securities.[68] As *The Economist* stated in 1895 "in many cases the securities are only dealt in locally, comparatively few of them being quoted on the London market."[69] The main market in coal shares centred on Cardiff, which by 1914 listed twenty-four companies.

Several local utilities had for long been supplied by companies many of which had equally well established connections with the local stock exchanges. In 1884 provincial markets quoted a dozen canal and dock enterprises with a paid up capital of £3.4 million, mostly Midland canals quoted at Birmingham. During this period docks, of the two, provided the main area of expansion, both private and municipal. An example of the former was the construction of Barry docks by coal interests represented by D. Davies and William Cory to gain an alternative outlet for South Wales coal so evading the high dues of the Bute docks at Cardiff. The only major canal venture involved a combination of private and municipal effort. The Manchester Ship Canal Co., after several false starts, was incorporated in 1885. The initial work was financed, not without some difficulty, by an issue of £2 million of ordinary shares the bulk of which were taken up in Lancashire and neighbouring counties, and in which Manchester brokers acted as agents. A further £2.4 million was raised in London through an issue on an offer for sale basis of 5% preference shares, handled by Rothschilds and Barings, and a debenture issue followed in 1809 on the same lines. The eventual cost of the canal approached £15 million, a third of which was borrowed from Manchester Corporation.[70] The market for the ordinary shares was at Manchester, with the fixed interest capital quoted in London.

Company water and company gas were also well represented on the provincial lists of the period. Most of these companies had been incorporated by act of parliament, with several of them dating from the 1820s. While the larger cities and towns displayed considerable municipal initiative in the provision of such necessities most of the lesser centres were content to rely on company water and gas. In 1884 fourteen waterworks were quoted on provincial markets mainly at Newcastle and Sheffield, with a total capital of £4.5

million.[71] Gas companies, on the other hand, were much more numerous, with thirty-nine quoted in the provinces in 1884, with a capital of nearly £5 million; Birmingham had fourteen in its list, while Newcastle had ten. Towards the end of the century increasing municipalization reduced the number of provincial quotations and by 1914 there were fewer private companies continuing in this sphere. The boom in 1882 in electricity companies did not touch the provinces where supplies were mainly provided by municipal concerns or by large national concerns quoted in London.[72]

One of the most prolific periods of company promotion before 1914 occurred in the 1890s when Bank Rate was unchanged at 2% during 1894-96 and the return on fixed interest investment as measured by Consols averaged only around $2\frac{1}{2}$%. Investors eagerly sought higher returns from other assets, while industry turned to the capital market to finance new technical advances. Company promoters aware of the weaknesses and needs of both parties found they could raise funds easily and they quickly took advantage of the position. All these elements were present in the cycle boom which centred on the Birmingham Stock Exchange, reaching its peak in 1895-6, and which quickly raised that market from its "lifeless state" and rendered "most of the members exceptionally busy".

The pioneer firm in the industry, the Coventry Machinists Co., had switched from sewing machine manufacture to making 'boneshaker' cycles many years before the invention of the safety frame in 1885 and Dunlop's pneumatic tyre in 1888.[73] While these developments were adopted by a few firms in the early 1890s, it was not however until the sudden surge of demand associated largely with an extraordinary craze for cycling among women that the pace of development took on boom proportions in 1895-96. Its pace is indicated by the following figures of cycle company registrations.

	Number of Companies	Total Nominal Capital	Average Capital per Company
1893	47	1,960,000	41,702
1894	31	1,280,000	41,290
1895	51	3,180,000	62,352
1896 Jan-June	103	14,324,207[1]	91,413[2]
July-Sept.	91	4,198,500	46,137
Oct.-Dec.	118	6,012,507	50,953

Source: *Statist*, May 9, 1896, p. 640.
Notes: 1. Almost half of this figure was for the Dunlop Tyre Co.
2. Excluding the Dunlop Tyre Co.

The most remarkable feature of the first cycle company promotion boom in 1893 was that it centred on the Dublin Stock Exchange while the Birmingham and London markets confined dealings to reasonably established cycle concerns. During the boom nearly fifty companies were promoted and the Dublin market had a merry time of it in the middle of 1893:

"No sooner does a company come with its £1 shares offered at par . . . than benevolent speculators push up the quotation to a big premium, in some cases as much as 200 or 300% in a very few hours and this inflation in patent rights must in a great many directions result in loss and disappointment. . . . We are given to understand that promoters whose antecedents are not altogether pleasant in regard to bringing out undertakings in London and the provinces in this country, have devoted their attention to the unsophisticated Irish. Their attitude to the Irish is really a *bouleversement* of the old fashioned cry of "No Irish need apply".[74]

Birmingham and local people did not give this "crowd of new companies a second thought". Following a lull in 1894 the pace quickened in 1895 and the boom got really under way in the early months of 1896 following a sudden rise in demand for cycles. In all, in that year, three hundred and twelve companies were formed, involving a nominal capital of £24.5 million. The boom continued into the early months of 1897 when promoters and manufacturers continued to bring out companies at the rate of four a week. Thereafter the boom tapered off and share prices dropped drastically, and the total nominal capital for the year was only £6 million.[75]

A flourishing trade grew up astonishingly quickly in promoting businesses to be "put off to the public":

"A favourite method of founding a business is for a man engaged in some other occupation to get hold of a practical person, and find money for the start. Premises, often ramshackle in character, are taken, men are set to work, and a trade is got together. This latter is not difficult, indeed, in the last 12 months the difficulty has been not to do a business. The profits are made to appear large in amount. This too, is easy, for recompense to the principal persons employed in the business can take the shape of deferred pay to come off when the concern is sold. Then the capitalist goes to the company promoter ring, and they arrange the issue, or sometimes, a promoter buys outright".[76]

In the case of large companies the directors were drawn from the ranks of well known names, but for smaller companies local business men were usually recruited. Most of the early promotions, especially those of 1893, were formed to acquire patent rights of dubious legality at very large sums and most of them resulted in heavy losses for participants.[77] When new ventures failed promoters often bought them up and refloated them with larger capitals. The small capitals of such companies were already heavily watered up, but promoters, particularly the two most famous, were expert at apportioning a "loading factor" for the further inflation of the paper capital of the companies. Capitals were usually calculated on the basis of profits earned at the height of the boom, while 'goodwill' figured prominently in the balance sheets. In fact, the average return on capital in these highly speculative investments was only $5\frac{1}{2}\%$, and a few years later it was down to $3\frac{1}{2}\%$. The only average investments were reckoned to be firms in the accessories side of the industry, such as the saddle makers J. D. Brooks & Co., B.S.A., and Alldays & Onions "who possess more than one string to their bow", and all paid regular 10% dividends.[78]

The two leading promoters were without doubt Ernest Terah Hooley and Harry J. Lawson. Hooley, a Nottingham lace manufacturer, began his meteoric financial career in 1895 and in three years promoted twenty-six companies, not all in the cycle industry, involving a nominal capital of £18.6 million, of which £5 million was his profit.[79] He was purely a company 'promoter' in that he bought an undertaking from the vendors usually choosing one that was well established and paying good dividends. He then kept on the previous management at higher salaries, put ornamental directors on the board as "front sheeters", obtained the most favourable reports he could as to its position and prospects, window dressed it to the public and loaded it with as much profit as he thought the public would swallow. His most famous floatation was the Dunlop Tyre Co. in 1896 which he bought for £3 million and sold within a few weeks for £5 million.[80] He finished up bankrupt in 1898, going "under as he had sailed, well in the public eye". Lawson enjoyed an equal reputation for loading on capital and making promises to shareholders. His prospectuses were extremely flowery and he paid little attention to underwriting his issues, indeed many of his prospectuses stated that no part of the issue was underwritten. He was responsible for the flotation of Humber, Rudge & Whitworth, and the less fortunate Beeston companies, Beeston Tyre, Beeston Rim and the new Beeston Cycle Co., all with "absurd inflation of the capitalisation".[81]

Although a few London jobbers did their best to create an active market in cycle shares the business never really caught on there. The chief dealings took place in Birmingham, and Dublin with its furious speculation also did a big business since the £1 cycle shares became popular with small investors.[82] By mid 1896 speculators had gained the upper hand and a Birmingham broker commented that "it isn't a question at all of merit or position, but market." Naturally, in such unusually speculative conditions there was considerable divergence in prices between the dealing centres. The range of price movements is reflected in the experience of the £1 shares of the Beeston Tyre Co. which were unsaleable at 2s. in January, but which reached £8 in May, 1896. In January 1897 the premiums on cycle shares ranged from 25% to 400%, giving cycle companies an estimated market capitalization of £30 million.[83] This rapid rise in prices had been stimulated by the Dunlop offer, an achievement which greatly impressed speculators. Other deals and rumours of amalgamation and absorption also helped. By the end of 1897 cycle shares reached their lowest point, at a time when the rest of the market advanced (see graph below).

During the years 1896–97 the Committee of the Birmingham Stock Exchange granted special settlements to 159 cycle companies, but only fifty-two of these were admitted to an official quotation. Frequently there were long delays in fixing a special settlement since companies were not very forthcoming with the required information.[84] At the end of 1897 the Birmingham daily list carried quotations for seventy-five cycle and cycle component companies, seventeen tyre firms, and sixteen tube undertakings, many of which were soon in the process of liquidation; twenty-eight companies in 1898.[85] The price quotations given for many companies were more nominal than real, such quotations being furnished by those entrusted with the business of "making a market". In addition, some of the companies were more in the nature of private than public companies with very few market dealings taking place. By the middle of 1897 it was doubtful if "free dealings could be effected in a tenth of the issues quoted".[86] The collapse of the boom came with overproduction, reduced cycle prices, increasing foreign competition, and the low dividends paid on the irresponsible capitalisations of the boom years. The unloading of a "vast mass of paper capital", the share blocks of promoters and vendors, provided an additional sharply depressing influence.

As an appendix to his cycle flotations Lawson extended his financial expertise to the infant car industry, launching in 1896 the Daimler Motor Co. with a capital of £100,000 in £10 shares which were taken up by over 500 shareholders with only two investing over £1,000.[87] The patent for the Daimler car was acquired a year earlier by Lawson's British Motor Syndicate who sold it for £40,000 profit to the Daimler Motor Co. In all twenty-six motor companies appeared in 1896, but only ten had capitals in excess of six figures.

Manchester Stock Exchange.

The Council of Associated Stock Exchanges, Windermere, October 1913.

Back Row: A. J. Harrison (Newcastle), A. M. Sing (Liverpool), H. A. Gifford (Secretary, Glasgow), E. W. Crammond (Secretary, Liverpool), E. E. Lamb (Birmingham).

Middle Row: E. Hunter (Newcastle), W. A. Moore (Birmingham), G. W. Todd (Belfast), W. F. Coates (Belfast), J. H. Wilkinson (Halifax), T. K. Mellor (Huddersfield), A. Stables (Glasgow), W. Ridehalgh (Liverpool), K. H. M. Connal (Glasgow), W. N. Tribe (Bristol), A. Middleton (Bradford), J. Burbridge (Birmingham), A. Macindoe (Glasgow), E. H. Roylance (Manchester), M. M. Speakman (Manchester), E. H. Lyddon (Cardiff), F. M. Tennant (Leeds).

Seated: J. N. Cain (Secretary, Manchester), T. K. Holden (Liverpool), J. R. Ward (Manchester), J. Corbett Lowe (Liverpool), C. K. Aitken (Glasgow), Edward Rae (President, Liverpool), William Bell (Manchester), R. M. Watson (Edinburgh) R. Oates Wever (Sheffield), G. H. Hodgson (Sheffield), A. L. Davies (Cardiff), W. Webster (Aberdeen).

Among these were the Great Horseless Carriage Co., with £750,000 of capital and some 3,000 shareholders, and the British Motor Car Syndicate Ltd., the basis of Lawson's operations, with a capital of £1 million; all these shares later fell below the offer price in market dealings.[88] Other Lawson flotations included such famous concerns as Rover and Humber, which by writing down capital and improved management survived. The number of firms in the industry also increased as cycle firms turned to car manufacture to escape from the saturated cycle market, among them Alldays & Onions, Sunbeam, and Singer. By 1906 some £12 million had been invested in the industry, and this total was increased by £2.4 million from new issues in 1906–7, the funds coming mainly from small investors.[89] All the leading car companies were quoted on the Birmingham Stock Exchange where motor shares had their main dealings.

Birmingham was not the only market in the 1890s to experience a sudden demand for quotations from newly formed joint stock companies. All the larger markets were similarly afflicted, for example, the number of commercial and industrial companies quoted in the Manchester list increased from seventy in 1885 to nearly 220 in 1906. Most of these were small companies with capitals ranging from £50,000 to £200,000, reflecting the gradual reduction in the average capital of companies at the turn of the century.[90] Moreover, many were in effect no more than private companies since no shares, or very few, were issued to the public. Such companies made considerable use of provincial exchanges as against London for two important reasons. Firstly, a provincial quotation was cheaper, and secondly, London jobbers simply could not "keep them all to the front". The London quotations for similar companies tended to be rather wide since once the initial premium hunting was over "the floating supply to the market was too meagre in quantity to admit either of free buying or free selling". Jobbers were therefore reluctant to keep books in them. In the case of stocks infrequently dealt in the provincial markets had a "manifest advantage over Capel Court . . . hence the notable fact that the smaller industrials are betaking themselves from London to the provinces".[91]

Cheap money in the nineties and the widespread desire to limit "the discomforts of a too free competition" resulted in the formation of several large combines whose shares were actively dealt in on some of the leading exchanges. This merger movement was particularly significant for the provincial markets since many of the companies brought together were unquoted private concerns, and the stock exchanges were always eager to add local firms to their lists. A few of the combines remained unquoted afterwards since although they had large capitalizations they had few shareholders, published no

K

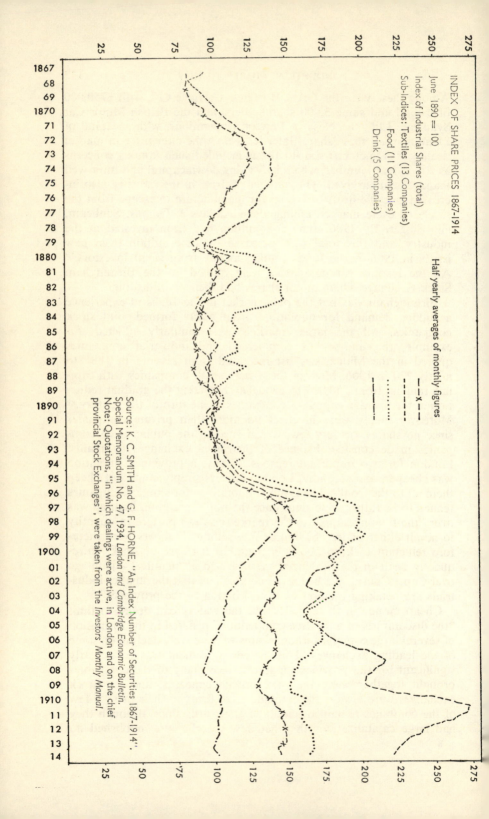

INDEX OF SHARE PRICES 1867-1914

June 1890 = 100
Index of Industrial Shares
Sub-indices: Textiles (13 Companies) (total)
Food (11 Companies)
Drink (5 Companies)

Half yearly averages of monthly figures

Source: K. C. SMITH and G. F. HORNE, "An Index Number of Securities 1867-1914",
Special Memorandum No. 47, 1934, London and Cambridge Economic Bulletin.
Note: Quotations, "in which dealings were active, in London and on the chief
provincial Stock Exchanges", were taken from the Investors' Monthly Manual.

information, and remained in effect private limited companies. A beginning was made in 1888 with the formation by a London syndicate of the Salt Union, the first great English amalgamation, followed in 1891 by United Alkali. The Salt Union consisted of sixty-four firms, mostly in Cheshire, and controlled 90% of domestic salt output. It had a capital of £4 million and 4,000 shareholders; the shares were eagerly sought after and went to a premium before allotment but subsequent results were extremely disappointing. United Alkali had an equally unhappy history. It included forty-eight firms, half of them in Lancashire, and out of the capital of £8.5 million the vendors commendably took £7.0 million in the aftermath of the Baring crisis. More successful from the shareholders viewpoint was the progress of Brunner Mond & Co. formed in 1881 and which expanded to absorb several rivals.[92] The above three companies constituted the salt and alkali section of the Liverpool market where they were actively dealt in.

A far more prolific programme of amalgamation occurred in the textile industry which brought considerable business to the Manchester Stock Exchange. Between 1897–1904 there were nineteen textile combinations involving by 1906 a total capitalization of £45.6 million.[93] Details of some of the larger ones are given below.

	Date of Formation	No. of Firms Involved	Capital £m.	Amount allotted to Vendors £m.
English Sewing Cotton Co.	1897	14	2.2	1.7
Fine Cotton Spinners and Doublers	1898	36	4.0	1.3
Bradford Dyers Assoc.	1898	22	3.0	1.0
Yorkshire Woolcombers Ltd.	1899	38	1.9	0.9
Calico Printers Assoc.	1899	46	8.2	2.5
British Cotton & Wooldyers Assoc.	1900	46	1.8	0.5
Bleachers Assoc	1900	53	6.7	2.1[1]

Source; H. W. Macrosty, *The Trust Movement in British Industry,* pp. 117-179.
Note: 1, Vendors also took up all ordinary capital £2.25m.

The flotation of these combines gave little cause for complaint. The valuations were undertaken by firms of accountants with the Manchester firm of Jones, Crewdson & Yorath being particularly prominent. Most of the actual promotions were done by Mr Scott Lings; less active was Mr Ernest Crewdson who contented himself with a commission of only $2\frac{1}{2}\%$, a mere fraction of that appropriated by E. T. Hooley. Because most of capitalization was done during a prosperous year, 1899, a little water crept into a few of the companies, but nothing like the huge amounts loaded on by Hooley. Only in the case of the Yorkshire Woolcombers Ltd., did it lead to final collapse when bad trading conditions later hit the industry. Also the vendors, as the table indicates, took large slices of capital and they generally took the ordinary shares leaving the safer preference and debenture capital to the public.[94]

Further south the threat of American competition in 1901 brought together thirteen tobacco firms, of which W. D. & H. O. Wills represented £7 million of the total purchase price of nearly £12 million of the Imperial Tobacco Co. Of the issued capital of £14.5 million two thirds was taken by the vendors which included all the ordinary shares.[95] The publicly issued securities were taken up for the most part by investors in Bristol and the south west all of which helped to raise Bristol from a "lifeless Exchange" to the most important market in tobacco shares.[96] By 1914 the capital of the Imperial Tobacco Co. reached £18 million and even the deferred shares stood at a premium of nearly 100 per cent.

By the turn of the century provincial company formation was undertaken by professional promoters, who had long since replaced the vendor in that role, and increasingly by ad hoc syndicates got up for one or two issues and which then split up. Small issues of about £50,000 were placed among wealthy local investors by a solicitor or a broker who was also prepared to make a market in the shares subsequently. For larger sums a prospectus issue was usually used. A marketing organization of varying quality extended all over the country with underwriters drawn from the ranks of banks, trusts, financial companies, insurance companies and financiers of all descriptions. The brokers who lent their names to the prospectus frequently did the underwriting on payment of an "overiding commission" and also carried through many of the technical details including requesting a special settlement and quotation on a provincial exchange.[97]

The problem of securing a full subscription in order to go ahead with allotment was eased by resorting to underwriting. Initially it was only usual to underwrite a portion of an issue, but the practice became common of underwriting the whole issue which involved an additional cost. Many provincial brokers strongly disapproved of the latter practice since some parties obtained preferential allotments marginally below the market price. Also, with the growth of underwriting the time allowed for applications became unduly short, a more important consideration in the provinces than in London.[98] Prior to legislation in 1900 the payment of underwriting commission and brokerage out of capital was illegal since it was regarded as equivalent to the issue of shares at a discount, but the law was easily evaded by such devices as issuing shares at a premium, issuing founders shares, etc.[99] The Companies Act, 1900, legalized underwriting so that thereafter companies were able to contract directly with the underwriters provided such contracts were disclosed in the prospectus.

Lavington in his classic study suggested that in provincial markets "local knowledge on the part of the investor, ensured that securities were sold at prices fairly near their investment values."[100] He had been particularly impressed by the conditions prevailing in Oldham where he claimed that local knowledge resulted in honest conditions of sale and realistic prices. Even for small local issues however the essential imbalance of the bargaining position of seller and buyer remained; the former remained in a superior bargaining position but less so perhaps than his London counterpart. There were of course plenty of opportunities for financial promotions and promoters were not slow to take advantage of them.[101]

The conventional costs of a public issue of shares expressed as a percentage of the proceeds were usually very large for small firms. An unknown company coming forward with an issue needed to buy the reputations of a broker and others supporting the issue. The costs of issue depended on the number of prospectuses sent out, the fees paid to banks, solicitors, accountants, brokers, and the underwriting commission. Even for a modest issue just before 1914 these hardly amounted to less than £2,000. Many brokers demanded fees of 1,000 gns, while advertising a prospectus might cost several thousands. The rates paid for underwriting was frequently around 10%, and occasionally rose to more than 50% on the portion of the issue underwritten. The cost of launching a relatively obscure issue certainly exceeded five figures so that on "small issues of £50,000 or £100,000 the expense is proportionately burdensome".[102] It can be reckoned that for the usual size of provincial issue which were seldom in excess of £250,000 the costs of an issue were probably of the order of 10%. If such an issue was made directly on the London market where it would be exceedingly obscure the figure would probably have been easily doubled. London, of course, was "much better adapted to supply capital to such bodies as foreign states, railways and other large undertakings than to meet the demands arising from small industrial ventures"; these found a cheaper and more receptive welcome in the provinces.[103]

Early provincial requirements as to special settlements and quotations involved little more than exhibiting the 'scrip' to the committee of an exchange. With the growth of company formation following the limited liability legislation the exchanges at Manchester and Liverpool laid down fairly detailed requirements as to special settlements so as to protect the interests of investors; the smaller exchanges continued for some time on an ad hoc basis. In 1863 Manchester drew up a list of "General Questions to be asked . . . of all companies seeking a special settlement", while Liverpool soon followed the lead. Details were required of the name of the company, whether it was registered under the limited liability acts, the number of shares and the amount of the nominal capital; amounts allotted to the public and promoters, amounts of deposits paid, whether promoter shares, or any part thereof, had been issued as paid up and the privileges they enjoyed; the amount of the promoter's consideration, and if there was any intention of issuing more shares within six months; a certified copy of the share applications and a copy of the allotment. Further they adopted the London requirement that they would not recognize transactions in any company shares unless half of the capital had been issued and at least 10% paid.[104]

Rarely were applications for a special settlement refused, but a company was not automatically quoted on the granting of such a settlement. To secure a quotation it was necessary for two-thirds of the capital to have been conditionally allotted to the public, submit a copy of the prospectus, the memorandum and articles of association, the certificate of registration, a list of shareholders and directors, copies of the latest report in the case of existing companies, while new companies were required to submit the Bank Pass Book, and the correspondence between the company and the broker. The articles of a company had to provide, inter alia, that company funds could not be used for the purchase of the company's shares, that directors' powers were not unlimited, that there were limitations on powers to increase capital, and state that there was no lien on fully paid shares. Most companies seeking a quotation were prepared to alter their articles so as to conform to these requirements which were a few steps ahead of company law in affording protection to investors.

Companies were however frequently admitted to a quotation without meeting the above requirements.[105] If it was quoted on London or another large provincial exchange this of itself was "sufficient evidence of bona fide character", while exchange committees were very sympathetic to members' requests for quotations when it was shown to be "to the benefit of the Association". For example, the Manchester Committee in the 1870s were willing to suspend their standing orders on quotations and were content to see merely the last available balance sheet and the articles of association in order to attract local companies onto the list.[106] As share lists became increasingly crammed towards the end of the century the Exchange became increasingly selective in granting quotations and while they would not adopt the London requirements in their entirety they were prepared to apply any provisions which were suitable to local needs. To discourage the quotation of exceedingly small companies Liverpool decided in 1890 not to quote companies with share capital of less than £50,000, while Manchester rejected quotations of small companies whose shares were "insufficiently in the public hands".[107]

Any assessment of the provincial contribution to the finance of home industry during the nineteenth century must be essentially qualitative rather than quantitative; to echo Lavington's anguish, "information with regard to the provincial issue of new securities is almost entirely lacking". Even in national terms the contribution of all the stock exchanges was relatively marginal, some £30 million out of the £150 million spent annually in the pre-1914 period on net home investment.[108] The provincial contribution was of course small; for companies formed with a prospectus during 1911–13 some £9.5 million was obtained from the public of which only £2– £3 million came from the provinces. However, over half the companies were floated in the provinces. To this may be added many companies formed without a prospectus with securities privately placed and markets subsequently being made which according to Lavington was around £12 million for the provinces.[109] A more impressive figure for the provinces does, however, appear if the boom years 1896–97 are considered since Manchester alone managed nearly £7 million, while figures for the cycle boom have already been quoted. However this was an exceptional phase and the figure of £4–£5 million per year is probably a fair reflection of the pace of financing through the provincial stock exchanges at the end of the century and up to 1914.

Obviously the provincial market facilities were of considerable value to the smaller provincial companies through the provision of a market for shares, while a quotation conferred greater borrowing power at lower cost. Quantitatively, it is not known how many companies and how much capital was raised through provincial exchanges during the period since the limited liability acts; qualitatively the position is a little easier to state in that there was "never any difficulty in raising capital locally or privately for the creation or extension of any business which offers a reasonable probability of large profits. A really good thing from Glasgow or Yorkshire, or Lancashire, or the Midlands seldom comes to London to be floated on the public. The insiders naturally keep it to themselves and their friends".[110]

NOTES

1 *Burdett's Official Intelligence*, 1884, p. CXXIV.
2 Quoted in J. B. Jeffreys, "Trends in Business Organisation in Great Britain since 1856", Ph.D. Thesis, London, 1938, p. 341.
3 F. Lavington, *The English Capital Market* (1921), p. 221.
4 Jeffreys, op. cit., p. 6.
5 H. A. Shannon, "The Coming of General Limited Liability",*Economic History*, Vol. 3, 1931, Reprinted in *Essays in Economic History*, ed. E. M. Carus-Wilson, Vol. 1. p. 360.
6 4 & 5 William IV, c. 94; 1 Vict. c. 73.
7 Shannon, "The Coming of General Limited Liability", op. cit., p. 367.
8 J. H. Clapham, Vol. 2, op. cit., p. 135.
9 Quoted by G. Todd, "Some Aspects of Joint Stock Companies, 1844–1900", *Economic History Review*, Vol 4, 1932, p. 61.
10 H. A. Shannon, "The Coming of General Limited Liability", op. cit., pp. 370-1.
11 H. A. Shannon, "The First Five Thousand Limited Companies and their Duration". *Economic History*, Vol. 2. 1932, p. 420, Table A.
12 Ibid., p. 397.
13 H. A. Shannon, "The Coming of General Limited Liability", op. cit., pp. 375-78.
14 H. A. Shannon, "The First Five Thousand . . .", op. cit., pp. 397-8.
15 H. A. Shannon, "The Coming of General Limited Liability", op. cit., pp. 378-9.
16 H. A. Shannon, "The First Five Thousand. . .", op. cit., pp. 401-2.
17 Todd, op. cit., p. 68.
18 H. A. Shannon, "The First Five Thousand. . .", op. cit., pp. 401-2.
19 Ibid., p. 408. By an amending statute in 1867 companies were allowed to reduce nominal capital.
20 Figures from *The Times*, January 1862; D. M. Evans, *Speculative Notes and Notes on Speculation*, (1864) Appendix, p. 325-27; *Economist, Commercial History and Review* of 1864 to 1867.
21 Liverpool Stock Exchange, Minutes, December 1, 1880.
22 Manchester Stock Exchange, Minutes, December 23, 1862, May 18, 1871.
23 Ibid., March 15, 1864.
24 Clapham, Vol. 2, op. cit., p. 321.
25 Quoted from C. Walford, *Insurance Guide and Handbook* (1857), by Jeffreys, op. cit., p. 46.
26 *Economist, Commercial History and Review* of 1866, p. 35.
27 Clapham, Vol. 2, op. cit., p. 331.
28 *Burdett's Official Intelligence*, 1890. In 1888 the seven Liverpool marine insurance companies underwrote liabilities amounting to £156 million on a premium income of £1 million. Liverpool at the time was "the most flourishing and steadily profitable centres of underwriting in the three kingdoms"; *Economist*, February 2, 1889, p. 144, 'Marine Insurance in Liverpool'.
29 *Economist, Commercial History and Review* of 1871, pp. 49-50.
30 *Royal Commission on the London Stock Exchange*, 1878, op. cit., evidence of Richard Withers, Q.7999. Thomas Skinner's *Stock Exchange Year Book* for 1879 noted of leading insurance shares that while quoted in the London list "the principal dealings in the shares take place in Liverpool".

31   *Economist*, April 19, 1884, p. 48. See also *Economist*, October 2, 1886, p. 1223; from this date onwards *The Economist* published a selection of provincial share prices.

32   Jeffreys, op. cit., p. 66. Shares in these companies tended to be concentrated in few hands.

33   *Burdett's Official Intelligence*, 1884. Some 5/6 of the capital of the British Shipowners Co. Ltd., came from Liverpool. Several other steamship companies obtained a special settlement and quotation on the Liverpool Stock Exchange during the years 1863-65. Among them were the National Steam Navigation Co. Ltd. with a capital of £200.000. 2/3 of which was subscribed from Liverpool; the British and South American Steam Navigation Co. Ltd., capital £1.0 million; the British and American Steam Navigation Co. Ltd., capital £250,000; and the Channel Steamship Co. Ltd., capital £240,000: Liverpool Stock Exchange, Minutes, 1863-65.

34   *Burdett's Official Intelligence, 1890* p. 1375; Clapham Vol. 2, op. cit., p. 139.

35   *Economist*, October 2, 1886, p. 1223.

36   Although they were not officially quoted on the Liverpool Stock Exchange dealings took place in the shares of single ship companies. A very large number of these were formed in Liverpool in the early 1880s. They first appeared there in 1878, and between 1879-1883 392 companies were formed. They were also found in fewer numbers in Cardiff, Bristol and London. Very few were formed after the 1890s following changes in the Merchant Shipping Acts and the much larger capital requirement as ships grew in size. They were the product of owners of small fleets splitting them up into small units for insurance reasons thus confining liability for loss to one ship. Others were formed by ephemeral promoters attempting to appeal to a wide range of investors. The shares issued were usually between £10—£50, and confined to a few shareholders. For further details see Clapham, Vol. 3, op. cit., pp. 205-6; H. A. Shannon, "The Limited Companies of 1866-1883", *Economic History Review*, Vol. IV, 1933, p. 306: *Economist*, 1886, pp. 1350, 1440; Jeffreys, op. cit., p. 67-8.

37   J. Sykes, *The Amalagamation Movement in English Banking 1825-1924* (1926) p. 35.

38   Clapham Vol. 2, op. cit., p. 351.

39   By the provisions of 21 & 22 Vict. c. 91.

40   Jeffreys, op. cit., pp. 100-2.

41   The National Provincial Bank obtained a London connection in 1864.

42   Clapham, Vol. 3, op. cit., p. 284.

43   Jeffreys, op. cit., p. 76-78.

44   D. L. Burn, *The Economic History of Steelmaking 1867-1939* (1940), pp. 254-5.

45   A. Birch: *The Economic History of the British Iron and Steel Industry 1784-1879* (1967), p. 207.

46   Burn, op. cit., p. 254, n.2.

47   *Report from the Select Committee on the Company Acts, 1882 and 1867*, B.P.P., 1877, VIII, evidence of David Chadwick, Q. 2041.

48   *Economist*, April 19, 1884, p. 480. The London Daily official list quoted 34 Iron, Coal and Copper companies in 1883 with a paid up capital of £13.4 million.

49   Ibid., p. 480.

50   Jeffreys, op. cit., p. 78.

H

51 *Economist*, March 9, 1878, p. 62. Average called up capital per company fell from £270,000 in 1863-65 to £58,000 for 1872-73.
52 *Accountant*, 1887, Quoted by Jeffreys, op. cit., p. 75.
53 *Burdett's Official Intelligence* ,1890; Newcastle Stock Exchange Weekly List, 1898.
54 The companies built and leased railway rolling stock, and are the ancestors of the modern hire-purchase companies.
55 *Economist*, April 19, 1884, p. 15.
56 Clapham Vol 3, op. cit., pp. 208-9.
57 *Burdett's Official Intelligence*, 1884.
58 Clapham Vol. 3, op. cit., pp. 390-91.
59 *Burdett's Official Intelligence*, 1890, p. 142-49.
60 Clapham, Vol. 2, op. cit., p. 204. Total paid up capital in tramways increased from £1.2 million in 1876 to £10.2 million in 1886; *Burdett's Official Intelligence*, 1887, pp. 100-4.
61 Many of the tramway companies had very small capitals with a few under £20,000.
62 H. O. O'Hagan, *Leaves from my Life* (1929), Vol. 1, p. 68.
63 A. B. Freeman, *Bristol Worthies;* also information kindly supplied by Sir George White, Evans & Co., Bristol.
64 J. Vaizey, *The Brewing Industry 1886-1951* (1960), pp. 8-9.
65 Clapham, Vol. 3, op. cit., p. 258.
66 *Burdett's Official Intelligence*, 1897. The Manchester list in 1895 carried 17 brewery quotations.
67 *Economist*, January 18, 1908, p. 111.
68 *Burdett's Official Intelligence*, 1897; Clapham, Vol. 3, op. cit., pp. 264-65.
69 *Economist*, March 25, 1895, p. 383. A few collieries were also quoted in Bristol.
70 Clapham, Vol. 3, op. cit., pp 365-69; *Burdett's Official Intelligence*, 1890, p. 693; Manchester Stock Exchange, Minutes, February 16, 1887.
71 Some of these enterprises were quite large, for example, Bristol Waterworks, capital £1.2 million; Newcastle and Gateshead Water Co. capital £703,398; *Burdett's Official Intelligence*, 1884.
72 Only provincial quotation in 1884 was the listing in Manchester of the Manchester and District Ellison Electric Light Co. Ltd., an 1882 promotion with a capital of £140,000.
73 A. E. Patrick, "Cycle Factories", *Journal of the Insurance Institute of Great Britain and Ireland*, Vol. 4, 1901, pp. 273-4. The Coventry Machinists Co. was bought by Hooley and Du Cros in 1896 for £250,000 and sold to the Swift Co. for £375,000, less £20,000 working capital; *Statist*, April 24, 1897, p. 642-3.
74 *Statist*, June 3, 1893, p. 604-5, "The Pnuematic Boom".
75 *Economist*, February 19, 1898. Several Birmingham brokers were involved in the marketing of the shares, among them W. J. Cuthbert, G. W. Beech, Edwards & Burbridge, Margetts & Addenbrooke, and especially H. C. Willis.
76 *Statist*, May 20, 1897, pp. 446-7, "The Inflation of Cycle Shares". E. T. Hooley in a letter to one Mr Hellewell of Manchester in Oct. 1897 promised to pay a 2½% commission on the purchase money if Hellewell secured for him the promotion of a company or the sale of a business to a company to be formed by Hooley. I am indebted to Mr. P. L. Cottrell, University of Liverpool, for this reference.
77 For example, £150,000 of the £170,000 capital of the Persil Flexible Wheel & Tyre Syndicate (Ltd.) was purely for patent rights. Other such

companies were Seddons Pneumatic Cycle & Tyre Co. Preston Davis
Tyre and Valve Co Ltd., and Cork Cycle Co.; *Statist,* June 3, 1893,
pp. 604-5.

78 *Economist,* December 10, 1898, p. 1761.
79 *Economist,* June 11, 1898, p. 869, put his turnover at £25 million, and
    his profit at £3 million—'sufficient unto the day'!
80 On the Bovril and Schweppes flotations he made a profit of 20% of
    the capitalization; *Economist,* June 11, 1898, p. 869.
81 *Economist,* October 2, 1897, pp. 1392-3.
82 *Economist,* May 22, 1897, p. 743, Cycle companies were also dealt in
    at Nottingham.
83 *Economist,* February 20, 1897, p. 274. Estimated nominal capital was
    put at £20 million.
84 Birmingham Stock Exchange, Minutes, 1896-7. The committee would
    not grant a special settlement in the vendors shares until the publication
    of the first balance sheet; Minutes, May 20, 1897.
85 *Statist,* October 14, 1890, p. 601.
86 *Economist,* May 22, 1897, p. 743.
87 S. B. Saul, "The Motor Industry in Britain to 1914", *Business History,*
    Vol. V, 1962-3, pp. 31.
88 *Statist,* November 21, 1896, pp. 767-7. The vendor of these companies
    was Lawson's British Motor Syndicate.
89 *Economist,* November 17, 1906, pp. 1864-5; Saul, op. cit., p. 23.
90 Clapham, Vol. 3, op. cit., p. 267.
91 *Statist,* July 9, 1887. pp. 38-9.
92 H. W. Macrosty, *The Trust Movement in British Industry* (1907), pp.
    181-94; Clapham, Vol. 3, op. cit., pp. 215-17.
93 Macrosty, op. cit., p. 124.
94 Clapham, Vol. 3, op. cit., pp. 225-29. The Yorkshire woollen combines
    were also listed and dealt in on the Bradford Stock Exchange.
95 Macrosty, op. cit., pp. 229-30.
96 *Financial News,* May 6, 1902.
97 Lavington, op. cit., p. 184. In the experience of one group the "average
    calls upon the members of the underwriting clubs run to about 14%",
    Western Mail, December 2, 1895.
98 Council of Associated Stock Exchanges, Minutes, October 23, 1914.
    Cases were cited in the discussions of whole allotments going to under-
    writers with the shares going to a quick premium on the market.
99 For further details see A. K. Cairncross. *Home and Foreign Investment
    1870–1913* (1953), pp. 99-100; D. Finnie, *Capital Underwriting* (1934),
    pp. 45-49.
100 Lavington, op. cit., p. 208.
101 Ibid., pp. 208-9. Lavington quotes the evidence of a Sheffield broker
    to this effect.
102 H. Lowenfeld, *All about Investment,* p. 175, quoted by Lavington,
    op. cit., p. 219.
103 Lavington, op. cit., p. 219.
104 Manchester Stock Exchange, Minutes, August 24, 1863. February 12,
    1864; Liverpool Stock Exchange, Minutes, March 20, 1863.
105 The smaller exchanges had virtually no requirements at all at this
    time. From the mid-nineties the larger exchanges were very conscious
    of this and attempted through the Council of Associated Stock Ex-
    changes to standardize requirements.
106 Manchester Stock Exchange, Minutes, September 17, 1873, May 8,

1878, The association was angling for quotations of many of the leading cotton spinning companies.

107 Liverpool Stock Exchange, Minutes, May 6, 1890.

108 F. W. Paish, "The London New Issue Market", *Economica,* 1951, p. 2. The remainder came from ploughed back profits and personal savings directly invested.

109 Lavington, op. cit., pp. 202-5; Cairncross, op. cit., p. 97.

110 F. W. Hirst, *The Stock Exchange* (1932), p. 175.

7 The Oldham Stock Exchange and the "Limiteds"

The Olham "Limiteds" were a remarkable phenomena in many ways. In the manufacturing sector they were the first to take full advantage of the provisions of the limited liability acts. Their system of finance, with share capital and loan money, was unique in the industrial capital market, engendering much criticism as a fair weather means of finance. The degree of local participation in capital provision was generally reckoned to be very great, a feature partly attributable to the thrifty habits of the local people. The advent of the joint stock mills also produced a local stock exchange which specialized in cotton mill shares, its fortunes being closely linked to the rise and decline of the "Limiteds". They deserve a corner to themselves.

Regionally, the companies were clustered in the Oldham, Manchester and Rochdale areas where the co-operative principle was already accepted and well tried. One of the first such ventures in cotton spinning was the famous Sun Mill Co., formed in 1861 from the Oldham Building and Manufacturing Society promoted in 1858, but it was not until after the Civil War and the end of the cotton famine that the Sun Mill, along with other companies formed between 1861 and 1870, began to pay out handsome dividends.[1] In 1871 the Sun Mill declared a dividend of $34\frac{1}{4}$%.[2] Their success, coupled with the general prosperity of the cotton industry and the widening "margins" led to a gradual increase in the promotion of new mills after 1871, culminating in the boom of 1874–75. The boom was at its height in the spring of 1874 when according to John Kidger, a local stockbroker, "there was quite a mania for new companies, no less than 30 being registered in two months, all of which, with the exception of two were formed for building new large mills".[3] In Oldham itself, forty-five new mills were projected with a nominal capital of £2.6 million, while in surrounding areas there were a further 140 companies with a nominal capital of £7.0 million .[4] Promotional activity fell off in the late 1870s following the depression in trade, but was resumed in the 1880s with a boom in 1883–84. This latter activity was encouraged by the low construction costs of mills and the high dividends paid by existing mills.[5] By 1885 there were eighty-five mills in operation in Oldham alone, most of which had been built at about £1 per spindle.[6] Thus between 1866 and 1885 the total number of spindles in the Oldham area increased from an estimated 3 million to 10 million.[7] Promotional activity centred largely on the formation of new companies, and less so on the conversion of existing companies to the joint stock form. Of these "turnover" companies thirty-two were floated in Oldham between 1873–75, and eight between 1884–89.[8]

The conversions were partly intended to offset competition from the new "Limiteds". The new companies were more efficient and larger than the old, having increased from around 10,000–20,000 spindles, the smallest of the two optimum levels of spindleage, in the 1873–74 boom to between 70,000–100,000 spindles in the 1884–85 period. They had the advantage of new machinery and the usual economies of scale arising from their size. Construction costs were also lowered since mills merely copied existing ones, a practice encouraged by mill and machine builders. The bulk of the machinery was supplied by two local firms, Platt Bros. and Asa Lees. Joint stock ownership secured the emergence of the larger units and the small concerns either went out of business or expanded through gradual growth.[9] With regard to the ceiling on size of around 100,000 spindles it has been suggested that given the dependence on loan money, the frailty of investors' confidence discouraged large experiments.[10]

Promotional activity in the boom periods was particularly feverish and essentially local. Promoters were drawn from a wide variety of occupations, and companies were formed "without the aid of [outside] professional floaters." In the 1874–75 boom promoters were drawn from mill workers, architects, contractors, cotton waste dealers, managers, accountants, and sharebrokers. Most of the mills were promoted by parties who were interested in their construction and subsequent operation.[11] The success of existing mills encouraged "gangs of promoters" who "hankered after directorships".[12] One of the most active of the promoters, who were also christened "floating secretaries," was William Nuttall, a leading Oldham sharebroker of the period, who is described by one authority as being "the greatest Lancashire promoter of his age." During the period 1873–75 he was associated with twelve mills, and "hoped to assist in forming many more." Unfortunately he lost heavily in some of his later flotations and emigrated to Australia in 1883.[13] Three other Oldham sharebrokers who were involved in floating activity were John Winterbottom, J. Brierley and John Bunting. Bunting was a blacksmith turned broker and was associated with several companies from 1884 to the first world war.[14]

No difficulty was encountered in issuing shares during boom periods. As John Kidger relates, "the shares were subscribed for without even a prospectus being issued, all that was wanted being an application form."[15] At the height of the 1874 boom projects had only to be brought "before the public almost in the way of suggestion in order to be fancied and sought after by parties anxious to become shareholders". The subscription list was frequently opened at a local hotel, a deposit being paid on application, followed by a further sum on allotment. Such a rush developed on one occasion at Shaw that a market sprang up in application forms outside the house of the company secretary, with sharebrokers anxious to "stag" the issuing buying forms from the public. A full subscription was thus fairly easily obtained; the issues were of course underwritten to a great extent since such people as architects, contractors, cotton brokers, etc., took blocks of shares in order to obtain their contracts. The "floating secretaries" were also accused of stagging issues, and of getting the shares up to a quick premium and then selling out.[16] This latter activity of helping to create a premium was normal market practice at the time.

The total number of shares subscribed in ninety companies by 1886 was just over 950,000 involving a called up share capital of £3.4 million. The nominal share capital was greatly in excess of this figure, the uncalled capital being used as security for the loan money which constituted the other major source of funds. Of the ninety companies listed by Kidger in his statement to the 1886 *Royal Commission* only two had share denominations of £100, neither of which was fully paid, seven mills had share denominations ranging from £10 to £50, while the remainder had £5 shares, and of these only eight were fully paid.[17] The attraction of small share denominations and low paid up capital for the small investor were to some extent diminished by the large uncalled liability outstanding on the shares; uncalled liability encouraged speculation rather than long term investment. Some companies also insisted on minimum holdings of shares, ranging from 10 to 100 units.

The early "Limiteds" drew the bulk of their capital from local sources. There was a certain amount of outside participation in the 1873–75 flotations, but the main source of capital was Oldham where "Every class of trade is represented . . . all found investing at par or if need be at a premium."[18] It has been estimated that there were 10,000 shareholders in Oldham in March 1874, many holding shares in several concerns, and "scores had shares in nearly all the concerns." About three-quarters of the shareholders were wage earning labourers.[19] Collectively, this investment involved approximately £1 million of paid up capital, a remarkable achievement in itself. This degree of local support could hardly have persisted; with the onset of depressed trade in the late 1870s and companies making calls on shares, working class holdings were soon down to a half. By 1885 only some 7% of mill workers were shareholders. As William Nuttall observed, "the cotton operative will not invest where he is employed, but prefers to invest in other companies"; risk spreading is by no means a recent discovery.[20]

A distinctive feature of the 1883–84 boom was the increasing participation of wealthier capitalists drawn from the ranks of the local professional classes, for example, shopkeepers, publicans, and trades people. The 1883–84 boom also brought in outside capital to a greater extent than in the 1870s, but it was never the "vast amount" pictured by the *Oldham Chronicle* as coming from all parts of the United Kingdom. In any case participation for outside capital was confined to the ordinary share capital.[21]

Given the above characteristics of the flotation of a large number of limited liability companies, active share dealing was bound to arise. Shares of small denomination, low paid up values, large numbers of local shareholders, and the practice of quarterly company stocktakings were features which made for active sharedealing, particularly speculative activity. In 1874–75 the whole town was reported as "rapidly becoming one huge joint stock concern", – the three "grand things" being "divis, premiums and shares."[22] According to the *Oldham Chronicle* "share transactions are executed every day in the week in some corner of the town."[23] The first share lists compiled by local stockbrokers to appear in the *Chronicle* in the early months of 1874 contained some thirty spinning companies, all standing at a premium, along with half a dozen other companies. By January 1876 over 160 spinning mills were so listed but by 1880 the list was down to half this number. During the initial months of the boom brokers made extensive use of newspaper advertisements in the form of "wanted and on-offer" lists as a means of attracting business, but reliance on this source of business declined as their numbers increased in the spring of 1874 and as several centres of share dealing sprang up in the town.

The 1875 *Commercial Directory* for Oldham listed nine brokers and three share dealing companies, but this is almost certainly an understatement since between 1874–77 some forty sharebrokers advertised in the local press. Among the "old veterans" were William Nuttall, J. Brierley, and J. Greaves (described in 1876 as the largest broker in Oldham), D. Thorpe, J. Winterbottom, and J. Hood. From the point of view of background they were a particularly varied assortment. The sharebrokers of 1875 included a "skilled coal hewer, policeman, weaver, spinner, wastedealer, corn miller, jeweller, mechanic, cordwainer—nay, the medical profession and even the law can claim to be represented in its ranks."[24]

Numerous share markets sprang up in Oldham with two things very much in common, their somewhat loose organization and their location in pubs. Amongst the first was the "Share Exchange" in Union Street, which commenced business in April 1874, and was organized by John Winterbottom, who was also a mill furnisher. "All persons wishing to buy or sell shares should at once subscribe to this Exchange, which will open every evening from 6–9.30," the subscription was 10s. 6d. and visitors paid 2d. per visit.[25] Within a few months another market appeared, possibly a more ambitious and optimistic form of the above. In May the New Share Exchange Co. Ltd. was formed with a capital of £500 in £1 shares, and meeting at the Masonic Hall in the Angel Hotel. About a hundred "gentlemen" subscribed to the shares, and the plan was to construct their own Exchange. The Chairman was W. Wilson, and the directors were all likewise local sharebrokers, namely, H. Stafford, R. Buckley, D. Thorpe, J. Hood, J. Cooper, and W. W. Winterbottom. Within a year it had neither supervisory functions nor place of business, and in 1876 it was wound up when all were "happy to wash their hands of the concern."[26]

A market also sprang up at Bottom o'th Moor where the old brokers, among them Nuttall and Thorpe, had offices, and where the market in waste cotton was held. Initially the share market was held on the "flags" in front of the Black Swan Hotel, "a house largely frequented by persons who dealt in shares," but later the enterprising landlord (also a broker) offered rooms to accommodate the market. "The inroads that sharebrokers and their clients have made upon the domain previously held sacred to waste dealing has rendered this step necessary and judging from what was said on all hands . . . the change is decidedly for the better and no less satisfactory to those interested in shares than to the older established dealers in that ticklish article which comes under the name of shoddy. A large, commodious, and comfortable room is thus concentrated to the purposes of a share exchange." Nearby another enterprising broker, William Schoffield, ran the Sharebrokers' Dining Rooms, which was open for share business all day.[27]

Another share exchange was located at the Market Hotel, Curzon Street, while members of the United Stock and Sharebrokers' Association, formed in November 1875, met every evening at the Kings Arms Hotel "where they can be seen by buyers and sellers of shares". These nightly markets were well patronized and fittingly boisterous, dealing being done by shouting bids and offers, usually in round lots of 10, 20, 50 and upwards of 100 shares.[28] The gather-

L

ings consisted of some very miscellaneous newcomers to the trade along with the "old veterans" who had floated some of the successful mills. Business was facilitated by the presence of several brokers who ran jobbing books. It was probably this group who took the lead in May 1874 in pressing promoters not to project any more companies since at that time they held large amounts of shares "the calls on which if made they would be unable to meet", and the prospects for the market of further issues would have been very bleak.[29]

Deals were mostly done on a cash basis, and where bargains for future settlement were made the date was fixed by the parties since there was no regular settling day in Oldham, and neither was it the practice to send out contract notes. There was no arbitrating authority in disputes and a request to the Manchester Stock Exchange for assistance in this respect met with no success. In one case, involving non-delivery of shares between Nuttall and Greaves, the County Court was resorted to for a decision.[30]

With the general depression in the cotton trade in the late 1870s and the falling off in promotional activity both the number of brokers and mushroom share markets declined. The main meetings became centred at the Black Swan and the "nocturnal gatherings at a more commodious establishment called the Market Hotel", but they still consisted of a "number of brokers, dealers, speculators, investors, and a crowd of loafers . . . and of pseudoloafers, who really are on the look out for small jobs at a small commission between buyers and sellers". However, by this time a Manchester group of dealers in cotton shares had been formed, influenced no doubt by the proximity of the cotton clientele of the Manchester Exchange which had a membership of nearly 7,000, and by all accounts this group of brokers operated on more formal lines. They met every Tuesday and Friday in a "formal and businesslike manner. It settles between buyers and sellers the prices of shares of the day and facilitates business by mutual information and counsel". A weekly list was issued and members could be "called to account morally" for their transactions.[31]

In November 1880 some of the Manchester brokers and brokers from the Oldham United Stock and Sharebrokers' Association met at Manchester to form the Lancashire Sharebrokers' Association. The "old veterans" were well represented, among them were J. Hood, J. R. Baines, John Kidger, John Chatham (who was appointed Secretary), J, Stott and John Bunting. Judging by later developments the objects of the new Association were to regulate entry into the ranks of the brokers, to formalize dealing and settlement procedures, and to obtain greater control over their own affairs. The rules provided for election by ballot on the recommendation of three members and an entrance fee of £10. The hours of business were fixed, with a daily call over at 2.30 p.m. Unless otherwise arranged all settlements were to be made within seven days of a transaction (later increased to seventeen). The Association was managed by an elected committee, and William Cornell was elected the first President.[32]

Change, however, came but slowly. It was not until 1883 that they obtained their own premises "apart from a licensed house" for the transaction of share business "under the control of this Association."[33] A room was rented in the Oldham Lyceum, but they were not very successful in confining share activity to their own market. Markets continued in the Black Swan and the Market Hotel, and another started in an unlikely place, namely Robinson's Tea Rooms. Later, fines were introduced in an attempt to deter members from patronizing such "nocturnal markets", and after 1890 frequent offenders became liable to the penalty of expulsion.[34] Such measures to kill off the outside competition were not entirely successful since the public continued to enjoy free access to the Lyceum market. It was not until July 1888 that the market was closed to the public.

The Manchester members of the Lancashire Sharebrokers' Association continued to meet twice a week at the Falstaff Hotel, but not without attracting the attention of the Manchester Stock Exchange. The latter, concerned "that some outside brokers advertise their meetings as held in some tavern in this City", hastily inserted an advert in the local press in 1882 stating that their members were not allowed to advertise.[35]

Share prices during this early period displayed some interesting characteristics. After the flotation boom prices fell off rapidly from 1876–79, a decline associated with the general depression in the industry and the fall in dividends. The annual average dividend for forty companies in 1877 was down to $3\frac{3}{4}\%$, while in 1878 some sixty mills ended the year with debit balances of varying amounts.[36] One of the main influences on changes in profits was the fluctuations in spinning margins, that is, the difference between the price of raw cotton and the price of yarn, per lb. Margins in the coarse and medium section of the industry, which centred largely on Oldham, fell from $5\frac{3}{8}$d. per lb. in 1875 to $2\frac{3}{8}$d. per lb. in July 1879.[37] During the 1880s and early 1890s share prices moved gradually upwards, fluctuations from this trend being associated with variations in profit performances. Individual share price movements were particularly closely linked to profit changes because of the high degree of capital gearing used by many of the mill companies. As already noted most companies relied heavily on loan money, and the smaller the equity element in the company capital the greater the scope for dividend increases with rising profits. Mill managements could therefore show very high rates of return on capital, particularly during periods of prosperity. They were not averse to concealing the full extent of a profit fall in bad years by diverting funds which should have been used for depreciation to other uses. Albert Simpson in his statement to the 1886 *Royal Commission* claimed that many mills did not depreciate by the appropriate 5% and that if the "books of these concerns had been kept on a proper basis, the dividends paid would have been reduced".[38] In the majority of cases dividends were declared on a quarterly basis, a feature which induced continuing market interest in the shares. The spinning companies were, in fact, extremely prompt in publishing their results, usually two or three days after the stocktaking.[39]

A major feature of the market was that both the rise and the fluctuations in prices occurred in most cases below the paid up values of the shares. In 1879 most mill shares stood at a discount, while in 1886 only fifteen mill shares out of eighty-two were at a premium.[40] This can only be explained by the liability of the uncalled share capital; it cannot be reconciled with the profits earned by many of the companies. Presumably local investors preferred the high interest rates on loan money and the short calls on the shares.[41]

Under the terms of the 1844 Joint Stock Companies Act, and indeed subsequent acts, companies were allowed unlimited borrowing powers, and cotton companies quickly took advantage of this provision by establishing loan accounts which were equivalent in function to the modern debenture and preference capital. Such borrowing permitted a rapid enlargement of capacity at little cost to the shareholders, and it quickly became an integral part of mill finance; companies failing to obtain adequate loan money seldom stayed for long in the industry.[42] The extent to which the spinning companies relied upon loan money is illustrated by the following figures; in 1877 the loan capital of seventy-two mills amounted to £2.3 million out of a total capital of £4.1 million, in 1886 the figure for ninety mills was £3.4 million out of a total capital of £6.8 million, and in 1891 the figure for 101 companies was £3.9 million out of a total capital of £8.9 million.[43] Most companies placed a restriction on the amount of loan capital to total capital and regarded a figure in excess of the value of the ordinary paid up capital as reckless financing. Quite a few paid little heed to such caution. In Kidgers' 1885–86 list, which contains ninety mills all of whom had loan accounts, there are numerous instances where mills had loan money equivalent to twice the ordinary capital, while Cavendish mill loan money was six times the ordinary capital. The loan money involved ranged from a few hundred for small mills to £122,000 for the large Whitelands Twist mill of 125,000 spindles. While the use of loan money provided relatively cheap finance and enabled higher dividends to be declared on the share capital, it was not in the early years of the "Limiteds" abused in the search for high dividends, and by 1903 many of the older mills had reduced their dependence on it by calling up additional capital or using the depreciation provision to that end.[44]

Deposits were placed with a mill in very much the same way as they would with a joint stock bank. The loans were invited by advertising in the local press before the mill was built. A pass book was issued to the depositor and deposits were made of £5 and upwards, small sums being withdrawable on demand and larger amounts with notice.[45] The depositor enjoyed the same security as an ordinary creditor to the company, an important part of this being the uncalled portion of the share capital. The system attracted depositors because of the simplicity of the arrangement and the fact that higher interest rates were paid than on comparable investments. Loan money acquired the reputation of gilt-edged, particularly in companies with managements of repute. One of its remarkable features was that despite the ease of withdrawal and the fluctuations in the fortunes of the industry there were few, if any, panic withdrawals of funds in the early period. Withdrawals occasionally occurred due to bad stocktaking results, but most mills were able to keep up dividends for prestige purposes in order to maintain loan funds. In the face of a large withdrawal companies could always call up share capital, but frequently this only came from withdrawal of loans to meet the calls. Funds were seldom withdrawn when removal would place a mill in jeopardy.[46]

Rates of interest paid on loan funds ranged from 4% to 7% depending on the state of the money market, the state of the industry, and the standing of individual firms. The older mills could generally command money at lower rates than new ones, since investors demanded an additional risk premium for the latter. Many mills stuck to the long standing and "dearly loved 5%"; loan rates were certainly above bank rates, savings bank rates, and those offered by the local co-operative societies.[47]

Investors of loan money were drawn mainly from the ranks of the "working class in the immediate vicinity", from minor officials at the mills, and also from local societies such as the Oldham Sick and Burial Society. The Stock Exchange Committee also put its surplus funds on loan with the Shiloh Mill.[48] The largest investors, however, were the successful mills with funds in excess of their own requirements and who lent them out at higher rates than they paid themselves. They regarded these funds as liquid assets which could be lent out on special withdrawal terms. It was, however, a practice which added to the vulnerability of the loan system, particularly during periods of depression, but there are no recorded instances of difficulty involving reinvested funds. The practice certainly led to an element of double counting in assessing the total volume of loan money used by the spinning companies. By the end of the century several Oldham mills sought their investments outside the cotton industry; the Lion Spinning Co. in 1900 held seventy-two separate investments in various sectors of industry at a market value of over £100,000. The income from such investments enabled the payment of higher dividends and loan interest during periods when their own trading record was not very successful.[49]

Apart from a brief interruption in 1892–93 the cotton industry experienced a long spell of prosperity from 1887 to 1901. During this period the pace of mill promotion was unexciting, while on the Oldham Share market prices moved to reflect the gradual climb in dividend levels. The years 1902–03 brought another brief interruption, but it was followed by a further period of prosperity in 1904–07 which brought with it hectic mill promotion and the associated problems for both the industry and the share market. During this short time over 12 million spindles were installed, the bulk of the expansion taking place in the mule spinning section. By 1904 Oldham already boasted the largest concentration of spinning mills in the world, and the 1905–07 boom merely confirmed the lead. But even in the middle of the boom there was widespread apprehension as to the ensuing depression. It was felt that neither home nor foreign markets were likely to absorb the additional production without lower prices.

Promotional activity lasted for three years and resulted in the floating of forty mills in 1905, twenty-three in 1906, and thirty-nine in 1907. The procedures and motives behind the promotions were very similar to those of earlier Oldham booms, with the major difference that on this occasion much greater emphasis was placed on the use of loan money in the search for high dividends. Promoters were drawn from the ranks of cotton mill managers, machine manufacturers and other parties with a vested interest in mill construction; one firm of local accountants successfully floated six mills in the boom.[50] The pace of promotion and building was indeed hectic. One observant visitor to the area in 1907 recollected that new mills were "put up with such rapidity that the machinery was being moved into the ground floor and started to work long before the top was finished. People were drawing their dividends from one mill and investing them in a new mill beside it and drawing their dividends from that within a year after that mill had started."[51]

Most of these mills had an authorized capital of around £80,000 in 1,600 £5 shares, and the paid up capital was held by relatively few shareholders. The marketing of so many blocks of new shares, even at low paid up values, on what was essentially a very small and narrow share market, proved a difficult problem and no doubt generated even greater reliance upon loan finance. Even in the early stages of the boom the public were only buying new mill shares "sparingly and with great caution". The position was not improved when large blocks of shares were thrown onto the market at a loss presumably because the holders could not meet impending calls. Consequently share prices fell rapidly and by the middle of 1905 the market was in an extremely "nervous state."[52] The prospect of some of the new mills going into production in the near future prompted John Bunting to comment that the share market was "ripe for a rise", but he added that the "reports of new mills check the effects of the good stocktaking. Were it not for these reports, a very important rise in prices would take place."[53] The flow of mill shares continued into 1906 and kept prices low, but even with low prices promoters were "as determined as ever to push new mills on the market". Toward the end of 1907 the boom tapered off and the share market felt the effects of the new mill issues which "accelerated the speed to bottom prices". The accompanying stringency of the banks in lending on margin for share speculation also contributed to the downward slide.[54]

From the promoters' point of view the fact that loan capital could be obtained at low rates and with comparative ease more than compensated for the nervousness of the share market and spurred on their "desire to rush up new mills". The dependence of some new mills on loan finance led to extremely high rates of gearing, few of which excelled those engineered by John Bunting, one of the leading sharebrokers in Oldham. The Iris Mill at Hathershaw paid an 80% dividend, with the aid of £103,320 loan money on a paid up share capital of only £6,250.[55] Another mill controlled by Bunting, the large Times Mill, had a called up capital of £8,000 and loan money of over £250,000 (20s. loan money and 10d. paid-up capital per spindle). Bunting, in fact, could re-deploy loan money between the mills under his control thereby ensuring financial certainty for his new promotions.[56] During the ensuing depression a few mills defaulted on their loan repayments but they managed to obtain powers to freeze the loans so as to prevent liquidation. Other mills adopted less extreme remedies to meet withdrawal of loans by calling up capital, while Bunting introduced a new financial innovation, at least in cotton mill finance, by way of an enlargement of capital in the form of fixed interest preference stocks.[57] Most mills, however, managed to retain the bulk of their loan money by keeping up dividend levels as a prestige symbol despite the falls in profits. With the regular payment of the dividend it was not surprising that shares in the large spinning companies were, in pre-war years, regarded as a good industrial investment.

With the onset of the first world war the industry soon felt the effects of the loss of export markets and a reduced home demand. The fall in exports was concentrated in the cheaper classes of cotton goods so that the 'coarse' section of the industry – the American section spinning the lower and medium counts – faired worst than the Egyptian section.[58] Average profit per company fell off abruptly reaching a low point in 1915, but dividend levels remained almost unchanged. During the second half of the war the position of the industry improved, and by 1918 average dividends had reached over 16%, double the previous year's level.[59] The large profits earned on restricted outputs were attributable to the widening margins, especially in the American section of the industry. Following a slight interruption early in 1919 both output and profits expanded rapidly, and the boom continued until the middle of 1920. While average profits did not increase greatly compared to 1919, dividend levels exceeded 20%.

As has already been noted the pre-war response to a rise in profits took the form of an expansion of existing firms and the building of new mills. In the prevailing conditions of 1919 such a response was impossible because of the shortages of equipment and building supplies. The actual response took the form of a hectic and speculative financial reconstruction of a major portion of the industry, affecting some 46% of total spindles. Nearly all the joint stock mills were involved because with quoted share capital they were amenable to financial manipulation. The cost of erecting a mill in pre-war years was around £1 per spindle compared with an estimated £3 after the war. It was therefore thought to be cheaper and quicker to acquire existing mills than start up new ones. The prices paid were not closely related to replacement costs, but more so to the expected earnings which promoters hoped from their investment.[60] In some cases prices were as low as 7s. per spindle, while other mills reached £5 per spindle. A great deal depended on timing since once the "orgy of faith" had commenced prices climbed very quickly.

Financial reconstruction took two forms, both of which served to increase the nominal capital value of the mills. The most common form was a reflotation of a company which involved the purchase of shares by speculators at high prices with the intention of forming a new company with a capitalization based on the high profits already earned, and which were expected to continue. Some two hundred spinning mills were refloated in this way, along with seventeen spinning and weaving concerns. The other method used was that of recapitalization which entailed increasing the share capital by the issue of new bonus shares. This method was used because shareholders were anxious to benefit from revaluation and they subsequently disposed of the bonus shares at a profit through the market. Thirty-two spinning mills were recapitalized, along with two spinning concerns.[61]

The bulk of the reconstructions took place between March 1919, and July 1920. The movement began slowly with seventeen instances between March – August 1919, quickening to forty-seven between September – November 1919, followed by 197 between December 1919 and April 1920 (an average of about thirty a week) and falling off to forty during the period May to July 1920.[62] The pace of the reconstruction is also apparent in the changes in the average prices paid per 1,000 spindles which rose from £1,400 in two mills in 1919, to over £4,000 in twelve concerns in April 1920, falling back to £2,250 in four mills by June of that year.[63] The prices paid were influenced by such considerations as the expected profit, the age of the mill (newer mills commanded higher prices), and the amount of loan money held. It was assumed that the new mill would retain the use of the latter because of its low cost.

It did not take long for the rumour to spread that shareholders were receiving "fat cheques" from the activities of the earliest financial syndicates on the scene, and share prices rose quickly. Exhorbitant prices were paid for some of the mills which were frequently sold at eight times their old value. The size of the deals varied greatly, but the largest single deal was probably the acquisition of the famous firm of Messrs Horrockses & Crewdson & Co. by the Amalgamated Cotton Mill Trust Ltd. at over £5 million for 300,000 spindles and 10,000 looms.[64]

The buyers of the mills were mainly syndicates of local people connected with the industry. Syndicates of local businessmen existed in Oldham, Shaw, and Rochdale, while a few sharebrokers were also active in the bids. Granville Mills was involved with a group of Oldham businessmen, while one of the leading figures in the whole episode was S. F. Mellor, "and it is safe to say that almost all the better companies which have been turned over had offers from him".[65] Ernest Platt was involved with a syndicate drawn from the Platt family. Outside interests were also attracted by the prospects of high dividends from reorganised mills. Among them were a London syndicate, a syndicate of London, Leeds, Nottingham and Bradford businessmen, another of Manchester and Oldham businessmen, a syndicate of "Liverpool gentlemen who are interested in the raw cotton trade", and the powerful Amalgamated Cotton Mill Trust Ltd. with directors drawn from a wide spectrum.[66]

The character of the financial reflotation is illustrated by the following aggregate figures for 129 mills covering the period 1919–1920. Of the total purchase price of £38.2 million, paid-up capital and premiums on shares contributed £21.4 million, the rest coming from loan money, mortgages and bank overdrafts.[67] Shareholders, therefore, provided only about 55% of the money needed. The shares issued to them were usually of £1 nominal value, 10s. called up, with a premium of about 2s. 6d.[68] They were eagerly taken up by the market, old shareholders absorbing a good proportion of them. However, the marketing arrangements did not meet with total approval, as it was alleged that directors and brokers received unduly large allotments and that the latter sold shares at a premium before allotment had taken place.[69]

Throughout the episode the share market was particularly active with plenty of promoters' money and the activities of "large dealers" giving share prices a quick lift, and even the "long neglected mills are wanted at the highest prices for many years." By June 1919 the market was "wild and excited", while expectations of further purchases kept it poised for a further advance; everyone was busy guessing which mills were up for reflotating.[70] The rise in prices was reinforced by the investment of record dividends paid out by some mills. However, by early 1920 there were signs that the boom was fading. Scarcity of loan money and a clamp down on bank finance to the principal operators brought a fall in share prices. The downward drift was accelerated when brokers and mill directors, favourably treated in the reflotation, started unloading large blocks of shares to the alarm of smaller holders.[71] By June 1920 the fall in prices was so marked that the Lancashire Sharebrokers' Association suspended publication of the weekly list for a few weeks, claiming that prices no longer reflected intrinsic values and that it was desirable to deprive speculators of them; it was, they held, "an advantage to keep developments from the public."[72]

Sharedealing in Oldham during this period was certainly not monopolized by the relatively small membership, twenty-five in 1919, of the Lancashire Sharebrokers' Association.[73] In the early months of the boom members of the public visited the market and dealt with the recognized brokers with the result that "the market became overcrowded and at times it was impossible to carry transactions through."[74] It was decided therefore, to close the market to the general public, a move which generated much criticism. The old brokers were no doubt protecting their interests, but the newer entrants to the profession felt that they were entitled to deal if they could make a living out of it. For a time the outside brokers returned to the old haunts of the Market Hotel and the Black Swan at Bottom o'th Moor. However they soon organized themselves into the Oldham and District Share Exchange, with G. Astbury as Chairman, and by early 1920 the membership was over 300. Rooms were rented in the Lyceum buildings and following the repeal of the restriction on entry to the Association's room many of the members operated on a jobbing basis between the two markets. Attempts to prohibit the members from dealing with the "upper room" failed and in June 1920 the new market itself was forced to restrict entry because of overcrowding.[75] With the fall in prices and turnover in the summer of 1920 many of the new brokers turned to other lines of trade. The Share Exchange continued in existence for a few more years but never got far with its attempts to merge with the Association. The latter, as a result of the reflotation boom, had received a permanent enlargement of its membership, which by 1925 had reached seventy-one members.[76]

Expectations of high profits in the industry were never realised during the inter-war years. The flotation boom was quickly followed by a depression in the industry, and a period of very low share prices. It was the beginning of a long and painful period of adjustment. Because of reduced exports, especially to India and the Far East where Japanese and Chinese competition was edging out Lancashire products, an inadequate expansion of the home market to compensate for this, and the gradual infiltration of synthetic fibres in the late 1920s, the industry found itself with considerable surplus capacity. Britain's percentage of world trade in cotton goods fell from 58% before the First World War to 28% before the Second World War, and her percentage of world production over the period fell from 84% to 46%.[77]

The process of adjustment to a reduced demand for cotton goods and increased foreign competition was made considerably more difficult by the legacy of debt financing left by the reflotation boom. Loan finance was soon seen to be totally unsuitable for an industry in depression. The prices charged for cotton goods had to cover not only the prime costs of production, but also heavy fixed interest charges, which made Lancashire prices uncompetitive in world markets. The problem was greatest in the American section where very little had been done by 1927 to reduce the fixed interest burden. At that date fixed interest capital per 1,000 spindles for re-floated mills amounted to £1,700, compared with only £592 for original companies.[78] The character of the debt, however, had changed somewhat. Unsecured advances had been converted into debenture and mortgages; the latter did not guarantee immunity from liquidation since mortgagees resorted to appointing receivers. The most important change was an increase of nearly 50% in bank overdrafts between 1921 and 1927; at the latter date twenty mills had overdrafts of well over £100,000, a sum far in excess of their uncalled capital.[79] The increase was associated with additional help in the depression and the persistent drain of loan money after 1921.

It was not until 1927 that the drain of loan money became serious, and soon several companies were placed in difficulties by withdrawals. The surprising fact was that so few went under, there being thirteen liquidations of spinning concerns in 1927. Other mills managed to survive because they went to the courts to obtain relief from their obligation to pay interest, while many more resorted to calling up capital. Between 1921–26, 171 of the refloated companies called up a further £6 million, a factor which exerted a permanent depressive influence on share prices.[80] During this period "many hundreds of families were ruined. Those who had loaned money to the mills found out that their loans were totally unsecured. Those who were shareholders were called upon to pay up the unpaid share capital. Those who were both shareholders and loan holders found that they were not able to set their loan money off against their calls."[81]

These critical developments produced some interesting, almost unique, features in the share market. Dealing in shares at a discount was one, and dealing in loan money was another. The circumstances which gave rise to dealing in shares at a discount are illustrated by the following example. In 1927 the Lilac Mill had a paid up capital of only £7,500 out of an authorized capital of £100,000, while the balance sheet showed liabilities of nearly £500,000. On its dividends the company had done well in 1925 and 1926 paying out 26%, but the sudden drop in 1927 coupled with the debt position of the company led many shareholders "to part with their (share) holdings without any payment in order to avoid liability of the uncalled portion," which was £4 12s. 6d. on the £5 shares.[82] This was by no means an isolated example. The practice began in 1924–25 and by 1927 the Oldham share list contained sixty-eight shares at a discount, ranging from a few pence to 5s. per share, and all drawn from refloated companies. From the share markets point of view paying to get rid of shares involved the danger of deals taking place without registration of new ownership. The Oldham Committee therefore passed a rule stipulating that the principal disposing of the shares should deposit through his broker "such amount of discount as shall be in excess of the amount paid per share" with the Secretary, and this sum was not paid over to the taker of the shares until he had furnished proof of registration to the Secretary.

The Committee also deemed it a moral obligation on the part of the broker taking the shares at a discount to see that every effort was made to present the transfer to the company for registration.[83]

Dealings in loan money were also a sympton of the financial difficulties of the spinning mills. Holders of loan money, realizing that they had little hope of getting it back, frequently sold their deposit through the market at very nominal prices. The buyers were usually those faced with calls on their shares in that mill, and who then tendered the loan money against the call. By 1930 the volume of this business going through the market was sufficient to justify members using the call over system to deal in it. Bids made by buyers were usually subject to the company accepting the loan money and transferring it to the share capital account.[84]

Three methods were open to the industry to reduce its scale, the process of bankruptcy, the formation of a cartel, or amalgamations. During the early years of the depression the industry resorted to short time working by all units, an expensive approach to the basic problem of surplus capacity since it involved increased overhead costs. The object was to hold up prices to cover prime costs plus interest charges, but even the mills with largest debt problems cut prices in an attempt to increase their revenue. More permanent solutions followed. By the mid-twenties bankruptcy was gaining its own momentum at the instigation of mortgagees and other creditors. A formal cartel arrangement, advocated by J. M. Keynes, was formed in 1926 and soon had a membership of 221 firms, all of whom agreed to adopt output restrictions and minimum prices. However, mills outside the cartel were able to attract additional business by undercutting cartel prices, and a return to free competition soon ensued.[85] Voluntary co-operation which retained individualism was seen not to work. The surest method therefore was amalgamation, a solution supported by the largest creditors of the mills, namely the commercial banks; it was claimed that most of the mills affected were "practically in the hands of the banks."

In the American spinning section this led to the formation, under the auspices of the Bank of England, of the Lancashire Cotton Corporation. Incorporated in 1929, its objective was to acquire between 9–10 million spindles and concentrate production in the most efficient mills, using between 6–7 million spindles, and scrapping the rest. Mill assets were purchased on the basis of an exchange for the Corporation's debentures and shares. Prices paid ranged from 10s. per spindle for old mills to 25s. per spindle for new mills, with stock taken over at market values; once a scheme was sanctioned the mill company was then wound up.[86] Although it examined some 200 mills during the early years of its operations, by December 1939 it had acquired only 104 mills, many of which were scrapped as being unsuitable for production.[87] These operations were financed by a paid up capital of £3.0 million, and loan capital of £1.5 million, with a quotation in London, Manchester and Oldham. In Oldham the Corporation was not particularly popular since in its early years it had "no Oldham man on the board", and because, as the *Stock Exchange Year Book* for 1939 pointedly states "No ordinary dividend yet". In fact, many of the Oldham mills only approached the Corporation after considerable pressure had been put on them by some of the creditor banks.[88]

In the Egyptian section, which was not so seriously burdened financially, the initiative for amalgamation came from within the industry. Following incorporation in July 1929 the Combined Egyptian Spinners had absorbed nineteen mills by 1939 in Oldham and surrounding towns. Its issued capital at that date was £7.4 million, with a quotation at Oldham.[89]

The effect on the industry of the activities of the combines, of the Cotton Spindles Board, set up in 1936 to buy and scrap spindles, and of the bankruptcy of over fifty mills, was to reduce the total spindles in the Oldham area from 19.8 million in 1927 to 10.9 million in 1939.[90] The effect on the share market was equally great. The number of mills listed fell from 296 in 1927 to 117 by December 1939; the total quoted paid up share capital (excluding the two combines) fell from £55 million in 1927 to £23 million at the end of 1939.

It was appreciated on the Oldham market that the enlarged membership of the twenties would require additional scope for business following this steady decline in the number of mill shares. As early as 1925 the Committee organized a bureau to facilitate dealing between members in unlisted securities. Although a useful departure, the amount of interdealing done was small and merely served to emphasize the fact that dealings in national securities could only be done by depending almost entirely on outside quotations.[91] To assist in this, a regular price service, operating alternatively with a London firm and the ubiquitous Nicholson's of Sheffield, was arranged in 1927, and the Oldham list was enlarged to include a selection of the leading shares in home railways, mines, oil, rubbers, and commercial and industrial companies. However, the volume of business arising from these innovations was very disappointing, and simply confirmed the early doubts of some members as to the wisdom of a purely "artificial attempt to increase business".[92] Nevertheless, the policy was continued and by 1939 the share list carried prices for well over a hundred national securities; at least the business that was generated acted as a supplement for the declining turnover in mill shares.

It was, of course, fully realized that in the matter of dealings in national securities the market was dependent upon the terms and treatment obtained at the hands of London and the larger provincial markets. To get the best possible terms, therefore, determined efforts were made to improve the standing of the Oldham market so as to get it recognized as a Stock Exchange throughout the country. Several measures were adopted to this end between 1925 and 1929. In 1925 admission requirements were brought into line with those practised by the major provincial exchanges; new members were required to obtain the personal guarantee of five members, while the principals in a firm had to become members of the exchange.[93] Dealing was successfully confined to one room, and the call over was made more orderly, only one member calling at a time.[94] A minimum scale of commissions for cotton shares was laid down; from 1934 onwards the London minimum was adopted for all transactions. Fortnightly settlement procedures were also introduced in 1925, a move which "tended to discourage undesirable speculation." In 1924 a permanent secretary was appointed, while in 1927 the market moved to more suitable premises in Priory Buildings, Union Street. To give an additional boost to its status, in 1929, the Committee changed the name to the Oldham Stock Exchange.

Following the adoption of these improvements an approach was made in 1931 to the Council of Associated Stock Exchanges requesting membership, but it met with little success. The application was rejected on the grounds that Oldham was an Exchange in name only with a very dispersed membership, while the method of conducting business was "not on all fours with the usual method of Stock Exchanges." Also, while it had adopted various rules in operation elsewhere they were not effectively enforced.[95] No doubt, the telling argument was the ultimatum from a neighbouring market that if Oldham joined they "could not possibly meet in this Council."

A further approach was not made until 1941 when London introduced new rules on commissions and country business. To get into the Council, and to secure the concessions that London extended to other exchanges under the new rules, several major changes were deemed necessary. These involved tightening up of rules on membership, quotation requirements, commissions, and several other matters. Also, it required the end of the Manchester call over and the removal of members' offices from the Manchester postal area. This move had been contemplated in 1926, but it was then felt that it was "a great advantage not only to the outside members, but also to those in Oldham that the market should be held in Manchester every Tuesday and Friday."[96] Only two firms were involved in the move out of Manchester, which took place shortly afterwards, although it was agreed that certain members could continue to attend Manchester's Royal Exchange at limited and specified times. The end result of the changes was that Oldham failed to gain entry into the Council because of the "dispersed nature of its membership." Some benefits, however, did follow in that both London and the Council were prepared to grant commission concessions and restricted dealing facilities to the Oldham members.[97]

The history of spinning since the last war is that of a contracting industry, and also one of low profitability compared with other manufacturing activity. The total number of spindles in the Oldham area fell from 10.7 million in 1945 to 6.1 million in 1958, and to 1.6 million by 1965. This was the result of amalgamation after the war to meet labour shortages, and the selling out of mills rather than waiting for better times. Official policy also had an influential hand in the contraction. Concentration and restriction of domestic output, rather than import restriction, became the official line in the face of growing imports of cotton goods. Assistance was given to the industry to modernize and concentrate production in the larger units, but the 1948 Cotton Spinning (Re-equipment Subsidy) Act made such assistance conditional on the closure of smaller mills.[98] Additional incentives were offered in the 1954 Budget by way of investment allowances but investment in the industry remained inadequate in relation to replacement costs; subsidies in themselves failed to stimulate investment levels in the face of low expectations.[99] Further rationalization followed in 1959 with a Government scheme for scrapping surplus machinery. The cumulative effect of these measures for the Oldham share market was to reduce the number of mills quoted from sixty-two in 1950 to a mere twenty-five in 1965, the last year of a separate Oldham list. Apart from a burst of bonus issues in the early fifties the market has seen a gradual decline in mill share activity, alleviated by the occasional bout of public interest in a few companies.

Over the post-war years the membership of the Oldham Stock Exchange has also fallen. Business in general securities did not increase to compensate for the contraction of the mill share market; proximity to and dependence on the larger provincial markets made this inevitable. From thirty-six in 1956 the membership fell to nineteen in 1965 and to twelve in 1968, only half of them being located in Oldham itself. As far back as 1947 the Stock Exchange discarded its larger premises and became a market operating through a telephone switchboard, but since the advent of Federation even this activity has ceased.

NOTES

1 J. H. Clapham, *An Economic History of Modern Britain* (1932). Volume 2, pp. 143-4.
2 T. Ellison, *The Cotton Trade of Great Britain* (1886), p. 134.
3 *Royal Commission on Depression of Trade and Industry*, BPP 1886, Third Report, Appendix A, VIII, p. 308. Statement from John Kidger, an Oldham stockbroker, described by J. H. Clapham as the "Oldham apologist".
4 Ellison, op. cit., p. 135. Many of the 140 companies were in close proximity to Oldham.
5 D. A. Farnie, The English Cotton Industry 1850-1896, University of Manchester, unpublished M. A. Thesis (1953), p. 268.
6 R. Smith, "An Oldham Limited Liability Company 1875-1896", *Business History*, 1961, p. 36.
7 Oldham Master Cotton Spinners' Association Ltd., Centenary Booklet, 1866-1966, p. 39.
8 Farnie, op. cit., p. 268.
9 T. S. Ashton, "The Growth of Textile Business in the Oldham District", *Journal of the Royal Statistical Society*, 1926, p. 136. By 1914 there were 184 joint stock mills in Oldham, but only 27 private ones.
10 F. Jones, The Cotton Spinning Industry in the Oldham District from 1896-1914. University of Manchester, unpublished M. A. Thesis (1959), pp. 77-8.
11 Farnie, op. cit., pp. 259-60. These ties, eg, with cotton brokers were not always to the best advantage of the mills.
12 Jones, op. cit., p. 13.
13 Farnie, op. cit., pp. 59-60. W. Nuttall was the first paid secretary of the central Co-operative Board, and a director of the C.W.S. At one time he was auditor to the Sun Mill Co. Among his successful mill promotions were the Greenacres (1871, nominal capital £70,000), Albert (1873, £40,000), United (1874, £100,000), Gladstone (1875,£112,000), Landsdonne (1875, £36,000). He was also secretary to four unsuccessful concerns. In 1875 he promoted a paper works and a colliery; he lost heavily in both.
14 Farnie, op. cit., p. 295. See also Jones, op. cit., p. 47. Bunting promoted the Eagle (1890), Moss (1890), and had a controlling interest in several mills. including one of the largest promoted, the Times No. 2, with 174,000 spindles.
15 *R. C. on Depression of Trade and Industry*, op. cit., p. 308.
16 *Oldham Chronicle*, February 21, 1874, April 11, 1874, and October 16, 1875. Personal application seems to have been a feature of the share issues; proxy, nominee or bank shareholding were greatly discouraged; see Smith, op. cit., p. 41.
17 *R. C. on Depression of Trade and Industry*, op. cit., pp. 310-11.
18 Quoted by Farnie, op. cit., p. 260.
19 Ibid., p. 261.
20 Farnie, op. cit., pp. 262-3.
21 R. Smith found that in four companies he examined that outside capital was comparatively small; pp. 40-41.
22 Farnie, op. cit., p. 286, p. 294.
23 *Oldham Chronicle*, November 8, 1874.
24 Farnie, op. cit., p. 281; quote from the *Oldham Chronicle*, January 16, 1875.
25 *Oldham Chronicle*, March 28, 1874.

M

26 *Oldham Chronicle*, January 23, 1875, July 15, 1876.
27 *Oldham Chronicle*, February 6, 1875, January 22, 1876.
28 *Oldham Chronicle*, January 2, 1875; "A Night with the Sharebrokers", February 26, 1876. There were also local markets in the surrounding towns, at the Duke of York in Shaw, the George Hotel in Moseley, the Feathers Inn in Ashton, and there was a market at Rochdale, probably in a "consecrated" pub.
29 *Oldham Chronicle*, May 9, 1874.
30 *Oldham Chronicle*, May 20, 1876.
31 *Oldham Chronicle*, October 23, 1880.
32 Rules of the Lancashire Sharebrokers' Association, 1881.
33 Oldham Stock Exchange. Minutes of the Committee and Monthly Meetings, March 6, 1883.
34 Ibid., August 3, 1888, November 4, 1890.
35 Manchester Stock Exchange, Minutes, January 18, 1882.
36 *Economist*, February 2, 1878, p. 122; Ellison, op. cit., p. 136.
37 R. E. Tyson, "The Cotton Industry" in *The Development of British Industry and Foreign Competition 1875-1914* (1968), ed. D. H. Aldcroft, pp. 101-2.
38 *Royal Cimmission on Depression and Industry*, op. cit., pp. 378-9. R. Smith, op. cit., p. 47, notes that for the Moorfield Mill considerable variation occurred in amounts set aside for depreciation, nothing being allocated in some quarters.
39 Kidger, op. cit., p. 309. He states that the balance sheets were published in the local press "and every opportunity is given for criticism . . . the few that are not considered up to the standard are well known, and the market value of the shares are governed accordingly." By the 1905-07 boom mill companies were far less forthcoming with financial details, and by 1919 only 42 mills out of 153 issued balance sheets.
40 *Royal Commission on Depression of Trade and Industry*, op. cit., p. 379.
41 R. Smith, A History of the Lancashire Cotton Industry 1873-1896, University of Birmingham, unpublished Ph.D. Thesis (1954), pp. 195-99.
42 Smith, "An Oldham Limited Liability Company 1875-1896", op. cit., p. 43. Firms failing to get sufficient loan money usually fell back on mortgages and bank finance. In 1886 some 35 mills had mortgages of £610,735; Tyson, op. cit., p. 229.
43 Farnie, op. cit., p. 275.
44 Jones, op. cit., p. 45. See also G. W. Daniels, "The Balance Sheets of Three Limited Companies in the Cotton Industry", *Manchester School*, 1932, pp. 82-3.
45 F. Lavington, *The English Capital Market* (1921), p. 291-2. Loan money was not used in other industries to anything like the extent that it was in cotton; local authorities however made extensive use of it.
46 S. J. Chapman and F. J. Marquis, "The Recruiting of the Employing Classes from the Ranks of the Wage Earners in the Cotton Industry." *Journal of the Royal Statistical Society*, 1912, pp. 302-3.
47 Farnie, op. cit., p. 277.
48 Clapham, op. cit., p. 141.
49 Smith, "An Oldham Limited Liability Company 1875-96," op. cit., p. 46.
50 Jones, op. cit., p. 13.
51 J. C. Stamp in discussion of S. J. Chapman and D. Kemp, "The War and the Textile Industries", *Journal of the Royal Statistical Society*, 1915, p. 230.
52 *Oldham Chronicle*, April 22, July 22, 1905.

53 *Oldham Chronicle,* September 9, 1905. The high profits earned would certainly support his view; average profits per mill (72 mills) in 1905 were over £7,000; see R. Robson, *The Cotton Industry in Britain* (1957), p. 338.

54 *Oldham Chronicle,* November 17, 1907.

55 Farnie, op. cit., p. 229.

56 Jones, op. cit., p. 47, pp. 87-8.

57 Ibid., p. 61.

58 G. W. Daniels and J. Jewkes, "The Post War Depression in the Lancashire Cotton Industry", *Journal of the Royal Statistical Society,* 1928, p. 157. The American section comprised some ⅔ of the total spindles in the industry.

59 Robson, op. cit., p. 338. Many companies also made "bonus calls", which was a bonus distributed from profits but credited as a call on a share, thus writing up the share capital out of profits.

60 Daniels and Jewkes, op. cit., pp. 171-73. Attempts were made to justify the reconstruction on the grounds that replacement costs had greatly increased, and that nominal capital should faithfully reflect such inflated figures. The apology was both disingeneous and misleading. See also E. B. Dietrich, "The Plight of the Lancashire Cotton Industry", *American Economic Review,* 1928, p. 472.

61 Ibid., p. 173. Forty companies were also reconstituted, but it was not clear as to which category they fell into; they were mostly outside the Oldham area. Many companies at the time also issued a large amount of bonus shares in order to reduce liability for excess profits duty. See *Oldham Chronicle,* January 11, 1919.

62 Ibid., p. 171. During this entire period (March 1919–July 1920) 76 reconstructions took place in the weaving section.

63 Ibid., p. 172.

64 *Economist,* November 29; *Oldham Chronicle,* December 27, 1919; details of other deals are given in the *Economist,* October 25, 1919.

65 *Oldham Chronicle,* December 27, 1919. Mellor had been involved in fifteen reconstructions by the end of 1919 alone.

66 By the close of 1920 the Amalgamated Cotton Mill Trust Ltd. had total assets of £8.9 million, of which £6.9 million represented cotton mills; this was at "cost" and in later years there was considerable reluctance to write this figure down in line with the depression in value of mill property.

67 Bank overdrafts were particularly important during and after the boom. By January 1921, 129 companies had over £5 million of bank overdrafts; See Daniels and Jewkes, op. cit., pp. 176-7.

68 *Oldham Chronicle,* December 27, 1919. It was alleged that most of the premium money went towards promotion expenses, especially gifts to old directors.

69 *Oldham Chronicle,* August 16, October 11, 1919.

70 *Oldham Chronicle,* March 8, June 28, 1919; weekly market reports of John Bunting.

71 *Oldham Chronicle,* June 9, 1920.

72 *Economist,* June 19, 1920, p. 1337. The Oldham and District Share Exchange, the rival market, continued to issue a list.

73 Thirteen members resided in Oldham, three in Manchester, and the rest in surrounding towns.

74 Members of the Association were allowed at the time to conduct share auctions. S. F. Mellor was particularly active in this sphere; Oldham

Stock Exchange, Minutes, December 11, 1919.

75 *Oldham Chronicle,* December 27, 1919, January 17, 1920.

76 Oldham Stock Exchange, Minutes, December 18, 1925.

77 Robson, op. cit., p. 2.

78 Daniels and Jewkes, op. cit., p. 177.

79 Cotton Spinning and other Companies; Summarized Accounts. Bank overdrafts were usually secured with debentures; the largest individual bank debt was that of the Howe Bridge Mill with £428,000 in 1927. The general state of the mills in this regard at August 1927 was that 194 recapitalized mills showed a loan debt of 16s. per spindle, and over 14s. per spindle to the banks, each of these being greater than the share capital per spindle before the days of recapitalization; "Cotton Mill Finance", *Economist,* August 27, 1927, pp. 350-51.

80 Daniels and Jewkes, op. cit., p. 179.

81 Oldham Master Cotton Spinners' Association Ltd., Centenary History 1866-1966, p. 26.

82 *Economist,* May 14, 1927, p. 1017; Cotton Spinning and other Companies, Summarized Accounts.

83 Oldham Stock Exchange, Rule Book 1936, Rule 108; Minutes, July 18, 1933. Some of the mills declined to register shares at a discount; Minutes, June 3, 1932.

84 Oldham Stock Exchange, Minutes, February 4, June 30, 1930.

85 *Economist,* April 20, 1929, p. 846. See also R. F. Harrod, *The Life of John Maynard Keynes* (1951), pp. 379-386.

86 *Economist,* February 23, 1929, p. 392.

87 Robson, op. cit., p. 158.

88 Local banking interests, particularly Manchester banks, had been strong supporters of the Corporation, and were very critical of the reluctance of some national banking institutions to give immediate support to the project; *Economist,* December 29, 1928, p. 1210.

89 Robson, op. cit., p. 159. The capital was divided into £2.8 million of ordinary and £4.6 million of fixed interest. Again no dividend had been paid by 1939; bank and other debt was £4.8 million.

90 *O.C.M.S.A. Ltd.,* Centenary History, op. cit., p. 39. The area covered by the Association's statistics include Oldham, Chadderton, Failsworth, Lees, Middleton, Royton and Shaw. The reduction was concentrated largely in the 'mule' spinning section in the industry. The Cotton Spinning Board was empowered to impose a levy on the industry to assist in financing its operations; by 1939 it had acquired just under 2.0 million spindles, ibid, p. 27.

91 Oldham Stock Exchange, Minutes, May 11, December 18, 1925.

92 Ibid, May 10, 1926.

93 Ibid., December 18, 1925. In 1931 the surety requirement was changed to a £300 security held by the committee for one year.

94 By the mid-thirties an increasing amount of the dealing seems to have gone over to the telephone.

95 Council of Associated Stock Exchanges, Minutes, October 14, 1932.

96 Oldham Stock Exchange, Minutes, May 10, 1926. The Manchester call over was brought to an undistinguished end when a bomb fell on the Douglas Hotel in December 1940.

97 Ibid., March 5, 1941.

98 Robson, op. cit., p. 161.

99 Ibid., p. 219.

8 Gilt Edged, Local Authority, and Foreign Stocks

Despite the rapid increase in the volume of railway securities during the two railway manias Consols remained the largest and certainly the most homogeneous block of securities on the market. In 1853 the total of gilt edged quoted on the London Stock Exchange amounted to just over £850 million (nominal value), which represented about three quarters of the total of quoted securities. Of this total £370 million was in 3% Consols, £116 million in 3% Reduced, and £217 million in New 3%.[1] Even when other sectors of the market outgrew Consols during the second half of the nineteenth century, with over £3,700 million of overseas securities in existence, and although gilt edged came to represent only 5% of the total of all securities outstanding, they still retained the position of being the largest market in a single security and certainly the best market on the London Stock Exchange.

One reason for the liquidity of the Consols market was that it had more jobbers than any other sector of the Stock Exchange, and not only that, but they had command over very large financial resources with which they were prepared to take positions in large lines of stock. In addition, the market was patronized by numerous and well endowed speculators. Jobbers could therefore operate on a narrow turn, the narrowest on the Stock Exchange, and the market was superior to any other with respect to marketability and stability, while brokers' commission on gilt edged was only $\frac{1}{8}$%.

Consols of course were held by a very large number of investors, by no means all large. In 1830 it was estimated that some 250,000 holdings received under £100 in half yearly dividends. This meant an average holding of about £6,000 nominal value, although most of the holdings were probably very much less than this.[2] By the end of the century the amount of gilt edged in private hands had fallen, partly because investors had turned to more remunerative investments. On the other hand there was an increase in institutional holdings, notably by insurance companies and banks. As a result of the rapid accumulation of funds in the first half of the century insurance companies by the 1850s held large sums in gilt edged, although they later diversified into other trustee stocks. The banks held gilt edged as part of their investment portfolios. Indeed Consols were widely regarded as the most suitable security for this purpose given that banks were open to the possibility of a run on their deposits. George Rae in his book *The Country Banker* advised the manager of a country bank not to place his reserves in any other security, because

> "Consols stand unrivalled and alone in the supreme quality of convertibility. They are the one security which you can, with absolute certainty, turn into cash at any hour of any business day, even in the worst throes of panic. You cannot rest assured of this in respect of any other description of securities – not even of the British Government itself. Your Consols are virtually so many Bank of England notes in a latent form, but with this advantage – that they yield you three per cent whilst practically forming a portion of your till money".[3]

Up until the First World War Consols could be dealt in for monthly settlements or for cash. Most nineteenth century dealings were conducted for the account, while speculation within the account undoubtedly exercised a stabilizing influence on prices. Even professional bankers used the facility to borrow cash by selling for cash and buying for the account, or alternatively they lent cash by buying and selling for the account.[4] The Bank of England also operated in the Consol market within the account. As the government broker told the *Royal Commission on the London Stock Exchange* in 1878, "you may call it a speculative transaction . . . it is, as far as I am concerned, merely borrowing money upon security".[5]

The Consol market was the only one where it was possible to execute quickly large bargains for cash. The procedure for this was quite simple. The buying broker made out a ticket stating the amount of stock, the price and the name of the person to whom it was to be transferred. The ticket was then handed to the dealer who lodged it at the Bank of England before one o'clock. The transfer was then made, and upon receiving a copy of the transfer by 3 o'clock the buyer handed over the cash. The stock was transferred by attendance of the seller or by his attorney at the Bank of England to sign the transfer form made out in the bank ledgers. As can be appreciated this procedure placed the provincial investor at some disadvantage and throughout the second half of the nineteenth century the provincial stock exchanges directed considerable efforts towards removing obstacles to free dealings in Consols in the provinces.

Provincial dealings in Consols in the middle of the nineteenth century were very limited indeed. The official lists of the exchanges did not contain any quotations for Consols, although several gave the London price. Even if there was no local market, Consols were widely held throughout the country and orders which were put through local brokers were passed on to London agents; according to Richard Withers "We have very little dealing in Consols. If we get orders in Consols we send to London because we have not dealers enough in Liverpool to make a close price in Consols". Also a considerable amount of provincial business in Consols was transacted through the agency of the banks.[6] It is conceivable that some business was done in Birmingham since in 1846 the Committee ruled that the sureties of members would also cover losses sustained while dealing in Consols.[7] Also in Bristol, a stronghold of trustee investment, the Committee indicated that account periods in Consols would be the same as London and that at the option of the seller bargains could be made for delivery either in Bristol or London.[8] Basically, however, provincial markets were channels for putting business through London. The provinces certainly had no dealers in Consols; an examination of the transfer books for 3% Consols for the period 1851–60 did not reveal any country jobber and the holdings that provincial brokers had were obviously trustee accounts and certainly not jobbing accounts.[9]

The first attempts to obtain additional facilities for Consol dealing were made in 1855. The timing may have been significant in that it was during the Crimean War and the Manchester Committee, and later that of Liverpool, may have wished to capitalize on the emergency to increase the effectiveness of their appeals for improved facilities for the transfer of Consols. Certainly the Chancellor of the Exchequer, Sir George Cornwall Lewis, favoured loans as opposed to additional taxation to meet increased expenditures so that requests to widen the market in gilt edged might have appealed to him.[10] Manchester's first approach to the matter took the form of an attempt in April 1855, to get more frequent reports of the price of Consols in London, and accordingly they set up a small sub-committee to confer with the English and Irish Magnetic Telegraph Company to see on what terms they "would be willing to furnish . . . throughout the day . . . half hourly or hourly Quotations of Consols on the London Market".[11] It was hoped that such a continuous price service might induce some shunting activity. In the event the telegraph company refused the request stating that it could not occupy the wires at stated times, but would furnish some additional prices gratis. Not having had much success in getting good London price facilities the Manchester Committee turned to explore another avenue. This was to secure "increased facilities in the mode of transfer of Consols in the provinces". Such a measure would bring additional business to provincial markets and also enhance the value of Government obligations. To expedite progress in the campaign it was decided to enlist the support of the Liverpool Committee and as a result each market set up a small sub-committee, led by Richard Withers in Liverpool and C. Grindod in Manchester, to discuss the most effective procedures.

The sub-committees undertook a considerable amount of work and enlisted the support of local members of parliament (Mr Bright of Manchester submitted a memorandum to the Treasury on the subject), local chambers of commerce, and numerous other professional bodies. Letters were also sent to Leeds and Birmingham requesting support in the campaign. In addition, evidence was obtained of practices abroad, particularly the successful use of provincial transfers of French Rentes.[12] By the New Year sufficient ground work had been done to justify a request to the Chancellor to meet a joint deputation from Manchester and Liverpool to discuss a memorandum which they had submitted to the Treasury. Unfortunately the memorandum has not survived and neither have the objections raised by the Bank of England to the proposed scheme of Consol dealing.[13] The general tenor of the memorandum can probably be seen in the following extracts from a separate one sent to the Chancellor by the Birmingham Stock Exchange who took up the campaign with great enthusiasm;

". . . your Memorialists have often had occasion to take notice of the fact that the right to transfer Government Stocks and receive dividends in Great Britain is attached exclusively to the City of London, and having attentively considered the subject, are humbly of opinion that this privilege is capable of being extended (under Limits) to the Provinces without injury of any kind, and with great public and private advantage.
. . . if the transfer of government stocks with the receipts of dividends could be affected in Birmingham, an extent of local negotiation for the sale and purchase of the same securities would certainly follow.
. . . it would be for the interest and convenience of the town of Birmingham and the wealthy district of which it is the centre if money could be here invested in English Funds without the expense of journeys to the capital or the risk and expenses of multiplied agencies.

. . . the limits of fraud would probably be narrowed by the more frequent personal identification of the Country Stockholder; also by giving him more perfect control over his own property, and by doing away with long outstanding powers of sale".

The Birmingham Committee requested the Chancellor to consider and to implement a scheme for transferring stock and paying dividends in all towns where there was a branch of the Bank of England; there was no reason why they should be at a disadvantage compared with their "London brethren".[14]

Despite influential support nothing came of these provincial requests. The nature of the Bank of England's opposition to the scheme is not known in detail but presumably it was associated with the convenience of the inscribed system and the disadvantages and additional cost of operating a double register. There was of course a precedent in that there was a separate office in Dublin for the transfer of Consols. London jobbers opposed the provincial moves for obvious reasons, and ardent opposition also came from the London banking interest. They opposed any scheme involving a double register because it would entail considerable risk of fraud. More important was the fact that "by the present system the whole of the Consols go through their hands and therefore the bankers of London are the bankers as regards Consols for the country".[15]

The appointment of a new Chancellor of the Exchequer in 1860 brought renewed hopes to Liverpool and Manchester that a fresh approach might succeed. But a new Chancellor in the middle of preparing his Budget was not likely to be very interested in the needs of the provinces. A shaft of light suddenly appeared in 1861 when Mr Gladstone announced that he was to grant the payment of Government dividends through the branches of the Bank of England. However, the pressure of other business, and the fact that the Chancellor was too busy, led to the postponement of further approaches on the subject of provincial transfers.[16] In 1869, Manchester attempted to stimulate interest among all exchanges where there was a branch of the Bank of England but this move came to the same end and for the same reasons as the previous one.[17] Apart from the statement by Richard Withers to the 1878 Royal Commission "that the country markets are very desirous that wherever there is a market, and a branch of the Bank of England, there should be a means of dealing in Consols in those markets with a transfer department branch of the Bank of England in that town to grant a title and registration", little is heard of provincial transfers until it is taken up by the Council of Associated Stock Exchanges at the end of the century.[18] The coming of limited liability and of foreign loans no doubt diverted investors interests, and the enthusiasm of the stock exchanges.

Beginning in 1904 the persistent effort of the provinces brought eventual change in the Finance Act of 1911, but it was another decade before the provisions of the act were to have any appreciable practicable effect. Compared with previous attempts the provinces operated through the agency of the Council of Associated Stock Exchanges, which gave their efforts more cohesion and certainly greater weight in discussions with the authorities. The interested groups within the Council were drawn from the main centres, notably Liverpool, Manchester, Birmingham, and the Scottish exchanges, while the smaller markets exhibited little enthusiasm in this attempt to widen the scope of provincial investment opportunities.

The early approaches by the Council and the response from official quarters were both marked by a certain degree of uncertainty. The Council in 1904 could not make up its mind whether to ask for greater facilities by way of the adoption of a registered system of transfer as used by public companies generally, or to ask the Bank of England to provide registers where there was a branch of the Bank of England. Eventually it was decided to ask the Bank for the latter facility. The Bank responded by inviting the President of the Council, then Sir George White of Bristol, to attend an interview with a senior Bank official who pointed out that by statute the registers had to be kept in London.[19] The Bank, however, indicated the possibility that transfers could perhaps be made in the same way as for some local authority issues, whereby after giving notice at the local branch of the Bank of England and allowing two or three days to expire the stock could be transferred. Such facilities would not, however, be as rapid as those available in London. While the Bank sympathized with provincial requests they were reluctant to initiate any major changes and shifted the responsibility onto the Treasury who they felt should make the necessary moves towards change.

Provincial dissatisfaction with the system of transfer, with the transfer books located at the Bank of England, sprang from many sources. There was the long standing irritation about powers of attorney. Under the system of registration of Government stock by inscription, transfers of stock had to be effected in the books of the Bank of England by the seller personally, or by his attorney appointed for the purpose. This latter requirement was irksome for provincial holders, a deterrent to prospective holders (it was stated that country investors found it "comparatively difficult to execute correctly a power of attorney"), it involved additional expense in the form of a 10s. stamp duty, and it involved risks in delegating authority to unknown parties. Not only did the Bank require power of attorney but they also wanted twenty-four hours to verify it.[20] Also it was held that provincial investors had to fight to get powers of attorney in the name of a provincial broker since officials of the Bank seemed to feel that it should only be given to one of their own staff, or a member of the London Stock Exchange.[21] Another dissatisfaction arose from the fact that the Bank did not issue a certificate as evidence of continued ownershp, and if verification was needed it was necessary to apply to the Bank, but the verification was only applicable to the date specified. This defect of course applied to London holders, but the precedure gave rise to much greater inconvenience in the case of country investors. An additional annoyance was that it was "practically impossible owing to the arrangement for transferring stock, to do business in Consols without employing a London broker, who, of course, has to be paid. The result is that except in the case of large orders the business is not worth doing, and brokers discourage their clients from investing in Consols".[22] Thus the absence of adequate provincial facilities for Consols had diverted a large volume of small savings into local authority temporary deposits "which in the opinion of the Council is fraught with much danger to the whole community".[23]

In accordance with the Bank of England's view that action should more suitably come from the Treasury, the Council directed their appeals to the Chancellor of the Exchequer. The approaches made in 1905 and 1906, however, met with little positive response. While sympathizing with provincial grievances the Treasury stated that the proposed changes would require special legislation, a point on which the Bank did not altogether concur, and that it would not act until "more evidence as to the practical inconvenience of the present system" from the public had been submitted.[24] In accordance with this request the Council in 1907 sent specific instances of frauds associated with the existing arrangements to the Treasury. The Treasury also confessed that "the abolition of a stamped power of attorney would be at the expense of the Revenue".[25] The rather negative response from the authorities convinced Edward Rae that it would all take a long time, and that they had to deal with influential parties, the Bank, Treasury, and the London jobbers, who were in very close contact with each other. The problem was simply that inscription suited London market needs, while deed transfer suited those of the provinces. It was accordingly decided that they would probably obtain greater success by concentrating on getting the Government to adopt "the method of issue of certificates common to public companies generally". What was wanted was not a general change, on which they had got nowhere, but rather a supplement to the existing system and thereafter they concentrated their claims on this, justifiably thinking that it had greater prospects of acceptance.

Although by the time of the annual meeting of the Council in October, 1907, the drive for improved facilities for Consol transfers had become a hardy annual, the President for that year was reluctant to make further approaches to the Treasury. However, when Asquith became Chancellor of the Exchequer in 1908 he consented to meet a deputation on the subject provided it included outside interests as well as stock exchange representatives, but before they got anywhere with this attempt to illustrate the public demand for such facilities, Lloyd George replaced Asquith, and it was decided that they would get little response from official circles during the lifetime of that administration.[26] Three more years elapsed with little in the form of results, but in 1911 the continued activity of the Council – aided by a good deal of press comment, parliamentary questions, and even a nudge from the City Notes of *The Economic Journal* – brought forth proposals in the Finance Act of that year to bring in registered stock transfers. The authorities might also have been swayed by the widely used argument that every chance should be taken to extend the market for Consols particularly in view of the fall in their price from 98 in 1903 to 82 in 1911, a decline not altogether explained by interest rate policy.[27] The Council was satisfied that the principle for which they fought had at last been recognized in official quarters. The act received the Royal Assent in December and in March 1912, the Bank of England put out the appropriate regulations.

The relevant clause from the Finance Bill read as follows:

"Notwithstanding anything in Section 22 of the National Debt Act, 1870, any stock belonging to a stockholder shall, if registered for the time being as stock transferable by deed in manner provided by regulations under this section, be transferable by deed instead of the manner provided by that section".

"...the Treasury shall provide by regulations for a separate stock register being kept for stock which is for the time being transferable by deed, for the conditions upon which stock is to be entered in or removed from that register, for the mode in which the transfer by deed is to be carried out, and for the payment of any fees in respect of the entry or removal of stock from the register and the carrying out of any transfer of stock by deed".[28]

The new procedure meant that a seller of Government stock registered as transferable by deed merely signed the common form of transfer in favour of the buyer, and this transfer, accompanied by the certificate of ownership issued by the Bank of England, was delivered to the buyer who deposited it at the Bank for registration.

These provisions remained "practically a dead letter" for many years. This was because of the regulations drawn up by the Bank and the Treasury, and the hostile attitude taken by certain London financial interests. Dissatisfaction with the regulations and the interpretation put on them by Bank officials soon became evident in the provinces. The Bank of England would not recognize the signature of a holder of stock upon a transfer deed, and would not allow the transfer of deed stock to take place until a confirmatory reply was received from an inquiry sent to the transferer, or until the lapse of ten days, whichever was the sooner, an action interpreted by the provinces as "obstructive". Even when every possible speed was taken it normally took several days after the transfer deed had been completed and lodged at the Bank before the seller could obtain payment. During this interval the seller not only suffered loss of interest but he also parted with his security absolutely. The Council attempted to enlist the support of the London Committee with a view to getting the ten day period reduced to three, a reduction of administrative delays, and also of charges, but the Committee were not inclined to intervene, although a few London jobbers protested to the Bank about the length of time required for transfers, but got nowhere.[29] The Council then went ahead with a direct approach to the Treasury but the only response they got was a statement that the charges seemed reasonable compared with those of commercial companies. This negative official attitude made Edward Rae extremely despondent about the whole project, and he was convinced that the Bank and the Treasury, along with the Stock Exchange were against any development of Consol business in the provinces. Indeed *The Economist* reported that "some Stock Exchange members sniff at the idea of the small investor buying Consols at all".[30] Accordingly, the Council allowed the matter to rest for two years.

One important consequence of the time element laid down by the regulations was that London jobbers would not pay for deed stock on delivery but insisted that settlement would only take place when registration in the transferees name had been completed. In the case of inscribed stock jobbers paid for stock immediately on delivery because they were in a position to re-sell or borrow on it from the banks. With deed stock, however, given the regulations, the commercial banks would not take a transfer as a satisfactory "floater" (collateral for a loan) and jobbers were thus unable to get finance to pay cash against transfers of such stock. Consequently London jobbers regarded it as an "act of grace" to accept registered stock, while the London rules relating to the delivery of gilt edged were based on the assumption that all dealings were in inscribed form. The Council pressed London to amend its rules so that a buyer would pay for stock on delivery of a transfer and the relative stock certificate, or of a certified transfer. The buyer would then not be able to make the seller wait ten days for his cash.

In 1915 there were "no dealings on the London Stock Exchange in Government securities in Registered Stock", but even when there were some in normal times "the market is not identical, either as to price, closeness of price or freedom of markets with that for the Inscribed securities owing to the attitude taken up by the Dealers on the London Stock Exchange. A seller had to wait ten days before he can demand payment for the stock sold, and as a consequence of this the Dealers add to or deduct something from the prices of Government securities in the Registered form as compared with the prices of Inscribed securities, the amount of such addition or subtraction being based upon the market value of money for the time being".[31] The Bank of England itself did not exactly encourage the use of registered stock since the Government broker would not accept delivery of stock or bonds registered transferable by deed when making Sinking Fund or other purchases for the Treasury but insisted on bearer or inscribed stock.[32]

Continued dissatisfaction with the lack of a free market in registered stock, and the knowledge that the number of holders were increasing, led the Council in 1916 to request a further meeting with Treasury and Bank Officials. At the end of the year a deputation from the Council met the Financial Secretary to the Treasury, Lord Cunliffe and Sir John Bradbury. The high powered reception would seem to indicate some official anxiety about the need to widen the market for Government securities and that they now took the Councils proposals a little more seriously. The meeting brought several important concessions for provincial holders of gilt edged. The authorities promised to improve the arrangements for the publication and distribution of new issue prospectuses which in the past had left the provinces at a considerable disadvantage. The Bank of England promised to abolish some of its fees regarding registered stock and the Treasury promised the abolition of the 10s. stamp duty on powers of attorney for the transfer of inscribed stock. Although these were important concessions the delegation did not really get what it wanted, "that the Bank of England as registrar should act in every way similar to other Registrars of Companies" and not insist on the existing procedure whereby they refused to recognize a buyer until the actual formality of registration and the issue of a new certificate in the buyers' name was complete. With this time delay it was impossible for a free market to develop in registered stock.[33] A request that the Bank of England should issue a transfer receipt pending the preparation of a new certificate which would speed up delivery was rejected by the Treasury since it was regarded as creating a document of "indeterminate value". However in 1917 the Bank did introduce a modification in that they would recognize a purchaser of stock and the transfer would be registered forthwith, if the stockholder when notified by the Bank that a transfer deed had been lodged then signified approval. It was understood, but probably only by the Bank, that in such instances that London jobbers would pay for stock immediately. The Council had grave doubts as to the effectiveness of these changes but they were prepared to try them out and indeed by the end of 1918 they were of the view that they had been of some benefit.[34] London jobbers, however, remained adamant about dealings in registered stock and continued to suspend payment pending the issue of a new certificate by the Bank of England.

The reluctance of the authorities in meeting provincial requests is a little difficult to fathom. They did not seem to attach much weight to the claims of the Council that additional facilities for registered stock would help sales of Government stock, which in the early years of the war represented the main borrowing medium. The first War Loan issue was made in 1914 amounting to £350 million, followed in 1915 by a $4\frac{1}{2}$% loan which raised £900 million, and the Third War Loan followed in 1916 which amounted to £2,075 million at 5% and £52 million at 4%.[35] Various attractive conversion rights were attached to these loans, and attempts were also made to attract small investors by selling stock through the Post Office in small denominations. Presumably the authorities felt that this would take care of provincial needs. After 1916 they resorted to other forms of financing and naturally they were not thereafter particularly concerned with the attractions of registered stock. While nothing was done to reduce the ten day delay period they did at least issue the 1915 War Loan in inscribed and registered form, but imposed a charge of 2/6d. on allotees who wished to have their scrip placed directly on the transfer by deed register, to the considerable annoyance of the provinces.[36] Despite the charge many investors took advantage of this facility and it was reported in 1918 that registered holdings had greatly increased in number. By 1920 the number of transfers were rising and ran to between 1,200 to 1,400 per day.[37] The authorities, however, used such figures to justify continuation of the ten day delay on the grounds of the increasing volume of work involved.

The market in the newly created registered stock was concentrated in the provinces, in particular in the larger markets. As early as 1915 a Glasgow shunter was reported to be making close prices in registered stock. By 1917 an Edinburgh firm, Watson, Forrest & Watt, were jobbing in the 5% War Loan and promised that in the case of registered stock they would pay cash at once against transfer with the certificate attached. This was a particularly difficult role to play since provincial jobbing in gilt edged was at a distinct disadvantage compared with London counterparts. If a provincial jobber was left short or long of stock he had few fellow jobbers to square with, and could not count on the constant flow of brokers' orders as in London. To compensate for the additinal risks involved in running a jobbing account in registered stock the Edinburgh firm took a small additional commission of $\frac{1}{16}$%.[38] South of the border the gilt edged scene was dominated by the Liverpool firm, Wall & Lloyd, and their failure in 1921 came at a particularly unfortunate moment as far as developing provincial gilt edged dealing was concerned. There were also a few other markets where members were prepared to deal in 5% War Loan at around $\frac{3}{16}$ to $\frac{1}{4}$ prices with payment on delivery. This was the case in Manchester and Bristol. In half a dozen other markets a fair amount of business was done between members but there were no dealers making regular close prices. The larger markets in fact listed registered stock on a separate line in their lists.[39]

Wall & Lloyd of Liverpool had been active in Consol dealings since the turn of the century. As early as 1905 W. G. Wall had put forward a scheme for local adoption. This involved changes in the rules which would make "an order on the Bank of England (or other bank satisfactory to the buyer) against payment a good delivery for Consols or other inscribed stocks, which are transferable only in London at the present time". The Bank of England apparently approved the scheme but the Liverpool Committee while agreeing that it might facilitate dealings between markets did not see any prospect of large scale dealings in Consols between London and the provinces. The Liverpool Committee thought that they should await the results of approaches being made by the Council to the Treasury, a suggestion which W. G. Wall did not readily approve of; neither body moved fast enough for this industrious and eccentric broker.[40]

With the large issues of War Loan stock Wall & Lloyd had greater scope for their gilt edged operations. In registered War Loan he was prepared to make prices at any time in moderate amounts, with bargains for cash against transfer. In large amounts special arrangements could be made. He was also prepared to do business in inscribed stock and to obtain powers of attorney when required, paying for stock the day after such power had been transferred in London. Wall maintained that his prices compared favourably with the net prices at which business could be done in London, and if brokers were prepared to give him all their War Loan business he was prepared to guarantee that in no individual case would prices be worse than in London.[41] In 1918 he used a scheme for getting small lots of inscribed stock transferred through the local branch of the Bank of England without the aid of a London broker, and he did this by using the stock receipt issued by the local branch. The Bank of England and the Liverpool Committee, however, were reluctant to commend this system as a regular means of dealing in inscribed stock. His ingenuity and expertise were lost to the market in 1920 when he was suspended and later declared a defaulter. This arose following his taking in some £30,000 of 5% War Loan financed by loans, mainly from the Union Bank of Manchester and Parr's Bank, and a quick fall in the price of War Loan meant that the additional cover required for the loan was beyond his resources.[42]

Despite early provincial hopes very little progress had been achieved. The position of the Bank of England was clearly set out during an interview between Council representatives and the Chief Accountant, who indicated that they remained adamant on the vital point which caused delays, that nothing would satisfy the Bank that there was no fraud except a communication from the transferer in reply to the Bank's letter of advice. Again, it was emphasized that the specified period was necessary because of the increased use of registered stock. The President also made a further attempt to enlist the aid of some London jobbers but they merely pointed to the obstacles involved in dealing in registered stock. The banks would not accept them as "floaters", the Government broker would not take them, and they would not take them without absolute title.[43] It was apparent that very little change had occurred in London attitudes during the previous ten years, and W. G. Wall might have been near the mark when he told the Liverpool Committee in 1916, "we hear that the London jobbers have combined not to pay for Registered Stock".

It was decided that the remedy was to deal in the provinces and by 1921 a very large amount of business was being done, to such an extent that London dealers were getting concerned at the development. It was of course unfortunate that Wall & Lloyd left the scene at the time, which probably caused a set back to the growth of business. It did not, however, greatly dent provincial hopes. When, in October 1922, the Chief Accountant of the Bank of

N

England announced that they were considering a scheme to reduce the transfer delay to a maximum of four days, the Council stated that the matter no longer retained the same degree of urgency. "One reason is the very large market which we have now in the provinces for deed stock with cash payment against delivery. The second is that the London brokers are now agreeable to deal in this deed stock and pay cash against delivery and transfer. They have been forced into that position solely . . . on account of the very large market which has now been created in the provinces".[44] The attitude of London jobbers was however rather changeable on this score and during the inter-war years, in the face of unchanged transfer regulations, they tended occasionally to insist on the ten days before paying.[45]

Inscription finally disappeared in 1943 when the new Government Stock Regulations amalgamated the inscribed register with the deed register. Thereafter there was only one category, namely, stock transferable by instrument in writing in any usual or common form, and the issue of certificates to all holders of Government stock. Inscription had for long been recognized as a cumbersome and wasteful process and the removal of the relevant department of the Bank of England to the country during wartime rendered it totally impracticable.[46]

The complaints of the provinces were not confined to difficulties associated with transfers of existing stocks. After almost every major issue of Government and Commonwealth stocks, a stream of complaints descended on the Bank of England from individual exchanges and from the Council of Associated Stock Exchanges. They centred on the unsatisfactory facilities available for provincial applications for new issues. On many occasions provincial brokers lodged applications at the local branch of the Bank of England only to find them returned with a note that the list had been closed. Apparently branches were only empowered to act as forwarding agents and not as bankers, which had not been made abundantly clear beforehand. By the time the applications reached London the list had closed, which provided another cause for complaint. From the standpoint of the provincial applicant the lists were open for too short a period, particularly when as happened with the Local Loans Stock issue of 1922, the Bank issued the prospectus on a Sunday! The time allowed was often insufficient to permit the provincial broker to wire his London agent who would then put in an application on his behalf. Brokers and investors were understandably annoyed if the stock later went to a premium. The Bank argued, however, that they could only hold the list open for a short time because they wanted to minimize the amount of money held from applications, some of which had to be returned, and further, that the issues were for fixed sums and not unlimited issues. Following repeated and pressing requests for an improvement in the situation the Bank of England in 1922 promised not to let such oversights occur, but on occasions it has strayed somewhat from its promises.[47]

The departure of Wall & Lloyd from the provincial gilt edged market was particularly unfortunate, but it was not the end of provincial dealings. Another Liverpool firm, Hardie B. Martin & Co., took over the business and ran a jobbing account in gilt edged. To assist them they took on the market dealer employed by Wall & Lloyd. Their business during the inter-war years was mainly in 5% War Loan, together with occasional transactions in War Bonds. They drew their orders from all over the country, but very little of it was institutional business; by this time most of the investment departments of the larger local financial institutions had moved to London. They were prepared to deal freely in amounts up to £10,000 of War Loan, and over this sum they were prepared to negotiate a price, or put it through their London correspondent. There were no other provincial jobbing accounts in the twenties, although there were gilt edged shunters in Birmingham, Manchester and Glasgow. During the thirties another Liverpool firm ventured into gilt edged but with little success. Hardie B. Martin & Co. ceased trading just after the beginning of the Second World War. The existence of jobbers and shunters along with the network of telecommunications developed in the inter-war years meant that the price differences which previously existed tended to disappear with the result that the average provincial investor suffered no disadvantage from being at some remove from the centre.[48]

Since the last war the Liverpool firm of Rensburg and Company have become the most important gilt edged jobbers outside the London market. Prior to nationalization they were mainly interested in the home rail market, but with the issue of gilt edged as compensation stock they moved over to that market. They maintain very close links with London through the usual broker channels, and they are recognized by London as outside jobbers able to make net prices. The Bank of England also assist their operations by providing local facilities for certifying stock thereby reducing time delays, an important factor in a cash market. They deal in a wide range of stocks and provide provincial investors with an alternative market to London, who with the preponderance of large institutional business tends to shade prices against smaller deals.

Although corporation loans were basically centred on London they also featured prominently in the lists of the leading provincial exchanges, particularly from 1880 onwards. The real beginnings of local authority borrowing date from the first issue of Metropolitan Board of Works 3½% stock in 1869 which amounted to £2.6 million. Early issues by provincial authorities were not, however, so large and were generally associated with their taking over gas and water undertakings. For this purpose many local authorities obtained parliamentary acts, for example, in 1875 Birmingham issued perpetual annuities under such powers in exchange for the capital of the Birmingham and Staffordshire Gas Light Co., while in 1870 Leeds issued Gas Companies Stock to acquire the Leeds New Gas Co., and the Leeds Gas Light Co.[49] As early as 1850 Liverpool issued bonds under the authority of various local improvement acts, and by 1856 some £2.4 million was outstanding; the bonds were of ten years maturity and were quoted on the Liverpool Stock Exchange for a number of years.

With the rapid growth of municipal expenditure on capital projects local authorities followed each other to the market in search of funds. Manchester between 1872 and 1882 raised £3.7 million at 4%. Leeds followed in 1877, and in 1880 so did Birmingham, Liverpool, Nottingham and Lancaster. With the inclusion in 1882 of "model stock clauses", which authorized the creation of local stocks, in local acts, many corporations quickly took advantage of such general provisions. By 1884 the amount of corporation stock outstanding had reached over £50 million, compared with only £5 million in 1873. From a market standpoint stock issues after 1880 were certainly larger and therefore made for wider markets, while the passing of the Trustee Investment Act of 1889 brought certain corporation stocks within the scope of trustee managers. By 1913 there was about £190 million of corporation stocks outstanding.

The local stock exchanges took a keen interest in the financial plans and activities of their respective corporations. When Birmingham decided in 1876 to make an issue of stock to consolidate its loan position, the Committee of the Birmingham Stock Exchange was very quick to protest at certain features of the proposed scheme. The corporation asked the Bank of England to introduce and manage an issue of £1.5 million of 3½% stock. On hearing of this the Committee sent a forceful memorial to the corporation finance committee urging that such functions should be allocated locally. They objected to the use of transfer by inscription at the Bank, which involved personal attendance or granting powers of attorney, and urged transfer by deed on the common form. Further, that it would "place all new issues of stock . . . in the first instance in the hands of London men . . . [and] . . . discourage the subsequent distribution of the stock among small capitalists of the country, including of course the small capitalists of our town". The memorial went on to elaborate on the "evils immediately attendant upon the separation of a Debt from the community indebted" which involved loss of local prestige and the loss to the community "of all that money which goes away into the pockets of the Managers of the Debt [which was £2,000 per annum in 1881 when the loan eventually appeared] and into those of the London Stockbrokers and other middlemen who must be employed whenever any business connected with the stock takes place . . . [and] . . . to restrict business in all financial centres but London".[50] In response to this plea the corporation promised that the transfer books would be kept at Birmingham. However, the terms of the issue were not very attractive and when the tenders were opened it was found that only about a fifth of the issue had been applied for, and no allotment was made. The proposed loan was hastily dropped with the corporation borrowing heavily from the Bank of England.[51] Eventually an issue of £2.0 million at $3\frac{1}{2}\%$ was made in January 1881, which was taken up within a month notwithstanding the unfavourable state of the money market.[52] Unfortunately, the corporation had forgotten their earlier promises on local transfer facilities and the Bank of England were appointed agents for the issue.

In the case of the early stock issues the work of issuing and registration was usually carried out by the Bank of England. By the eighteen nineties many corporations took on the work themselves, much to the approval of local brokers, while the joint stock banks also took on registration to the detriment of the Bank of England. Liverpool Corporation used the Bank of England as agents for the 1880 issue, but handled subsequent issues themselves, the 1894 one being transferable by inscription. In fact this caused some concern among London jobbers because of the absence of transfer facilities in London.[53] By contrast, Manchester brokers in 1892 were complaining to the corporation about the concentration of transfer facilities in London, and the necessity to use a London broker.[54] Later, where local authorities did the registering of their own stock they used the more suitable method of issuing registered certificates, while they provided London jobbers with facilities by way of separate ledgers for keeping a running account for which no certificates were issued.[55]

Several methods of issue were used for local authority stocks. Up to about 1900 the usual method was to offer stock for public subscription by tender, and judging by the amounts applied for corporation stocks were well in demand. Issues of between one and two millions made by the larger corporations were usually tendered for twice over and they tended to go quickly to a market premium.

The Manchester issue of £1.0 million in 1875-76 soon reached 103 on the market, which helped in attracting applications from mortgage holders who wanted to convert their claim into a marketable stock.[56] Smaller issues of around half a million did not attract a large over-subscription despite the relatively attractive terms offered. The narrowness of the market particularly for large investors provides a partial explanation of the cool reception for smaller issues. The tenders were invited over and above a minimum official price and allotments were made at offered prices until the issue was fully taken up. The coupon rate for the majority of such issues was 3½%, well above the current yield on Consols.

The Liverpool Corporation issue of 1880 provides an example of the tender method in operation. The issue of £2.0 million of 3½% stock drew applications for £4,192,900 at prices ranging from £105 to £98%. Applications at £100 were allotted about 50% of the amount applied for, while tenders above £100 were allotted in full.[57] As is evident from the following list, London interests dominated the subscription; the Liverpool stake was comparatively small with individuals taking up only an eighth of the issue and two Liverpool banks taking £136,000. The bulk of the loan went to London investors with a good measure of institutional interest, banks and insu-

Allocations of Liverpool Corporation 3½% Irredeemable Stock.

			£	No.
Individuals	–	London	471,500	47
		Liverpool	253,300	20
		Other provincial	28,100	10
		Scotland	3,100	2
Banks	–	London	173,000	8
		Liverpool	136,800	2
		Other	20,000	1
London Insurance Offices			67,000	5
Members of the London Stock Exchange			322,700	72
Bank of England			518,200	4
Other			6,300	7
			2,000,000	176

rance offices being quite prominent. An interesting feature was that about a quarter of the loan seems to have been 'taken in' by the Bank of England, and on the evidence of the transfer books later transferred in blocks to the Government broker, H. A. Daniel, and disposed of through the market. Members of the London Stock Exchange took a substantial interest in the stock, possibly for stagging purposes, while twenty-four members operated jobbing accounts during the early years of the stocks life. The big jobbers in the stock were Francis Livermore, Algernon Henry Mackworth Praed, and Francis Ricardo, who ran the biggest jobbing book. No provincial broker ran any jobbing account in the stock.[58]

The tender system was replaced by a fixed price system at the turn of the century. For the delicate matter of deciding on the terms of an issue a corporation usually employed a leading London issuing house and broker. The former also took responsibility for underwriting the issue, and in this matter at least the provincial stock exchanges took an active part. In the case of a Bristol corporation issue in 1909 the main underwriting was done in London but a portion of the stock was set aside for underwriting by members of the Bristol Stock Exchange.[59] Similarly, in 1934, thirty-six Liverpool firms agreed to underwrite a quarter of a £4.0 million issue on a pro rata basis.[60] This practice continues on most exchanges to the present day.

Provincial brokers also participated in getting stock out to the public by receiving applications and recommending the stock to clients, for which they received a commission from the corporation. It was an established practice in the provinces, although apparently not on the London Stock Exchange, that in conversion operations the corporation would approach stockholders through the original broker. Manchester's violation of the tradition just before the first war led the Committee to strike local stocks from the list. The problem of conversion, however, did not arise for many of the issues made in the eighteen nineties since irredeemable stocks were regarded with favour by trustees and investors as offering permanent security at premium rates. With rising interest rates irredeemable stock fell into disfavour and corporations took to issuing only redeemable stock.

Although some limited markets were made in corporation stocks on some of the larger exchanges in the nineteen twenties, the market for them has always been firmly centred on London.[61] All the provincial exchanges included the relevant local stocks in their lists, but there were no brokers who operated jobbing accounts to provide a quotation. This perhaps seems something of an oddity in view of the essentially local nature of corporation activity, but the lack of turnover in a few local issues has been inadequate to make a jobbing account feasible on a single floor.

For the London Stock Exchange the period from 1850 to 1900 was dominated by a surge of activity in overseas investments, which more than made up for the contraction in the size of the gilt edged market and for the fact that large scale domestic company borrowing did not start until the eighteen nineties. In terms of nominal values, which overstates the position, the holdings of publicly issued overseas securities in 1913 amounted to over £3,700 million, of which 40% was in railways, 30% in loans to foreign governments, 10% to mines and plantations, and the rest divided between public utilities, banks, and financial institutions.[62] Provincial participation in this vast capital raising operation was relatively small compared to the scale of activity in London. The provinces, however, had played an important part in the financing of early United States railway construction, but it did not involve active participation by the stock exchanges. Much of the finance for the early railroads of the eighteen thirties was obtained from the state governments who raised the capital by the issue of bonds, and L. H. Jenks has estimated that about £170 million of them had been issued by 1838, most of which found their way to Britain. The usual procedure was for the bonds "to be had of the merchant-bankers by favored country banks for distribution to favored clients".[63] There was no public issue and the practice of placing them with firm holders was as detrimental to provincial broking business as it was to their London counterparts.

The first big boom in foreign investments occurred in the period 1860 to 1875 when over 150 governments loans were issued in London, involving a nominal capital of over £720 million, and which attracted from British investors £320 million in cash. In addition there was a further sum of £390 million for colonial governments and railways, and companies operating abroad.[64] This led to the growth of extensive markets in overseas securities on the London Stock Exchange, but very few of them found their way into the quotations of the leading provincial markets. The Liverpool lists for the period contain quotations for some half-dozen foreign government loans, mostly small issues by such countries as Mexico, Egypt, Brazil and Spain. The same was true of Manchester, as the Chairman stated to some London brokers in 1868, "dealings in this market were unimportant and the influence of the Manchester Committee in such matters was small".[65] This stemmed partly from the fact that provincial participation in the issue of foreign stocks was very small indeed. The agents were invariably London merchant banks, although it is interesting to note that the Manchester County Bank acted as agent for an issue in 1863 by North Carolina, but it only involved £300,000.[66] Heywood, Kennard, who dealt in many issues, had strong Liverpool connections, as indeed did Barings, but they do not appear to have used those outlets to channel foreign issues into the provinces.

Provincial markets enjoyed much closer contact with companies operating overseas in railway and mining activity. For example, the Leeds list for 1852 contained seventeen foreign mines, which was not far short of the number listed in London, while Sheffield had the same a year later. Between 1852 and 1860 several foreign companies sought and obtained a Liverpool quotation. Frequently such a request came from a local broker who was anxious to attract more business to the local market. The Liverpool brokers, Ashton and Todd, and the Manchester firm, Mewburn and Barker, acted as agents for a few foreign company issues. Where London refused to grant a quotation to a foreign company attempts were often made to obtain a provincial one, but provincial markets after corresponding with London regarding "the respectability of the schemes" also refused to grant a quotation. The best example of such an incident was London's refusal in 1864 to quote the Australian and Eastern Navigation Co. Ltd., and when Liverpool subsequently refused several proprietors withdrew from the company since "a quotation was not available in recognized markets".[67]

The flow of British capital overseas slackened off during the late eighteen seventies and was not resumed on a large scale until the late eighteen eighties. In this renewed boom in foreign issues the provinces played a more prominent role, but of course they were still very insignificant compared with London. The activity which brought additional business, particularly to the leading markets, was the speculation associated with South African gold mining. Gold was discovered there in 1884 and within a few years numerous companies were listed in provincial lists, although the boom in mining shares did not materialize until 1889, and the even larger wave of speculation in 1895, when Liverpool had its own "Kaffir Circus", albeit on a miniature scale.

Mining shares were dealt in extensively in Liverpool from 1886 onwards. During the 1894–95 boom nearly fifty such companies were listed on the "Unofficial Mining Board" which was called over immediately after the official boards since members were dealing freely in South African mining shares. In such a speculative market the prices quoted fluctuated greatly, and the accuracy of some of the quotations was often in doubt; at times they were so wide as to be useless.[68] Settlements in mining shares were not of an official character, but were done privately between members, "transactions being settled from contract to contract without a clearing", but members were allowed to buy-in or sell-out to enforce completion of contracts. Market interest in mining shares was fairly widespread, indeed, some two-thirds of the Liverpool membership requested the Committee to set up a Kaffir sub-committee to obtain all possible information on mining and other shares not officially quoted, stating that it was "highly necessary and important seeing that a very large proportion of the business of the Exchange is at present centred on these securities". The sub-committee also had to keep out of the unofficial list "worthless concerns for fear of the crash they inevitably brought".[69] A considerable amount of speculation went on and it was usual to carry over several times. In Birmingham a firm opened a line with the London Kaffir Circus and "made close prices in mining shares which greatly facilitated business in this class of share".[70]

Towards the close of the century a large volume of American railway shares appeared on the market, and by 1913 over £1,700 million was quoted on the London Stock Exchange. Liverpool participated in this development and had a substantial market in "Yankees", and also in the shares of South American railways which appeared on the market at the same time. Manchester also did a lot of business in American shares but the main provincial market centred on Liverpool which actively competed with London. In fact, during the 1914 emergency Liverpool did not adopt a minimum price in "Yankees" since dealers felt confident of being able to stabilize prices. This was partly a reflection of the large holdings of Liverpool shipping and commercial interests with their extensive trading contracts who held American and Argentine rails for investment purposes.[71]

NOTES

1 C. Fenn, *A Compendium of the English and Foreign Funds.* 4th Ed., (1845), p. 17.
2 E. L. Hargreaves, *The National Debt.* (1930), p. 137; see also G. R. Porter, "The Accumulation of Capital by the Different Classes of Society", *Journal of the Royal Statistical Society*, 1851, pp. 195-6.
3 George Rae, *The Country Banker*, 5th ed., (1906), p. 222.
4 J. W. Gilbart, *History, Principles and Practice of Banking* (1922 Edition), Vol. 1, p. 298.
5 1878, *Royal Commission*, op. cit., Qq 857-8.
6 Ibid., Qq 7950, 8009.
7 Birmingham Stock Exchange, Minutes, August 19, 1848.
8 Bristol Stock Exchange, January 21, 1848.
9 Bank of England Record Office, Stock Transfer Books.
10 Hargreaves, op. cit., p. 170.
11 Manchester Stock Exchange, Minutes, April 23, 1855.
12 Ibid., December 6, 1855.
13 Liverpool Stock Exchange, Minutes, March 12, 1856. The Bank of England have no record of these early negotiations.
14 Birmingham Stock Exchange, Minutes, December 20, 1855. Manchester Council sent a similar memorial to the Chancellor in January, 1856. It pointed to the "greater expense, the seeming mystery and the actual distance" which hindered the provincial public from investing in Consols. Improved facilities would divert interest "from local bubbles and hazardous speculations, in which a considerable portion of their savings has hitherto been placed and lost": *Manchester Council Proceedings*, January 9, 1856, pp. 100-1.
15 1878, *Royal Commission*, op. cit., Qq 8006-09.

16 Manchester Stock Exchange, Minutes, April 3, 1860; Liverpool Stock Exchange, Minutes, February 8, 1861. In 1864 the Bank of England announced that they were prepared to give in exchange for inscribed stock of Consols and other issues, stock certificates to bearer, with coupons for dividends attached, and obtainable in sums of £50, £100, £200, £500 and £1,000. While it was not possible to split the certificates, such Consols became eminently transferable, but were not widely used; *Burdett's Official Intelligence* 1884; see also *Economist.* February 28, 1863, pp. 225-6.

17 Manchester Stock Exchange, Minutes, August 5, 1869.

18 1878, *Royal Commission,* op, cit., Q. 8003.

19 Registers were also kept at the Bank of Ireland but Government securities inscribed in the Bank of England books could not be transferred in the books of the Bank of Ireland without powers of attorney being granted by the Bank of England.

20 Council of Associated Stock Exchanges, Minutes, October, 19, 1906.

21 Ibid., October 9, 1908.

22 Ibid., October 21, 1904.

23 Borrowing on deposit loans on security of deposit notes for short periods (six months, usually at 3% p.a.) was used mainly by the smaller towns of the north of England. In 1905 about 150 boroughs in England and Wales had about £3 million of such loans outstanding: J. R. Johnson, *Loans of Local Authorities,* (1925), p. 25; Lavington, op. cit., p. 292, n. 69.

24 Council of Associated Stock Exchanges, Minutes, October 20, 1905.

25 Ibid., October 19, 1906.

26 Ibid., October 9, 1908.

27 Hargreaves, op. cit., pp. 223-25.

28 Finance Act, 1911, 1 & 2 Geo 5, ch. 48, s. 17.

29 Council of Associated Stock Exchanges, Minutes, October 11, 1912.

30 *Economist,* June 17, 1911, p. 1293.

31 Liverpool Stock Exchange, Minutes, October 5, 1915.

32 Council of Associated Stock Exchanges, Minutes, Resumé 1921-22.

33 Liverpool Stock Exchange, Minutes, December 1, 1916.

34 Council of Associated Stock Exchanges, Minutes, Resumé, 1917-18.

35 E. V. Morgan, *Studies in British Financial Policy 1914-1925* (1952), pp. 106-12.

36 Liverpool Stock Exchange, Minutes, September 14, 1915. The financial press advised readers against taking up stock in registered form because of the lack of a market in London.

37 Council of Associated Stock Exchanges, Minutes, October 15, 1920.

38 Liverpool Stock Exchange, Minutes, September 14, 1915, Birmingham Stock Exchange, Minutes, April 3, 1917.

39 Liverpool Stock Exchange, Minutes, November 1, 1920; Survey of Provincial Dealing Facilities in Gilt Edged.

40 Liverpool Stock Exchange, Minutes, February 14, 1905; September 4, 1906; January 22, 1907.

41 Ibid., March 4, 1917.

42 Ibid., July 29, August 13, 1918, November 18, 1920.

43 Council of Associated Stock Exchanges, Minutes, Resumé, 1919-20.

44 Ibid., October 6, 1922.

45 Ibid., October 14, 1932.

46 *Stock Exchange Official Year Book,* 1943, pp. 13-14; *Economist,* January 2, 1943, p. 22.

47   Manchester Stock Exchange, Minutes, February 1, 1922.
48   *Economist*, February 27, 1941, p. 250-51.
49   *Burdett's Official Intelligence*, 1884, pp. 972-986. Full details are given of issues up to 1884.
50   Birmingham Stock Exchange, Minutes, December 6, 1876.
51   J. Thackeray Bunce, *History of the Corporation of Birmingham*, (1885), Vol. 2, pp. 35-6; Clapham, vol. 2, op. cit., pp. 304-5.
52   A. Briggs, *History of Birmingham* (1952), p. 344.
53   Liverpool Stock Exchange, Minutes, December 7, 1894.
54   Manchester Stock Exchange, Minutes, February 2, 1892.
55   Johnson, op. cit., p. 39.
56   Manchester Council Proceedings, 1875-6, Report of the Town Clerk to the Finance Committee, August 10, pp. 330-32. In 1875-76, Manchester had 3,615 individuals with £3.3 million in mortgages, of which 1,812 people with £1.3 million of mortgages applied for conversion into stock.
57   Liverpool Corporation, Finance Committee, Minutes, October 15, 1880.
58   Scrip Register and Transfer Books of the Liverpool Corporation 3½% 1880 Stock: Bank of England Record Office.
59   Bristol Stock Exchange, Minutes, March 30, 1909.
60   Liverpool Stock Exchange, Minutes, March 2, 1934. Parr & Rae handled the allocation of the underwriting between members; 70% was left with the underwriters.
61   Lavington, op. cit., p. 221.
62   Morgan and Thomas, op. cit., p. 80. Edgar Crammond, the Secretary of the Liverpool Stock Exchange from 1912-18, was a considerable authority on these matters. In an article in the *Quarterly Review*, 1910 he estimated that British overseas securities amounted to some £3,300, divided equally between empire and foreign countries. A Fellow of the Royal Statistical Society he read papers to them in 1911, on "The Economic position of Scotland and her financial relations with England and Ireland", in 1913-14 on "The Economic relations of the British and German Empires", and in 1915 on "The Cost of the War". He also gave evidence to the 1929 *Committee on Industry and Trade*.
63   Jenks, op. cit., p. 78.
64   Morgan and Thomas, op. cit., p. 88.
65   Manchester Stock Exchange, Minutes, January 8, 1868.
66   Jenks, op. cit., Appendix C, p. 421.
67   Liverpool Stock Exchange, Minutes, April 18, 1864.
68   Ibid., December 6, 1887, November 20, 1894.
69   Ibid., April 2, 1895.
70   Birmingham Stock Exchange, Minutes, October 24, 1894. During the 1895 boom they had a separate 'mining' room.
71   *Economist*, October 13, 1914, p. 787.

9 The Formation of the Council of Associated Stock Exchanges, 1890–1914

Co-operation among provincial stock exchanges can be traced back to their earliest years. Since the railway period, it occurred in various degrees, on such matters as special settlement dates, exchange of information on defaulters, buying-in and selling-out between markets, and the settlement of disputes between brokers. Although these, and lesser matters, were common to all the exchanges, they were not really of sufficient importance to merit the creation of a formal association. The dangerous implications arising from the forged transfers episode provided the necessary stimulus, albeit a little delayed.

The frauds perpetrated by Samuel Barton took place between 1874 and 1885, when, without the knowledge of Ann Barton, who was a joint trustee under the will of one Samuel Barton of London and North Western Railway Co. stock, Barton sold portions of the holding and signed and executed transfers to the buyers. He forged the signatures of Ann Barton, and also those of the attesting witnesses. Since Barton had signed the dividend warrants and also accounted for all the dividends that were payable, the frauds remained undetected until he absconded in 1886 and new trustees were appointed. The latter brought a successful action against the company who were ordered by the court to replace the names of the trustees on the company's register as the owners of the stock. The company duly obliged, and informed the transferees under the forged transfers that their names would be removed from the register; one of them had held the stock since 1874, while "all were bona-fide purchasers for value, innocent and ignorant of the fraud."[1] Legally, the company's action was quite correct but it caused widespread alarm, especially since railway stocks by this period carried the status of first class investments.

It was not until four years after the discovery of the Barton fraud that provincial brokers began to concern themselves seriously with seeking a measure of protection, for themselves and for shareholders, against the misfortunes which befell innocent victims who found themselves holding a stock certificate issued by a company under a transfer which turned out to be forged. In February 1890 six firms of Liverpool stockbrokers, prompted by the Barton case and by letters in *The Economist* on the same subject, expressed concern to the Liverpool Committee as to their vulnerable position, since they, unlike Manchester and London, had no rules to define the extent or nature of brokers' liability in such circumstances. The suggestion to establish a local committee was taken up and a small sub-committee commenced consultations with the Manchester and Glasgow stock exchanges. Both agreed to co-operate and to accept Liverpool's lead in the matter. Such joint action would pool experience, advice, and not least, economize on Counsel's fees. Counsel's opinion was, in fact, immediately sought on the question of brokers' liability to each other and to their clients.[2]

Positive action was not long in coming. An agenda for a meeting between the three exchanges was quickly agreed upon. It proposed the formation of an associated committee of provincial stock exchanges that would attempt to clarify the laws on stockbrokers' liability, establish a basis for joint action, invite the participation of stock exchanges with over fifty members, and proceed to get a "common understanding and recognition of such laws by association among Provincial Stock Exchanges."[3] On May 9, 1890, representatives from Glasgow, Manchester, and Liverpool met at the Stock Exchange in Liverpool, with James Lappin of Liverpool presiding. Having considered the issues and the general desire among the brokers of the three exchanges to form an associated body, the decision was taken to form the Council of Associated Stock Exchanges. At the same time it was decided to enlist the support of various financial and professional bodies with a view to joint action to get an act of parliament "making companies fully responsible for their own certificates when once issued." The conference also approved the principle that there should be the "closest possible assimilation of the Rules and Bye-laws of the several Associated Stock Exchanges", an ambition which was never fully attained.[4] The first full meeting of the Council was held in Liverpool in October 1890, by which time the Birmingham, Dublin, Edinburgh, Leeds, and Sheffield Stock Exchanges had become members.

The Council was not alone in wanting to see legislation enacted to provide for the indefeasability of transfers. The newly formed National Association of Shareholders had already introduced a bill into the Commons through Mr Pitt Lewis, containing the same objectives as those pursued by the Council. It was decided therefore to support this bill in order to save time and expense, and Council members succeeded in mobilizing some impressive support for the bill.[5] The leading figure in this campaign, indeed the "moving spirit throughout", was Edward Rae. However, his attempts to enlist the full support of the London Stock Exchange Committee were not very successful, possibly because a new committee had only just been elected to office. Other professional bodies proved more responsive, as did many influential individuals, among them George Rae, Inglis Palgrave and Joseph Chamberlain.[6]

The "Act for preserving Purchasers of Stock from Losses by Forged Transfers" received its third reading in August 1891. It empowered companies or local authorities to compensate shareholders for losses arising from forged transfers and allowed both bodies, if they thought fit, to "provide a fund to meet claims for such compensation".[7] In order to make the provisions of the act retrospective a minor amending act was passed in 1892. Once the act had reached the statute book, the Council directed its attention to getting companies to adopt the provisions of the act, while also urging them, in cases where insurance was used, not to pass the costs of the premium onto the shareholders. In Liverpool, the Stock Exchange combined with the Law Society, the Chamber of Commerce, and the Chartered Accountants, to form a Forged Transfers Committee whose task was to exert pressure on companies who were slow to adopt the provisions of the bill. Manchester Stock Exchange also participated in similar local canvassing. Within a year companies with £230 million worth of stock had adopted the bill's provisions, and by 1904 some £1,000 million worth of stock was so covered. Most large companies did not pass on the insurance costs and recognized that stockholders were entitled to good title to their holdings. Companies, by adopting the act, thereby rendered their certificates absolute evidence of title.

The constitution of the Council was fixed at the first meeting. One representative was allowed from each "properly constituted Exchange", with an additional representative for every fifty members in excess of the first fifty on the roll; the representation was modified in 1912 in favour of the larger exchanges.[8] A President was elected for one year, with three vice-presidents, and the administration was to rotate among the stock exchanges with the secretary of the Exchange acting also as Secretary to the Council; in practice it was mainly confined to the larger ones for administrative reasons. Bristol (1903–4, 1957), Sheffield (1911), and Leeds (1955) were the only small stock exchanges to take on the "administration". It was felt at the time that a President drawn from a small exchange did not lend as much authority to the Council as one from the larger brethren. Attempts to locate the administration permanently in

Liverpool failed since the leading figures were strongly of the opinion that equal status for the larger elements was an essential feature if the movement was to hold together. A Consultative Committee drawn from members of the Council was set up to deal with "expenditure . . . obtain legal advice when necessary, collect information, and recommend questions of general policy for consideration by the Council".[9] In addition to organization the general objects of the association were also spelled out. They were "to discuss and consider all questions of general business interest, to interchange views upon and devise methods for the convenient execution and settlement of business, to assimilate the practice of the several Exchanges, and generally to promote the interests of the Exchanges and their Members".[10]

At the time of its formation the Council consisted of eight exchanges, with a total membership of just over 550 brokers. Many of the smaller exchanges were diffident to join because their rules did not fully conform to the Code of Laws of the Council, particularly since many of them still allowed members to advertise and issue circulars without restriction. Bristol and Cork joined in 1899, with Bradford, Cardiff, and Swansea joining in 1908, all having changed their rules to comply with the Code Laws. Swansea, however, withdrew in 1911 claiming that the extent of outside competition made it essential for members to resort to advertising, but was re-admitted after the First World War.[11] Aberdeen, Halifax, Dundee, and Huddersfield joined in 1912, while Newport and Greenock delayed until 1918, with Nottingham coming in last of all in 1922; a grand total of 22 exchanges with 1077 members.[12]

With the Forged Transfers Act safely in use the Council quickly turned to discussing one of the basic objectives of its constitution, the drawing up of a general code of laws which would apply to all member exchanges. The object was not to bring all markets into absolute agreement, which would clearly have been impossible at that date, but rather to secure "uniformity of principle in the conduct of exchange business". It was appreciated that local variation did not permit of exhaustive legislation on matters of detailed rules or domestic management. The general principles of conduct were taken from the London rules and were slightly modified to suit the Council's needs. Such matters as local exchange constitution and management, and quotation requirements, were left to be dealt with by local bye-laws. The first code, presented at the Preston conference in May 1891, was circulated to the member exchanges for consideration.[13]

All went well until some dissenting voices were heard from north of the border. The dissent came from Gasgow who indicated that whilst they were prepared to make a few changes in their practices so as to fall in line with general practice, they were not prepared to adopt changes in wording which might give rise to doubt as to the precise meaning and intent of the rules. Further, they claimed that differences in Scottish and English law complicated adjustments. Such faltering on the part of a major exchange caused Edward Rae to resign as Liverpool's representative to the Council, but he subsequently resumed his position when Glasgow in October 1891, decided to adopt the 'Preston Code'.[14] Following further "exhausting committee work" a redrafted Code was circulated to the member exchanges, on the understanding that objections would be met as far as possible in the final version. It was then hoped that it would meet the requirements of the "Provincial Stock Exchanges in the transaction of business". However, in January 1893, Galsgow decided to reverse its previous decision to adopt the Code. While they were anxious to continue as members of the Council they were not prepared to do so "on the basis of a Standard Code forming an object of the Constitution". Rae had expected this, but certainly not the general feeling of many of his English colleagues that the Council should abandon the whole Code Law project. However, he eventually managed to persuade them to proceed on an English basis, and that this was a feasible and worthwhile pursuit. At a meeting of the Council in February 1893, Glasgow successfully proposed that all reference to the Standard of Code Laws should be omitted from the constitution. The English exchanges then proceeded with the adoption of the Code, which, it was hoped, would approximate "the Laws and Practices of every Exchange adopting it to those of the London Stock Exchange".[15] Manchester adopted the Code "en bloc" in February 1894, and Liverpool followed suit a few months later, with the other exchanges soon falling in line.

The Code Laws did not pertain to quotation requirements. It was not long, however, before the Council attempted to introduce some degree of uniformity in this area. A beginning was made in 1895 when the Council indicated to all member exchanges that it would be desirable for them to require companies seeking a quotation to include certain clauses in the Articles of Association. The articles should restrain a company from using the funds of the company for the purchase of its shares; that the amounts and intervals of calls should be limited, along with the borrowing powers of boards of directors; directors' interests in contracts should be disclosed and that their power to refuse transfers should be limited to shares not fully paid up, as should also the company's right of lien; directors' reports and balance sheets should be printed and circulated to shareholders before meetings.[16] Most of the large mem-

o

ber exchanges already had similar rules, but they did not always adhere closely to them.[17] By 1910, however, uniformity on a few points was superceded by a desire to see the adoption in its entirety by all exchanges of the London quotation rules. Four exchanges, Manchester, Birmingham, Cardiff, and Belfast, immediately protested, pointing out that they could not do so since many local companies could not, and need not, conform exactly to London rules. Manchester, for example, noted that many local companies could not attain the $\frac{2}{3}$ requirement in the matter of the amount of capital to be issued to the public.[18] Faced with some dissension the Council decided to seek limited uniformity based on the London requirements, allowing local committees to waive certain rules where local needs dictated. There the matter rested until it was taken up after the war.

The other issues which occupied the attention of the Council up until 1914 included relations with outside brokers, commission levels, relations and negotiations with London (mainly on commissions and dealing links), the running of the Preston Enquiry Bureau, and the need to get improved facilities for the transfer of Government securities in the provinces. This latter issue has been dealt with in Chapter 8.

Individual exchanges had a long history of relationships with outside brokers. It ranged from occasional downright hostility in the early days to a more accommodating attitude towards the end of the century, when, in some instances, outsiders were given access to market floors, daily lists, and even telegraphic facilities under the control of the exchange. Attitudes to outsiders differed markedly, however, depending as to their precise location. Those carrying on business in towns without an associated exchange were generally regarded as legitimate feeders of business, but those operating within a five-mile radius of an associated exchange were viewed with disapproval, which gave way to hostility by the turn of the century. This was because markets were annoyed by the "touting" activities of such outsiders, and the fact that they frequently gained easy access to market facilities without incurring any of the costs or responsibilities of memberships.

The first concerted attempt to limit the "facilities of which advertising Outside Brokers are possessed for executing orders in the various provincial centres through the medium of our Exchanges" came in 1904, when Sir George White of Bristol, the President of the Council at the time, urged all associated exchanges to adopt a common policy to that end.[19] Some member exchanges had already passed the appropriate rules. Bristol, for example, had for some two years refused to deal at all for local outside brokers or for those carrying on business within a five-mile radius of an associated stock exchange. Both Leeds, in 1903, and Sheffield, in 1904, had adopted similar policies; the effect in Sheffield was to drive all but one out of business.[20] In 1901 Birmingham introduced a rule whereby members could only deal with outside brokers in the town on a minimum commission, a provision later extended to cover those within thirty miles of the Birmingham Stock Exchange.[21] However, the effectiveness of unilateral adoption of such measures was undermined by the outside broker "getting his business done in his local exchange, but through the agency of a broker in another town". In fact, some outside brokers paid a salary, rather than commission, to the man acting as agent for them on the floor of a stock exchange.[22] It was hoped that concerted action through general adoption of the five-mile limit would effectively diminish opportunities for outside broking, and either force such brokers out of business, or else into the stock exchanges.

The probability of immediate success was soon seen to be small. Some exchanges were afraid that such a measure merely diverted outside brokers to London, at a time when it was claimed that London was already competing with them to a "considerable extent". Opinions varied as to the outcome of such a drift. London might well regard them as more of a nuisance than an advantage and would soon put up obstacles to their dealing there. Further, the outside broker would probably only go to London for deals in national stocks, while those brokers near to the smaller provincial markets probably went there anyway. Even if some business in local stocks, which was the main dealing activity of outside brokers, drifted to London it was invariably passed back to the provinces since dealers made no real markets in such shares.[23] If business threatened to go to London the solution was to get the co-operation of that market and thereby keep out outside brokers from all markets. Edward Rae was particularly keen on enlisting London co-operation for this purpose but realized that their interest in outside competition began and ended with the activities of certain city financial houses.[24]

Little progress was accomplished by way of concerted action. At the October 1906 meeting a resolution was passed urging member exchanges to take steps to prevent outside brokers from having the same facilities for dealing as members of a stock exchange, but little came of such a general motion.[25] It was not until the following year's meeting that the Council urged member exchanges to adopt the Manchester practice of charging full commission for all outside brokers carrying on business within a five-mile radius of an associated stock exchange.[26] Again there was a marked lack of enthusiasm for the proposal. Glasgow stated outright that they would not, on any account, drive business to London. Liverpool, while admiring their neighbour's "courageous measure" felt that without London's agreement on minimum commissions little success would follow from such action; "You will never get rid of the outside broker so long as the [London] Stock Exchange countenances the attendance of the representative of an outside broker in the Stock Exchange as a broker to transact business for a salary. Evidently London does not intend to do anything".[27] At the time London had their own difficulties with outsiders and internally the delicate problem of the uneasy relations between brokers and jobbers.[28]

The longer the matter delayed the more difficult it became to ensure joint action, let alone hope for London's co-operation. By the 1909 annual meeting the issue had become another hardy annual on the agenda. Bristol brokers, who had hoped for an early lead from the Council on the matter, became very dissatisfied with the loss of business and important connections, and decided to revert to unrestricted dealings with outside brokers.[29] On the other hand, Birmingham adopted more rigorous rules designed to "stamp out" outside brokers in the city. Those within ten miles of the Stock Exchange were charged full commission, and those between 10-30 miles half commission. Also if the Birmingham committee felt that any outside brokers were dealing in a way prejudicial to the interests of any associated stock exchange they would debar them from access to prices and information. In an attempt to increase the effectiveness of these provisions all other Exchanges were urged to maintain strict surveyance on access to trunk telephone lines for outside brokers.[30] Again, the proposals received a very mixed reception at the Council meetings. Manchester agreed, but Liverpool would not act on similar lines without a guarantee of general action, a guarantee no one was in a position to give. Other exchanges were equally cool in their response to Birmingham's moves: the matter was allowed to rest for a while.

Subsequent proposals designed to secure greater approval had little success. An extreme suggestion that members should not deal with any outside brokers brought immediate opposition. To include London outside brokers in such a rule was unacceptable to most exchanges. However, a compromise suggestion that minimum commission levels should be charged for outsiders gained more support, especially from the smaller exchanges who complained bitterly of outside touting activity. Later this was coupled with a suggestion for the reciprocal adoption of a five-mile protected area around each exchange, but even this proposal did not obtain the support initially hoped for. Glasgow refused to adopt it, Liverpool and Manchester co-operated in its adoption, but little further progress was made and the outbreak of war in 1914 led to the shelving of the whole issue.[31]

Most exchanges agreed in principle with the protected area scheme, but anxiety about obtaining reciprocity daunted its success. The Council could not impose its decisions on member exchanges, while concerted action seemed impossible on a voluntary basis. In fact, long before the outbreak of the war other weightier matters increasingly diverted the attention of both individual exchanges and the Council of Associated Stock Exchanges. These were the relationships between the provinces and London.

The protracted negotiations with the Committee for General Purposes of the London Stock Exchange arose directly from the introduction in 1908 of rules designed to enforce the separation of jobber and broker functions. Such a separation had been commended by the *Royal Commission* of 1878, but since then the distinction had become less sharp. Brokers dealt with each other and also with outside financial houses, while the jobbers, following the development of the telegraph and telephone, built up arbitrage links with New York and continental markets, and established direct lines to the offices of many provincial brokers.[32] The London committee declined to interfere when various test cases were brought before it in the 1890s, but a proposal to repeal the rule prohibiting dual capacity provoked a "storm of indignation" among members. Finally, following lengthy consultations with the members, the Committee in 1908 passed new rules, which also included provisions affecting provincial markets. They provided that members should declare in what capacity they were acting, and that they could not carry on business in a dual capacity; that a dealer "shall not deal for or with a nonmember. He shall not carry on Shunting business"; that a broker "shall not make prices or otherwise carry on the business of a dealer. He shall not carry on Shunting business". Brokers could deal with a non-member if this was to the advantage of the client, but they were forbidden to take two commissions when doing so. The rules became effective in 1909; the necessary corollary of the decision to keep the two classes of members separate was that Shunting between London and the provincial exchanges had to be abolished.[33]

London's proposals, designed according to one exchange to "put the clock back fifty years", were discussed at the Council in July 1908. The assertion that "Shunting is to be abolished" was seen as leading to a reduction in the amount of business coming from London, a widening of dealing margins, and a drift to London of richer clients.[34] Their reaction was to seek means of reducing depen-

dence on London, and to increase the amount of business transacted in the provinces. It was pointed out at the time that the
volume of business between the larger provincial markets was
smaller than was one time the case, and that they should aim to
get it back; while they could not entirely do without London,
neither should they spoon feed them. The President claimed that "if
the smaller exchanges would try the three larger exchanges they
would find jobbers springing up there".[35]

However, the only action taken towards keeping business in the
provinces was a scheme to exchange lists of miscellaneous securities,
wanted and on offer, compiled at the close of daily business by the
secretaries of the various exchanges. Any business thus arising was
put through the usual correspondent network. The scheme was not
very successful. The intention was to deal mainly with London
stocks, but the lists were dominated by local stocks, usually the
"refuse of orders" by way of odd lots of unsaleable stocks doing the
rounds. Also little attention was paid to the lists since those who
wanted to execute their business speedily, usually found that this
was best achieved by going through London, and London had no
minimum commission scale at the time to act as a disincentive to
deal there.[36] Suggestions for transforming the list arrangements into
a more formal bureau were not taken up until 1914 because of
virtually continuous discussions with London on the issue of dealing
facilities.

The Council was convinced that London would do all that they
could to prevent shunting through their members. In practice this
was not difficult since there were only a few firms involved, a
fact which of itself was an important reason for London's action.[37]
As Sir Robert Inglis put it at a later confrontation,

"Formerly, business of county Brokers was transacted in London through a number of London Brokers, and their business
as a result was spread over many different Dealers on our
Exchange, to the benefit of markets generally. The introduction
of private telephone wires, coupled with the absence until
recently of any strict distinction on our Exchange between
Brokers and Dealers, tended to alter this. In course of time
the business became centred largely in the hands of a comparatively few firms, who controlled the private telephone wires.
Dealers on our Exchange were encouraged to arrange joint
accounts with members of country Exchanges, with the result
that business in Stocks which had their chief market in London
was carried on locally, to the detriment of our Exchange".[38]

It was realized in London that it was "impossible to enforce the rule restraining a Dealer from dealing with a non-member if he is able to employ a Broker at a nominal remuneration to pass his bargain through". To make the rule absolutely effective it was necessary to adopt a compulsory minimum commission payable by the non-member on every transaction carried out by the Broker acting between the dealer and the non-member. In 1909 a sub-committee reported to the Committee for General Purposes in favour of a minimum scale for the public and a minimum scale for inter-market dealing. Although the proposals were accepted by the Committee for General Purposes they were rejected at a general meeting of the members, and for a time the matter was allowed to rest. While the Council welcomed London's intention of adopting a minimum scale for the public, they deprecated any action in the matter of restricting inter-market dealing. It was felt that it would seriously restrict business between markets, "and lead to a cessation of provincial orders to London," a slight overstatement of the likely effects. In 1910 a delegation from the Council received a most "cordial hearing" from London on the commission issue, and following London's inactivity in implementing its proposals the provinces decided to allow their plans for a clearing house to lie dormant.[39]

In the following year the Committee for General Purposes again brought proposals for commission rules before the members, only to have them rejected. At the same time another deputation from the Council went to London to put their views and hear London's aims. Edward Rae on returning to Liverpool commented that it had been more of a "tribunal than a Conference". Certainly, there could have been no misunderstanding of London's aims, which were clearly expressed by Sir Robert Inglis. London recognized

> "that all our Exchanges are, and must remain, in competition one with the other, but that each Exchange is, for varying reasons, the principal market for certain Stocks and Shares, and is entitled therefore to protect such market in the interest of its own members who have developed it. So far as concerns Stocks in which London is the principal market their idea would be to give members of your Associated Stock Exchanges access to these markets on better terms than anyone else. I hope that I have made the position clear, and convinced you that any suggestion of free trade between your Exchanges and ours is . . . quite impossible."[40]

This categorical statement that there could be no return to free trade was not regarded by the provinces as too serious, partly because of the promise of preferential terms, and partly because they knew that the London market was divided on the whole commission issue and that this would prevent any hasty action.[41]

Seeing that a return to free trade with London was out of the question the Council decided to concentrate on obtaining a negotiated brokers' scale. The proposed scales were regarded as particularly unsatisfactory. The levels were such that provincial brokers felt they would be unable to retain their London connections. In particular, on small business from the country, where most of the costs were incurred, a 50% division with London would certainly make it unprofitable.[42] In addition, the Brokers' scale was very similar to the scale for the public, even for a change of investments and speculative business. A request for a deputation to be received by London went unanswered. Perhaps this was because London had not been over-impressed with previous provincial delegations; the Council could not promise to bind the constituent exchanges, and most of the delegates were Shunters.

The London commission rules were finally passed by a slender majority in March 1912. Edward Rae was convinced that London had no further intention of altering their views on provincial ties, and the last thing he wanted was another snub to the Council. However, many of the smaller exchanges were extremely anxious that further approaches should be made. to London, while by the autumn of 1912, even the larger ones were beginning to feel the effects of the new scales. A leading Liverpool broker of the day, W. G. Wall, commented, "So far, we have found very little difficulty in continuing our business in railway and American shares, but in Africans the larger commissions are undoubtedly reducing the volume of business and widening markets here."[43] In Manchester business had been very considerably restricted, with people taking pains to try all other markets. The problem was that deals had to be put through in the course of a day which left shunters with little time to shop around provincial markets. London, in fact, was the only market with sufficient turnover to absorb such operations without causing delays. It was suggested, therefore, that they should indicate to London their willingness to accept the new scales for the public, but use this as a bargaining counter on intermarket rates. The prospect of uniformity, it was hoped, might induce London to give them "fair and reasonable treatment". Their desire to negotiate was conveyed to London, but they did not exactly plead for a conference.

London responded with an invitation to send a deputation to discuss possible revisions to the commission scales with representatives from the Committee for General Purposes. London's decision to review the scale, and willingness to consult the Council, probably sprang from several causes. After a few months' experience of the new scale several London brokers questioned the wisdom of charging a "stiff commission between markets". The rule prohibiting any charge below full commission on transactions under £1,000 had seriously hampered small business, while business from country brokers was also seriously affected. Instead of carrying out their orders in London, country brokers dealt with members of the provincial exchanges who were "running books, or, in other words, jobbing on London prices".[44]

Edward Rae was anxious that the deputation should present a strong united front rather than several unrelated suggestions, but he had considerable difficulty in getting the other large exchanges to accept such a strategy.[45] The deputation was accorded a cordial reception and the London representatives were extremely surprised at the simplicity of provincial demands; they had expected a plea for free trade, and they also were determined not "to look at any proposition which would have the effect of damaging or restricting the freedom of the London market". As William Bell of Manchester pointed out, it was in everybody's interest to maintain London's position, since it was the market of last resort for the provinces. In the event London agreed to a reduced brokers' scale, fixed at about 37½% of the clients' scale. Also, further concessions were given to the provinces on specific points; a bona fide change of investments could be done for one commission, and charges for small deals were to be reduced.[46] In return for these concessions the Council delegates promised that the Council would advocate general adoption of a minimum scale for the public, based on London rates.[47]

The ensuing euphoria was short lived. In the new year the Council received notification from London that "after due consideration of the report, and representations made to them by members who do a large provincial business, the Committee regret that they have been unable to adopt the recommendations embodied in the report". Accordingly, a revised brokers' scale was laid down, 50% of the clients' scale, compared with the 37½% agreed at the conference. The main reason for London's rejection of the recommended scale was the fear that it might encourage shunting when the objective was its abolition. The Council was bitterly disappointed at this reverse, but Edward Rae was convinced that no more deputations should be sent to London. The Council therefore decided that they would not urge member exchanges to adopt uniform minimum commission scales to the public.[48]

The introduction of the new scale, and the attitude of the London market, encouraged a large volume of business to flow to the provinces. Liverpool reported a record volume of business coming from Birmingham and Manchester. In order to encourage provincial dealing further the Council decided to set up a Central Enquiry Bureau so that as much investment business as possible could be done without resorting to London.[49] However, there were doubts in many minds; the failure of the scheme for the interchange of lists did not provide a happy augury for the proposed clearing house.

The Bureau, located at Preston for reasons of communication, was to operate experimentally for three months, and it began operations in July 1913. It did not undertake transactions, but merely acted as a central clearing house for the receipt of enquiries and the sending out of replies. Communication was by telegram, and orders arising from information received from the Bureau was put through the usual agency channels. About a third of the total membership made some use of it during the first weeks of operation, but within a few months only the smaller exchanges used it. This led to a dispute regarding finance, the larger exchanges who made little use of it claiming that the costs should be borne directly by the 200 or so users. The Council underwrote its activities for a while, but it was eventually closed down in the autumn of 1914.[50] At the outset some business in London stocks had been kept in the provinces by its operations, but increasingly its activity centred on local stocks, which stayed in the provinces anyway. Its procedures were slow and cumbersome, while little use was made of either tape machines or telephones. The experiment certainly indicated the reluctance of the larger exchanges to subsidize for any considerable length of time the activities of their lesser colleagues.

In its first twenty-five years the Council lived up to most of the intentions of the founders. It certainly provided a lively forum for the interchange of views on several matters affecting all the member exchanges. The annual meetings, usually held in the autumn at Windermere, proved to be something more than a place for "nice talk". The lines of communication between the Council and the individual exchanges did not always operate as smoothly as they might have done, but considering that it was only a consultative body a united front on all issues was clearly impossible. It was appreciated at an early stage that if the Council attempted to enforce decisions on the member exchanges dissolution would have been the end result. However, inability to bind members probably deprived it of power when negotiating with other bodies; at no stage in the negotiations with London could the Council promise complete compliance from the member exchanges. The representatives on the Council always had to report back to the parent exchange. It was also a disadvantage in matters affecting member exchanges, since they were occasionally reluctant to adopt a particular policy for fear that their sister institutions might not reciprocate.

Generally, relations between the member exchanges were exceedingly amicable. The larger ones certainly held the main sway; a threat to their dominance in 1912 by a "combination of the smaller Exchanges" was quickly overcome.[51] The interests of the smaller exchanges were not of course always synonomous with those of the larger ones, and where serious conflict arose the former usually opted out of the Council, only to rejoin later. Relations between the larger exchanges were particularly close; they were only marred by the disagreement over the Code Law issue.

It was in the entanglement with London on the commission issue that the Council was least successful during these early years. To a large extent the provinces were aggrieved by the fact that in order to enforce the separation of broker and jobber they were deprived of important London connections. Also, well established practices were ended quickly without much regard for provincial feelings. The Council was, of course, at a disadvantage in that it could not guarantee compliance with any bargains it made, but it is doubtful if London's attitude would have been markedly different anyway. London, at the time, seemed to regard the provinces as totally dependent on them for a market, and therefore, they should not seek to set up an independent position but be content with whatever London laid down. This attitude was seen by one observer as resulting "in too little give and take on the part of the Central Institution; too much cast iron opinionativeness and determination to legislate for the good of London whatever effect this may have on the Country Exchanges". Naturally, the provinces did not share London's interpretation as to their position, and felt that they could if neccessary get along by themselves; "if the mother adopts a hostile attitude the children in their turn will break away from their old ties, and in so doing seriously damage the fabric of the house".[52] The long-term effects of the rift were clouded by the onset of war; London lost some feeder business, while provincial attempts to remedy the loss of London facilities were not entirely successful. However, without the intermediation of the Council the provincial exchanges would have fared far worse at the hands of London, and amongst themselves co-operation would have been very haphazard.

NOTES

1 *Economist*, October 25, 1890, pp. 1350-51.
2 Liverpool Stock Exchange, Minutes, February 4, 17, March 10, 1890.
3 Liverpool Stock Exchange, Minutes of the Law Sub-Committee, March 10, 1890.
4 Council of Associated Stock Exchanges, Minutes, May 9, 1890.
5 Liverpool Stock Exchange, Minutes, January 6, 1891.
6 Liverpool Stock Exchange, Minutes of the Law Sub-Committee, October 23, 24 1890, May 14, 1891.
7 54 & 55 Vict. c. 43. A fund to meet compensation claims could be provided for by imposing fees on transfers, reservation of capital, accumulation of income, by insurance or any other "manner which they may resolve upon".
8 Council of Associated Stock Exchange, Minutes, November 22, 1912.
9 Liverpool Stock Exchange, Minutes of the Law Sub-Committee, October 23, 24, 1890.
10 Liverpool Stock Exchange, Minutes, February 28, 1893.
11 Council of Associated Stock Exchange, Minutes, October 9, 1908, October 6, 1911.
12 In 1912 the Council was anxious to achieve closer ties with the newly formed Association of Provincial Stockbrokers (membership about 400) in the hope of diverting some business away from London, with whom the A.P.S. did most of its business; Council of Associated Stock Exchange, Minutes, October 4, 1912. Details of the A. P. S.'s attempts to join the Council during the inter-war years are given in Chapter 10.
13 Council of Associated Stock Exchanges, Minutes, May 4, 1891. Among the matters covered by the Code Laws were transaction of business, settlement of stock, buying in and selling out, transfers, registration, defaulters, options, dividends, principals in default, liability of brokers, and contracts of members.
14 Liverpool Stock Exchange, Minutes, June 31, July 6, September 22, October 6, 1891. The Council's early meetings were at Preston.
15 Liverpool Stock Exchange, Minutes, February 28, June 24, 1893.
16 Council of Associated Stock Exchanges, Minutes, October 25, 1895.
17 Ibid., Minutes, October 7, 1910.
18 Ibid., Minutes, October 4, 1912.
19 Ibid., Minutes, October 21, 1904.
20 Leeds Stock Exchange, Minutes, December 21, 1903; Sheffield Stock Exchange, Minutes, October 21, 1904.
21 Birmingham Stock Exchange, Minutes, October 17, 1901; Council of Associated Stock Exchanges, Minutes, October 18, 1907.
22 Council of Associated Stock Exchanges, Minutes, October 21, 1904, October 19, 1906.
23 Ibid., October 19, 1906.
24 The London market was particularly worried by the direct contacts which some jobbers had with outside dealers, notably the foreign banks operating in mining (South African) and Indian securities; London Stock Exchange, Minutes of the Committee for General Purposes, September 24, 1906, February 21, 1907.
25 Council of Associated Stock Exchanges, Minutes, October 19, 1906.
26 Ibid., October 18, 1907; Manchester adopted this rule in November 1905.
27 Ibid., October 1908. This loophole in the London commission rules was corrected in 1912 when it was passed that a broker could not commute

his commission for a fixed payment or salary; *Economist,* December 16, 1911, p. 1255.

28 E. Victor Morgan and W. A. Thomas, *The Stock Exchange: Its History and Functions,* (1962), pp. 146-7.

29 Council of Associated Stock Exchanges, Minutes, October 18, 1907.

30 Ibid., Minutes, October 8, 1909. Very few brokers had such lines at this time.

31 Some of the smaller Yorkshire markets proceeded on their own. Three of them reached an "honourable understanding" not to do business "directly or indirectly, with a broker carrying on business in Huddersfield, Halifax, or Bradford, who is not a member of the Exchange of the town in which they carry on business"; Huddersfield Stock Exchange, Minutes, April 13, 1915.

32 Morgan and Thomas, op. cit., pp. 146-7.

33 London Stock Exchange, Minutes, January 1908; Hartley Withers, *The English Banking System,* U.S. Monetary Commission, 61st. Congress, 2nd Session, Senate Document, No. 492, Washington (1910), pp. 118-9. It was the London dealers who were mainly concerned in shunting activity with the provinces.

34 One observer noted that the prohibition had "made a good deal of difference to the volume of business", *Economist,* February 6, 1909, p. 269.

35 Glasgow had at that time a better market than London in some of the South African Shares, with a closer price and a faster growing turnover. Council of Associated Stock Exchanges, Minutes, July 6, 1908.

36 Ibid., October 9, 1908, October 23, 1914.

37 Effective shunting required "a costly system of private telephone wires". The few, however, were not immediately put out of business by the 1908 rule. London firms doing broking and jobbing (shunting) business split up into two parts, a jobber firm and a broking firm. Jobbing firms with country connections then put transactions through the books of the broking firm, thus obeying the "letter of the law, while evading the spirit". The latter was suitably christened "dummy brokers". "Through it shunting has been revived in some degree. Jobbers still deal with the country, although under the flimsy veil of a broker through whose books they pass all their transactions, instead of making them direct with the provincial Stock Exchange man"; *Economist,* September 16, 1911, p. 569.

38 Council of Associated Stock Exchanges, Minutes, October 6, 1911. Shunting business at the provincial end had also fallen into fewer hands; ibid., October 8, 1909.

39 Ibid., February 21, 1910, October 7, 1910.

40 Ibid., October 6, 1911.

41 Liverpool Stock Exchange, February 18, 1912; Liverpool received a circular from fifteen London firms indicating that only a minority of London members had been consulted on the commission proposals. Many London jobbers were annoyed since the commission rules would prevent them from undoing their business in the country, and it would also prevent them from making prices in many country stocks; they felt that the loss to the House was greater than the gain.

42 One estimate put the costs of a small deal at 8s. out of a £1 commission.

43 Liverpool Stock Exchange, Minutes, October 1, 1912.

44 Council of Associated Stock Exchanges, Minutes, November 22, 1912. In August 1912 about 200 country brokers petitioned the Committee for

General Purposes and protested against being charged full commission because they advertised or issued circulars. They pointed out that advertising was frequently the only method of dealing with unquoted local securities, and that London brokers were in the habit of sending to country brokers orders in unquoted securities which could not be executed in London. There were about 400 country brokers and many had depended on extensive advertising for some fifty years or more; *Economist*, August 31, 1912, p. 403.

45 The provinces wanted, of course, to get back to free trade, but Edward Rae saw little point in pressing the matter because London felt "that the provinces had been making more of the business than they had"; Liverpool Stock Exchange, Minutes, November 5, 1912.

46 The £1,000 limit, however, was not changed. Under this a London broker could rebate to his client ½ commission on orders over £1,000. The provinces pointed out that if their client demanded the rebate on a transaction done through London there was nothing left for them. They felt that the "collector of business" should get better treatment; *Economist*, March 28, 1914, p. 757.

47 Council of Associated Stock Exchanges, Minutes, November 22, 1912; Liverpool Stock Exchange, Minutes, November 26, 1912.

48 Council of Associated Stock Exchanges, Minutes, January 16, 1913; Liverpool Stock Exchange Minutes, January 16, 1913. By 1913 17 out of the 19 members of the Council had instituted minimum commission scales, but without any uniformity. While the Council still thought it desirable to have a uniform scale, they were certainly not willing to be hurried into its adoption.

49 Council of Associated Stock Exchanges, Minutes, January 23, 1913.

50 Ibid. May 16, October 24, 1913, October 23, 1914; Liverpool Stock Exchange, Minutes, May 27, 1913, October 5, 1913.

51 Liverpool Stock Exchange, Minutes, November 18, 1912.

52 *Economist*, February 17, 1912, p. 348.

10 The Council of Associated Stock Exchanges, 1914–1960

The constitution of the Council of Associated Stock Exchanges remained virtually unchanged until after the Second World War when a significant alteration was made in the powers of the Council which transformed it from a consultative body into a representative one. Such a change had been mooted in the thirties by the reformists on the Council in order to strengthen its power in negotiations with London, so that all agreements arrived at could be made binding upon the member Exchanges. But at the time a good sprinkling of the old liberal view persisted claiming that such a move was a direct contravention of the original purposes of the Council, that it was never intended as a coercive body but rather one aimed at obtaining harmony by consultation.[1] If such a change had been accomplished then, it would undoubtedly have improved the bargaining position of the provinces in their negotiations with London later in the decade. The experience of those meetings and the closer association with both the Treasury and the London Stock Exchange during wartime, and especially the post-war attempts at a greater uniformity of regulations, brought matters to a head. Accordingly in 1947 the Council introduced new rules whereby all member exchanges were required to adopt all decisions passed by the Consultative Committee. If a member exchange did not agree then the matter would be placed before the full Council, and if carried by a majority of three-quarters of the total voting power the new rules became binding on all member exchanges; the alternative was to leave the Council. The smaller markets overlooked their reservations about the new procedure in exchange for better representation on the Consultative Committee. The Council thus had powers to "make and to enforce decisions", albeit, a little delayed in coming.

A few years before this the Council had formalized its links with both London and the Provincial Brokers Stock Exchange by participating in the Joint Advisory Committee on Stock Exchanges set up in 1941–2. It was an off-shoot of the 1939 Conference and was intended to provide a "permanent organization for the interchange of opinion and discussion of all matters of interest to the constituent bodies, to promote greater unity of policy and to make recommendations from time to time to the constituent bodies."[2] Initially, both London and the provinces had four representatives, with two from the Provincial Brokers Stock Exchange, but in 1943 the provincial representation was increased to six because of conflicts of interests between the large and the small exchanges, who thereby gained a voice in the Committee's deliberations.[3] Despite its admirable intentions it seems to have been defunct by 1947. A more enduring, and certainly successful, link along similar lines was organized in the late fifties in the form of an Ad Hoc Joint Committee of seven representatives from London and the Council.[4]

The only important provincial stockbroking bodies which remained outside the Council were the Oldham Stock Exchange and the Association of Provincial Stock and Share Brokers.[5] The latter body was formed in 1912 and incorporated by charter. It comprised some two hundred members, with large geographic coverage who co-ordinated the investment business of nearly a hundred smaller towns and offered marketing facilities for a large number of predominantly local shares which rarely found their way to London. The Association was quickly recognized by London since its representatives, along with those of the Council, attended the 1915 conference on commission levels. As a result the Association adopted a bye-law fixing a minimum commission scale, but the Board of Trade refused to sanction its adoption since the proposal was in restraint of trade and contrary to the conditions laid down in the Association's charter of incorporation. Negotiations with both London and the Council for a minimum scale could obviously proceed no further. However, the Association felt that their inability to impose a minimum scale seriously prejudiced their negotiating position. They decided therefore to seek a way around the respective provisions of their charter, and the unwelcomed supervision of the Board of Trade. A new organization for this specific purpose could not be formed by the Association, but the members themselves were free to do so provided there was no financial or administrative connection between the proposed Stock Exchange and the Association. The members accordingly formed the Provincial Brokers Stock Exchange in September 1924.[6] Since it was a recognized Stock Exchange the members could withdraw from the Somerset House List, and they were also not liable for stamp duty on contract notes sent to each other. More significant was the fact that the new organization could adopt regulations prohibiting advertising by members, impose a minimum scale of commissions, adopt the Code Laws of the Council, and impose the five-mile rule.

Following the reorganization, an application for affiliation was made to the Council which was rejected. The Provincial Brokers Stock Exchange had hoped that the new constitution removed all obstacles to membership of the Council but the grounds for rejecting the application turned on more basic issues. The Council claimed that the new set up was an exchange in name only, not in function. Members, it said, were "too jealous of the dignity and the position which this Council has assumed to consent to the admission of members who are not members of a legitimate and properly organized Stock Exchange". In addition, one of the largest exchanges on the Council voiced strong objections to admitting an organization of outside brokers, because giving access to net prices and commission free dealing facilities would lead to a large loss of business.[7] A further request for affiliation in 1932 met with a similar rebuff.

The Council also strove to attain uniformity in the treatment of outside brokers. During pre-war years some exchanges had adopted provisions which imposed full commissions on outside brokers operating within a five-mile radius of an associated exchange. However, those exchanges were soon regretting the decision. Liverpool abandoned such a rule in 1915 because it was found that local outside brokers could get business done through stock exchanges free from such restraints.[8] The Scottish stock exchanges were not prepared to adopt the five-mile rule since they regarded the outside broker as an important feeder of business, while some of the English exchanges found such a rule unacceptable because they had high commission levels, and did not rebate to agents anyway.[9] The provinces were hesitant in moving in the matter as long as London's treatment of outside brokers was fairly liberal. Although formally London distinguished between outside brokers who issued circulars relating to purely local shares and those brokers who advertised indiscriminately, in practice, London brokers were alleged to deal with everybody on minimum terms.[10]

The number of outside brokers involved was by no means negligible. In 1923 there were over seven hundred on the Somerset House List, representing a widespread network of business. With the contraction in share dealing business in the early thirties the Council decided to curtail opportunities for competition from this large mass of outsiders and discussions were held on means of restricting the access of outside brokers to market facilities. It was pointed out that dealing at net prices, free of commission, practically brought outside brokers into the market without their making any contribution to market expenses, while they were also in a position to cut commissions to clients since they were not subject to any minimum scale. Even so, the smaller exchanges felt that to come down too harshly on outside brokers would seriously diminish provincial

P

business by driving it to London thereby undoing some of the solid achievements of previous years, when an "enormous lot of business which previously used to go to London is now being done in the provinces by the marrying of orders, so saving double London brokers' commission and on London jobbers' turns and in that way the provincal public are getting a better service than they used to".[11]

As a step towards greater uniformity the Consultative Committee of the Council suggested in 1935 that all member exchanges should charge full commission to all outside brokers operating in towns and cities where there was an associated stock exchange, in the hope that London would fall in line. Surprisingly, strong opposition to the proposal came from one exchange only, Birmingham, while the smaller exchanges were curiously silent on the issue. Birmingham's case was that free trade was far preferable to using artificial props to bolster up the stock exchanges, and that "the genesis of this proposal is found in a desire to prevent provincial jobbers dealing with outside firms on the same terms as they do with members of the Associated Stock Exchanges".[12] Provincial free trade it was argued should not be allowed to go the same way as London free trade. The proposed measures were unfair to the longstanding outside brokers and would merely encourage the growth of outside dealing facilities; it was putting brokers' interests before those of clients. However, Birmingham agreed not to veto the move and a united provincial front was presented to London.

Long negotiations were held with London in an attempt to obtain a reciprocal agreement regarding the charging of full commission on all business conducted for outside brokers. However, the existing London rules relating to agents left a gap since outside brokers who did not advertise and were on the Stock Exchanges' Country Register were entitled to a rebate. The County Register had been introduced in 1936 so as to regulate the return of half commission to county brokers not members of a recognized exchange. Prior to the introduction of this list the test for the sharing of commission between London Stock Exchange members and country brokers had been the latter's inclusion on the Somerset House Register, "admittance to which appears to have been if anything, more easy to obtain than a motor-driving licence". By 1937 there were only 137 outside brokers on the Country Register, and a large number of accountants who did not do any legitimate stockbroking business had been deprived of rebates; the Register was abandoned in 1941.[13] Until the agency rules could be changed little progress was possible.

Both issues were eventually dealt with at the 1939 conference of representatives from the Council and the London Stock Exchange.

The agency position was clarified and agreement reached on the treatment of outside brokers. It was agreed that all member exchanges would adopt a rule whereby "a member shall charge full commission on any transaction for a broker carrying on business and/or having a place of business in the London postal area or in the postal area of an Associated Stock Exchange who is not a Member of such Exchange or who, . . . was not a member of the Provincial Brokers' Stock Exchange".[14] It was felt that this would induce outside brokers to apply for admission to an exchange, or at less expense, join the P.B.S.E. By this means the outside broker could be driven into the stock exchanges or out of business: general stock exchange opposition was not against the outside broker as such, but against those indulging in highly questionable advertising methods.

Another area in which the Council sought greater uniformity was that of quotation requirements. Little advance had been achieved since the pre-war resolutions on the subject and the pace of standardization was not much quicker in the twenties. Some of the larger exchanges, notably Liverpool and Manchester, had adopted London requirements in their entirety, while other markets did so "as far as practicable", with variations dictated by local needs. However, there was an even greater lack of uniformity in so far as the actual requirements were pursued in practice. Companies refused a quotation in London sometimes managed to obtain one in the provinces, while the reverse also happened with London obliging where the provinces had declined, all of which arose from differences in interpretation.[15] The most common regional variation concerned the proportion of an issue allotted to the public. London laid down two-thirds, while many provincial markets exercised their own discretion with respect to applications from small companies.

When London introduced new regulations on permission to deal and quotations after the First World War the provinces soon followed suit, but with the difference that many exchanges had no formal process of granting permission to deal, they merely had a provision whereby anyone could object to the making of bargains in the shares. This procedure drew criticism from both within and outside the stock exchanges. Exchanges who insisted on formal application resented the fact that a few others dealt extensively in shares where no explicit permission to deal had been given, while from outside the Cohen Committee on Company Law, reporting in 1945, saw it as a means for what they termed the "backdoor" entry into London.[16] While the main provincial markets moved rapidly towards the adoption of full London requirements, the remainder were catching up by the late forties. The introduction of new London requirements in 1946–47 was followed in the provinces by a decision of the Council, now armed with greater powers, to request individual exchanges to follow London, but the traditional proviso was retained whereby an exchange could waive certain rules to meet special local needs.[17]

The other major issues confronting the Council during the inter-war years were those relating to commissions, intermarket dealings, and country jobbing; in other words, the level of brokers' income and the quality of market facilities. Discussions on these themes occurred throughout the entire period and they were not satisfactorily resolved until the 1939 conference.

The commission issue was inherited from the pre-war years. The much prized feature of uniformity had not been achieved and although by the twenties most of the provincial exchanges based their commissions on London, some clearly did not. Birmingham, for example, maintained a very independent line on the subject with a higher scale than London. They claimed that they bore greater risks, had higher working expenses, and that they did not suffer by it. The post-war discussions on the subject however took in not only the need for greater uniformity but also proposals for higher commission levels to cover increased costs. Unless London could be persuaded to move with the provinces they could not act alone since such action would merely invite loosing a great deal of business to London.[18] At that time London refused to move in the matter on the grounds that the jobbers were strongly opposed to it, as were the larger broking firms doing considerable business with the banks.[19] An alternative course, persistently advocated by one of the larger provincial exchanges, was that they "should not divide" with agents, and although this provided part of a later solution it received very little support at the time.

Before any progress was achieved on the above question the Council started negotiations with London on a specific point, "For the purpose of inducing them to permit their members to resume the time-honoured practice of transacting business for members of the Associated Exchanges for half the commission chargeable by members of the London Stock Exchange to their private clients, or alternatively, to come as near thereto as possible".[20] The genesis of the suggestion lay in provincial disaffection with the effects of London's £2,500 rule whereby a client was entitled to a rebate of half commission on the amount of the consideration in excess of this sum, at the broker's discretion.[21] Provincial brokers complained that they had little by way of discretion once the concession had become generally known to the public. It also meant that provincial brokers had to pay on nearly all large transactions, except the first £2,500, the same commission as paid by the clients of London members. The matter was finally settled as part of the 1939 conference package agreement. It was then established that the commission charged to provincial brokers should be uniformily half the scale chargeable to clients, while provincial brokers were also to receive the benefit of the £2,500 rule.[22]

The general problem of rising costs was not tackled until the 1939 conference. Several possible means of relief were open to the stock exchanges, the most obvious being an overall increase in charges to the public. It was generally felt however that such a move would be strongly criticized so long as brokers continued to return to agents such a large proportion of gross commissions. It was therefore decided to seek relief by revising the basis upon which commissions were divided between broker and agent. The amounts of rebates were strictly set out in the rules, but there was no effective restriction on admitting outside parties to the privileges of agency. In the absence of such controls many "private and casual persons and firms who are not professionally or even habitually engaged in handling stock exchange business" had obtained rebates of commission.[23] London was anxious to cut out this casual element, while the provinces were even keener to do so since they had lost a lot of business as a result of direct dealing between such agents and London brokers.[24] Some of the diehards in the provinces were against giving back anything in the nature of a rebate, but most exchanges were prepared to rebate to banks and the public trustee, both of whom introduced a great deal of business. The main offenders in provincial eyes then were a certain class of half commission men who practised some rather dubious business and who seldom came under the effective control of a member firm.

It was agreed at the 1939 conference that the agency rules should be revised, and subsequently the Consultative Committee of the Council and the London Committee reached agreement on a scheme of registration of agents which aimed at eliminating the undesirable element. Five categories were established with a register for each; banks, remisiers, attachés (these were the former half commission men who in future had to be "regularly and normally located in his employer's office"), clerks (full-time clerks to a stock exchange member), and a general register for those not falling into the other categories, but who were "professionally or habitually employed in handling Stock Exchange business".[25] The registers were kept in London in order to avoid duplication, and provincial applications were submitted through the appropriate stock exchange. The other measure was the reduction of rates of rebates to agents. As they stood the rebates were 50% of gross commissions to banks, remisiers, and clerks, and 33⅓% of gross commission to all others. It was estimated for the immediate pre-war years that average costs were at least ⅓ of broker's gross commissions which left him with a mere 16⅔% when 50% was rebated. It was therefore decided to rebate 33⅓% of gross commissions to those on the registers of banks, remisiers, attachés, and clerks, and 25% of gross commissions to those on the general register.[26]

Provincial brokers with their heavier telephone and other expenses, and the smaller average size of their bargains, were soon urging the Council to exert pressure on London to amend their commission rules again so as to deal with the problem of rising costs. As with previous moves there were two suggestions, reducing the amount of commission "given away" to agents, and raising overall commissions. By the end of the war there had in any case been a general reduction in the scope of agency business and it was increasingly limited to definite professions. In 1947 London amended its commission rates which in effect eliminated the sharing of commissions with solicitors, accountants, and others. This measure received full provincial support, with Manchester who for decades had advocated ending all rebates being understandably jubilant; banks, however, retained a firmly entrenched claim on rebates. These rules were rescinded in 1949 since the majority of London members disapproved of them, and the commercial banks threatened retaliatory measures.[27] The case for an overall increase in commission levels was not allowed to rest. In 1950 the Council received, and acted upon, a suggestion from Glasgow and Birmingham to press London for a general rise in commissions which had been virtually unchanged for forty years, and also a further reduction in the percentages of commission rebated to agents. In 1952 London adopted new commission scales and also reduced the allowances to banks to 25%, and that to persons on the general register to 20% of gross commissions. All the provincial exchanges adopted the new scales without any complaint.[28]

Without doubt the main issue of the 1939 conference was that of country jobbing. It was London's main concern at the discussions and the major bargaining counter of the provinces in getting their demands met. For some years beforehand London had expressed concern about the "decline of the relative predominance of the central London Market", and with certain provincial developments which they regared as being organized "not in co-operation, but in competition with the London Market". Neither were some of the larger provincial exchanges over enthusiastic about such developments. Those with self-sufficient floors were opposed to country jobbers making net prices to outside brokers, which meant a loss of "remunerative and satisfactory" agency business to broker only members. They were therefore anxious to get back the volume of inter-market business – "get it back to our rooms" – and they were quite prepared to accept limitations on the scope of provincial jobbing activities to attain this end.

Country jobbing involved three types of activity. In the first place, jobbing occurred, to a greater or lesser degree, in all provincial centres in the securities of local companies. London had no quarrel with this sort of activity, while provincial markets were keen to retain it. The only complaint about it related to London markings in such stocks which showed considerable discrepancy in price compared with quotations in provincial official lists. Putting business in local stocks through London gave clients a raw deal in what were very limited markets; "in any case, the business is shunted to our [provincial] market at all times at a good profit".[29]

The second kind involved shunting which was a modification of the classical shunting activity of the pre-1914 period when provincial markets were in direct contact with the London jobber, and business was frequently conducted on the basis of a joint account. The direct link was terminated following the introduction of new London rules in 1908 which effectively enforced the separation of jobbing and broking functions and which stated categorically that "Shunting is to be abolished". During the inter-war years provincial links with London developed between London brokers specializing in country business and provincial specialists in London and inter-market business, connected together by direct private telephone lines and teleprinters. It was handled by a comparatively small number of firms with highly specialized organizations; it was a matter of substantial business done on very fine dealing margins on a highly professional basis.[30] These specialists now took over the label shunters from the original jobber shunters. London had no objection to this development and regarded it as a normal function of the London broker to supply the closest market quotations to his country correspondent, who "sometimes with the help of other similar inter-market connections, makes prices based thereon to the members of his Exchange." The price service provided by the London broker thus projected the facilities of the London jobbing market onto provincial floors and helped to "unify and bind together the dealing machinery" of the stockbroking profession; some provincial dealers however looked back with nostalgia to days when the links were stronger and far more direct. The prices made in the provinces by the shunting organizations were based on London.

"which possess the only true and the only ultimate market in stock and shares".[31]

The third kind of country jobbing activity, and the offending one as far as London was concerned, was a new species of "predatory extra-mural competition". It involved firms specializing in lists of active securities, the composition of which was varied from time to time in line with shifts in market interest and which were widely circulated so as to attract business from provincial exchanges and from brokers all over the country. Country jobbers used prices based on London and usually kept in step with London fluctuations in order to attract business. London's objection was that they skimmed off the best business and that they did not pass business onto London. By attracting a sufficient volume of business it could be married at a jobbing turn, and if any balances of stock were left on a country jobber's books these could be undone on the London floor, the last resort market. London declared that they had no objection to the operation in the provinces of genuine jobbing markets but they stipulated that they should be "entirely on their own feet, and independent of London"; if carried far enough this kind of jobbing "would seriously undermine and weaken the London jobbing market, by diminishing its volume and its liquidity". With the prevailing paucity of business London was very conscious of anything that reduced turnover. The main culprit in all this, of course, was the Sheffield firm of J. W. Nicholson & Sons, whose enterprise had "matured into a masterpiece, and there is not a single Provincial Broker in the country who has failed to benefit"; they were a great convenience to the provinces but in so doing they had greatly provoked London.[32]

Assertions as to the central importance of the London jobbing market were not altogether accepted by some of the provincial exchanges, or indeed, by some outside commentators. *The Economist,* for example, held that "though still mainly feeders to the London market [the provincial exchanges] today transact between themselves a larger proportion of their own business".[33] Birmingham, of the larger exchanges, was particularly vocal in its criticism of the London jobbing mystique and feared the creation of a London monopoly in a business in which no one held the right of monopoly. At the Council discussions on the Blue Book proposals the Birmingham delegate strongly repudiated the assertion that all country jobbers relied regularly on London as a last resort market. He cited the case of a prominent Birmingham jobber in insurance shares who ran a large business, making a price on his own book. The London insurance market at the time had only two jobbers and "often quotations are given on a nominal basis and it is frequently impossible to deal"; certainly he did not unload in London, he did not even have a direct line there.[34] The feeling of many provincial dealers was that there was no need to acquiesce in driving provincial business to the London jobber; he could protect himself against any unloading by country jobbers by not dealing, and by making greater efforts to put his own affairs in better order by attending to capital resources, rather than try to create a monopoly of jobbing activity.

The main reason for the growth of this variety of country jobbing was associated with the pre-war London commission rules and the abolition of the jobber-shunting link. The imposition of high commission scales had thrown a curtain around the provinces who were forced to get their business done at more favourable terms. Besides, the provincial jobber was prepared to do business at *net* prices, while they disliked doing business through London since they had to pay the stipulated half commission. The provinces by contrast had the free trade principle.

Another reason was the stamp duty concession extended to provincial dealers by the 1931 Finance Bill. Under the provisions of Section 42 of the 1920 Finance Act dealers were permitted to pay ten shillings maximum duty on the transfer of stock, but the concession was confined to dealers not carrying on any other business. Provincial brokers also acting as dealers were thus debarred from the concession and were obliged to pay £1% stamp duty. The Council made representations to the Treasury urging an extension of the concession to the provinces.[35] It was pointed out that provincial dealers were reluctant to buy shares for some days prior to the end of an account because of stamp duty reasons. Prices were thus adversely affected "owing to dealers restricting their purchases", while their profits were swallowed by the stamp duty. Granting the concession would thus improve markets in local securities. After several requests to the Treasury an amendment was included in the 1931 Finance Bill, to the effect that the expression dealer meant a person who "being a member of a stock exchange in Great Britain is recognised by the committee of that exchange as carrying on the business of a dealer". The concession applied only to members who had a "regular and habitual practice of dealing"; it did not apply to carry-over transactions, arbitrage, or shunting dealings. By persuading the Treasury that they would not lose by it, and London that it was not an unfriendly act, the Council gave provincial dealers an opportunity to expand markets in local securities, and indeed others.[36]

Following informal approaches from the President of the Council, London agreed to a conference for an exchange of views on major matters where they had grievances. The conference was held in London in June 1939, with Sir John Braithwaite in the chair and with six representatives from the Council and five from the London Stock Exchange.[37] The main provincial grievances were the £2,500 rule, the need for a clear definition of the term "agent", the necessity for rules governing relations with outside brokers (these points have been discussed above), and London's interpretation of Rule 88 which prevented London brokers from dealing with their country agents unless they could do so on more favourable terms than with their own jobbers. A fair measure of agreement was reached on these issues and the subsequent Blue Book proposals gave effect to them. London's only important request was that the provincial stock exchanges "should not permit . . . members to issue lists or make prices to anyone outside the Associated Stock Exchanges".[38] London, of course, was in a stronger bargaining position since the Council could only recommend acceptance of the new rules to the constituent exchanges, "who alone can take the necessary action". In the event four exchanges adopted the proposals in their entirety, while thirteen adopted them subject to an amendment, conceded by London, that members should be allowed to issue jobbing lists to their correspondents in other Associated Stock Exchanges.[39]

After lengthy discussions on the country jobbing question the conference agreed that members of the London and of the Associated Stock Exchanges should not make or deal at net prices with non-members, and that strict control should be placed on facilities for direct access to London by provincial firms who engaged in *jobbing activity other than in securities of a purely local nature*. These general principles were subsequently embodied in specific rules which were adopted by both London and the provinces. The Committee for General Purposes of the London Stock Exchange took powers to declare any non-member firm a non-member jobber "and to prohibit or regulate the business relations of members with such firms". Also, that members could not "establish, maintain or use direct private telephone lines, or teleprinters" with any non-member resident outside the London postal area without the consent of the Committee.[40] The Council recommended that member exchanges should adopt rules to prohibit members from dealing at net prices, or as principals, with anyone except members or the Associated Stock Exchanges. Also, a rule to

"prohibit their members from having telephone services, or private telephone lines or teleprinters to Stock and Share Brokers other than members of the London, Associated or Provincial Brokers Stock Exchange; and from allowing their offices to be used by third parties for transmitting messages relating to Stock Exchange business to any broker who is not a member of such Exchanges, or who, being a member, issues lists and/or makes prices, or otherwise carries on the business of a jobber, other than in securities of a purely local nature".[41]

These proposals as they stood did not prohibit a member of an Associated Stock Exchange from having a direct link with a country jobber declared by London to be a non-member jobber. This gap was not left open for long since the Council recommended member exchanges to adopt further provisions to the effect "that a member shall be prohibited from having a private line or teleprinter to a firm declared by the London Stock Exchange to be a non-member jobber", a rule aimed at severing provincial links with the main offender in the eyes of London, Nicholson's of Sheffield. Also, members were prohibited from having booked time calls to or from a non-member jobber for the purpose of providing a collective service to a stock exchange.[42]

The Associated Stock Exchanges reluctantly accepted the proposals but not before giving vent to some of their antagonism. Strong opposition came from the smaller exchanges, from Sheffield, Cardiff, Huddersfield, Newcastle, Bradford, Bristol, and Belfast, while Birmingham was particularly critical of the restrictions on country jobbing, pointing out that London knew full well that a jobber could not exist on the basis of business generated within one provincial floor. The smaller exchanges were annoyed at giving up their direct links with Nicholson's, after London declared it to be a non-member jobber. With no shunting lines to London, and with only limited markets in local shares, they no longer had facilities for dealing at net prices since the larger exchanges would only deal on a gross basis. They liked the "alternative and competitive" market offered by country jobbers, not only for the dealing facilities but also because "immediately the Country Jobber puts on his List a Share or a Stock in which he is prepared to deal, from that very moment the London Jobber begins gradually to close in his price".[43] They felt that the larger exchanges had imposed the agreement on them and then deprived them of net dealing facilities, and since they could rarely put business through on their own exchange floors they had to go to London, which may have been London's intention but certainly not that of the provinces. The larger markets were not very worried about such matters since they had their own shunting lines, more floor trading, and looked upon the restrictions on country jobbing as bringing business back to their floors; giving a non-member jobber a private line, or booked time calls, was virtually making him a member of that market.[44] No doubt the larger brethren agreed with *The Economist's* view that "while at first blush, this may appear an undue limitation of individual initiative and of competition, it is perhaps more usefully regarded as a practical acceptance of the fact that telecommunications have made the country one circuit, with one market, and that jointly fixed rules for all those who use it whether in person or by teleprinter, are a necessity".[45]

The position of the smaller exchanges was not made any easier by a subsequent understanding reached between London and the Consultative Committee whereby country jobbing would be confined to purely local securities. A rule was adopted which required country jobbers to seek the approval of their committee before listing securities not of a local nature.[46] In practice, the jobbing activity that went on in the provinces was a little wider in scope than certainly London had intended, particularly in exchanges with specialized markets, such as iron and steel shares at Sheffield. By 1947 London was somewhat alienated on this score and the matter was allowed to rest for some time.

The other aspect of inter-market dealing discussed at the conference related to London's interpretation and operation of Rule 88, which stated "that the broker in London should satisfy himself that he cannot deal on the London market before he goes outside". It was aimed basically at outside dealings in gilt edged and Australian securities by finance houses and others, but in the event inter-market dealing had suffered by it although no such effect had originally been intended. In the late thirties several exchanges raised the matter at Council meetings, pointing out that business in provincial securities had been retained in London after London brokers had obtained bids in the provinces and then reported back to their own jobbers who gave them the same bids. The provinces disliked such practices since a day or two later a London jobber would undo his position in the provinces to his advantage. Also, when the rule was introduced London brokers cancelled all their traditional "retaining orders in local securities", and in addition reduced the volume of reciprocal business done with country brokers.[47] It was agreed at the conference that the London broker was under no obligation to disclose either to the jobber or the non-member the price quoted by the other, while he was allowed to deal with country brokers in local securities on the same terms as those they obtained from their own jobbers.[48]

Provincial jobbing and shunting came in for further attention in the early fifties and arose from London's continuing concern about outside competition. Where provincial firms had direct links with

London they were anxious that information gained thereby was not made available to outside brokers, and particularly to non-member jobbers. In their discussions with the Council London urged that shunters should "close their books every day where practicable", and "undertake not to have or accept Direct Private Telephone lines, omnibus circuits (except those already in existence connected to and authorized by London) or teleprinters, nor will have or accept fixed time calls, or reimburse the cost of telephone calls or telegrams, to, with or from any member or member firm, of the Associated Stock Exchanges, or of the P.B.S.E. or the Oldham Stock Exchange". London, of course, had complete control over its own shunters, and also had a fair degree of influence over provincial shunters with direct links with London and who had a desire to retain the connection. Provincial shunters with omnibus circuits which they had operated for some fifty years, but with no direct London link, were the concern of the provinces. London was prepared to permit direct links with London markets, and approved of shunting activity which provided "a service of prices from London in all securities for the floors of each of your Exchanges large enough to make such a service a mutually paying proposition". What they objected to were provincial links which "enable your Shunting members to extend their business beyond their own floor and build up a country-wide business on the back of London". Most exchanges agreed with London's attitude in protecting its own floor and ultimately acquiesced with their demand to lay down conditions for provincial links with London firms. The important point was that country correspondents had to give an undertaking to London that they "would not make prices directly or indirectly (except in securities of a purely local nature) or otherwise act as Jobbers or Shunters except to members of their own individual Exchanges".[49]

Provincial attitudes to competition seem to have waned compared with pre-war years, while the disappearance of any serious country jobbing of the Nicholson type removed the main reason for the protests of the smaller exchanges. The telephone links were thus kept, while little change occurred in subsequent years. In exchange for accepting London's demands for restricting telephone links the provinces at least got a gilt edged concession. This involved treating gilt edged as local securities and was requested by the smaller exchanges after the issue of gilt edged stock as compensation for local shares taken off the market by nationalization. Accordingly, it was agreed that London shunters should be free to make prices in British Government securities to members of other exchanges who cared to get in touch with them at their own expense.[50]

NOTES

1   Council of Associated Stock Exchanges, Minutes, October 16, 1936.
2   Ibid., Resumé 1941-2.
3   *Economist,* December 25, 1943, p. 856.
4   Council of Associated Stock Exchanges, Minutes, Resumé 1958-9.
5   The unsuccessful attempts of the Oldham Stock Exchange to join the Council have been noted in Chapter 8.
6   The Association continued in being but only had advisory powers. The new Stock Exchange was in fact formed out of the existing Provincial Brokers' Bureau. The Exchange was located at Hull and controlled by a committee of seven. H. Goodes of Hull was elected Chairman, and Sydney Laking, honorary secretary. It sent out a daily list; some of the members of the Associated Exchanges had participated in the Provincial Brokers' Bureau's lists but they were requested to withdraw from the new arrangements; Council of Associated Stock Exchanges, Minutes, October 16, 1924.
7   Ibid., October 16, 1924.
8   Ibid., October 8, 1915.
9   Ibid., November 18, 1915. Some exchanges were very reluctant to cut out outside brokers, particularly during the years 1914-18, since the latter were able to deal in shares which members of stock exchanges could not deal in without the consent of their own committees, a requirement laid down by Treasury regulations; ibid., October 17, 1919.
10   Ibid., October 6, 1922. London abolished the distinction between outside brokers who advertised purely local shares and those who advertised more generally in 1924.
11   Ibid., October 19, 1934.
12   Ibid., October 18, 1935.
13   *Economist,* November 28, 1936, pp, 420-1; March 6, 1937, p. 534.
14   Report on the Conference between Representatives of the Committee for General Purposes, the Stock Exchange, London and the Council of the Associated Stock Exchanges. June 14-16, 1939. Members of Associated Stock Exchanges were to charge half commission to P.B.S.E. brokers; also they could render net contract notes to them.
15   Council of Associated Stock Exchanges, Minutes, October 15, 1920.
16   Ibid., October 26, 1945.
17   Ibid., Resumé, 1946-7.
18   Ibid., April 20, 1920.
19   Ibid., October 18, 1921.
20   Ibid., October 12, 1923.
21   Ibid., October 10, 1924. London introduced the concession in order to combat competition from the large outside financial houses operating in the city.
22   London Stock Exchange, "Alteration to the Rules", (Blue Book Proposals 1941), p. 4.
23   Ibid., p. 2.
24   It was alleged that some London broking firms had come into the country and made agents of all kinds of people, thus taking provincial business to London by offering rebates quite indiscriminatingly.
25   Blue Book Proposals, op. cit., p. 3. Outside brokers on the White List of the London Stock Exchange were transferred to the General Register, provided they were not located in the postal area of an

Associated Stock Exchange, or that of the London Stock Exchange.

26 Ibid., pp. 2-4. In 1945 there were nearly 4,000 agents on the General Register, with solicitors and accountants representing over 80% of the total. By 1956 the General Register had increased to well over 5,000.

27 Council of Associated Stock Exchanges, Minutes, Resumé 1947-8; *Economist,* December 27, 1947, p. 1056; January 29, 1949, p. 210.

28 Council of Associated Stock Exchanges, Minutes, Resumé 1950-1, October 24, 1952; *Economist,* August 9, 1952, p. 357.

29 Council of Associated Stock Exchanges, Minutes, November 1946. Cardiff particularly complained bitterly in the Council about this kind of dealing which they said had been going on for a few years.

30 *Economist,* July 29, 1939, p. 225.

31 Blue Book Proposals, op. cit., p. 5.

32 Council of Associated Stock Exchanges, Minutes, March 7, 1941.

33 *Economist,* April 22, 1939, pp. 202-3.

34 Council of Associated Stock Exchanges, Minutes, March 7, 1941.

35 Ibid., October 7, 1927. The Treasury's reluctance to move on this score does not seem surprising given their ignorance of the workings of the provincial exchanges. When the Controller of Stamps visited a few of them to inquire into the use of the ten shilling stamp duty concession in the 1940s he "appeared to have little knowledge of the manner in which Associated Stock Exchanges function"; ibid., Resumé 1948-9.

36 21 & 22 Geo. 5. ch. 28, s. 42. Finance Act 1931; Council of Associated Stock Exchanges, Minutes, Resumé 1930-31. Most of the work in securing the concession had been done by J. E. Winder, Manchester Stock Exchange. Apparently London agreed to the extension of the 10/- jobbers stamp facility on the understanding that provincial jobbing would be restricted to local securities. This undertaking was given by the administration of the Council of Associated Stock Exchanges but somehow it was never notified to the member exchanges; Liverpool Stock Exchange, Minutes, September 25, 1944.

37 Representatives from the Provincial Stock Exchange came in on the latter part of the discussions.

38 Council of Associated Stock Exchanges, Minutes, March 7, 1941.

39 Ibid., Resumé 1941-2. The initial proposals precluded the sending out of lists to members of other exchanges. Some of the members of the Council were extremely annoyed at this since they had been under the impression that such restrictions would apply only to the sending of lists to outside brokers.

40 Blue Book Proposals, op. cit., p. 6.

41 Ibid., p. 7.

42 Council of Associated Stock Exchanges, Minutes, Resumé 1942-3.

43 Ibid., March 7, 1941.

44 Ibid., October 10, 1942.

45 *Economist,* February 15, 1941, p. 220.

46 Council of Associated Stock Exchanges, Minutes, Resumé 1942-3.

47 Ibid., September 29, 1938; Report on the Conference . . . June 14-16, 1939, op. cit., section 3.

48 Blue Book Proposals, op. cit., Appendix A.

49 Council of Associated Stock Exchanges, Minutes, Resumé 1950-1. Liverpool Stock Exchange, Minutes, May 14, 1950.

50 Ibid., Resumé 1950-51.

11 Organization of the Provincial Stock Exchanges, 1914-1960

While the consequences of the outbreak of the First World War in August 1914 were serious enough for the provincial stock exchanges they were certainly not on the scale experienced by the London market. The provinces did not have London's large volume of international business and they were therefore more or less free from the difficulty of obtaining payment on foreign transactions. Neither were they involved in as much dealing on the basis of borrowed money and were thus less open to problems arising from calls for additional cover for margin loans, or at worst outright recall of the loans. They were not entirely without speculative activity, but contemporary accounts apportion the bulk of their business to investment activity in local and national securities.[1]

The outbreak of war between Serbia and Austria on July 28 1914 produced a sharp fall in prices on the London Stock Exchange, and on the following day London jobbers by tacit agreement declined to deal so that prices became nominal. By this time nearly all the continental markets had closed, while the news on the thirtieth that Paris was about to do the same, which would have meant that firms involved in foreign deals would not be able to fulfil their obligations, prompted the Committee for General Purposes to post a notice in the market on the thirty-first closing the Stock Exchange indefinitely and postponing the settlement until the end of August.[2] The decision by London dealers on the twenty-ninth not to make prices induced both Liverpool and Manchester not to make up the opening boards for that day and await for further moves from London. The decision of the Liverpool Committee was quickly endorsed by a weighty petition from the members urging that no prices should be altered or made during the afternoon call. The Official List was put out but it merely carried a statement that "No Official prices have been made today".[3] It was later decided to bring quotations into line with London, a task completed by members of the Committee on the thirtieth. On the morning of the following day the Liverpool market opened for business and a few transactions took place but immediately news was received of

London's closure the market was closed and the settlement postponed. Manchester did not react quite so promptly to the London move but decided to defer action until they had received full details of the London position. The Stock Exchange was therefore not officially closed until August 4, and even then it was decided to keep the Settlement Room open for the convenience of the members.[4] A similar train of events occurred at Newcastle where the Committee suspended the daily list on the thirty-first, but members continued to negotiate bargains privately until the Exchange was officially declared closed on August 4.[5] Birmingham followed London since under its byelaws it closed automatically upon any move from London; Sheffield also closed on the thirty-first, as did all the remaining markets.

In order to alleviate the financial difficulties of the general business community the Government proclaimed a two-day extension of the Bank Holiday period, and on August 31 quickly passed the Postponement of Payment Act which postponed most commercial payments, including those involving stock exchange transactions for one month, a power which was later renewed for a further two months. Under the terms of the Royal proclamation stock exchange members were able to charge interest at Bank Rate where their principals took advantage of the moratorium and refused to make payments which were falling due.[6] The problem remained however of firms holding securities on borrowed funds; brokers had loans from banks and other sources on behalf of clients who had bought stock and then carried it over in the usual way; jobbers of course depended largely on borrowed money to finance their holdings of stock. The London Stock Exchange quickly ascertained the extent of such borrowing, which came to £81 million (see Table below for details). The London Committee was also anxious to know the precise country position but the leading provincial markets declined to make such information available, claiming that the serious problem evident in London did not apply in their case.[7] However, sometime later they were quite prepared to supply the relevant information when the Treasury requested a full statement as to the amount of loans outstanding so that they could assess what assistance could be offered to the stock exchanges. The total borrowing of the provincial exchanges came to nearly £11.0 million. The following are the detailed figures for Liverpool, Manchester, and London.[8] This was not of course the entire loan position of the markets since large amounts of stocks and shares stood in the names of brokers and their clients who had taken in stock as a means of getting a good rate of interest.[9]

At the end of October the Government announced a scheme to

Q

Outstanding Loans

Amount owing to London Clearing Banks and branches:-	With Margin £	Without Margin £	Total £
Liverpool	1,850,176	10.000	1,860,176
Manchester	322,200	130,000	452,200
London	36,331,190	786,420	37,117,610
All other Banks:-			
Liverpool	893,560	—	893,560
Manchester	531,390	79,000	610,390
London	19,891,374	3,709,008	23,600,382
Other institutions, firms or individuals not members of the Stock Exchange:-			
Liverpool	391,281	133,514	524,795
Manchester	182,311	62,084	244,395
London	10,810,401	9,232,967	20,043,368
Total loans outstanding:-			
Liverpool	3,135,017	143.514	3,278,531
Manchester	1,035,901	271,084	1,306,985
London	67,032,965	13,728,395	80,761,360

help the Stock Exchanges but it did not apply to lenders who were members of a stock exchange. The scheme was drawn up "with a view to avoiding the necessity of the forced realisation on a large scale of securities held as cover for account to account loans", which it was feared might occur once the moratorium ended and as soon as any semblance of a free market was re-established. The main provisions of the scheme were that the joint stock banks agreed not to press for repayment, or request further margin, on stock exchange loans; the Bank of England was empowered to make advances to other lenders up to 60% of the value of the securities held as collateral, at one per cent above Bank Rate (varying), provided they likewise did not press for payment (an obligation which extended to twelve months after the end of the war); the stock exchanges were to ensure that the benefit of the scheme should be passed on to the ultimate borrowers. Early repayment of loans was allowed for upon the liquidation of the borrower, or if the securities pledged as collateral reached the valuation price of July 27 for Consols and July 29 for other securities.[10]

Provincial reactions to the aid offered were varied. They accepted it but not without some caustic remarks. They were annoyed that the provinces had not been asked to participate in the discussions between the London Stock Exchange, the Treasury, and the Bank of England, and claimed that provincial interests were not identical with those of London. They shared in the general annoyance that members themselves had been omitted from the scheme which

thereby left out an important group of lenders. Also they disliked
having to agree not to re-open the stock exchanges without sub-
mitting the date and conditions for Treasury scrutiny.[11] Manchester's
objections were much more strongly put; "its application is not
suitable to the needs of this Exchange, nevertheless, in view of the
interdependance of the various Exchanges, it is essential that Exchanges should adopt one common scheme . . . [but] . . . the
severity of the crisis and the need for assistance is not common to
all the Exchanges, but was brought about by over trading and over
speculation on borrowed resources in London – that the length to
which the system of so-called underwriting has been carried in
recent years has led to the pawning of masses of undigested securities with Banks and other money lenders – that the Members of this
Exchange generally and their clients, the investing public, have no
responsibility for the state of things brought about by these operations".[12] This fervent disclaimer does not altogether square with
their annoyance at not being consulted about the scheme, nor perhaps
with the fact that nearly a quarter of Manchester's outstanding loans
had no margin at all. Birmingham added similar strictures, referring to the "careless and evil producing system in some markets
of carrying over stocks".[13] A more restrained provincial broker
however noted that the problem was not margin lending but loans
without a sufficient margin, which if used would have taken borrowers out of the danger zone.

After the official closure of the stock exchanges share dealing
went on in a variety of circumstances. In Liverpool it was suggested
in September that the Stock Exchange should open for a limited
time each day since members were dealing in the street. A petition
to the Committee emphasized that there was a fair deal of investment
business (insurance shares were beginning to pick up) on a cash
basis, and that, as the Chairman put it, they "had been long enough
on the pavement and in the gutter for the reputation of the Liverpool Stock Exchange". Accordingly, members were allowed access
to the Clearing House which proved unsuitable and shortly afterwards they were given limited access to the market on condition
that it was not regarded as officially open, that no prices were published, cash deals only, no telegraph facilities, and that trustee stocks
be dealt in at fixed prices.[14] Manchester members however had not
really left the premises. In October the Committee allowed access
to the floor for two hours daily, with a small call-over in a very
limited range of stocks, and of course, all cash business. A request
to the Treasury for permission to reopen the market in December
was turned down since the authorities were anxious to reopen all
the markets simultaneously.[15] After the closure of the Birmingham

Stock Exchange members met to do business by private negotiation on the premises, but the Committee were very anxious to keep quiet about such activities, and all transactions were unofficial. A request to the Treasury in October to reopen the market for "unofficial dealing" was turned down, but it was later granted in December.[16] The Sheffield Stock Exchange was one of the first to resume business, on a strictly cash basis, after the closure. This arose because of the large number of enquiries coming in for armament shares. Business was negotiated through brokers and the Committee put out a list for the information of the public.[17] Newcastle brokers were provided with a room to meet for unofficial dealing; by October they found that there was a "fair amount of speculation passing".[18] On August 6 Cardiff members reopened dealings on a small scale in their offices, and a fortnight later the Committee announced that "although the Exchange was officially closed, the members were meeting daily, with the view of arranging business between buyers and sellers for cash settlements."[19]

On September 14 the Committee of the London Stock Exchange issued a list of recommended minimum prices (as on July 30) for some 800 trustee securities, and within a short space of time this action was widely copied in the provinces. Liverpool went a stage further and fixed minimum prices for local securities, and members were invited to recommend local stocks for inclusion in such a list; Liverpool however did not adopt the American share minimum.[20] By contrast Manchester was rather reluctant to accept London's lead "to guard against attacks upon the National Credit". The Committee maintained that they had no power to restrict members in their dealings and they merely posted the London list in the market.[21] Sheffield accepted the London minimum in the case of investment securities but continued to negotiate daily prices in armament and other local stocks. This was the general policy adopted by most markets.[22]

Improved war news brought prices nearer to the recommended minimum, and to the valuation prices fixed under the relief scheme. The difficulties in the way of reopening the exchanges were rapidly receding, while the November settlement passed without difficulty. Provincial exchanges were increasingly concerned that they were losing business to outside brokers over whom they had no control, and nobody else seemed to have any either. By the use of widespread advertising outsiders were able to obtain a large amount of business which had previously gone to the stock exchanges, and this was especially the case in the shares of companies securing armaments contracts.[23]

The authorities however were concerned about much more

general matters, such as, measures to prevent a drastic fall in prices, the need to deny market facilities to the enemy, to prevent neutrals from selling securities and take out gold and to see that Government loans were not exposed to competition from other borrowers. On the basis of these considerations a scheme was finally agreed upon between the Treasury, the Bank of England, the London clearing banks, and the London Stock Exchange, for reopening the stock exchanges. The date of reopening was fixed as January 4, 1915, on condition that markets accepted the temporary regulations which had been drawn up. Among the main points in these were that minimum prices should continue for a time, that the recommended list could be altered by the London Committee but that any reduction in prices needed Treasury approval, cash bargains and no speculative facilities, all new issues to be subject to Treasury consent, and that "no member shall be allowed to bid for or offer stock openly in the market". In view of the fact that the "absence of Dealers in most of the provincial Stock Exchanges would render this provision almost prohibitory", the Chairman of the Council of Associated Stock Exchanges met Sir John Bradbury and Lord Reading of the Treasury, and secured the relaxation of this provision for the provinces.[24]

The system of minimum prices was as unpopular on the provincial exchanges as it was on the London floor. It was certainly the least approved of the reopening conditions. Manchester spoke particularly strongly on the matter stating that they were "prepared to consent – though not willingly and under strong protest – to conform to these conditions. . . . We recognize that it is possible that it is in the interests of certain powerful financial houses and banking institutions to endeavour to keep up prices in this way".[25] In general provincial dislike of minimum prices stemmed from the following points; that the position of the stock exchanges became very nominal if business was to be restricted arbitrarily to the quotations ruling at the end of July; that it interfered with the freedom of trustees and executors; that in some cases minimum prices had been fixed at too high a figure thus making stock unmarketable; and that outside organizations had no restrictions to abide by.[26] Unrestricted prices in the provinces however were not fraught with the same dangers as such a policy would have involved had freedom been quickly resumed on the London market; there was after all some difference between the "retail transactions in a country Stock Exchange and the wide freedom of a real market in London". The general idea of the authorities of course was to protect members, and the public, against violent falls in prices following the receipt of bad war news.

An additional element in obtaining the removal of a minimum scale was that such a move was expedient for the Treasury. Heavy official borrowing forced up rates and if the market was to be kept from "freezing" up it was necessary to allow for the revision of prices. Accordingly, prices were marked down in March and June 1915, and in November British Funds and several other trustee stocks were removed from the list. The provinces applauded these moves and claimed that since investors had now been given an opportunity to sell they might transfer into Government securities. In January 1916 a further group was removed from the list (including Bank of England stock), and in July all prices became completely free again.[27]

Another area of stock exchange operations which was controlled by temporary regulations were new issues. After January 1915 dealings in new issues needed the sanction of a stock exchange committee and the approval of the Treasury. In this matter the Treasury was advised by a newly formed committee, and domestic issues had to satisfy it that they were "advisable in the national interest". After an initial rush of applications the flow of new issues was reduced to a trickle by 1916, and thereafter the Government became very jealous of the new issue facility.[28]

With the ending of the war the authorities and the stock exchanges were anxious to remove all controls as soon as possible. One of the first to go was the one relating to new issues which was removed in March 1919. It was to take a while longer to bring back normal dealing facilities, that is, account dealing, carryovers and options. One procedure however was quickly restored to provincial floors. In January 1919 Manchester resumed calling over the price boards, without seeking Treasury permission; in February such consent was given to all provincial markets provided the chairman of the stock exchange presided at the call-over.[29] Although they were also anxious to resume account dealing and carryover facilities they could not do so without similar action by London, and approval from the Treasury. One stumbling block to this was the fact that office staffs depleted by war recruitment could not cope with the additional burdens of extended dealing facilities. The major difficulty was that the Treasury would not permit account dealing to resume until the pre-war loan position had been settled. As far as the provinces were concerned this was not a serious problem. At the end of October 1921 Liverpool had loans of £72,000 outstanding to banks, and just over £9,000 to other lenders; the Manchester figures were £26,000 and £2,000 respectively.[30] Matters were not pressed very hard at this juncture since markets were relatively depressed. However, by 1922 markets had improved and the pre-war debt position was virtually cleared, and in May the temporary regulations came to an end. Fortnightly settlements were resumed, options were henceforth limited to three months, gilt-edged dealings were put on a cash basis, while 'permission to deal' in new issues replaced the twin regulations of special settlements and quotation requirements.[31]

The war also had a marked effect upon the membership of the provincial stock exchanges. Within a few months of its outbreak half of the "possible effectives" of the Liverpool Stock Exchange had enlisted, that is, thirty-one members and ninety-four clerks. Following further recruiting drives by the National Service Department the number of Liverpool members in the forces increased to forty-seven by 1917, along with 199 clerks. Birmingham by the same date had lost 109 members and clerks. By 1916 Manchester had lost 138 persons, with a further 138 "attested" but not yet joined.[32] As a result of this drain the total membership of the three exchanges fell from 359 in 1914 to 302 in 1918. The loss of clerks, telegraph operators and other personnel was to some extent compensated for by the increased employment of women. The smaller exchanges suffered loss of members and other staff but nowhere near the scale of the larger markets.

During the inter-war years the membership of most exchanges remained fairly constant. Reduced turnover, loss of local share markets, and the introduction of labour saving devices all played a part in this. Only two markets displayed any large increases, Manchester and Birmingham. The former increased from 88 in 1918 to 142 in 1938, while the latter increased from 60 to 105 over the same period. The Second World War had a similar impact to the first, the three largest markets suffered a reduction in membership of about 50 each, while the smaller markets each lost a few members; the total personnel of the Associated Stock Exchanges fell from a pre-war level of just over 4,000 to around 2,000 in 1942.[33] Since the war the membership of the exchanges has remained more or less constant.

The inter-war period witnessed a further decline in the importance of the call-over as a mechanism by which provincial markets did their dealing, and the trend persisted after the last war until eventually it was abandoned by one exchange after another in the nineteen sixties. Increasingly dealing took place between the official call overs and this tendency was accelerated with the rapid adoption of improved telephone facilities after the First World War. The call-over was also made less important by the emergence of country jobbing facilities which provided a superior service by way of continuous dealing opportunities. The decline in the importance of the call-over is also evident in the attempts made by several exchanges to bolster it up. For example, absence of members from the floor certainly militated against its efficiency and this problem was particularly bad for the smaller markets, such as Leeds and Newcastle, who attempted to improve attendance but with no lasting success.[34] Sheffield by contrast in 1936 regarded the call-over as an "interruption to ordinary business", and accordingly from that date they ceased to call the list for quotations.[35] Other markets found that many securities on their lists were seldom dealt in and pruning followed so as to cut out the deadwood, for example, Birmingham in 1936 decided not to call inactive stocks. Earlier in 1931 the Manchester Committee indicated to the members that they would welcome lists of what were regarded as active stocks. Meanwhile the importance of local jobbers in the dealing process was greatly increasing. Markets urged their jobbers to provide current prices of active stocks, and in Liverpool the jobbers who did so in order to provide better price information were given the protection of the chair.[36] In 1936 Birmingham decided, following an evaluation of the call-over procedure, to request their jobbers to give prices to the boards. Ultimately then the call-over became merely a means of ascertaining an official price of the most current business and little more than this. It was certainly not a dealing mechanism any more since that role had been taken over by continuous floor dealing and the facilities provided by country jobbers and shunters.

The overall structure of country business during the early inter-war years may be summarized as follows. Deals for local clients in purely local stocks could be handled on the spot. If a client wanted to deal in national stocks this could be done locally by finding another broker with a complementary order, or through the local jobbing market, a procedure which was greatly favoured by provincial spokesmen at the time. If it could not be executed locally then it could be put through the agency channels to another provincial market or to London, and the commission would in this instance be divided between the initiating broker and the one who actually executed the deal. Alternatively the order could be accommodated through Shunting channels, that is, by one of the specialist firms in the provinces who maintained a nationwide network of private lines and teleprinters. During the inter-war years this structure was modified by the appearance of very active country jobbing which developed in the late twenties, and which lasted until the early years of the Second World War.

Provincial jobbing activity in the early twenties was relatively limited in nature being mostly confined to local stocks. One reason for this restriction (limited jobbing in this sense meant jobbing within an account) was that country brokers were excluded from the concession on stamp duties handed to 'dealers only' in the 1920 Finance Act. Under this concession dealers could hold stocks without payment of an ad valorem stamp duty for a period of up to two months.[37] Provincial jobbers deprived of this concession were therefore reluctant to buy shares towards the end of an account which tended to narrow local markets. In 1931, following country pressure, the Finance Bill granted the concession to members recognized by the committee of a stock exchange as carrying on the business of a dealer, that is, engaging in the regular and habitual practice of dealing.

Within a short space of time six Liverpool firms had claimed the concession, among them H. E. Rensburg & Co., J. Arnitt Dear & Co., and Hardie B. Martin & Co. Six Manchester firms requested their Committee to be recognized as dealers, and among these were Henry Cooke & Son., F. W. Staveacre & Co., David Q. Henriques & Co., and Kerr, Leather and Hollows, with a further four firms obtaining the concession during the period 1932–35. Over the years 1933–38 four Bristol firms obtained the 10s. jobber stamp, including H. C. Woodcock & Co. The largest crop of applicants came from Birmingham with its expanding market in industrial shares. In the 1930s thirteen firms requested recognition by the local Committee, including T. & H. Wheelock for insurance shares (they had been specialists in them for thirty years), Smith, Keen, Barnett and Son for rails and general shares, Gibbs and Viney, and E. A. Collis, in motor company shares. However, several of these had withdrawn from the 10s. stamp list by 1938; application for permission to use the concession had to be renewed every six months. The resulting provincial jobbing network proved to be more extensive than London had envisaged and outside commentators were soon attesting that "London is naturally feeling the competition of provincial jobbers".[38] Generally, they operated in a limited range of securities which changed periodically to accord with current market interest. They made net prices which in the case of local shares were based on local markets, while prices in national stocks could be locally based or else taken from London. Using net prices was of course the accepted convention in the provinces where the free trade principle was fully accepted. Undoubtedly the leading proponent of this form of business was the Sheffield firm of J. W. Nicholson and Sons.

The firm was formed in 1909 by J. W. Nicholson who had joined the Sheffield Stock Exchange in 1899 as a member of the firm of F. E. & S. Smith. In 1912 Cyril Nicholson joined his father and in 1927 four more partners were admitted into the firm, namely, W.

A. Nicholson, G. F. Booker, F. P. Nicholson and A. G. Wall. The possibilities of provincial jobbing were first appreciated during the shunting activity they conducted in the early post-war boom, and more so, during the rubber boomlet of 1925 when they used a machine for printing jobbing lists which were sent out daily to numerous provincial brokers. These circulars gave lists of net prices at which Nicholson's were prepared to deal up until 11.00 a.m. on the next morning. The practice of quoting fixed prices was a great convenience to provincial brokers since it gave them a definite price up until the opening of markets; the practice was later dropped however. Gradually the firm increased its coverage and by the early 1930s it was sending out some 900 circulars. An important step which greatly facilitated the growth of their jobbing business was taken in 1927 when they moved their offices into the Telephone Buildings where they had the full co-operation of the Post Office in building up an elaborate communications network. By 1928 they had connections with London and all the main provincial markets. In order to improve their efficiency they contracted Ericssons, the telephone and electrical experts, to build an up-to-date dealing room with an electrical display board which formed the centre of their jobbing operations.[39] Through a network of private lines covering the main industrial centres in the United Kingdom provincial brokers were able to contact the nearest local centre which was in direct communication with the dealing room in Sheffield, from which they could obtain a dealing price immediately and complete the transaction quickly, and for a much smaller telephone charge than putting a call through to London or a major provincial exchange. The prices made by the dealers in Sheffield were radiated to all the local centres by girls in the dealing room, and by 1936 facilities for the execution and completion of up to 3,000 bargains a day were installed, including a punch card system of accounting.

Some of the facilities offered by Nicholsons were very beneficial to the smaller markets who lacked their own shunting links with London, who had no local jobbers, and who were not over enthusiastic as to the service they got from the larger exchanges through the traditional agency channels. Nicholsons it was claimed "will give you a price in any security", a service not altogether to the liking of the larger markets who lost business as a result. This type of operation is characterized by what one rather testy representative to the Council of Associated Stock Exchanges called "the Belfast Venture". In that instance Nicholsons had a teleprinter link to the office of a Belfast broker who then allowed other brokers "to ascertain prices". When any business resulted the exchange of contracts and the completion of the transaction was done directly between the initiating broker and Nicholsons. The Bradford Stock Exchange also benefited from a similar collective service in which the business was originated by the local members, not by Nicholsons.[40]

The decline of this impressive and efficient organization came at the beginning of the Second World War when the G.P.O. terminated the private line facilities owing to the national emergency. Unfortunately this masterly operation had provoked London's hostility, while the larger provincial exchanges were basically hostile as well. London had been aroused on two counts, one general the other specific. On the general count London held that such jobbing operations in a wide range of securities diverted business from them, that London prices were used, and that they could always get out in London (and not infrequently at a loss). Hence the proposals in the Blue Book for regulating country jobbing which resulted in London adopting rules which enabled them to declare any country jobbing firm a non-member jobber and accordingly to "prohibit or regulate the business relations of members with non-member jobbers". In practice this meant that London members had to give an assurance that they would exclude such parties from their direct private telephone lines. Following this declaration in the summer of 1941 the firm was divided into two with J. W. Nicholson & Sons concentrating on the private clients business, and Cyril Nicholson & Co. continuing with the jobbing side.

The specific count came a little later and resulted in the ending of Nicholson's links with provincial markets. It arose following "the discovery of the existence of a circuit line connecting a non-member jobber with four of the larger Exchanges, the same brokers have a separate circuit to London". The upshot was a proposal from the Council of Associated Stock Exchanges to member exchanges that they should adopt rules which "preclude your member from having a private line or teleprinter to a firm declared by the Stock Exchange, London, to be a non-member jobber".[41] The rule was not at all popular with the smaller markets, and Bradford only relinquished its link with Cyril Nicholson & Co.[42] after a threat by the larger exchanges to charge Bradford and Sheffield members full commission on all business done with them.[43]

The outbreak of war in 1939 did not produce a repetition of the 1914 financial crisis in London or in the provinces. The stock exchanges were less involved in international business, and they had a warning of things to come during the crisis of 1938, when, on some provincial exchanges they had to abandon the call-over for a time because "it was impossible to obtain current prices of securities".[44] When the outbreak of war came the provinces quickly followed London's lead, more or less pursuing the Birmingham policy that "any special regulations put into force in the London Stock Exchange governing the transaction of business shall be considered binding upon members of this Exchange". The ruling by London on August 24 that no member should deal in gilt-edged, corporation and dominion stocks below the previous day's prices, and that all bargains in such securities should be for cash, was adopted in the provinces. Also, the provincial exchanges closed between September 1–7, and they adopted the same temporary regulations as London as to the governing of business, namely that all bargains be for cash, no options or contangoes, and that permission to deal in new issues would not be given unless such issues were approved by the Treasury and the committee of a stock exchange.[45]

When business settled down to the new conditions in the spring of 1940 the provincial stock exchanges were anxious to return to fortnightly settlements since they experienced considerable delays in getting names. They alleged that London brokers were "reluctant to sell out for fear of creating ill-will with the jobbers"; something of a perenial problem. Such a resumption however was delayed for many years because the responsible authorities (the Treasury and the Bank of England) were "reluctant to make any change at the present time, owing to the dangers of encouraging speculation and with depleted staffs, the difficulties of settling account bargains in the course of a few days".[46] Another problem for provincial markets who relied heavily upon telephone networks, which they had built up at some expense in the thirties, was the reduced facilities they enjoyed, especially after the introduction of 'priority calls' in 1941. With regard to minimum prices the provinces accepted the necessity of a floor to prevent collapse with bad war news, but they found that a partial floor covering only Government securities created problems for industrial shares. The latter tended to bear the brunt of forced sales to raise funds, and even small transactions tended in wartime to produce disproportionate falls in prices.[47]

The restoration of a free market at the end of the war took rather a long time considering that there was not the problem of a pre-war settlement as in 1914 to cope with. Certain quarters were, however, somewhat suspicious of the resumption of speculative facilities. Even before the war ended the exchanges exerted continuous pressure aimed at an early resumption, and when peace came difficult conditions were created "by the continued application of daily cash settlements to the heavy volume of post-war business". Fortnightly settlements were re-introduced early in 1947, but without contangoes or free closing. The speculative facilities were not reintroduced until later; restricted contangoes were allowed in 1949, but broker-to-broker contangoes did not come until 1953 while options were not reintroduced until 1958.[48]

As to the question of provincial dealing facilities the post-war period witnessed a gradual reduction in their scope, a trend basically dictated by London's fear of a repetition of the sort of competition which Nicholson had provided in the thirties. During the immediate post-war period shunting activity was undertaken on an extensive scale particularly by the larger shunting exchanges. At this time there were eight shunting exchanges, namely, Glasgow, Manchester, Liverpool, Birmingham, Edinburgh, Leeds, Newcastle, and Bristol. The larger markets had about six shunters each. The smaller exchanges had single shunting lines while the larger market had omnibus circuits which made "Manchester, Liverpool, and Birmingham, to a considerable extent, one floor". Three firms of shunters operating from Glasgow, Bristol, and Liverpool made prices in a very wide range of stocks, much wider than they were supposed to, and they in effect jobbed to members of other markets using fixed time calls and basing their operations on London prices. As a result a considerable volume of business was married in the provinces and thus never reached London. There were also some London shunters who did the same. Up to a point London had been prepared to acquiesce in a few smallish imitators so long as the scale was very modest, and no more. By 1950 London was very concerned at this development and saw it, understandably, as a potential return to the Nicholson technique. Accordingly rules were introduced in that year and agreed to by the provinces, but not without a storm of protest from the smaller exchanges whose access to dealing facilities had once more been curtailed. The effect of the new rules was to confine shunting during the ensuing years to much more rigid channels. A shunter served his own exchange and gave it a London price service in a wide range of securities, but he could not deal off his own book to any broker outside his own exchange except in local securities and in gilt-edged, both of which were subject to qualification. Local securities were those of companies which then or previously had their head offices within a radius of thirty miles of the exchange in respect of which they were claimed as local. By agreement with London certain other securities were also classified as local, such as insurance shares in the case of Liverpool and Birmingham, where two firms ran jobbing books in them. With regard to gilt-edged a shunter was permitted to have one declared correspondent on each of the twenty-one Associated Stock Exchanges with whom he could make prices or deal off his own book, but time calls to other markets were specifically prohibited.[49]

On commission charges the general pattern was for provincial markets to follow London. Most of them felt that they could not afford to be below London, especially on small deals and at a time when expenses absorbed an increasing portion of commission income, while pitching rates above London would merely result in a loss of business for the provinces. However, there were two notable exceptions to this picture, although they too were soon to follow London's lead. Manchester had traditionally maintained a very distinctive approach to the commission question particularly as to rebates of commissions to agents. Their own commission levels were "based on the fact that we do not divide with anyone", and they justified such a practice by stating that division was "detrimental to the interest of both principal and broker".[50] It led however to some curious and not particularly cheap channelling of business. For example, Manchester banks sent business to London brokers and in the case of local stocks they then sent it back to Manchester.[51] By 1926 the drift of business away from Manchester was causing concern to many of the members and in a strongly supported petition to the Committee they stated that they "viewed with much anxiety the diversion of important business from this market to others", and urged that the situation be reviewed. As a result certain minor amendments were made but the position of agents remained unchanged. Dissatisfaction persisted and following another widely supported petition a year later the Committee agreed to allow members to grant rebates to banks and the Public Trustee.[52] Final conformity with the London scale came in 1936 when some "petty irregularities" between the two markets were removed. However, although Manchester followed the general practice of rebating to agents they persistently urged its general abandonment and they were positively euphoric when the number of agents were reduced as a result of the 1939 conference proposals.

Birmingham was the other provincial individualist. Their level of commissions was generally higher than that of other markets and they claimed at the end of the First World War that they did not suffer by it, indeed they urged others to come up to them. However, in 1926 it was decided to adopt the London level, a decision which did not please all the members. Birmingham also operated for a number of years a "protected list" of securities on which members were compelled to charge the Birmingham scale of commissions. Evasions obviously occurred by putting the business through another market, but in 1917 the Committee fixed a minimum scale for business in such stocks coming from other markets. The protected list was abolished in 1923 and a more flexible policy pursued.[53]

NOTES

1 *Economist*, October 31, 1914, p. 786.
2 Morgan and Thomas, op. cit., p. 217; *Economist*, August 1, 1914, pp. 220-21, "The Stock Exchange Crisis Day by Day". In the event the settlement was further postponed until November when it passed relatively smoothly; only £0.5 million was advanced for all markets through the relief scheme.
3 Liverpool Stock Exchange, Minutes, July 29, 1914.
4 Manchester Stock Exchange, Minutes, July 31, August 4, 1914.
5 Newcastle Stock Exchange, Minutes, July 31, August 4, 1914.
6 Liverpool Stock Exchange, Minutes, August 11, 1914.
7 Ibid., September 1, 1914.
8 Ibid., October 13, 1914; Manchester Stock Exchange, Minutes, October 7, 1914. The loans were probably used to carry stocks on the London list. Unfortunately a full breakdown of the total provincial borrowing figure is not available.
9 *Economist*, October 17, 1914, p. 634.
10 E. Victor Morgan, *Studies in British Financial Policy 1914-1925* (1952), pp. 26-7.
11 Liverpool Stock Exchange, Minutes, November 3, 1914. See also *Economist*, January 2, 1915, pp. 4-5; "the provincial stock exchanges have not been unanimous in their endorsement of the Treasury's dictation", particularly so Glasgow, Edinburgh and Manchester.
12 Manchester Stock Exchange, Minutes, November 9, 1914.
13 Birmingham Stock Exchange, Minutes, November 18, 1914.
14 Liverpool Stock Exchange, Minutes, September 22, 29, October 8, 13, 1914.
15 Manchester Stock Exchange, Minutes, October 1, November 30, 1914.
16 Birmingham Stock Exchange, Minutes, October 27, November 12, December 11, 1914.
17 Sheffield Stock Exchange, Minutes, August 7, 1914; *Economist*, November 7, 1914, p. 834.
18 Newcastle Stock Exchange, Minutes, September 9, 1914, *Economist*, November 7, 1914, p. 834.
19 *Economist*, November 7, 1914, p. 835.
20 Liverpool Stock Exchange, Minutes, September 15, 1914; *Economist*, October 31, 1914, p. 787.
21 Manchester Stock Exchange, Minutes, September 15, 1914.
22 Sheffield Stock Exchange, Minutes, November 11, 1914.
23 Birmingham Stock Exchange, Minutes, October 27, 1914; Manchester Stock Exchange, Minutes, November 30, 1914.
24 Liverpool Stock Exchange, Minutes, December 31, 1914.
25 Manchester Stock Exchange, Minutes, December 31, 1914.
26 Liverpool Stock Exchange, Minutes, February 16, 1914, February 28, 1916; Birmingham Stock Exchange, Minutes, February 15, 1915. Outside brokers and financial houses dealt below the minimum prices.
27 Liverpool Stock Exchange, Minutes, November 29, 1915, February 1, 1916; Morgan and Thomas, op. cit., p. 220.
28 Morgan and Thomas, op. cit., p. 220.
29 Liverpool Stock Exchange, Minutes, January 14, February 7, 1919.
30 Liverpool Stock Exchange, Minutes, October 11, 1921; Manchester Stock Exchange, Minutes, May 5, 1920; September 30, 1921.

31 Manchester Stock Exchange, Minutes, May 19, 1922; Liverpool Stock Exchange, Minutes, May 17, 1922.
32 Liverpool Stock Exchange, Minutes, March 20, 1917, Birmingham Stock Exchange, Minutes, March 20, 1917. The Manchester Stock Exchange complained to the National Service Department in 1917 that their establishment had now been reduced to a minimum level and could not be reduced any further; Minutes, March 21, 1917.
33 Liverpool Stock Exchange, Minutes, June 18, 1942. Thirty-one firms had ceased to exist and there had been ten amalgamations.
34 Leeds Stock Exchange, Minutes, January 18, 1928; Newcastle Stock Exchange, Minutes, March 12, 1947.
35 Sheffield Stock Exchange, Minutes, October 27, 1936.
36 Liverpool Stock Exchange, Minutes, December 9, 1924.
37 Liverpool Stock Exchange, Minutes, August 18, 1931; see also Chapter 10.
38 Birmingham Stock Exchange, Minutes, July 23, 1935.
39 In 1932 two of the partners went to Wall Street to look at American practices but returned unimpressed by what they saw. Their dealing room in Sheffield was certainly superior to anything in this country and well ahead of its time. Nicholson's also had a "fine statistical department".
40 Sheffield Stock Exchange, Minutes, August 30, 1939.
41 Sheffield Stock Exchange, Minutes, November 12, 1942.
42 Bradford Stock Exchange, Minutes, October 12, 1943. This particular line could be switched through to the offices of all Bradford members.
43 I am greatly indebted to J. W. Nicholson & Sons, Sheffield, for providing details of the firm's history.
44 Manchester Stock Exchange, Minutes, September 27, 1938. London gilt edged jobbers fixed minimum prices at the time, a move widely followed in the provinces. They only lasted for two days, but even so there was an appreciable loss of business to outside houses; Economist, August 26, 1939, p. 411.
45 Unofficial business was conducted on some markets during this period.
46 Liverpool Stock Exchange, Minutes, March 12, 1940.
47 Liverpool Stock Exchange, Minutes, June 20, 1940. London had discussions with the authorities on these points but no action was taken.
48 Morgan and Thomas, op. cit., pp. 236-7.
49 Liverpool Stock Exchange, Minutes, February 14, March 14, July 4, October 17, 1950. It was easy to identify shunters who went beyond jobbing in local securities since if they asked for the 10/- jobbers stamp facility they had to declare the shares for which they wanted the concession.
50 Manchester Stock Exchange, Minutes, January 19, 1920.
51 Economist, August 12, 1916, pp. 282-3.
52 Manchester Stock Exchange, Minutes, October 6, 1926, March 16, 1927.
53 Birmingham Stock Exchange, Minutes, January 31, 1917, February 23, 1923, August 10, 1926.

12 The Industrial Share Market in the Provinces since 1918

At various times since the end of the First World War the share lists of the provincial stock exchanges have undergone certain bouts of contraction. The first of these occurred with the railway grouping of 1923, under the provisions of the 1921 Railway Act. This programme of amalgamation was largely inspired by the experience of unified working during the war which had brought greater efficiency and various operating economies. Under the Act "about six score companies have been turned into four companies". These were the Great Western Railway (nominal capital £136.5 million), The Southern Railway (£145.0 million), the London and North Eastern Railway (£348.0 million), and the London, Midland and Scottish Railway (£430.0 million). The advantages of the change to the shareholders were those of "comparative stability of prices and of readier marketability".[1] However, as far as provincial stock exchange lists were concerned it meant a reduction in the range of railway shares they carried. For example, in the case of the Manchester Stock Exchange List the number was reduced from twenty-eight lines to seven. This of itself did not result in reduced market turnover but with subsequent public loss of interest in railway shares after the conversion and the gradual concentration of dealing in London, the former prominence of provincial railway markets, especially its shunting activity in debentures, gradually disappeared. As from January 1, 1948 the four main railway companies were vested in the British Transport Commission, along with several other quoted transport undertakings, and the shareholders received in compensation British Transport 3% Guaranteed Stock 1978–88.[2]

Other major acts of nationalization also occurred after the Second World War. The first was the Coal Industry Nationalization Act of 1946 which provided for the public ownership and control of the coal mining industry and certain other allied activities, and for the establishment of the National Coal Board. The total value of the assets transferred amounted to £164 million, the largest transfers involving companies operating in Yorkshire, Nottinghamshire, Durham and Northumberland, Scotland, and South Wales. Compensa-

R

tion took the form of Government guaranteed stock. Since the mining activities of numerous companies were vested in the N.C.B. as from January 1947 this involved a reduction of assets and earning power of many of the large quoted companies, and led in the case of specialized mining markets, such as Cardiff, to a considerable reduction in share activity.

Also among the quoted securities taken off the market during the nationalization programme of the post-war Labour Government were those of companies acquired by the British Electricity Authority, which was set up under the provisions of the Electricity Act of 1947. Compensation in this instance took the form of British Electricity Authority stock issued on the basis of the "average market value" for quoted securities, while unquoted securities were a matter for arbitration. Some 130 companies were involved throughout the country, many of which were quoted in provincial lists, particularly the smaller local concerns.[3] Another fuel industry nationalized at the same time, the gas industry, also led to the loss of numerous gas companies from the lists of provincial exchanges. Many gas works had of course long been municipalized but by no means all of them. The Gas Act of 1948 set up area boards to develop and maintain local gas supplies and on vesting day in May 1949 the assets and liabilities of over 620 companies, whose securities were still in the public hands, were vested in the appropriate area board, while compensation was in British Gas stock.[4] The steel industry was also for a time subject to nationalization. Under the provisions of the 1949 Steel Act ninety-five iron and steel companies were taken over, but following the change of Government in 1952 the industry was de-nationalized. However, it was again re-nationalized in 1967 with the result that the shares of the leading steel making companies disappeared from provincial lists resulting in a marked loss of business for a specialist market such as Sheffield.

If certain specialized lines of stock were taken out of provincial lists this was more than compensated for, in terms of numbers at least, by the increase in the industrial and commercial sector after 1918. Admittedly this growth did not provide as homogeneous a group of securities as some of those which had been taken over by the state constituted, but periodic surges of activity and the gradual growth of provincial companies to a 'national' standing kept up a steady stream of business, particularly in areas of the country where the newer industries were fast taking root. Rapidly growing companies were quick to exhaust the traditional sources of private capital and accordingly resorted to the market for an increasing proportion of their capital needs.

The immediate post-war years certainly witnessed such a company boom. The rapid relaxation of wartime new issue regulations in the early part of 1919 meant that issues for domestic purposes could proceed without restriction.[5] Conditions were such that the supply of securities was quickly taken up. Money market rates were low and the public had large sums of money at their disposal, while wartime propoganda had popularized the advantages of investing in securities. If the traditional high income investor was on the decline, the number of small investors had not only increased but they had also become more enterprising and speculative.[6] They readily took up ordinary shares, particularly those offered by the more speculative undertakings, while the more prudent investor only took up preference and debenture issues. In addition, while such sophisticated activities as underwriting, or even sub-underwriting, was not readily accessible to the majority of outsiders as a means of obtaining shares, large scale "stagging" on the other hand became extremely popular.[7] On the supply side it was predominantly a boom in home industrials. Companies were quick to take advantage of market conditions to undertake capital reorganizations by conversion issues. Others, in need of additional funds contributed to the flow of new shares, while promoters of new companies were never slow to seize a suitable moment to throw their "creations" onto the market.

The year 1919 provided a large number of company registrations, nearly 11,000, and particularly noticeable within the total was the relative increase in the number of companies with capitals in the range, £200,000 to £300,000, of which there were nearly 300 in the year. The amount of capital subscribed for the industrial and commercial category was £70.1 million, a figure which rose to £157.8 million in 1920, but which declined to £32.7 million in the following year.[8] The boom was mainly associated with the provision of industrial capital through the issue of ordinary and preference shares, which represented 84% of all issues in 1919 and 68% in 1920. Only when the boom collapsed and when speculative issues had fallen off did fixed interest stock come onto the market in any quantity. A feature of this was the large number of short-term notes which appeared towards the end of 1920. Generally they matured within 5 to 12 years and were issued on generous terms, 8% issued at 98%, which indicated the difficulties companies experienced in raising capital. The hope of course was to fund in the future at a lower rate. At this time, however, market conditions were such that even with fixed interest stock yielding up to 9%, and with high class guarantee, underwriters were left with an increasing proportion of their commitments.[9]

Provincial participation in this boom activity involved both the market for popular industrials and that in new issues. In the early months of 1919 *The Economist* noted that "Liverpool is pressing up insurance shares to prices that appear extravagant and Manchester goes on buying textiles insatiably. The West of England has again taken a hand in the hotel share market, fed by demands from South Wales".[10] Provincial buying at this time also involved taking up shares connected with local industries which were being sold in London; London it was said is "so accustomed to leaning upon Sheffield, Cardiff and other provincial centres to provide buyers of shares connected with local industries that the refusal of the country exchanges to take stock could lead to difficulties on the market", which was in fact the case later in the year.[11]

With regard to provincial new issues there was a general increase in activity, with some markets displaying a marked upsurge in business.[12] Birmingham, for example, witnessed a rapid increase in the number of flotations by companies in the motor car and associated industries. In January 1919 the motor industry had a total nominal capital of £32 million, while during the course of the year "capital emissions" from the industry reached the figure of £16 million.[13] This consisted of a "large number of increases in the capital of local companies" and the appearance of new companies. An indication of the volume of local activity is given by the figures of applications for quotation on the Birmingham Stock Exchange, which were thirty-seven in 1919, 103 in 1920, and seventy-five in 1921. The volume of new issue work was such that the Stock Exchange set up a sub-committee to consider applications for permission to deal and for quotations. All this served to increase the importance of the Birmingham market, which was confirmed by the receipt of applications for quotation from several companies "not in any way local".[14]

Some hectic activity was also evident in shipping, with a big crop of issues especially of the one ship type in the latter half of 1919. With high freight rates and earnings being three or four times the pre-war level, "another orgy of speculation broke out in Cardiff, and in one month alone 30 companies were floated with £4.0 million capital. . . . The experienced shipowner sold, the ignorant man bought, and the banks financed the deals". The usual procedure was to invite subscriptions for the purchase of a vessel on the stocks or one that had already seen service. The latter method was by far the most common, and in some instances vessels nearly fit for the breakers yard were sold to the public.[15] Several shipbuilding yards also changed hands at high prices, and some sections of the shipbuilding industry went ahead and capitalized their wartime profits rather than keep them "to offset the inevitable fall in the value of the new tonnage built to replace war losses".[16]

The next period of active new issues starts at the end of the post-war depression in 1924, and from 1927 onwards there was the "beginnings of a conspicuous burst of new issues activity for the home market", reaching its height in the 1928 new issue boom. The boom in speculative issues was well under way by 1927 with the appearance of greyhound racing tracks and film issues; thirteen greyhound track issues were made, including several provincial ones. In 1928 there were 277 issues in all involving a total subscribed capital of £114.9 million. Of these, fifty-six issues were by old companies, involving £43.7 million; seventy-four by new companies acquiring business where past profits were stated, involving £28.8 million – in several cases the capital raised was not used to purchase a business but was nothing more than a technical device used by vendors for ends other than a literal sale; there were twenty-nine issues by new companies acquiring business where profits were not stated, involving a capital of £8.0 million; and there were 109 new or virtually new ventures involving £26.7 million.[17] This flood of new companies represented for the most part new industries recently introduced into the country. Among them were gramophone and radio companies (twenty-one issues), artificial silk companies (ten issues), finance companies (ten issues), films, cinemas and theatre companies (eight issues), and portrait machine companies (seven issues).[18]

An index of the extent to which provincial brokers participated in this new issue activity is given in the following table of the number of issues with which they were associated. As the figures indicate, Manchester was the busiest provincial market, followed closely

	1926	1927	1928	1929	1930
Manchester	31	38	82	41	4
Birmingham	25	27	49	22	6
Liverpool	23	24	33	19	4
Bristol	9		11	51	15	–
Others (9 in all)	27	26	79[1]	28	1

Source: *The Issuing House Year Book and Financial A.B.C.*, 1934.
Note 1. This figure includes 19 issues for Nottingham, 15 for Cardiff, and 12 each for Leeds and Huddersfield.

by Birmingham, and then somewhat surprisingly Bristol. In the lists of the various brokers handling these issues the newer undertakings were well represented. The main brokers in Manchester in the new issue business at this time were D. Henriques & Co., F. W. Staveacre & Co., and Lowson and Ormrod; in Birmingham, Fyshe & Horton, and A. E. Bartlett & Co.; H. C. Woodcock & Co. in Bristol; and Crichton Bros. and Townley in Liverpool. Of the speculative issues mentioned thirteen of the gramophone issues had been brought to the market with the aid of provincial brokers, while eight of the

artificial silk issues made in 1928 also enlisted the marketing channels provided by provincial brokers.

The boom was characterized by several disquieting financial
practices. Most notable was the gross over-valuation of assets and
the accompanying declaration that "nothing is included for goodwill", a considerable reversal from pre-war habits when in some
companies goodwill was all. Over-valuation of assets, of course,
brought problems of meeting interest costs later during the slump
period. Companies were also characterized by high gearing ratios,
that is, they had a very large proportion of the total capital in debt
form with the public being allowed to participate only to a partial
extent in the ordinary capital and at hefty premiums. This policy
later resulted in conversions of debt to lower rates levels. Partly
arising from the above practices was the widespead use of the shilling share since its appearance was closely linked with the deliberate
restriction of the amount of ordinary capital. It proved very popular
with investors and served to widen makets in industrial issues, but
it also led to prices far in excess of what such shares would have
commanded had £1 units been used.[19]

It was of course essentially a boom in specialities both in the
area of new issues and on the stock exchanges. Repeated over-subscription for new issues resulted in large premiums, while deferred
shares in such issues were regarded as gambling counters. Prices
reached extraordinary proportions especially in gramophone shares.
For example, the shares of the Gamophone Co. rose from £3 to
£8$\frac{13}{16}$. The boom, however, proved unstable because of the nature
of the assets dealt in, and because a large volume of speculation
was carried on with bank loans. The rise in Bank Rate early in
1929, and mounting disappointment with the failure of speculative
issues to bring the promised returns, caused a break in the market
and its fall was further accelerated by the Hatry Crash and the Wall
Street Slump. *The Economist* commented that in "the purely speculative share, with no dividend yield and no known earnings there
is hardly any bottom to the fall when the market turns sellers".[20]
By 1931 the total market value of the 109 new companies floated
in 1928 had fallen to £4.6 million compared to their original subscribed capital of £26.7 million.[21] Companies with past records kept
up reasonably well; it was the new companies that collapsed.

The next few years were relatively unimportant for new issues. In
1931 provincial brokers were only involved in five issues. After 1933
industrial borrowers began to re-appear in the market but funds
flowed mainly towards established concerns in iron and steel, land and
buildings, and into the newer industries of aircraft and motor
vehicles. These categories in 1936 took just over 50% of the £109

million raised for general industrial enterprise.[22] The emergence
of these industries offered greater scope for new issues by small
growing companies whose undistributed profits proved insufficient
to finance expansion. It was found that by 1937 one third of total
issues was by new companies, compared with only a fifth in 1926.[23]

The main institutional channels by which new issues were brought
to the market during the inter-war period deserve some further
elucidation. The position was not particularly satisfactory, as the
Macmillan Committee noted in 1931, since with the exception of
the older issuing houses, a few first rate finance houses, and some
leading stockbrokers, "the public is not usually guided by any institution whose name and reputation it knows".[24] In the case of the
established issuing houses they were concerned, certainly up to the
mid-1930s, with the export of capital rather than with supplies to
home industry. Their resources were not at the disposal of home
issues and certainly not to the smaller firms. Even in the period
of very active new issue activity, 1927–28, only two of the established houses, Higginson & Co., and J. H. Schroeder & Co., handled
any home issues at all. A few had provincial offices at this time but
for trade reasons only, rather than for capital raising operations.

Some of the larger finance houses on the other hand played an
important part in the inter-war issue market. They had good connections, reasonable capital resources, and acquired reputations. In
issuing and underwriting activity they found that capital could be
turned over quickly, and that a substantial volume of new issues
could be financed by a group of companies with a modest total
capital. They certainly did reasonably well out of it since about a
third of the costs of issue represented remuneration to the finance
house.[25] One of the most resourceful provincial concerns in this
category was the British Shareholder Trust Ltd. set up in 1916, and
which by 1929 had a paid-up capital of £538,212.[26] It initiated, in
Lavington's words, "an interesting and important development in
the marketing of provincial securities". It was formed largely
because of dissatisfaction with the conditions under which new
capital issues were offered for subscription by London institutions.
Provincial interests felt that they had no voice in the shaping of
new issues and that they were only allowed to participate in issues
after the bulk of the profit had been taken in the metropolis. The
London issuing houses "most of which were not of British origin,
were in the habit of telegraphing to country brokers giving them a
few hours to decide whether they would participate in any imminent
issues. The country brokers had but small opportunity of inves-
tigating the inherent soundness of new issues thus referred for subscription".[27] It was felt therefore that the B.S.T. would enable

country brokers to investigate " the inherent soundness of new issues"
and that it would provide sound new issues at fair prices after
making due allowance for a reasonable commission.[28] Its operations
were detailed by Lavington as follows: —

> "The organisation consists of a central Trust company in
> London and five allied companies in the more important Pro-
> vincial centres. Its methods seem well adapted to reconcile
> the interests of promoter and investor and to facilitate the
> economical use of securities. At each centre is an executive
> assisted by an advisory body elected from brokers nominated
> by shareholders of the Trust. It undertakes the marketing of
> new securities, the underwriting of issues and the sale of large
> blocks of securities of deceased people. The shareholders are
> composed in a great measure of those connected with the
> management of large undertakings; on the one hand, they
> bring to the notice of the Trust opportunities for profitable
> business; on the other they form a market in which the Trust
> may quickly and economically dispose of at least a part of its
> issue. The organization is a powerful one the aggregate capital
> of the six allied Trusts amounting to nearly £2½ million. It has
> already [by 1920] carried through a number of important issues
> and in one case underwritten an issue amounting to £16
> million".[29]

Other active provincial finance houses during this period were the
Northern Territories Trust, which was mainly interested in small
local issues; the Midland Trust, formed in 1896, with an issued
capital in 1929 of £110,000; and Neville Industrial Securities of
Birmingham formed in 1936 as a private company by local business
and professional people. Another Midlands concern which was associated with some of the 1927–28 boom issues was the Midland
Industrial and General Trust, formed in 1910, and which had a paid
up capital of £400,000 in 1929.

A third group of participants in the new issue market consisted of
"syndicates of varying degrees of repute formed by company promoters for the purpose of launching certain particular issues". Most
of them appeared after 1924 and they were mainly a London phenomena; the country position was represented by the reply Manchester
gave to an inquiry from the Committee on Share Pushing of 1937 –
there is "no recorded instances of such activities being carried on
from headquarters in Manchester".[30] About a dozen or so appeared
during the immediate post-war boom with an equal number over
the next few years. Between 1924 and 1927 over sixty were formed,
with forty in 1928, and half a dozen in 1929. Of the 180 or so

"issuing houses, banks, promotion syndicates and other financial undertakings" formed between 1919 and 1929 one third had nominal capitals of less than £20,000, while some two-fifths had capitals between £21,000 and £250,000, with the remainder having capitals in excess of the latter figure.[31] They certainly had insufficient capital with which to take on unmarketable securities of any kind, and the majority were heavily involved with rather dubious underwriting activity in which syndicates acted as the main underwriters but passed on the entire issue to sub-underwriters who frequently defaulted on their obligations.[32]

Lastly, there were certain powerful stockbroking concerns who handled issues without assistance and who could place shares through their special contacts with clients, a procedure which also included placing blocks of unmarketable securities.[33] Their activities increased during the inter-war years, especially with the rise in the number of small industrial issues coming to the market. It is doubtful if there were many provincial brokers which fell into this category, but undoubtedly there were some. In the late twenties they handled several small local issues without the aid of either issuing houses or London brokers. As a rule, however, local issues were made in conjunction with a local issuing house, or a London issuing house or broker.[34] Provincial brokers worked very closely with London in most cases, although subsequently the share prices of popular local issues were often dictated by local markets.

Several methods were available to a company which wished to dispose of shares to the public through the market and obtain a stock exchange quotation. For large amounts the most common method used was a prospectus issue, while a variation on this was an 'offer for sale' in which case the entire issue was acquired by an issuing house or broker who then invited public subscription for the shares. In the former case the issuing house or broker acted as an agent for the company, in the latter as a principal. Both these methods involved underwriting, with the issuing house or broker acting as main underwriters but it became a common practice in the inter-war years to sub-underwrite issues.[35] The main underwriters to London issues frequently passed on some of the sub-underwriting to the provinces whose record in this respect was fairly respectable. Indeed, it was stated, to the Cohen Committee on Company Law that no case had been known "of a provincial broker falling down on his sub-underwriting".[36] The advantage of these two issue methods were of course that they involved widespread publicity, the offer of a fixed quantity of stock allocated on a non-discriminatory basis, a wide distribution of ownership, and a wide market.

A method which increased greatly in popularity during the inter-war years, especially for small issues, was that of a broker placing shares with various parties and then seeking permission to deal on a stock exchange. It was in fact a revival of an old established method and caused considerable controversy at the time. *The Economist,* for example, frequently expressed anxiety about its increasing use after 1925, not least, because it dispensed with the issue of a formal prospectus.[37] In the thirties it was widely used by the growing number of small companies which came to the market with the recovery from the depression. In 1936 the Midland Bank put the number of publicly advertised private placings at 240.[38] Criticism arose of course not only because of insufficient publicity, but also because of doubts as to the number of shares effectively available to the market, that they might not be widely held, and that the resulting market might be rather narrow. However, for the small firm it had the advantage of low costs, no direct underwriting costs, and low legal and administrative costs.

The requirements of the various provincial exchanges for granting permission to deal following a placing varied a great deal. The larger markets had specific rules, typified by that of Manchester, which stated that "no dealings in new issues or any securities placed on the market be permitted until the permission of the Committee had been obtained", unless such permission had already been granted by London or another Associated Stock Exchange.[39] The smaller exchanges tended to lack any formal process for granting permission but a member could object to any bargains marked. The Cohen Committee in 1945 hinted that the smaller markets were "possibly not applying the strict principles of the larger ones" and it accordingly urged that "it would be in the public interest for the rules and practice of the provincial exchanges to be brought into line with those prevailing in London".[40] In practice some of the smaller markets adopted the safeguard of not granting permission to deal or a quotation until this had been done by one of the larger neighbouring exchanges, or they used the vetting facilities of a larger exchange. Very occasionally, however, lapses occurred, but although the Cohen Committee expressed concern about possible 'backdoor' entry to the London list it is only fair to note that such evasions were not entirely a one way affair.[41] The provinces in the thirties were particularly anxious to avoid any episodes of the 1928 variety, and as a preventive measure sought close collaboration between themselves and with London.[42]

Unfortunately, there is no detailed analysis of all provincial new issues for the inter-war years and it would be an unenviable task to undertake one.[43] Neither are details available for provincial costs of issue. However, the general picture as to these ran along the following lines. In the middle twenties a public issue of the order of £200,000 cost about 13% (% of issue proceeds) which probably meant for an issue of half this size issue costs in the region of 25% since conventional costs for a public issue were reasonably fixed. By the mid-thirties it was estimated that a small offer for sale in the region of £100,000 involved issue costs of 20%. Certainly commentators seem agreed that issue costs fell during the inter-war years owing to the improved institutional arrangements so that the market was able to deal more efficiently with both large and small issues. The worst abuse of high marketing costs and over-valuation of assets were definitely on the decline by the late thirties.

In the case of placings followed by permission to deal, issue costs were not greater than that of a public issue or an offer for sale. Although there are no detailed figures available there is no reason to think that the cost of placings would have been higher, and indeed there were many creditable reasons for thinking them to be lower for small issues especially if made in the provinces; there were factors present there which made "possible issues of considerably smaller size, down to £50,000, at reasonable costs of issue".[44]

Among the factors making for lower provincial costs were the following. A company was known to local investors and therefore incurred less sales resistance. This was certainly Lavington's view in 1920; "It might reasonably be expected that in the Provincial markets local knowledge on the part of the investor, both of the business and the reputation of the vendor and of the prospectus of his undertaking, would do a great deal to eliminate dishonest promotion and ensure that securities were sold at prices fairly near their investment values".[45] Further, a provincial broker would be disinclined to sponsor a bad issue for his clients, while he might also have been content with reduced profits in the interests of keeping local clients from taking their business to London. Another attraction of a local issue was that the broker to the issue would probably make a better long term market in the shares than would a London jobber who might lose interest once the first flush of premium hunting was over. More directly on the cost side some of the constituent elements of conventional costs such as advertising, legal, accountancy and other professional fees were lower in the provinces than in London. Also, in the case of placings the absence of stagging on the London scale (although provincial stags had their day) would reduce costs if this was measured by the difference between the placing price and the opening market price. All these factors helped to keep provincial costs below London levels.[46]

The characteristics displayed by some of the main provincial centres in the thirties differed somewhat in terms of the sort of new issues they undertook. In Birmingham new issue activity was dominated by the financing of a large number of new enterprises, and the prevailing prosperous conditions made "considerable local funds available for investment". These were supplied mainly from private sources and through trade connections, with solicitors and accountants playing some part in this. In Manchester it was easier for established firms to obtain funds through the market while the reception accorded to new entrants was not as favourable as that given in the Midlands. They were, however, conscious in some financial quarters that "new issues are too frequently compelled to go to London, where often the cream of the underwriting is taken off although the particular issue may concern a Northern enterprise". For the most part the Liverpool position resembled that of Manchester, with the market favouring established concerns to new ones. During the inter-war years Liverpool experienced a reduction in the number of "small private capitalists", while the drift of many commercial pursuits to London also adversely affected the flow of local funds. Liverpool issues at this time were predominantly of existing business involving public issues made in conjunction with the London new issue market. Of the smaller centres Bristol displayed a good deal of activity by way of financing new firms associated with its rapidly growing commercial and engineering industries which were plied with funds from well-to-do investors with a strong urge to invest locally. In the case of the numerous other centres it was probably easier for an established firm to obtain funds through the market than it was for a new enterprise.[47]

The provincial share markets of the late thirties reflected several of the characteristics displayed in their new issue activity. Birmingham being the "economic focus of the prosperous Midlands" was the domicile of a large number of companies of first class investment status. Metal working concerns associated with the motor car industry, heavy engineering, and a wide range of consumer industries, provided a list of companies with enviable dividend records. Investors of the period did not look to Birmingham for high geared equities, "but rather for the share which provides a regular 15% dividend with a capital bonus at intervals"; in the dividend records of Birmingham companies the depression did not emerge as more than a passing inconvenience. In the list there were numerous shares, especially in the motor industry, "which are valued in London tomorrow according to Birmingham's view today".[48] In the case of the other large centres the lists had become more nationally orientated. Manchester had no definite block of shares, while Liverpool shares were for the most part those of leading companies well known to London and most other Exchanges. New industries were gradually emerging, but the Palatinate had not yet matched its pre-war strength. As for the smaller markets Bristol probably displayed greatest activity with aircraft and motor shares occupying a prominant place in the list alongside its important markets in tobacco and cocoa shares. Other markets had their local range of shares which reflected the dominant local industry, for example, Sheffield steels, Newcastle shipbuilding and shipping, and Cardiff coal. The market position of most of their shares was probably that none of them "enjoy a very free market, but the interest of the investor who is seeking opportunities in the provinces is not necessarily in free markets alone, when adequate yield and security is to be had".[49]

During the Second World War industrial new issues came to a virtual standstill. Under the emergency regulations such issues were restricted to private placings or to offers to existing shareholders. Permission to deal had to be sought from the Treasury, which if refused meant that Stock Exchange members could not deal in such unquoted securities. These arrangements however did not extend to certain outside houses who dealt not only in small issues but occasionally in quite large ones as well. Provincial members were not in any way barred from taking blocks of shares from outside bodies or persons, but if they wanted to sell them they had to get permission from the Capital Issues Committee. From the early months of the war the provincial exchanges co-operated with London in operating the gentlemen's agreement as to the 'grey market arrangements'. All market controls were lifted early in 1945.[50]

During the post-war period the provincial new issue market increased the scope of its operations, and thereby its importance in contributing towards the financial needs of industry. The general picture of the activity of provincial brokers during the period 1946–1968 is given in the following table. The number of issues for the immediate post-war years indicates the early resort to the new

Number of issues with provincial broker participation, 1946-1968

	Public Issues	Offers for sale	Placings	Intro- ductions	Rights Issues	Capital- isations	Conversions & Exchanges	Issues to Shareholders
1946 (Apr)– 1949 (Mar)	20	43	86	34	22	—	9	23
1950–1960	28	78	209	132	233	632	173	68
1961–1968	31	93	300	72	305	473	563	198

Source: *The Times Issuing House Year Books;* figures for England and Wales.

issue market, reflecting the prevailing need for external finance since the old established local sources had continued to shrink. It was difficult for companies to attract funds of course without a quotation, since prospective shareholders in its absence had little hope of realized capital gains. Over the period as a whole the majority of issues have been associated with capitalizations and share exchanges, while many of the other types of issue have also been of the "no new money" type, that is, the proceeds of the issue going to the vendor rather than for direct investment expenditure. Most of the issues given in the table were done in conjunction with London issuing houses and/or stockbrokers, the provincial broker providing the regional connection for the distribution of shares and not infrequently reflecting the regional origins and ties of the company making the issue.

Although several dozen provincial brokers participated in new issue work over the post-war years, two features deserve special note. There has been a gradual concentration of work among the larger firms following upon mergers and the emergence of stronger broking units with specialist new issue departments. The other feature has been the concentration of new issue activity in the larger centres, notably Birmingham and Manchester, followed at some remove by Liverpool, Cardiff, Bristol, and Sheffield. The importance of Birmingham is evident from the following figures; local brokers were involved with one-third of the issues given in the above table, while in the case of placings done solely on provincial markets between 1961–68 nearly half were handled in Birmingham. Manchester brokers handled a fifth of the total provincial participation indicated in the table. The leading Birmingham brokers during this period were Smith, Keen, Barnett, A. E. Sharp & Co., Murray & Co., Margetts & Addenbrooke. In Manchester the most active brokers were Henry Cooke & Son and D. Q. Henriques & Co. In the other centres Tilney & Co. at Liverpool, Christopher Barber & Sons and J. W. Nicholson Sons at Sheffield, Lyddon & Thomas, Freeguard & Co. at Cardiff, B. S. Stock Son & Co. at Bristol, Wise, Speak, Sherlock & Edmondson at Newcastle, and W. Chapman & Co. at Nottingham were the most active local brokers in the new issue field.

Until the early 1960s provincial new issue work was relatively neglected by issuing houses, with of course some exceptions. Of these the most important was Neville Industrial Securities of Birmingham which had a long standing reputation for floating companies whose shares subsequently went to substantial premiums.[51] Another important Midland house, the Birmingham Industrial Trust, formed in 1960 as a private company, has provided finance for private companies, assisted their growth and later aided their flotation on the appropriate stock exchange. In Cardiff Gwent and West of England Enterprises Ltd., a public company since 1955 with an issued capital of £3.5 million, has been active in sponsoring local companies and in making issues. Although some of the established London issuing houses had links with some provincial centres for trading purposes it is only comparatively recently that they have realized the importance of closer local connections. Accordingly such leading issuers as Singer and Friedlander, Hill, Samuel, and Kleinwort Benson have either acquired local connections or opened branch offices so as to provide a full range of services, ranging from financial advice to bringing companies to the market.[52]

Perhaps a more interesting picture of provincial new issue work is obtained by taking those issues which are handled solely by provincial agencies with no London broker participation. The figures in this case are small compared to those given in the table above, and certainly minute in comparison with the volume of work done in London. The main methods whereby shares were brought to the market involved placings, offers for sale, and introductions. As to the figures there were 328 placings and seventy-seven offers for sale during the period 1946–1968. Introductions probably numbered more than this since one calculation for the period 1956–1960 put the figure for the provinces at 243.[53] This form of issue is particularly important because for the most part it is the first contact of many firms with the market. It is, however, only available to companies with a pattern of shareholding which is capable of supporting an orderly market. Under the Federation rules on Admission of Securities to Quotation it may only be considered when "the security is already widely held and there are no other circumstances, including the disposal of a large block of securities, that make special marketing arrangements necessary". Also, sufficient shares have to be made available to the jobbers in the market to enable them to support dealings.[54] The rules also lay down minimum publicity requirements but it is still one of the cheapest methods of obtaining access to the market.

The placing method is used where the pattern of shareholding rules out an introduction. The preponderance of placings is explained by the fact that "a small new firm making a small issue is likely to have greater success if the securities are directly distributed by the issuing house or broker." Such a small amount made by an offer for sale would involve a prospectus issue which might not be so successful. Usually a placing takes the form of an issue of ordinary shares, and from the investors' viewpoint the risks involved are too some extent compensated by prospects of capital appreciation and dividend payments, while marketability is frequently aided by using small share denominations. Seldom are small preference issues made since the size of the firm would preclude the issue of a sufficient amount to make a viable market.[55] With a placing the issue house or broker acquires a percentage of the issued capital, which under the present Federation rules must be at least 35% of the voting capital in the case of an equity placing and 30% in the case of fixed income securities.[56] Also, at least 25% of the amount placed must be offered by the sponsoring broker to the market, that is, to other brokers who might sell them to clients, or to jobbers to enable them to sustain a market when dealings begin. In the case of a provincial issue with no other market except the one of the sponsoring broker, the investor may look to the sponsoring broker to buy stock back from him. If the sponsoring broker cannot find a ready market he can take the stock in for his own account with a view to placing it later where he can. In this instance the broker is viewed as performing more of the role of a "specialist" than of making a book himself.[57] A feature of such placings over recent years has been the growing importance of provincial activity, there being quite clearly a "collective dominance over London" in the sixties, which centred largely on Birmingham and Manchester.[58] Part of the explanation for this probably resides with the improved institutional arrangements available and the realization that cheaper facilities were available in the provinces.

The main purpose of a placing operation is the transfer of owner-ship from the original shareholders of a company. Certainly, during the post-war period the majority of placings have been of the "no new money" variety. For example, during the period 1951-60 90% of provincial placings were of this type, while for 1961-65 less than one-sixth of the total value passing by placings involved new money to the companies.[59] The bulk of the funds raised in the market thus went to the vendors. Such issues are of course easier to make since they do not involve persuading the investor that additional funds can be profitably employed, merely that things will continue as they are.

For larger issues of about £250,000 and over, the offer for sale method is usually used. In this instance an issuing house or broker acquires the issue from the company and markets it at a stated price to the public after a formal prospectus has been issued. Again the bulk of provincial offers for sale were not aimed at providing new finance but rather at obtaining a quotation. For example, bet-ween 1951–60 nineteen out of the twenty-five offers for sale done in the provinces were of the 'no new money' type.[60]

Prior to the introduction of the Federation Rules on Quotations in 1966 there was a wide distribution in the size of firms making use of the provincial new issue market. They ranged from those with net assets of around £30,000 to some with several millions, although the bulk of them had net assets of between £100,000 and £400,000.[61] However, there was little relation between the size of firm and the size of issue made. This lack of association in the case of provincial issues arose because the main motive was not to obtain funds so that there was little need to issue the maximum numbers of shares consistent with the size of a company, merely sufficient to ensure an active market in the shares. Over the post-war period the average size of provincial issues have increased only slightly, but it has been so slight as to offer little support to the belief that it was proving increasingly difficult for small issues to be made. Indeed, some two thirds of the placings made between 1961–65 were under £100,000.[62] An important facility accordingly existed for small issues, which was certainly not the general case in London. One regrettable feature of the Federation Rules on Quotations has been the uniformity of the provisions regarding issue size, which has meant the withdrawal of an important channel for small placings. Prior to Federation most provincial exchanges exercised some degree of restraint when granting small quotations, and they operated on the basis of a desirable minimum of the order of £50,000, but occasionally for special reasons they went below this. The Federation Rules, however, lay down that "no application will be considered unless the Company will have an expected market value of at least £250,000 and any one security for which quotation is sought will have an expected market value of £100,000".[63]

As to the costs of issue it is interesting to note that for issues of comparable sizes it has been estimated that the average costs of issue in London were significantly greater than for a provincial issue. Certainly the provincial exchanges "were able to make placings of small size for new firms more economically than could be done at London". This was not surprising since a small company going to London would be quite unknown and would be difficult to place and thus the cost would rise. In the case of an offer for sale "there does not appear to be any basis to discriminate between them".[64]

Despite this cost advantage there was a tendency during the fifties for firms to seek a London quotation rather than a provincial one. It is possible to suggest various reasons why this should have been so. Up to and including the early fifties, many of the provincial exchanges did not actively encourage local firms to seek a local quotation. There was a belief current among firms that London was 'the Exchange' with superior listing requirements. In fact, most provincial listing requirements were based closely on London with minor amendments to help smaller local issues, but the belief was there that they were intrinsically inferior. Perhaps companies viewed the additional cost of going to London as an annual charge in which case it appeared far less onerous. Also, they may have had London as the long-term aim, so why take any intermediate steps in the provinces. There may in addition have been the belief that the capacity of the provincial new issue market was limited in terms

S

of the volume of business it could handle, which might have deterred potential issuers.

Some of these disadvantages were more apparent than real, and the increasing importance of provincial placings during the early 1960s indicates that there was a growing realization as to the advantages of provincial facilities. Since the introduction of Federation there could be no claim as to the inferiority of provincial listing requirements, and even before then it was a largely spurious one. As to the capacity of provincial markets there were factors present making for increasingly favourable comparisons with London. The growth of large stockbroking units with specialist new issue departments, aided by the growing ranks of provincial issuing house connections, provided a wide range of expert facilities. The much mooted institutional investment ceiling of the early 1950s, that they were not interested in small firms due to lack of active markets, also became less rigid. There was growing institutional interest in the secondary list of securities so that investment policy became more discretionary and less mechanistic in the selection of new investments through underwriting and placing contracts. The important factor was not size, but past profit performance and future prospects. The experience of Birmingham with its enterprising issuing houses and brokers would indicate that the capacity was present. Certainly provincial facilities have grown in attractiveness for the smaller firm in comparison with London. With the growing internationalization of the London market small issues will inevitably involve higher costs simply as a means of rationing the time and services of the market so that the cost differential will probably increase in favour of the provinces. In view of this there would appear to be a distinct opportunity for provincial centres in attracting the smaller domestic issue below the million level.

The importance of the provincial new issue market should not of course be assessed on the basis of the volume of funds made available to companies directly. In this case their contribution seems small indeed, for example, some £3.0 million for the fifties,[65] and just over £2.5 million for the placings made between 1961–65. Such figures are an inadequate measure of its economic significance. Other considerations need to be taken into account. Marketability is conferred on the shares which greatly affects their attractiveness for the investor, while vendors might put the funds they obtain into other investment channels. Companies having secured a quotation can then proceed to make further issues at lower cost, especially rights issues to their shareholders. Indeed, over recent years provincial markets have been slowly loosing their image of being solely 'death duty markets'.

As a consequence of the growing volume of new issues the lists of the exchanges have increased in size, particularly the industrial commercial sections. Also, the policy of the exchanges in seeking quotations of national stocks with strong local connections helped to attract further business. The general industrial section of the list of the Northern Stock Exchange now numbers nearly 1,600 securities, while the Midland and Western Stock Exchange list carries just over 1,300 in that category. Neither rival London with its formidable total of nearly 8,000 company securities, but nevertheless they constitute important markets especially in some leading national stocks, a growing list of secondary stocks which London has tended to ignore, and in stocks which only have a provincial quotation, of which there were 207 on the Northern Stock Exchange, and 298 on the Midland & Western Stock Exchange in 1970.[66]

NOTES

1 *Economist,* January 6, 1923, p. 45.
2 Details of the transport undertakings taken over are given in the *Stock Exchange Year Book,* 1950, Vol. 1, pp. 79-82; see also D. H. Aldcroft, *British Railways in Transition* (1968), pp. 109-10.
3 A detailed list of the electricity companies acquired appears in the *Stock Exchange Year Book,* 1950, Vol. 1, pp. 65-70.
4 For a full list of the gas companies acquired see, *Stock Exchanges Year Book,* 1950, Volume 1, pp. 1375-1497.
5 A.T.K. Grant, *A Study of the Capital Market in Britain 1919-1936* (1937), p. 137.
6 T. Balogh, *Financial Organization* (1947), p. 282.
7 *Statist,* June 4, 1921, p. 1048.
8 These figures, from *The Statist,* were of annual capital subscriptions calculated at the price of issue and exclude conversions, bonus issues, and shares issued to vendors.
9 *Statist,* October 16, 1920, p. 614, December 4, 1920, p. 886, January 8, 1921, pp. 50-51.
10 *Economist,* January 18, 1919, p. 74.
11 *Economist,* July 26, 1919, p. 130.
12 For the extent and excesses of the cotton reconstruction boom see Chapter 7.
13 *Statist,* December 20, 1919.
14 Birmingham Stock Exchange, Minutes, October 22, 1919, October 27, 1920.
15 *Statist,* January 31, 1920, pp. 184-5.
16 H. W. Macrosty, "Inflation and Deflation in the U.S. and the U.K., 1919-1923", *Journal of the Royal Statistical Society,* 1927, p. 72.
17 R. A. Harris, "A Re-Analysis of the 1928 New Issue Boom", *Economic Journal,* 1933, p. 459.
18 Ibid., p. 458. During 1926-28, 23 issues by artificial silk companies appeared on the market; by 1931 all the portrait machine companies had been wound up.
19 Florin shares had been used in the pre-war rubber boom and proved very effective in attracting public subscription.

20 *Economist*, November 10, 1928, p. 854.
21 Harris, op. cit., p. 459.
22 Grant, op. cit., p. 149.
23 R. F. Henderson, *The New Issue Market and the Finance of Industry* (1951) p. 36.
24 *Committee on Finance and Industry*, Report, Cmnd. 3897, 1931, para. 167.
25 Balogh, op. cit., p. 296.
26 Edgar Crammond, one time secretary of the Liverpool Stock Exchange, was a managing director of the B.S.T., a post he held until after the Second World War. The original name of the Trust was the British Stockbrokers' Trust but the original broker members were forced to withdraw since as a share dealing agency with a London office they ran foul of the London Stock Exchange commission rules. London threatened to charge full commission to provincial brokers who retained an interest in the Trust.
27 *Economist*, February 9, 1918, p. 206.
28 It also had an unbridled nationalistic motive – "to ensure that British capital shall be applied to the development of British industry and not for the purpose of German economic penetration": ibid., p. 206.
29 Lavington, op. cit., p. 209. In 1954 the B.S.T. was absorbed into Phillips Hill, Higginson & Co. Ltd.
30 Manchester Stock Exchange, Minutes, January 21, 1937.
31 *The Issuing House Year Book and Financial A.B.C.*, 1930.
32 D. Finnie, *Capital Underwriting* (1934), pp. 69, 70.
33 Liverpool Stock Exchange, Minutes, June 28, 1927. Groups of provincial brokers also took blocks of unmarketable shares and distributed them by private placing.
34 Evidence of A.A. Fisk (representing the Council of Associated Stock Exchanges) to the *Cohen Committee on Company Law Amendment*, Cmnd. 6659, 1945, Q. 10,707.
35 For the abuses of subunderwriting in this period see Finnie, op. cit., Ch. 10. In the early twenties the public began to deal in underwriting "to an extent quite unknown even five years ago". Many were merely out to get commissions and if they were left with any stock they sold out immediately which was no help to a shaky issue; *Economist*, July 5, 1924, p. 13.
36 Fisk, op. cit., Q. 10,711; 10,715.
37 *Economist*, May 23, 1925, p. 1018.
38 Quoted by Grant, op. cit., p. 163.
39 This left a loophole if the issue came from a small provincial exchange with no specific rules of its own on permission to deal.
40 Cohen, *Committee on Company Law*, op. cit., para. 24; also evidence of A. A. Fisk, op. cit., Q. 10,683.
41 See Chapter 10.
42 Manchester Stock Exchange Committee in 1930 was very anxious to restrict the granting of permission to deal in shares of new companies issued as "consideration for services rendered in connection with the formation of a new company" until after the publication of the first annual account of the company; Minutes, December 17, 1930.
43 *The Issuing House Year Book* for these years does not give details of the amounts raised, while *The Times' Book of Prospectuses of New Issues* seldom contained provincial only issues.
44 Henderson, op. cit., p. 83. Compare the statement by Grant, op. cit.,

p. 223, "there appears to be no economical local stock market for providing local capital, the expense remains high just the same".

45 Lavington, op. cit., p. 208.

46 Henderson, op. cit., pp. 83-4.

47 Grant, op. cit., pp. 223-29.

48 *Economist,* February 15, 1936, p. 37, January 23, 1937, pp. 184-5.

49 *Economist,* April 18, 1936, p. 137.

50 Council of Associated Stock Exchanges, Minutes, Resumé 1944-5; *Economist,* February 12, 1944, pp. 220, 789.

51 Neville Industrial Securities is a wholly owned subsidiary of Neville Developments, a quoted company. When placings are made the shares are offered to members of Neville Developments, while in the case of an offer for sale a portion of the shares is reserved for the members; *Economist,* September 28, 1963, p. 1158.

52 P. Brackfield, "Merchant Banks in the Provinces", *The Banker,* 1967, pp. 129-33. In 1967 there were 26 merchant bank offices in the provinces.

53 The total number of introductions given in the table for the entire post-war period is 238. It would appear that *The Times Issuing House Year Book* does not record fully all provincial introductions. The figure given in the text is from J. K. S. Ghandi, "Some Aspects of the Provincial New Issue Market", *Bulletin of the Oxford University Institute of Economics and Statistics,* Volume 26, p. 259.

54 The number of shares involved is not made public.

55 Ghandi, op. cit., pp. 242, 251.

56 Provincial requirements as to placings prior to Federation varied between markets. No minimum percentage of the issued capital had to be placed, but there were varying requirements as to the amount to be made available to the market, e.g., in Liverpool it was suggested that 10% of the placed capital should be made available, while the Birmingham figure was a third; the amount was left to the discretion of the broker in Manchester; Liverpool Stock Exchange, Minutes, July 19, 1955.

57 Federation Document, Memorandum of Guidance to Exchange Committees on Prescribed Rules, p. 48.

58 G. W. Murphy and D. F. Prussman, "Equity Placings on the New Issue Market", *Manchester School,* 1967, p. 173.

59 Ghandi, op. cit., p. 244; Murphy and Prussman, op. cit., p. 176.

60 Ghandi, op. cit., p. 244.

61 Ibid., p. 248.

62 Murphy and Prussman, op. cit., p. 177.

63 Admission of Securities to Quotation, General Requirements, p. 2.

64 Ghandi, op. cit., pp. 254-5. It was estimated on a comparison with the period 1945-47 that for an average issue of £200,000 that the cost of a "no new money" placing in the provinces was 8.5%, compared to 24.0% if made in London. A similar difference in costs held for a 'new money' placing. For offers for sale of just over £200,000 the London cost worked out at 11.0%, that of the provinces at 10.0%.

65 Ghandi, op. cit., p. 256; Murphy and Prussman, op. cit., p. 175.

66 At December 1962 some 720 securities had a provincial only quotation, with a market value of just over £430 million; J. R. S. Revell, Market Values and Number of Securities Quoted on Associated Stock Exchanges (1964), D.A.E., University of Cambridge.

13   Federation and Regionalization

Provincial brokers, along with those in London, have had a long standing interest in attaining uniform standards and in improving the status of their profession. Steps towards these ends have from time to time taken the form of suggestions for a charter for stock brokers, the work of the Council of Associated Stock Exchanges in promoting the codification of certain provincial rules, and the informal discussions which the provinces have had with London since the pre-war years, and which developed into much greater and happier collaboration in the nineteen fifties. During the early sixties these discussions resulted in a desire to set up a closer and more permanent system of collaboration, and to this end in 1962 a joint committee (the Co-ordination Committee) was set up to investigate the best framework whereby this could be achieved. The members of the Co-ordination Committee were drawn from London and the provinces, including the Provincial Brokers Stock Exchange, and the provinces themselves were eager to participate in the venture since they felt that with developments in communications and share ownership, rising costs and the need for better research and statistical services, a great deal more could be done collectively towards improved services for investors than could be accomplished in isolation. One possible solution of course was the formation of a national or united stock exchange with common membership, but it was generally agreed at the time that conditions were not quite suitable for such a development. It was felt that the answer lay in a federal arrangement, with executive powers on specific matters being vested in, and exercised by, a federally constituted committee.[1] Following considerable discussion and three interim reports the final recommendations were put forward in the 'Federation Document', and after its acceptance by all parties the Federation of Stock Exchanges in Great Britain and Ireland came into being on July 1, 1965. Its objects were to "promote co-ordination of activities of Stock Exchanges in Great Britain and Ireland, to promote good service to and safeguards for the investing public, to promote facilities for companies having or seeking a quotation and to promote the interests of the Federated Exchanges and their members".[2]

At the outset the membership of the Federation consisted of London, the Scottish Stock Exchange (which was regionalized in 1964), and sixteen other stock exchanges, including the Irish ones. Following the regionalization of the English exchanges the provincial element in the Federation fell to three exchanges, plus the Irish markets and the Provincial Brokers Stock Exchange.[3] To be effective of course Federation required executive powers, and these are exercised by the Federal Committee. They cover matters on which the constituent exchanges are prepared to delegate authority, while the decisions taken at Federation level are then implemented by the constituent exchanges. The Federal Committee consists of twenty-six members, fourteen nominated by the London Stock Exchange, ten from the Associated Stock Exchanges, and two from the Provincial Brokers' Stock Exchange, while the Government Broker is also an *ex-officio* member. However, to ensure that executive powers are not exercised to the detriment of a substantial part of the Federation the constitution provides that a resolution to be effective must be carried by 75% of the votes cast. Thus when a resolution has been so adopted it becomes binding on the individual exchanges, with disciplinary action extending to expulsion from the Federation if they do not comply. The assumption of new executive powers by the Federal Committee requires reference to each member exchange which can grant its approval by a simple majority vote of the governing committee.

The initial regulations which were made, and implemented by the Federal Committee covered a wide range of activities. They were concerned with the provision of adequate compensation funds, quotation requirements, and branch offices. Rules which "Federated Exchanges will be required to adopt unless, in the case of a particular rule, an Exchange can satisfy the Federal Committee that it has already adopted a more stringent rule", covered matters such as comon entrance standards for new members, the control of partnerships, financial control of member firms, and finally, provisions designed to institute a limited control of dealing arrangements, "whereby the ability of Firms to act in the dual capacity of brokers and jobbers is defined with a view to the ultimate abolition of dual capacity".[4]

One of the first matters to concern the Federation was the provision of adequate compensation funds for the protection of members of the public. Outside comment from the Jenkins Committee on Company Law in 1962 had spurred on consideration of this issue since it had noted in its Report that "investors dealing with members of a recognised stock exchange should be protected by a compensation fund, or by insurance if this is a practical alternative".[5] At this time London had its own compensation fund, as had several of the provincial markets. During the late fifties the Council of Associated Stock Exchanges had continually urged member exchanges to move towards setting up their own funds, and by 1960 fifteen exchanges had made such provision involving a total of £220,000 for some 900 members.[6] Generally, the exchanges earmarked part of their general funds as a compensation fund. The smaller country exchanges however found it difficult to set up such funds since the length of time taken to accumulate a sufficient sum from annual contributions effectively prevented such a solution, while insurance cover was far too costly. Following Federation each Federated Exchange was required to have a compensation fund of an amount equal to £200 per member. If this sum proves insufficient to meet payments arising from a default on one exchange a call can be made on the resources of the other Federated Exchanges, while if that proves inadequate a further call of up to £,1000 per member can be made. Thus the total compensation fund is of the order of £5 million.[7]

The second regulation which came into effect on Federation dealt with requirements as to the granting of a quotation. The rules which were incorporated in "Admission of Securities to Quotation" were based mainly on the London Stock Exchange's Appendix 34, and the introduction of the new rules met the traditional complaint that uniformity was lacking, which was not perhaps altogether to be deprecated. Also, it met the point made by the Jenkins Committee that the smaller stock exchanges could not "scrutinize applications for quotations" as adequately as the larger ones. Each Federated Exchange is now responsible for ensuring compliance with the Federal requirements, and one exchange cannot grant a quotation to a share if it has been refused by another. The implementation of these regulations is supervised by a New Issues Panel, appointed by the Federal Committee, which can call for documents and which generally decides upon matters of interpretation in the administration of the quotation and permission to deal rules.

A further regulation introduced with Federation concerned the opening of branch offices by brokers. The traditional policy had been not to open branch offices except at discreet distances from another Associated Stock Exchange. Such offices as were in existence at the time of Federation were retained, while new offices subsequently opened are only permitted within a twenty-five mile radius of a Federated Exchange with its approval.[8] This condition was an important element in provincial acceptance of Federation, but little advantage has as yet been taken of the provisions.

Also among the prescribed rules of Federation were those aimed at improving the professional standing of stockbroking through ensuring a satisfactory standard of entry, with further rules to ensure that member firms maintained a minimum of financial strength for the conduct of their business. The first of these rules related to requirements for membership. In addition to following the tradition that a candidate requires a sponsor and a seconder, the rules also lay down that he should have completed not less than three years' training in a firm or firms of a Federated Exchange and that he should then proceed to attain a minimum standard in a written Federal Examination in subjects relating to stock exchange practice. In the provinces these provisions apply to prospective women members; indeed the provinces already have several women brokers, while London has yet to mend its ways in this matter. The rules aimed at maintaining the strength of member firms were those which prohibited partnerships with non-members, and which also restricted the membership of unlimited companies to members of the stock exchange. This continues the long standing practice of not diluting the liability of a member firm with outside commitments. Also prescribed was a rule which stated that a member may not carry on business "in the capacity of a broker or jobber as a sole trader", since it was generally felt that such concerns lacked adequate resources. The last provincial sole trader ceased trading in 1970. And finally, extensive requirements were set out as to the records to be kept by firms of their transactions with each other and their clients, and also on the compilation of an annual balance sheet. Every firm is now required to maintain a balance on capital account sufficient to ensure a minimum margin of solvency which must not be less than £5,000 per partner for a broking firm and £15,000 for a dual capacity firm. In this case a margin of solvency is broadly defined as those assets which are readily realizable to be set against specified liabilities.[9]

Finally, uniformity was aimed at in a more controversial area. Federation brought with it uniformity in dealing arrangements based on the London pattern. Without this condition London's co-operation in achieving Federation would have been more difficult to obtain. The London system involved two distinct categories of membership, both single capacity, with brokers acting as agents to the public and jobbers acting as principals and providing the market's dealing mechanism. The provincial practice in dealing matters prior to Federation was somewhat fragmented, varying from infrequent meetings on the smaller exchanges to the continuous auction markets which was basically a procedure of calling across the floor used on the larger ones, with bargains being done on a broker to broker basis, while some brokers also engaged in limited jobbing and shunting activities which provided a local price service based on London prices. From London's viewpoint provincial members enjoyed a privileged position since they were able to act in a dual capacity. Federation therefore required in the case of the provinces the adoption of separate functions for the membership.

However, it was obvious that independent jobbing units could not emerge immediately in the provinces. The firms already undertaking jobbing and shunting operations needed time to build up adequate business, and satisfy themselves of the viability of single capacity operation before they could cast aside their less risky broking activities. The original intention was to allow a transitional period of about ten years, but on reflection it was felt that fixing such a deadline was impracticable given the importance of dealing arrangements and the need to maintain a price service to the country exchanges if they were to survive as independent units. Accordingly it was decided that the Federal Committee should have discretionary powers as to when dual capacity operations should cease. This would enable a more timely assessment to be made as to whether the necessary adjustments to the new conditions had been made and allow sufficient time for increased turnover to develop on the new regionalized markets. It was readily appreciated that business on individual local floors would not make profitable single capacity jobbing viable.

During the transitional period those provincial firms already engaged in jobbing and shunting activities were encouraged to emerge as full time jobbers. These adopted dual capacity status, with the provision that the broking side and the jobbing side were to be kept separate, and that in the interests of increasing market business and protecting their clients' interests, the broking side of such a firm could not execute clients' business with the jobbing side. Each dual capacity firm registered with its own exchange committee, while new applicants for dual capacity must seek through their local committee, approval from the Federal Committee. The jobbing side of dual capacity firms are also required to specify the list of securities in which they deal since this is a matter of some consequence not only to them but also to certain members of the London Stock Exchange. Accordingly a list of securities in respect of which they deal and make prices has been drawn up and is supervised by a panel set up by the Federal Committee, to whom application is made via the local committee for any additions to the list. This is basically a list of nationally quoted stocks, the leading market securities, although jobbers also notify the Federal Committee of local stocks in which they deal.

The dealing channels for country jobbers were laid down in a fair degree of detail by the Federation rules. Such a firm may make prices and deal off its own book with members of its own exchange and those of its officially recognized region without restriction, and with a member of any Federated Exchange, except London and the Provincial Brokers Stock Exchange, in securities in which it has been authorised to deal. A country jobber may therefore deal with another country jobber, but although he can consult a London jobber he can only deal with him through the medium of his registered London correspondent who is obliged to charge commission at the appropriate rate. Similarly, a London jobber may deal with a country jobber through the former's country correspondent. However, the London correspondent must disclose to the London jobber that he is dealing on behalf of a country jobber or shunter, which follows the London practice when a jobber deals with another one through a broker.[10] An indication of the scope and the measure of success attained in country jobbing may perhaps best be deferred at this point since the inception of regionalization, which followed closely on the heels of Federation in England and Wales, made a considerable difference to the environment in which emerging jobbers had to operate.

The impetus behind regionalization came from two main sources. There had for some time been a growing realisation in some provincial circles that the smaller stock exchanges were inadequate from the point of view of providing an efficient service to members and maintaining proper standards of control. There were at this time fifteen exchanges with fewer than forty members. They did very little floor trading, while many of their member firms were too small to afford specialist staff, and also to meet the cost of providing an improved service to investors. The exchanges themselves certainly could not offer the range of services provided by the administrations of the larger ones. In particular, they did not publish regular lists, they could not adequately supervise the membership, and they lacked facilities for vetting fully applications for quotations, although on this last point they could call upon the assistance of neighbouring exchanges. Also, they could not operate their own compensation funds while the cost of insurance cover was prohibitive. It was felt that such exchanges could be closed down and the membership brought into regional units, while the damage caused to local pride and the loss of autonomy would be sufficiently compensated for by association with larger and stronger units. Indeed, in their evidence to the Jenkins Committee the representatives of the Council of Associated Stock Exchanges stated that they would "like the smaller exchanges to amalgamate, or join the P.B.S.E."[11]

Some of the comments made by the Jenkins Committee in their report in 1962 gave these internal thoughts some greater urgency. Although the Jenkins Committee had "received no evidence that the operations of these small stock exchanges have led to serious trouble or difficulties" it was of the opinion that the time had come "for some rationalisation of the existing exchanges, perhaps by the amalgamation of some of the smaller ones". Accordingly, it recommended "that the Board of Trade should re-examine the existing list of recognised stock exchanges with a view to reducing their number and increasing their size".[12] This explicit threat of intervention by a government department no doubt hastened the working of the forces already present.

It is interesting to note that the regional concept was anything but new in the north east of England. As far back as 1915 discussions had taken place between the Leeds Stock Exchange and its three immediate Yorkshire neighbours on the desirability of a merger in order to increase the size and turnover of the market, but no progress was made. A similar proposal was again mooted in 1946.[13] When the Federation proposals were under discussion, and when the Council of Associated Stock Exchanges could not reach agreement on a collective compensation fund, the idea of a Yorkshire exchange was again brought up, but it was eventually decided to join the proposed Northern Stock Exchange since this would constitute a much stronger unit. The arrangements for setting up the new regional exchange were completed very swiftly and the Northern Stock Exchange came into being in August 1965. The constituent exchanges were Liverpool and Manchester (with a combined membership of about 230) and the exchanges at Bradford, Halifax, Huddersfield, Leeds, Newcastle, Oldham, Sheffield and some members of the Northern Counties Brokers' Association, making in all a market with a membership of some 350. Executive authority resided with a council with members drawn from the various local associations. The main administrative work of putting out the daily list for the whole region and dealing with applications for quotation was centred in Manchester and Liverpool respectively. Since its formation the local associations at Bradford and Halifax have closed down. A year later in October 1966 the Midland and Western Stock Exchange was formed with a total membership of just over 200, and presided over by an executive committee of ten. The largest local association within this region is Birmingham with a membership of about 110, which accordingly undertook the main administrative work of putting out the daily list and vetting applications for quotations. The other local associations in this region are Bristol, Cardiff, Nottingham and Swansea.[14]

The benefits which were seen to flow from regionalization were several. Large size would mean administrative economies and greater efficiency, and these benefits extended to the work of settlement and the clearance of bargains. It was also felt that the resulting stronger units would more effectively support the activities of provincial brokers since they represented "the grass roots of British industry". They had background knowledge of it, access to sources of information, personal contacts, and intimate local knowledge. Further, if in the future a national or united stock exchange was contemplated then regionalization was a suitable step to take, and if successful it would place the provinces in a stronger position than otherwise in any preparatory discussions. The other benefit was the maintenance of strong independent provincial broking firms. However, in this matter it was appreciated that such firms required adequate dealing facilities. It was important that regional markets should have the two features of continuity and marketability. To this end therefore, an efficient jobbing system was deemed essential to the future development of provincial floors. Only if members could deal as effectively on their own floors as their counterparts did in London would they be content to keep most of their business in the provinces.

At the time of Federation twenty-five provincial firms requested dual capacity registration. The Liverpool market had seven firms, three of which were authorized to deal in a miscellaneous range of nationally quoted stocks, while four specialized in breweries, preference shares, insurance and bank shares. On the Manchester floor there were three firms, all dealing in nationally quoted stocks. Birmingham had eight dual capacity registrations, with four of them dealing in purely local stocks, and the remainder jobbing in national stocks. Bristol had two dealers one of whom had a list of over one hundred nationally quoted stocks. Cardiff's one dual capacity firm specialized in local stocks. There were three on the Scottish Stock Exchange, while Belfast had one dual capacity registration.[15]

It is apparent from this list that most of the firms registered for dual capacity operated in a fairly general range of leading industrial shares, while there were a few specialized markets running alongside. Liverpool, for example, continued its traditional interest in banks, insurance, breweries, and its important market in preference shares. With regard to these particular markets it was held at the time, even in London, that they were significant markets in terms of turnover and price leadership. In Cardiff the market in local finance issues is mainly associated with the activities of the Hodge group. Birmingham's dual capacity firms displayed an interesting characteristic in that several jobbers specialized in purely local stocks which stem from the amount of new issue work done on that market. To the extent that there are dealers ready to take a position in such stocks the issuing of carefully nursed local companies is therefore made easier. But from a jobbing viewpoint this is unlikely to provide sufficient turnover to sustain all the local dual capacity firms who wish to emerge as full-time jobbers in due course.

The new dealing arrangements were not introduced into the best possible climate. At the time business had fallen to a very low ebb, and the low turnover made it difficult for jobbers to run open positions in a large range of stocks. London, of course, suffered equally from the same problem which made their jobbing members very sensitive to the appearance of outside competition. Not only was the volume of business low, there was also a clear need to rationalize the number of firms on the provincial jobbing scene so that the strongest and most viable could be encouraged to emerge as soon as possible. For example, at the time of Federation there were some fifteen provincial jobbers authorized to deal in I.C.I. shares. The result was that many did not run any reasonable position in such stocks and could not be said to be really jobbing. Intense competition accomplished part of the rationalizing work, while others amalgamated to form stronger units. By 1968 the number of dual capacity firms on the three regional exchanges had been reduced to fifteen, a level at which they have since remained. The Northern Stock Exchange has four, the Midland and Western seven, and the Scottish three emerging jobbers. In 1971 the Liverpool firm of Edgar Henriques & Co. became a single capacity jobber/shunter. The question of number has not yet been entirely solved in that some small jobbing units remain, while if these felt able to drop out this would ease the problem for the stronger units of deciding whether to opt for single capacity operation in the near future. This would then leave each regional exchange with two or three very strong jobbing units.

From an efficiency standpoint the operation of provincial jobbing offices had to contend with various difficulties during the formative stages. Provincial jobbers faced greater problems than their London counterparts, and operated in certain areas with considerably higher expense ratios. London jobbers are mainly occupied with the most important clearing stocks and at the end of an account they are chiefly concerned with the administration of their long or short position. Country expenses, however, were obviously higher since they had to get stock from one corner of the country and perhaps dispatch it to another, all of which went through their office, while there were also delays in the receipt of cash for the same geographical reasons. To some extent this problem has now been eased with the introduction of regional clearing and the Central Stock Payment System, while the introduction of Federal clearing at some future date would serve to accomplish a great deal in terms of provincial handling economies.

Apart from these jobbing problems there was also a need for a great deal of re-education in order to alter certain long standing dealing practices. It was necessary to get brokers and their market dealers out of the habit of 'picking up' shares at random, and of 'trying elsewhere first', all of which involved time and not infrequently the end of the geographical search was that they missed the first and probably better local offer. Coupled with this was the practice under the old shunting system, that when a broker declared his position but found he was unable to deal he then went to London only to find that London knew all about the order, and not unnaturally the market had moved against him. There was a definite need to reduce the habit of relaying information, and gradually this practice is being whittled away so that London now has less knowledge of country dealings than used to be the case. A greater degree of mutual trust is developing between broker and jobber and the provincial dealing etiquette is designed to foster this trend.

Not only was there a problem of leakage of information, but there were also certain practices which kept stock off the market and so reduced turnover. This made it more difficult for a jobber to make close and competitive prices. In pre-Federation days when a broker with a 10/- dealing stamp made a price in a stock he often found that two brokers had got together at the middle price and merely left him the odd shares. Closely allied to this was the practice of some brokers, especially in nationally quoted stocks, of crossing them in their office if they had matching orders. Subsequently, rules have been introduced which are designed to give such a cross to the jobber who is making a book in the shares. The adoption of London rules 87–90 which relate to putting business through a jobber and therby keeping business on the floor, unless it is clearly to the client's advantage to deal elsewhere, have certainly brought gains in market turnover. Provincial jobbers have also been helped by the adoption of the London practice of brokers declaring to them what limits they have, even if they are above the market. This is helpful since it permits the jobber to know what the strength of the market is likely to be. Also, in the case of big orders the practice is gaining ground of giving it to one firm of jobbers and not as previously putting it around the country, which tended to ruin marketability since some half-dozen jobbers might be chasing the same stock. This served to make for greater difficulties in jobbing if turnover happened to be low.

Despite the early problems considerable benefits have flowed from the adoption of dual capacity. In particular, individual brokers have found dealing under the new system easier than under the rather loose arrangements which previously existed, and they are well satisfied with the service they have got especially for the small and medium sized orders. In general terms it has provided a price and dealing service, and removed some of the previous thinness of provincial markets. Certainly their activities over the past few years has meant that provincial markets have gradually moved away from the provision of mere 'daylight' trading towards being a more competitive and self sustaining market.

Certain pointers serve to provide a tentative measure of the degree of success achieved by the emerging jobber since Federation. Firstly, a comparison of London and provincial prices. In this area provincial jobbers developed an early reputation for giving very competitive prices, indeed offering consistently better net prices than their London counterparts. London's response to such competition has been somewhat on the negative side, amounting to the claim that the provinces were undercutting them by dealing within the London price margins. Perhaps their comments on this score have been a little overdone. If the provincial jobber is to emerge in a single capacity function, partly at the insistence of London, then he must build up turnover and in the short run the only way of doing this is to redistribute the existing total market turnover. Certainly in periods of low market activity there was no other way of attracting business, but it has meant on such occasions that London jobbers "licked their wounds and cursed the country". The provincial jobber however is only taking advantage of an accepted competitive move in what is reputedly a highly competitive market. Adopting a smaller jobbing turn, the difference between the jobber's buying and selling price, is therefore an obvious way of increasing turnover through attracting clients to the lowest cost market. In a sense the provincial jobber can afford to do this since London is there as a last resort market to balance his books, but no doubt he would not be permitted to 'get out' with any degree of frequency in London without taking a loss. In the long term the provincial jobber can hope to consolidate his position by taking a larger share of new investment business, but that is both long term and less certain.

A second pointer is the fact that as the number of jobbers in the provinces operating fairly substantial books stabilizes, and as turnover grows recourse to London by the provinces will diminish. It has been estimated that whereas before amalgamation most of the provincial business went through London, now up to about a half is dealt with more efficiently in the provinces, efficiency in this context meaning that it was done more quickly and at a better price, while there was no need to pay half commission to a London broker. Certainly the volume of provincial dealings is quite appreciable. A recent sample survey of some leading national stocks indicated that 22% of all purchases came through the provinces, and 26% of all sales.[16] Obviously London will continue to be the last resort market since total turnover is so much greater than that of the provinces, particularly for large deals.[17] But even in this area the growth of turnover could lead to a raising of the bar of size in terms of provincial operations. In effect therefore there has been a change in the size of the relative flows of business between London and the provinces, mainly to the benefit of the latter. This is probably not entirely attributable to the service provided by the emerging jobber but also to other developments as well. Among these should be noted the much larger stockbroking units which have been set up in the sixties.[18] These offer a wide range of investor services and with their specialist research departments they have attracted leading institutional clients who now also employ provincial brokers as well as London ones. In addition, there has been a growth of institutional interest in the range of secondary industrial securities many of which have a better market in the provinces than in London.

Once a bargain has been completed in the market between broker and jobber a considerable number of complex but essentially routine operations then follow. These include such matters as making out contract notes, changing clients' ledgers, payment of stamp duty, delivery of certificates, and so forth, while at the end of each account member firms settle their positions with regard to their dealings by delivering either cash or securities as the case may be.[19] A great deal of this accountancy and clearing work was highly labour intensive and the advent of computer facilities provided an opportunity for introducing cost reducing methods. However, the size and the volume of business conducted by provincial firms could not justify the adoption individually of computer facilities since the capital cost and subsequent operating costs would be prohibitive. But on a regional basis the capital cost can be defrayed over a large number of participants, with the long run prospect of linking up with the computer facilities of the London Stock Exchange. Attempts to start an inter-regional scheme proved unsuccessful and accordingly the regions went ahead separately. The Scottish Stock Exchange was first in the field with an inter-broker clearing system, while the Northern Stock Exchange started its computerized clearing system in 1967, but not using the same machine as the Scottish Stock Exchange. In 1968 the Midland and Western came into the

T

Northern scheme and as a result inter-regional clearing now operates between these two exchanges. Since the English regional exchanges have adopted the same computer system as London it is quite possible that a national system of clearing could be set up in the future so that original buyers and ultimate sellers could be put in touch wherever they happened to reside, with cash or stock going through a central agency.

With the successful development of inter-regional clearing on the English regional markets it was decided to follow this up with the introduction of a Central Stock Payment (C.S.P.) system so as to expedite the movement of stock from one broker to another in different parts of the country. This C.S.P. system came into operation in 1968 as a joint venture by the Northern and the Midland and Western Stock Exchanges. Stock and documents are now moved around the country by a special service and it has proved highly successful. However, with a system which involves stock going all over the country a broker might send stock to a distant broker who is relatively unknown to him. If the broker defaulted it was felt that it would be unfair on the sending broker to leave him without any form of protection and to this end the Council of Associated Stock Exchanges set up a Clearing Guarantee Fund to which every member contributes £200, with the possibility of a further call if additional funds were needed. The fund is to be used at the discretion of the Council towards compensating any member of the Associated Stock Exchanges "who may suffer loss through the default of any firm whose partners are members of the Council of Associated Stock Exchanges".[20] This then is essentially an internal compensation fund to cope with a particular regional problem, while the public who are covered by an entirely separate fund have no claim against it.

The progress achieved by the provincial exchanges over the past ten years has been of a very satisfactory order. The Federation of Stock Exchanges in Great Britain and Ireland has provided through its numerous rules and requirements uniform standards for stock-broking activities so that investors are guaranteed a minimum level of service. With the rapid and successful adoption of the regional set up the provincial exchanges met most of the points raised by the Jenkins Committee, while in addition bringing many important benefits. The dealing mechanism which evolved under Federation rules and in the regional environment has provided an efficient service which not only has been to the advantage of local investors but also served to enlarge the range of competitive market facilities to a wider circle of investors. This of itself has been an important contribution to the improvement of the investment services provided by the national security markets.

It has been numerously suggested in the recent past that local markets should perhaps concentrate on local shares and leave the national shares to the main market in London. There would seem to be little future for useful regional security markets in these terms. The turnover in local shares is totally inadequate to support an efficient dealing and broking mechanism, and it could only operate on the basis of large price movements which would be to no particular advantage. On the other hand, if the regional market's dealing agency, the jobber, can operate books in national stocks which have a large turnover then his income is to a much greater extent assured and he is more likely to run a book in some local shares as a side line. Also, to the extent that there is a market in the shares of existing companies new issues by local companies will be easier to make since investors will be more readily inclined to take up such shares which can subsequently be dealt in on the market. This provides shareholders in local companies with superior markets to that which would exist if they were solely locally orientated. An economically useful future for regional stock exchanges would seem to lie in continuing and strengthening present developments.

NOTES

1 With the implementation of Federation several administrative and policy matters previously dealt with by the Council of Associated Stock Exchanges passed out of its hands. However, it still continues to provide a useful forum for the discussion and expression of country opinion, and will continue to do so unless of course, a united stock exchange comes into being in the future.
2 Federation Document, 1965, p. 2.
3 As from April 1971 the Dublin and Cork Stock Exchanges will form the Irish Stock Exchange. The Belfast Stock Exchange will continue as at present.
4 Federation Document, op. cit., p. iii. There were also rules on some general matters.
5 *Report of the Company Law Committee,* 1962, Cmnd. 1749, paras. 257, 264.
6 Council of Associated Stock Exchanges, Minutes, Resumé 1961-2.
7 Federation Document, op. cit., pp. 13-15.
8 Ibid., p. 17.
9 Ibid., pp. 21-34.
10 Ibid., pp. 35-38.
11 Evidence of Mr C. T. Ockleston and Mr A. Owen to the Jenkins Committee, 8th day Q. 2543.
12 *Report of the Company Law Committee,* op. cit., paras. 256-7.
13 Leeds Stock Exchange, Minutes, February 19, 1915, June 25, 1946. These discussions probably did not get far since each exchange feared the loss of quotation fees, and that increased size might lead to the elimination of the numerous small firms.

14 The Newport Stock Exchange amalgamated with Cardiff in 1961. At one stage of the prolonged negotiations to set up the Midland and Western Stock Exchange, Cardiff and Bristol contemplated setting up a Western Stock Exchange.

15 Federation Document, op. cit., pp. 57-67; List of Authorized Securities and Dual Capacity Firms.

16 Report of the City Working Party on Securities Handling (Heasman Report), Appendix 2. The figures are based on a sample of stockbrokers transfer forms lodged with the registrars' departments of I.C.I., Courtaulds, Barclays Bank, and B.P. It was also noted that 54% of purchases were done through London and 50% of sales, while the London Stock Exchange estimated that one delivery there in five has a country element (i.e. buying or selling broker).

17 No turnover figures are available for the English provincial markets; The Scottish figures are given in Chapter 14.

18 Since regionalization the number of firms in the Northern Stock Exchange has fallen from 117 to 66 in 1971. There are 10 firms with 8 or more full-time partners. The Midland and Western Stock Exchange number of firms has fallen from 58 at regionalization to 40 in 1971. There are 6 firms with 8 or more full-time partners.

19 The end of account arrangements are very similar in the provinces to those of London. For a detailed account of the timetable of events see Morgan and Thomas, op. cit., pp. 262-66; also J. Dundas Hamilton, *Stockbroking Today* (1968), Chapter 3.

20 Council of Associated Stock Exchanges, Minutes, Resumé, 1968-9.

PART TWO

Scotland

14   The Scottish Stock Exchanges

A. *Origins of the Markets*

Glasgow's first stockbroker was James Watson, a founder member
of the Glasgow Stock Exchange, who in 1830 added share dealing
to his existing accountancy business. Until 1835–36 he seems to
have enjoyed a virtual monopoly of local activity, but the 1836
boom saw the entry into the trade for a few years of A. McTaggart.
The increasing number of railway promotions and the associated
growth of public interest brought new brokers onto the scene and
by 1842–43 five more had appeared. They were John Lang,
Buchanan and Aitken, MacEwan and Auld, J. C. Foulds, and Kerr
and Anderson, and they conducted their business by advertising
'wanted and on-offer' lists in the local press. By 1844–45 the number
of brokers in the city had risen to eighteen. In June 1844 a number
of them formed "a society under the title of the Glasgow Stock
Exchange Association". It was asserted in the local press at the
time that the "vast amount of business transacted in the city in
stocks has rendered such an association, more particularly of late
years, a decided desideratum; and there can be no doubt that it
will prove highly advantageous to the public. An accredited list
of prices founded on the actual transactions of the Association will
be regularly furnished to the members and to the different newspapers, and anything like misrepresentation as to the value of shares
for dishonourable or jobbing purposes will thus be effectively
checked".[1] The first meeting, called by Peter Wilson Dixon, a broker
since 1842, consisted of accountants who had also been acting as
brokers. It was held at the Exchange Sale Room and the decision
was taken to commence business early in July at No. 3, North
Court, Royal Exchange. Only brokers in public companies or
undertakings, insurance agents or accountants, were to be admitted
to the Stock Exchange, and they had to be resident in Glasgow.
Admission was by ballot and entry money was put at £5 but soon
raised to £25, and to £100 in April 1845. The Stock Exchange was
administered by a committee of five members, later increased to
nine, James Watson was elected Chairman and Andrew MacEwan
to the post of Secretary.[2]

The original membership of the Stock Exchange numbered twenty-eight, and by the end of the year a further six brokers had joined. The following year saw a sharp increase in membership; from January to April eighteen new members joined and a further fourteen during the rest of the year. By June 1846 the total membership was sixty-three, and two years later it was seventy. Although the accountancy profession was well represented, the bulk of the new entrants had no traceable professions in the local directories. Many only enjoyed a short stay in the market and by 1850 the membership had fallen to forty.

During the early months of 1845 a number of brokers who had been refused admission to the Stock Exchange, and certain other persons drawn from numerous occupations, set up a rival stock exchange. This was the City of Glasgow Stock Exchange, later called the Union Stock Exchange, which also met at the Royal Exchange Buildings. It was nicknamed the "Wee Room", although its membership exceeded that of the Stock Exchange; in January 1846 it had nearly eighty members, Alexander Morrison was chairman, and J. H. Hill, secretary. Not only did the Stock Exchange rules exclude the above parties from membership, but they also through the imposition of strict commission terms encouraged outside brokers to develop market facilities of their own. The Stock Exchange's minimum commission rules were to be "stictly adhered to by the members in relation to transactions in Scotland", and was calculated to preserve their status and respectability.[3] Another group which was also denied entry were members of the Faculty of Procurators, the local association of the legal profession. They had sent a delegation to discuss with the officials of the Stock Exchange the subject of the abolition of all entry requirements thus permitting members of the professions and those outside Glasgow, to become members of the Stock Exchange, and they also requested that the sixty-two members of the Faculty should be admitted at a reduced fee. The Stock Exchange refused to oblige and the Faculty in October set up the General Stock Exchange of Glasgow, referred to colloquially as the "Writers Room". It was under the auspices of the Faculty but its facilities were not confined to their members. They met every "lawful day" in the Exchange Room, No. 17 South Frederick Street. Both these rival bodies collapsed after a few years.[4]

The earliest reference to share dealing in Edinburgh directories is to be found in 1825–26 when John Hay and John Robertson added it to their existing activities. Ten years later they were joined by John Trench and Alexander Stevenson. By 1840–41 the number of brokers in the city had increased to seven, among them Reid and Nicholson, a firm founded by John Reid author of the *Manual of the Scottish Stocks and British Funds*. With the railway boom the number rose to thirty firms, most of which entered the trade in 1845 from untraceable professions.

The origins of the Stock Exchange are to be found in a meeting of seven brokers convened by Pillans and Horne, and held on December 16, 1844 at the Royal Hotel, Princess Street. Those present were, J. W. Pillans, A. Stevenson jun., T. Miller, Edward Mc-Callum, Albert Cay, W. Cleland and David Horne. The majority concluded that "considering the augmented number of Stock Brokers and the increasing importance of the trade it is expedient in order to facilitate the transaction of business to form a Stock Exchange in Edinburgh". A committee of three brokers was given the task of drawing up a series of regulations for the government of the proposed stock exchange. These rules were later approved at a general meeting held at the offices of Pillans & Horne in Princess Street. J. W. Pillans was elected chairman, and Albert Cay as secretary. Premises were obtained at 71 Princess Street in a "front Room first flat".[5] By October 1845 the membership had increased to twenty-six, and by a further ten a year later.

Among the rules adopted by the Stock Exchange were ones which required residence in Edinburgh, ballot procedures for admission, proposal by two members, and commission rules which lay down a minimum scale to be strictly adhered to in relation to transactions in Scotland. Those brokers who did not wish, or could not, comply with such requirements joined with those who had been refused admission, and early in 1845 they set up a rival exchange. In February of that year they had a meeting at the Royal Hotel and proposed the formation of the Edinburgh and Leith Commercial and Stock Exchange Association. *The Scotsman* commented that the

". . . want of an Exchange in the metropolis of Scotland has long been a matter of serious complaint, and we have therefore, no doubt of the success of the present undertaking. Some four or five years ago, several highly respectable and influential merchants formed themselves into a body with a view to the furtherance of a similar object, but from the peculiar circumstances of the scheme was, after a few weeks' trial, abandoned. The new Association propose to commence their operations upon a more extended scale – to add to the business of a commercial exchange that of a Stock Exchange, so that not only will merchants meet in the rooms for the purpose of mutual information, and to facilitate their transactions, but

sharebrokers and their clients will assemble there to their profit
and advantage. The mercantile community generally will find
it to their interest to become members of the Association, in
as much as there will be a perpetual amount of real intelligence
to be gathered daily 'on Change', while jobbers in stocks and
shares will derive incalculable benefits from their connection
with it. We have only to add, that . . . it is projected in no
hostile spirit towards the existing Stock Exchange, but purely
from a conviction that such an institution was desired by the
public".[6]

With the decline in share turnover after the collapse of the
boom, it was not long before the rival exchange approached the
Stock Exchange about the possibility of amalgamation, but the
ballot procedures described by the latter's rules prevented a whole-
sale merger.[7] The question lay dormant until 1854 when the Stock
Exchange Committee considered that it was "desirable and important that all transactions in stockbroking connected with Edinburgh
should as far as practicable be centred in one market", and
accordingly deputations from both markets discussed steps for a
future union. After several meetings the rival exchange agreed
to the necessity of admission rules and agreed to accept the terms
of the Stock Exchange. However, in October 1854 the Stock
Exchange went ahead with the election of officers for the coming
year, contrary to the agreement reached at the discussions. The
"proposed junction" fell to the ground and the brokers of the rival
exchange continued their daily meetings in the offices of one of
their number. Two years later amalgamation discussions were
resumed and finally in November the merger was speedily completed. On November 24, 1856 the members of the Stock Exchange
and the City of Edinburgh Stock Exchange "met together in one
association" under the chairmanship of Robert Allan.[8]

The activities of the earliest broker in Aberdeen, W. Gordon, can
be traced in the local trade directories back to 1834–35. During
1840–42 he was joined by George Oswald and W. Adamson. With
the increase in railway promotion the number of brokers rose to
well over a dozen, and in October 1845 fourteen of them held a
meeting at the Agricultural Societies Hall, Market Street, "for the
purpose of adopting measures for the formation of a Stock
Exchange in Aberdeen". W. Gordon was elected Chairman and
W. Adamson, Secretary. It was decided to adopt the rules of the
Edinburgh Stock Exchange.[9]

The Dundee and Greenock Stock Exchanges were formed later in
the century in response to local investment needs. The 1845 railway

boom did not altogether leave Dundee unaffected with a few brokers dealing in railway shares through periodic auctions. Among them were William Crockett, D. B. Niven, Baxter and Miller, and Andrew Ogilvie. By the 1860s there were six brokers in the town, increasing to nine by 1878–79. On March 25, 1879 it was decided to form a local stock exchange to provide for "establishing regular daily meetings". Naturally, Andrew Ogilvie was elected chairman, while J. R. Mudie was made secretary. The market opened for business on April 1, 1879.[10]

Some ten years later in 1888 a Stock Exchange was opened in Greenock following a desire "to afford facilities to those persons who being possessed of railway shares, Consols, Harbour Stock, or any other kind of stock were desirous to realise or invest and also those who wanted to buy". Essentially it was to provide an investment service for shareholders of local shipping and associated companies, certainly not for speculative business. All transactions were to be for bona fide purchasers and sellers and clients had to have either securities or cash on hand, or members would not deal. Premises were obtained in the Municipal Buildings and the membership consisted of accountants who engaged in share dealing on the side. In 1888 there were six members, with Lawson Walker as chairman. By 1914 the membership of the Greenock Stock Exchange was more or less unaltered.[11]

B. Organization

The main changes which occurred in the membership of the Scottish Stock Exchanges since their formation are summarized in the following table.

	Glasgow	Edinburgh	Aberdeen	Dundee	Greenock
1845	49	26	15	–	–
1848	70	32	15*	–	–
1850	40	17	n.a.	–	–
1864	51	21	n.a.	–	–
1880	114	40*	14*	12	–
1900	188	61*	13*	15*	6
1914	265	72	13	19	7
1939	249	64	11	13	14
1946	206	56	10	12	19
1959	136	54	9	11	16

Source: Stock Exchange Minutes: *Glasgow Stock Exchange Association Records*
Note: * denotes figures for the nearest year available.

A feature of the table is the marked decline in the membership of the two main markets after the collapse of the eighteen forties railway boom. From the high point of 1848 both markets nearly halved their membership by the mid-fifties, a trend associated partly with the withdrawal from the market of the more speculatively inclined entrants of the mania era. During the last quarter of the century the membership grew quite rapidly, a fact linked with the growth of foreign investments and the widespread adoption of the limited company form, with peak membership being reached in 1914. War brought a reduction, but markets soon recovered in the early twenties. The Second World War brought a repeat performance but the post-war period witnessed, especially in the case of Glasgow, a very substantial fall in membership. Their large fall was probably associated with the reduced volume of dealing in overseas investments, while nationalization took many leading shares off the market, and perhaps the allegedly "punting population" of Glasgow was also less inclined to deal. Also, the elderly element spared the war retired and were not replaced by younger members. The membership of the smaller markets changed very little over the period.

In general the membership of the stock exchanges consisted solely of stock and share brokers. It is interesting to note however that during the railway period that the Glasgow Stock Exchange had rules permitting the admission of members wishing to act solely in a jobbing capacity. In 1847 the Committee agreed to admit jobbers on the understanding that: —

> "he shall bind himself to act strictly in that capacity, . . . that he will not either directly or indirectly act as a broker but that on the contrary all his transactions shall be on his own individual account, . . . that he will be prepared in ordinary states of the market, to deal in one or more stocks (to be named by him), . . . either as buyer or seller as may be required, at prices nearly the same as the latest quotations of the said stock or stocks in the London market, . . . or in Liverpool or Edinburgh, if the said stock or stocks be not in the London market".[12]

Unfortunately, it is not recorded how many took advantage of such provisions but presumably there must have been some demand for membership as jobbers for such rules to be formulated. With the growth of telegraphic markets later in the century many brokers turned to shunting activity; in 1878 Glasgow had "some members who systematically lay themselves open for that kind of business".[13] Edinburgh members also developed shunting activity, both markets becoming part of the shunting circuit of the present century. During the early years clerks were admitted into the market only if members were ill, but later accredited clerks were permitted to attend regularly.

The basic method of dealing was for broker to deal with broker during the various daily call-overs. In Glasgow the opening of the market was announced by the ringing of a bell "and the stocks were called *seriatim*; there is a moderate time allowed for transacting in each stock; and transactions must all take place when the stocks are being publicly called in that way".[14] An official called the list and the Chairman presided. Generally, the first person who accepted the buyer or the seller's price was entitled to the stock. If rival bidders appeared when a stock was offered and they called simultaneously the chair had to rule which one had precedence. If a member offered stock but did not name a price then usually it was held as dealing at the last quotation of the previous day's printed list. If no quantity was named it was held to be a market-able amount as set out in the rules. Special calls, that is a public call of a particular stock, were allowed in the case of pressing orders on the discretion of the chair. With the development of telegraphic facilities fluctuations in other markets became much more quickly known and special calls were more frequently allowed.[15]

During the eighteen eighties Edinburgh held three call-overs of the list at each of the three daily business sessions. During the first and last calling the Secretary called in regular rotation only the principal stocks, as determined by the Committee. The second calling could be interrupted by special calls on application to the Chairman. Growth in the size of the list and increased business soon led to the calling of only the principal stocks while special calls were allowed each time. By 1928 it was decided to curtail the calling of the list, and a few years later it was discontinued.[16] Glasgow also moved in the same direction, with the principal stocks being called at the 11.0 call-over, after which deals could be made without special calls, and in any order. The call-over had developed into a continuous auction market.

The smaller markets of Aberdeen and Dundee proceeded on similar lines. However, they were able to maintain the call-over system for longer because of their shorter lists and less active trading conditions. As late as 1945 the system was still used in Aberdeen; "From the bottom of the table the Secretary calls the list of Stocks, and from round the table comes a chorus of rapid responses, interspersed with calls of 'First Buyer' and 'First Seller'. For all the world like a quick fire auction sale".[17]

All bargains made on a stock exchange were in the nature of absolute transactions for purchase or sale, and brokers were regarded as principals to each other and so bound to carry out the transaction.[18] Once a bargain was made it was entered into the market books of both parties, and on the Glasgow Stock Exchange brokers initialled each others book, rather than exchange written contract notes stating the terms of the transaction. The practice of initialling entries was occasionally used on other markets but their rules lay down, and committees periodically insisted, that written contracts should be exchanged between members.[19]

By the time the main stock exchanges were well established in their own premises, the prices at which bargains were done were marked up on price boards in the market, and from the closing prices of the day the daily list was compiled. Earlier, in 1844, on the Glasgow Stock Exchange "all transactions done in Glasgow, by the members shall be daily reported in the list provided for that purpose in the Stock Exchange and the last quotation shall be considered as the price at 4 o'clock of the day". The first daily list was put out on March 11, 1845, and it gave prices which had been "reported" and those done "on change"; a few months later only the "on change" prices were given.[20] Edinburgh put out a daily list from March 1845 "in order to insure perfect uniformity in the printed or published prices of stocks".[21] These, of course, were records of price changes and not of the size of transactions. The smaller markets kept their own daily records, but Aberdeen contented itself with a fortnightly list, while much later Dundee published a list of quotations ruling at the close of business on the last day of the month.

Unlike most of the early provincial stock exchanges Glasgow did not settle bargains on a cash basis, but from the beginning used settling days. There were two settling days each week, Tuesday and Friday, when all transactions were completed, and all sales and purchases were considered as made for the first settling day after intimation of the transfer being ready, unless other arrangements existed. Dissatisfaction with this system, which was not all that far removed from cash settlements, led the Committee to initiate an examination of the practices used in London and on other provincial markets. However, it was decided in March 1846 to keep the existing system of weekly settlements but with one settling day instead of two. Tuesday was thus the settling day for all transactions done prior to the close of business on the Saturday preceding. It was held that weekly settlements suited the needs of their limited market and they liked the system whereby each transaction could be settled individually without the need to strike balances and settle differences.[22] The settlement commenced at

11.00 and stock and cash changed hands at the offices of the respective purchasers with payment made by cash or cheque, at the option of the seller. These rules also applied to transactions in registered stock with distant markets, such as London and Liverpool. As an Edinburgh observer noted, "this would appear . . . to be almost tantamount to putting a stop to all transactions with places at a distance". The Glasgow Committee, however, frankly stated that the rules were made "to prevent as much as possible all jobbing for the same account between Glasgow and other English markets, and thus compel brokers to confine themselves to sales or orders from private parties having the stock on hand ready for delivery".[23]

Following the decline in share turnover during the post boom depression, and the fact that the major English exchanges used fortnightly settlements, Glasgow in July 1847 abandoned weekly settlements and went over to fortnightly ones using the same dates as London.[24] Also, a ticket system was introduced to aid the settlement mechanism but it did not work smoothly until the setting up in 1853 of an effective Clearing House system which worked by settling differences in cash through the Secretary.[25] It was not until 1891 that exchange vouchers replaced cash for this purpose.

During the early years of the Edinburgh Stock Exchange bargains were settled on a cash basis. The buying client was bound to give the consideration immediately to his broker so that he could pay when presented with documents by the seller. In August 1846 the Committee decided to inquire into the expediency of setting up settling days and after examining the Glasgow and English systems they opted for fortnightly settlements on the London pattern as being more suitable to their existing and future needs. The volume of business done on the market did not merit the setting up of a Clearing House until the early eighteen eighties.[26]

Aberdeen also commenced business using cash settlements but in 1853 the Committee instituted a trial period of fortnightly settlements in a limited number of shares and it was "found a great convenience to the members in transacting business as well as an accommodation and benefit to their principals." As a result it was decided that all transactions would be for fortnightly settlement at the middle and end of each month, "and that the last purchaser or party taking up stock shall have the naming of the consideration money or purchase price to be inserted in the Transfer; but such price must be one at which the stock has been dealt in, in any Exchange, during the account in which the shares were bought".[27]

The Dundee Stock Exchange was of course set up at a time when Stock Exchange practices were well established and accordingly fortnightly settlements were adopted from the start.

A feature of dealings during the early years of the markets, when the bulk of the business was in railway scrip for cash settlement, was the frequent recourse to buying-in and selling-out because of the non-delivery of cash or securities. This was soon put on a regular footing and was usually done through the Secretary of the Exchange. The adoption of regular fortnightly settlements however afforded more time for the delivery of cash and securities, and the use of carry-over facilities also made buying-in and selling-out comparatively rare. On the Glasgow Stock Exchange it was soon found that dealing for the next account almost from the beginning of the existing one created confusion and considerable interruption to the regular business, and although private dealing between members for the next account was allowed, from 1848 onwards carry-overs through the Secretary could not be called until three days before the end of an account.[28]

Commissions were a particularly thorny subject which occasioned much internal debate and a great deal of external consultation. Generally, the exchanges laid down a minimum scale which was "to be strictly adhered to by the members in relation to transactions in Scotland", with fines for those found dealing below the scale. Commission levels were not however uniform between Glasgow and Edinburgh during the early years. Edinburgh rates were below those of Glasgow on small shares, perhaps reflecting the "punting population" of the latter and the more staid investment class of the former which occasioned less risk to brokers. Early attempts to establish a uniform scale were not immediately successful. In 1846 Edinburgh expressed a desire to put all Scottish rates on the same level as London, and also suggested that the level of rates should be raised since brokers guaranteed transactions, but the proposals were rejected which was not surprising in the depressed state of markets at the close of 1846. The Glasgow Stock Exchange and its rival exchanges however proceeded to arrive at an agreed scale without reference to Edinburgh, much to their annoyance, but ultimately Edinburgh fell in line with the new scale. The main change was an increase in the commission on small shares, and the scales worked out at $\frac{1}{2}\%$ for railway and miscellaneous securities, and $\frac{1}{4}\%$ for bank and insurance shares.[29] By 1878 the general commission charge on shares was $\frac{1}{2}\%$, still strictly enforced. The commission rules also contained strict provisions with regard to rebates. The general position was that members could divide with brokers on the English markets but with no others, while members were also

Birmingham Stock Exchange.

The Dealing Room of J. W. Nicholson & Sons, Sheffield in the mid nineteen thirties.

prohibited from making net prices to outsiders. During the early years of the Glasgow Stock Exchange this policy had the solid support of the great majority of members, and similar views prevailed in Aberdeen and Edinburgh.[30] Exposure to increasing competition from outside agents and improved telegraphic communications from the seventies onwards brought demands from members for some relaxation of the strict rebate provisions. In 1876 a number of Edinburgh brokers requested rebates for law agents because "much of the business of Edinburgh is being diverted to London and other markets".[31] This became a recurring complaint during the next sixty years. Aberdeen in 1899 relaxed its commission rules to remedy a similar concern. The situation was deemed to have become particularly serious by the nineteen thirties, and Edinburgh brokers were very conscious of the loss of business in bank and insurance shares to London and Birmingham. Even the markets in the shares of local Scottish banks were drifting southwards, while the more venturesome of the English country jobbers found the Scottish restrictions much to their advantage. Obviously Scottish business was particularly vulnerable to attack from the south where most brokers divided commissions. Persistent pressure from members eventually brought a change in the rules in 1941 and the Scottish exchanges agreed to rebate to solicitors, accountants, banks and investment trusts, as in the London rules. It was appreciated that some loss would occur on transactions of a purely local nature but they were confident that following the change the increased business would compensate for this.[32]

C. Domestic Matters

The exchanges followed the general practice of imposing entry fees, annual subscriptions and surety requirements, although naturally the amounts differed between the four exchanges. The early entrants to the Edinburgh Stock Exchange paid entry money of £10, and an annual subscription of £5, but with increased business and a growing demand for membership the entry money by September 1845 was raised to £100. In subsequent years the figure was varied depending as to the pressure for entry to the market. By the end of the century the entry money stood at £200, with concessions for the sons of members and experienced clerks. Later, entrants were also required to contribute a share of the general fund of the Association. The general pattern of entry money was the same on the Glasgow Stock Exchange, beginning with £5 at the time of its opening but it was soon up to £100 by April 1845. Thereafter it was increased, and occasionally decreased when it was thought to constitute a bar to new entrants, until by 1920 it reached £1,000 for outsiders, to-

U

gether with a share in the general fund. Entry money in Aberdeen was originally £25 but quickly rose to £50, and at the end of the century it took the form of a full share of the capital of the Association, plus a cash sum. Dundee began with an entry fee of £20, but soon raised it to £100.

New entrants also required to be proposed by members of the Association and be elected by ballot. The other major condition was the need to provide surety. On the Glasgow Stock Exchange it was decided in 1845 to require each member to find surety for £500 for 3 years, but "no member of this Association shall become surety for another". These provisions did not remain in force for long. The surety requirement was re-introduced in 1862, fixed at £1,000 for five years with power to the Committee to call a further £1,000. Edinburgh introduced in 1845 somewhat similar requirements to those of Glasgow, but they were dropped shortly afterwards to be reinstated in 1860 when it was fixed at £500 for three years. On both markets the surety requirement was gradually revised upwards following on increased business and "the responsibilities incurred by the members in the transactions of it".[33] By the end of the century the surety on both markets was around £3,000 for five years, somewhat above the requirements of the English markets. Aberdeen introduced a surety requirement in 1854 for the sum of £300 for three years, which was increased in 1884 to £500 for five years, at which level it remained for a long period. Dundee introduced a surety requirement in 1906 for the sum of £1,000 for three years.

The exchanges were managed by committees elected from, and by, the members. Edinburgh began with a small committee of three members plus a chairman and secretary, but by the end of the century the growth of business and of exchange membership necessitated a much larger committee of ten members. Glasgow also began with a small committee of five, but by 1884 it had increased to twelve members. The smaller exchanges at Aberdeen and Dundee managed with small committees of about half a dozen members. An exchange chairman was elected annually but very few of the Scottish ones served long terms in contrast to the pattern south of the border; Sir James Watson was Chairman of the Glasgow Stock Exchange from 1844–66 and 1875–78, while Andrew Ogilvie (1879–87) and W. M. Ritchie (1887–1911) served the Dundee Stock Exchange for moderately long periods. The early secretaries were drawn from the ranks of the members which imposed considerable additional burdens on them since they were required to attend during business hours, make up the price lists, keep the minutes and the books of the association, and generally perform such other duties as were conducive to the convenience of members. Glasgow appointed its first full-time secretary in 1871, and Matthew Shields, who gave evidence to the 1878 *Royal Commission on the London Stock Exchange,* held office until 1891. He was succeeded by Horace Gifford from 1891 to 1936.

With their gradual growth and changing requirements the stock exchanges exhibited a fairly roving existence. The Glasgow Stock Exchange started life at 3 North Court, Royal Exchange, but soon moved to a hall on the north side of St George's Place. In February 1847 it again moved its quarters to the National Bank Buildings in Queen Street where it remained until 1877 when the original portion of the present building was opened which provided particularly well appointed quarters for the market. In 1906 the premises were further enlarged in the French Gothic style of the main building. In the recent rebuilding of the Stock Exchange the external shell has been completely preserved and a new interior constructed to provide for the future needs of the market.[34] Edinburgh commenced business in a "front room first flat" on Princess Street but a short time later leased premises in South St David Street. The fall in membership at the time and the lack of entry fees brought a need to economize and smaller premises were thought desirable. However, by 1870 the membership and the business recovered and the Stock Exchange looked for new premises, leasing Craigie Hall in 1874, and in 1880 obtaining premises in South St David Street. In 1888 the decision was taken to construct a suitable building on the existing site as a permanent home for the Association and this building served such a purpose until the mid-nineteen sixties when the old building was replaced by a modern one which was opened in 1966.[35] The exact locations of the Aberdeen market are not certain but at various times it has met in premises in Market Street and in the Aberdeen Corn Exchange. The Dundee Stock Exchange retained until recently its original meeting place, nestled at the rear of the local Chamber of Commerce.

Probably the most important technical advance of the period as far as the Stock Exchanges were concerned was the development of the telegraph services. Both Edinburgh and Glasgow made early use of the new facility but it was not altogether a happy experience. In 1847 both obtained daily London prices by telegraph but the regularity of the service provided by the Electric Telegraph Co. left a great deal to be desired. Indeed Glasgow were soon regarding the transmissions as utterly valueless.[36] During the seventies and eighties telegraph facilities in the exchanges expanded greatly but congestion still led to delays, as did the ruling by the Post Office in 1887 to curtail the development of a network of provincial telegraph links.

During the inter-war years there was a gradual decline in the use of the telegraph and after the Second World War the installations were removed from the markets. After an initially cool reception the telephone replaced it as the main communications medium.

D. Scottish Share Markets

Early Scottish share markets centred largely around well established banks and insurance companies. The sort of investment opportunities available to local investors is evident in the following table compiled from the 1831 list of "Prices of Stock at the Offices of James Watson, Accountant" of Glasgow.[37]

		Total Capital Advanced £mn.
6	banks	5.5
7	insurance companies	2.7
3	water companies	0.5
2	gas light companies	0.2
2	canals	1.0
2	railways	0.1
22	Total	£10.0

Some of these activities were of very long standing indeed. The Bank of Scotland was incorporated by Act of Parliament in 1695, the British Linen Company of Edinburgh likewise in 1746, the Royal Bank of Scotland was incorporated by Royal Charter in 1727 and the Commercial Bank in 1810. Other early banks included the Dundee Bank, 1763, and the Dundee Union Bank, 1809. By 1836 the shares of thirteen banks were dealt in on local markets. A further increase in numbers followed in 1838 when there was a minor banking boom with the formation of seven banks, among them the Clydesdale, Southern, Eastern, Caledonian, and Edinburgh and Leith banks. John Reid notes in his *Manual* that applications for Clydesdale shares were "so numerous that not $\frac{1}{3}$ of the number applied for could be allocated, and the shares went to a premium of 15s. per share before the first call was paid", while a "great deal of speculation took place in the stock of the Edinburgh and Leith bank; the shares went to 5s. premium as soon as they were in the market, and 2,000 or 3,000 shares have been known to change hands in the course of a single day".[38] The shares of most of these Scottish banks were "but little known in the London market".

The other main category in James Watson's list, insurance companies, included companies of considerable standing, such as the Caledonian Fire and Life (1805), the Hercules Insurance Co. (1809), the North British Insurance Co. (1809), and the Fire Insurance Co.

of Scotland (1821). The period 1836–40 saw the formation of five new life insurance offices and this sector of the market represented in John Reid's opinion "a very good investment for capital", with existing companies paying dividends of between 5% and 11%. Also, during 1839–40, a crop of marine insurance companies came onto the market, eight in all, some of which paid dividends of 15%, but all except three of them had paid up capitals of under £15,000.[39]

The first major joint stock mania occurred in 1825 but it left no survivor for inclusion in James Watson's list. John Reid commented in his *Manual*; "We may notice the Alloa Glass Co., Caledonian Dairy Co., and many others that originated amidst the visionary schemes of 1825, all coming within the same category. The amount of capital actually squandered in such schemes, during these years in Scotland was enormous".[40] Numerous gas companies were formed in the 1820s which survived but most had capitals of less than £10,000. The increasing number of miscellaneous companies which appeared during periods of active company promotion in the following decade were a little more fortunate, as indeed were the participating investors. In this activity shipping and investment companies figured prominently. Among the shipping companies were the Leith and Hull Shipping Co. (1835), the New Clyde Shipping Co., and the Aberdeen Steam Navigation Co. The most interesting development however was the appearance of several overseas investment companies. John Reid lists the following; the Illinois Investment Co. (1837), with a capital of £100,000, the North American Investmnt Co. (1839) – capital £213,000, the Michigan Investment Co. (1839) – capital £30,000, and the Galena Investment Co. (1840) – capital £37,5000, all with £1 fully paid-up shares. They were concerned with investment in the United States, the last three being launched by Aberdeen financiers who risked a sum of £125,000 in the ventures. Three of the companies paid dividends of between 12–15% in 1841. The Galena Investment Co., a lead mining venture, failed to become a profitable concern.[41] The other investment company given by John Reid was the North British Australian Co. which was promoted and largely financed by Aberdeen interests in 1839, with a capital of £50,000.[42]

By 1841 the number of companies whose shares were publicly dealt in had increased greatly compared with 1831. The following summary of John Reid's Scottish stock list for July 1841 illustrates the size and composition of the market. An interesting contrast between James Watson's and John Reid's lists is the size of the share denominations. The former list is dominated by the large share units of the early banks, canals, and gas companies, relieved with a few low denomination shares of insurance companies. The promotional booms of the eighteen thirties saw the introduction of shares of lower values with a greater appeal to a wider circle of investors, a trend which was followed by the railways. It is noteworthy that in John Reid's list there are a number of very low denominations particularly in the case of investment companies and some of the gas companies of the late thirties which used £1 fully paid shares. Although Reid's list gives a selling price for practically every share he does add a cautionary note to the effect that since quotations in Edinburgh were left to "the option of one or two stockbrokers . . . whose knowledge is necessarily limited to the last prices obtained by themselves . . . it frequently happens that quoted stock has not been sold in the Edinburgh market for the space of a whole year", and that consequently some prices were purely nominal.

		"Advanced Capital"
		£
23	banks	10,064,200
15	insurance companies (Life and Fire)	2,001,500
10	marine insurance companies	368,166
16	railways	2,613,375
17	gas companies	537,893
24	miscellaneous companies	2,264,803
105	Total	17,849,937

Railways constituted the main class of shares which grew steadily in number in the thirties and which by the early forties was beginning to dominate share activity in both Edinburgh and Glasgow. Beginning with the Kilmarnock and Troon Railway, opened in 1810, most of the early lines were promoted in the late thirties and early forties, for example, the Edinburgh and Glasgow (incorporated in 1838), the Glasgow and Ayr (1837), the North British (1844). By 1838 some fifty miles of lines were operational in Scotland. The 1845 boom brought a surge of new companies; 423 miles of line were authorized for Scotland involving extensions of the Caledonian, and major links between Aberdeen and the south. In 1846 another 393 miles were authorized for some 22 railways in the south of Scotland, mainly small stretches, with 419 miles in the north for 14 companies, again mainly small stretches apart from the Inverness–Aberdeen link. Authorizations in 1847 were mainly for minor extensions.[43]

All this meant increased business in railway shares from the late thirties onwards but the big upsurge occurs in the spring of 1844 when the first rush of railway prospectuses appeared in the local press. Among Glasgow brokers who participated in the marketing of shares were MacEwan and Auld, Buchanan and Aitken, and James Watson, himself an interim secretary of the Glasgow and Ayr Railway, and secretary of the Edinburgh and Glasgow Railway. In Edinburgh Robertson & Co., Pillans and Horne, Robert Allan, and George Napier were prominent in receiving share applications. In March 1845 the Glasgow list included twenty-two Scottish lines; by December of the same year the number had risen to over seventy. In October there was "hardly a capitalist of any consequence . . . who has not invested more or less of his property in these great national undertakings". Nearly all descriptions of railway shares were eagerly sought after at "considerably advanced prices", the majority of transactions being in the scrip of newly brought out schemes. Prices were sent even higher by the fact that in the case of some lines investors felt that too little of the stock had been allocated locally and far too much sent south to London and Liverpool.[44] In the summer both Stock Exchanges decided upon a short break to abate the speculative fever, Edinburgh closing for a week, Glasgow for three days. At the height of the speculation in September the Edinburgh Stock Exchange resolved "that with a view to check the present excessive speculation in shares that this Exchange will after this date recognize no transaction in the shares of any new company made before the issue of the scrip," and members were cautioned not to engage in such dealings in their offices. Speculation was also encouraged by the setting up of local Exchange Banks which afforded "accommodation of the holders of railway and other stocks by advancing money on the security of such stocks", usually at about $6\frac{1}{2}\%$. Later, they also dealt in the stocks on which they had granted advances. Among these companies were the Glasgow Commercial Exchange Co. formed in 1845 with a capital of £1 million, and the Edinburgh based Scottish Exchange Investment Co. with a capital of £500,000. Nine such companies were quoted in the list of the Union Stock Exchange of Glasgow, most of which had £10 shares with about half of this amount paid up. By 1847, the shares of most of them stood at a substantial discount and several subsequently collapsed.[45]

Scottish markets followed English experience with the fall in prices from the peak of Autumn, 1845, and the excessive premiums soon disappeared. Railway shares, although depressed, continued to dominate the share lists of the Stock Exchanges. By 1860 there were 46 lines in the Edinburgh list, mostly Scottish; the Glasgow list at this date contained thirty-three Scottish railways. The bulk of the Scottish railway system had however been concentrated into the hands of five companies, the North British, the Caledonian, the Glasgow and South Western, the Great North of Scotland, and the Highland Railway. The dominance of the railway section in the share lists continued into the 1880s by which time railway stock acquired trustee status; "when the public are doing penance for a spell of unlucky speculation, the first sign of it invariably is a rush at railway preferences and debentures paying about 4%".[46]

Most of the pre-limitation joint stock companies in Scotland were not of an industrial nature but were concerned with such service activities as banking, insurance, transport, and a miscellaneous range of public utilities. Those that were not incorporated by royal charter or act of parliament were based on the system of co-partnery by which each contract, though renewable, was generally entered into for a relatively short period which thereby facilitated frequent withdrawals of capital. By the provisions of Scottish partnership law this system provided the three chief attractions of incorporation, namely, transferability of shares, separate legal personality of the company, and the limited liability of shareholders. This gave Scottish partnerships considerable advantages over the English variety, but the need for larger and more permanent capital led to the adoption of the provisions of the 1856 legislation which was the first Joint Stock Companies Act to apply to Scotland.[47]

The general progress of the adoption of limitation in Scotland before 1880 is indicated in the following table. Comparatively few companies were formed in the eighteen sixties and most of these languished quickly. Among those of permanent importance were two formed in 1866, namely, Young's Paraffin Light and Mineral Oil Co., and the Tharsis Sulphur Co., Scotland's first overseas mining company which was heavily sponsored by the Tennant family of Glasgow.[48] The seventies however brought a surge of both domestic and foreign investment activity. During the period 1872–74, 206 limited companies were registered in Scotland. Among these were conversions of existing companies as well as new ones. An important area in which such conversions from private to public companies occurred was the Scottish coal industry. Hitherto it had been mainly organized on a small scale basis but the years 1872–74 saw the conversion of numerous undertakings at a time when share prices were at their peak (see graph, Chapter 6), but the experience of some of them was however distinctly unfortunate. Among them were the Benhar Coal Co. (1872), the Niddrie Co. (1874), the Omoa and Cleland Coal Co. (1872), the Lochore and Capledrae Coal Co. (1872), the Rawyards Coal Co. (1873), the Cairntable Gas Coal Co. (1873), and the Arniston Coal Co. (1874).[49] Four of the above companies were quoted and dealt in on the Edinburgh market, and the

Companies Registered in Scotland Under the Companies Act, 1862

	New Limited Co's.	Other	Total	Total Share Capital (£mn.)
1863	24	7	31	1.8
1864	17	9	26	2.8
1865	29	8	37	2.9
1866	33	3	36	4.9
1867	14	4	18	0.6
1868	20	5	25	0.7
1869	13	5	18	0.7
1870	12	7	19	0.4
1871	42	5	47	1.8
1872	81	3	84	8.4
1873	62	1	63	5.8
1874	63	1	64	6.2
1875	45	3	48	4.6
1876	64	5	69	5.2
1877	83	5	88	11.6
1878	61	3	64	4.8
1879	58	7	65	4.0

Source: Return Relating to Joint Stock Companies, B.P.P. 1883, No. 190, p. 156.

rest at Glasgow. They continued to be provincial concerns dealt only in Scotland and the shares yield 10% in 1895, what *The Economist* in that year labelled as "Unclassified Investments".

Conversions also occurred in the Scottish iron industry. In 1872 the Monkland Iron and Coal Co. was constituted to take the place of the old co-partnery which failed in 1861. The new company was promoted by Alexander McEwan, Glasgow stockbroker and it displayed a somewhat chequered career.[50] Other important formations were the Lochgelly Iron and Coal Co., and the Glengarnock Iron Co. A year later Messrs Chadwick, McKenna and Adamson floated the unfortunate Blochairn Iron Co. for the vendors, Messrs Hannay & Sons.[51] More successful was the Steel Company of Scotland, which introduced the Siemens process to Scotland, and which was the offspring of the versatile financial genius of the Tennant family. Also incorporated by Special Act in 1871 was the famous Shotts Iron Co. Formed in 1802 it had been made a public company in 1825 and was among the first industrial companies to be listed on the Edinburgh and Glasgow Stock Exchanges.[52]

The activity which provided the "first notable craze of the Scottish investor was the Property Company". These accepted small loans and made advances on real property. They were used extensively in the cities to "help speculative builders to run up new Streets, mortgage them to the full cost or a little more, and, failing tennants, drop them on the hands of the property company". Also as a result of their activities it "was not an uncommon event in Edinburgh for a house to be sold four or five times over within twelve months, and for the last price to be double the first". Companies also invested on their own account instead of lending to others and these proved particularly insecure. The first crop appeared in 1872, among them, the North British Investment Co., the Caledonian Heritable Security Co., the National Heritable and Property Association, the Glasgow Heritable and Property Association was formed in 1873, while among the 1874 promotions were the Scottish Provident Investment Co., the National Property Investment Co., and the Union Heritable Security Co.[53] Property company shares "which were French *assignats* adapted to the climate, were run up at one time to 300 or 400 per cent premiums". By 1877 Edinburgh alone had seventeen such companies with a paid up capital of nearly £250,000 and with loans of nearly £4.0 million, a somewhat slender base for such lending operations. The collapse of the City of Glasgow Bank in 1878 crippled many of the companies and those which had financed excessive expansion were seriously affected. By 1884 fourteen such companies were listed by W. R. Lawson as being actively dealt in on the Edinburgh and Glasgow markets, with a total paid up capital of nearly £1.0 million, while five of them had paid up capitals of £20,000 or less. A year later *The Statist* remarked that these companies "now cut a very small figure in the market. Only about half a dozen of them remain on the official list . . . [and they] . . . are quoted nominally at from 3d per share upwards". This "notable craze" had cost Scottish investors "about a million and a half to say nothing of the fancy premiums".[54]

The "first notable craze" of the Scottish investor overseas involved the promotion of mortgage and investment companies, the first of which appeared during a period of depression in the United States when they were able to take advantage of low security prices to acquire investments. Edinburgh was the main centre for these early operations. The first companies formed, under the companies acts, were the Scottish American Investment Co. Ltd. (the first investment trust company outside London) of 1873, and the Scottish American Mortgage Co. Ltd. of 1874. By 1878 the former company had a called up capital of £340,934, a tradition of a 10% dividend had been established, and there was a reserve fund of £60,000. It was not until railway securities rose to high levels in 1879, too high for Scottish tastes, that the company placed some of its funds into real estate, again profitably.[55]

News that Scottish capital was available for overseas investment brought a demand from Chicago and Illinois for loans on the security of real estate. Accordingly in 1874 the Scottish American Mortgage Co. Ltd., was set up to receive money on loan for fixed periods and lend it, along with the paid up capital. It had a nominal capital of £1.0 million in £10 shares, with £100,000 called up. The main lending resources were acquired by debenture issues, offering from 4–5%, up to the amount of the uncalled capital (deposits were also accepted), and the funds were lent out in the U.S. at around 8%. This was the basic formula of all the Scottish mortgage companies. The largest shareholders came from Dundee and Edinburgh, while among the ranks of the smaller shareholders there were a number of merchants, lawyers, and stockbrokers.[56]

Dundee was the other centre of the early Scottish mortgage companies. The first was the Oregon and Washington Trust Investment Co. Ltd. which was registered in October 1873. Twenty-five men signed the memorandum of association, among them members of the local "juteocracy". In 1875 the Oregon and Washington had a subscribed capital of £150,000, with £25,438 paid up, and £44,150 in debentures as well as deposits. It was conservatively run from the start giving advances on only 33% of the value of the property, while its insistence on periodic repayments meant added security.[57] In 1874 William Mackenzie was made secretary to the company. He was a Dundee stockbroker, and later an original member of the Stock Exchange. However, although he found "that occupation profitable enough in its way" he gave up the business, but retained his stock exchange membership, and devoted his energies to building up the Mackenzie group of companies.

In order to undertake investments not permitted by the constitution of the Oregon and Washington a group of its directors formed in 1876 the Dundee Mortgage and Trust Investment Co. Ltd. with William Mackenzie as secretary. Its main activity was mortgage business but it had power to acquire preferred railway stocks and related securities. It had a subscribed capital of £300,000, and the public issue was over-subscribed three times. By 1879 its paid up capital was £50,000, with debentures and loans (which were not to exceed the uncalled capital) of £257,000.[58] In 1878 the same group formed a company for land speculation, the Dundee Land Investment Co., with a capital of £250,000, and William Mackenzie as secretary. In the following year the Oregon and Washington was amalgamated with the Dundee Mortgage and Trust Investment Co. Ltd.; both had the same board, engaged in similar business, and they paid a 10% dividend. A further merger followed in 1881 when Mackenzie consolidated the Oregon and Washington Savings Bank with the larger company. At this date the Mackenzie group administered between £800,000 to £900,000 of funds in the United States. Also, in 1881 Robert Fleming became a director of the group thus linking all the Dundee companies with interests in the United

States.[59] In 1882 the Dundee Land Investment Co. was reconstituted to permit of a wider field of investment activity and within a
few years its business was similar to that of the Dundee Mortgage
Company. With similar business and an identical board of directors,
an amalgamation seemed possible, and in 1888 the Alliance Trust
Co. was formed with an authorized capital of £2.0 million and £1.1
million subscribed.[60] The success of these pioneer trusts prompted
other groups of capitalists to try their hand. Prior to 1881, several
other companies were formed, mainly in Edinburgh, which not
only invested in the United States, but also in Canada, Australia
and New Zealand.

Between 1881–84 further mortgage companies appeared but these
late entrants were not so successful as their forerunners. A few
were wound up within a comparatively short period since they
could not meet interest payments on borrowed funds. Edinburgh
provided the main market for dealings in mortgage company shares
– "some even of the Land and Mortgage Companies quoted in
London find in Edinburgh a more congenial soil".[61] The first sign
of weakness in this sector of the market appeared in 1883, and by
1884 the falling trend in shares was well established, even in the
case of the leading Edinburgh companies: "The aggregate loss
on shares quoted on the Edinburgh stock list was £220,000 for the
year, and on Dundee shares over £400,000. There is practically no
market in Glasgow for investment and mortgage shares; while
Aberdeen, though a large dealer in Edinburgh shares has only two
or three Companies of its own. The aggregate depreciation in the
Investment and Mortgage Market for all Scotland including unlisted
Companies, will reach nearly three quarters of a million".[62] By
1885 enthusiasm for these companies had greatly waned, and what
money investors were prepared to part with went into the well
established companies with their safe dividends and 'showy reserves'.
In the next five years only two such companies were formed in
Scotland.

Scottish investment overseas, particularly in the United States,
was not confined to land and mortgage activity but also took the
form of institutional investment in stocks and bonds. The home
of the development of Scottish investment trusts in the eighteen
seventies rested firmly in Dundee. The emphasis was on the trust
form of organization rather than using a limited company with
extensive borrowing powers. Robert Fleming was the pioneer of
this movement. In 1870 he visited the United States and returned
greatly impressed with the possibilities for Scottish investment and
aware that the time was particularly opportune in view of the
depreciated state of the dollar. In July 1873 the Scottish American
Investment Trust made its first issue of £300,000 in £100 certificates

and it met with a flood of applications, a large part of which represented surplus funds from the local jute industry; holdings over £3,000 were predominantly those of merchants and manufacturers.[63] A second issue of £400,000 followed later in 1873, with a similar sized issue in 1875. This meant a total investment in the United States of over £1.0 million. The acquisition of the securities was in many cases a "matter of negotiation requiring special knowledge" which placed this form of institutional investment in an advantageous position compared to a private investor.[64] The trust deed used was modelled on that of the Foreign and Colonial Government Trust but following a legal ruling that such trusts should be registered as companies it was decided in 1879 to convert the trusts into three separate companies.

In the eighties Edinburgh took on the role of being the main Scottish centre for investment trusts. Up until 1887 the Scottish American Investment Co. was the only one in Edinburgh interested purely in securities, but soon numerous competitors appeared on the scene. The first was an investment trust promoted by some directors and several large shareholders of the United States Mortgage Company of Scotland. This was the Scottish Investment Trust Co. Ltd., formed in July 1887 with a nominal capital of £500,000 in £10 shares and whose investments were not confined to the United States. The success of this trust prompted the promotion in 1888 by the same group of the Second Scottish Investment Trust Co. Ltd., with the same capital structure and a similar investment policy. In that year Robert Fleming returned from London to organize, in conjunction with John Guild of the Scottish American Trust Companies of Dundee, the British Investment Trust Ltd.[65] It proved highly successful, a tribute to Fleming's stature, and the high price of trust shares along with a boom in trust flotations in London – 70 were formed between 1887–90 – encouraged the formation of many more.[66] By 1890 there were nine Scottish investment trusts in operation, the shares of which were actively dealt in on the Edinburgh and Dundee markets. However, these newer trusts earned only meagre dividends, "which the shareholders could easily have earned for themselves, without bearing the burden of heavy establishment charges".[67] Very few trusts were formed outside the two centres of Edinburgh and Glasgow during the pre-war years, the first in Glasgow appeared in 1907, and in Aberdeen a year later. The revival of investment trust promotion between 1909–14, when seventeen new trusts were formed in Scotland, was almost an entirely Edinburgh affair, eleven of the trusts being based there, which made it the most important share market in local financial issues.[68]

In the late seventies Scottish investment interest was captivated by reports of large profits being made by cattle ranch companies in the

United States. London, however, beat them to it as far as forming
the first cattle companies was concerned. In May 1879 London
promoters formed the Anglo-American Cattle Co. Ltd., and in
December, the Colorado Ranche Co. Ltd. was registered, both of
which were under-capitalized and came to a swift end.[69] In the following year Frank L. Underwood (of Underwood & Clark Co.), who
had placed numerous loans for the Edinburgh based Scottish American Mortgage Co., convinced the directors of that concern that
capital could be raised for a company which had the additional
novelty of cattle production and that large profits would flow from
it. In December 1880 the directors registered the Prairie Cattle Co.
Ltd., capitalized at £200,000 and with the prospectus claiming that
U.S. cattle ranchers were making between 25–40% annual profits.
The issued capital was in £10 shares, with £4 paid, and with a third
of them going to Dundee interests.[70] The company's agent acquired
range rights and herds along the Cimaron River and the Texas
Panhandle, and at the end of the first year investors learnt of the
company's success, profits being equal to 26% on the paid up
capital. A 10% dividend was declared along with a bonus of 9/6d.
per share. The success justified an increase in the capital to £500,000,
and the second year proved even more successful with the company
declaring the usual 10% dividend but with a bonus of 17 sh. per
share, a performance which greatly impressed Dundee capitalists
and which was well publicised in the prospectuses of subsequent
cattle companies.

Underwood then went to Dundee where in December 1881 he
formed the Texas Land & Cattle Co. Ltd., with an authorized capital
of £240,000. Several prominent shareholders in Dundee mortgage
and investment companies signed the memorandum of association
and invested heavily in the shares. Later the capital was increased to
£630,000 and a first dividend of 15% was declared. The success of
this company prompted Dundee interests to search for additional
ranch properties in Texas which were ready for "joint stocking". A
year later the Matador Land & Cattle Co. Ltd. was registered with a
capital of £400,000. On each £10 share £6 was called up and there was
a debenture issue of £160,000 which was equal to the uncalled capital. Robert Fleming, also a director of the Texas, played an active
role in the flotation of the Matador. Also launched at the same time
in Dundee was the Hansford Land & Cattle Co. Ltd., capitalized at
£210,000.[71]

Meanwhile back in Edinburgh further land and cattle companies
appeared. The directors of the Scottish American Investment Co.,
eager to keep up with the activities of the Scottish American Mortgage Co. formed in November 1881 the California Pastoral and Agri-

cultural Co. Ltd. with a capital of £250,000. In July 1882 the same group formed the Wyoming Cattle Ranche Co. Ltd. with an authorized capital of £200,000. Also launched in 1882 was the Missouri Land and Livestock Co. Ltd., but this was predominantly a land company. In January 1883 Western Ranches Ltd. was also formed in Edinburgh.[72]

The craze for cattle companies was not confined to Scotland; London financiers got equally excited. These companies attracted many Scottish shareholders just as the Scottish companies had to some extent attracted English capital. Among these were the Cattle Ranche & Land Co. promoted by Rufus Hatch, the Western Land & Cattle Co., the Arkansas Valley Land & Cattle Co. Ltd., the Powder River Cattle Co. Ltd., and the Maxwell Cattle Co. Ltd. Scots either promoted or sat on the board of directors of every cattle company registered in London in 1882. It proved a particularly active year with ten companies being formed involving a total subscribed capital of £2.2 million of which £1.6 million was called up. The speed with which this investment activity occurred was testimony to the surplus capital in Scotland, particularly in Edinburgh and Dundee, and to the euphoria of the Scots at the possibilities of large scale husbandry. In 1883 the pace slackened, six companies appearing in London and only two in Scotland, a subscribed capital of £2.1 million with £0.8 million paid up. The major Scottish flotation was that of the Swan Land and Cattle Co. Ltd. with a capital of £600,000. Most of the London ones proved of a very ephemeral nature, while between 1884–86 the citizens of Leith, Greenock and Glasgow attempted in a small way to emulate their neighbours by each forming a cattle company.[73]

The marketing of cattle company shares, usually £10 nominal with about half paid up, was handled mainly through local markets, and this was especially the case with Dundee companies.[74] This followed from the fact that when these companies were floated "it was the patriotic design of their promoters that the plum should be kept for Dundee alone". An example of this policy was reflected in the fact that 90% of the Matador shares were held in Dundee. Accordingly, share applications "from other quarters were declined with thanks, and the other quarters found very easy revenge in refusing a quotation to the carefully localized shares". Interest in shares however was not confined to the traditional surplus capital sector of merchants and professional men. As the *Dundee Year Book* for 1882 notes, "there have been signs of a growing tendency to speculation in shares by people who are not wealthy" and one result of this was that "the value of some well established investments has been depreciated by sales necessary to meet purchases in new undertakings, indicating a certain weakness amongst investors".[75] Dundee investors also had an interest in Edinburgh companies (a third of the Prairie Co.'s shares were held in Dundee), and in London companies, as well as in unquoted companies offered in Dundee by visitors "with ranches in their pockets". *Per capita* they were certainly heavily involved in the cattle craze. All this gave a spurt of activity to the newly formed Stock Exchange, where the firm of Andrew Ogilvie & Co. was the most active trader on the market. The other centre of dealing was Edinburgh where Laurie and Kerr played a leading part in introducing new companies to the market and in subsequent dealings.

Shares in the leading cattle companies continued to command a premium in the market into 1884 which reflected their success in maintaining the attractive dividends of earlier years, a feat due largely to the continuous rise in livestock prices. However, by early 1885 nearly all the shares had their premiums run off, and following the depressed state of the trade during 1885–86 the shares took a major tumble, the worst reaction taking place in Dundee. In 1886 nearly all the companies passed their dividends, which also happened during the following year. The share market suffered a total collapse and several companies were finished, among them, the Wyoming, Powder River, and the Dakota Stock and Grazing Co. Ltd.

Some of the factors which led to this collapse were of the industry's own doing, others were ones over which it had no control. Many companies had bought lands and herds, especially the late arrivals, at prices about four times their actual values. Many herds, had been bought on the standard range custom of the book count, a curious form of 'prairie arithmetic', which meant that often half the money was for a 'phantom herd'.[76] One of the basic difficulties however was over-production and the saturation by 1884 of both domestic and export markets. Problems too arose over the vendors participation in profit sharing schemes, while the mere fact of geography brought clashes between management and the Scottish domiciled directors. But some problems were way beyond their control. A series of bad winters. 1884–85 and especially 1886–87, brought heavy losses of cattle when severe blizzards on the open range caused whole herds to drift up against wire fences and, unable to get further, they died by the thousands. The subsequent calf crop was correspondingly lower. Disease took further toll of herds, while quarantine regulations in the northern states hindered the movement of southern herds to market, and strict quarantine regulations abroad reduced the export of live cattle. Also, loss of range rights and grazing on Indian reservations was a hard blow to an industry where scale was of the essence.

Glasgow Stock Exchange.

Glasgow Stock Exchange; the General Market in 1907.

Glasgow Stock Exchange; the new floor.

The depression did not cripple all the major Scottish companies. By 1890 they were recovering through adopting policies of more selective selling of cattle and better management, exemplified by Murdo Mackenzie of the Matador. Accordingly share prices recovered. In the long term many of the cattle companies proved to be reasonable investments since the shareholders received their capital back when the companies sold out their land holdings in the early 1920s.

Among other "frisky securities", as W. R. Lawson labelled them, dealt on the Scottish stock exchanges were a number of land and timber companies formed in the same period. These companies were set up to buy blocks of land from railroad companies which was then sold off in small lots. Between 1877–1881 several companies were formed by Scottish interests, but most of them passed their dividends and folded up by 1885.[77] Timber companies were also formed for much the same reasons. It was quickly realized that forest lands could be bought in large blocks and considerable profits made by cutting and processing timber. Again William Mackenzie was a leading promoter, forming in 1880 the British Canadian Lumbering and Timber Co. Ltd., and in 1882, the American Lumber Co. The latter had a called up capital of £212,000 with its shareholding concentrated in Edinburgh, Glasgow and Dundee, all the shares being privately placed without any public participation.[78] Several other timber companies appeared during 1883–84 but most of these soon found themselves in difficulties, and the heavy uncalled liability meant that the shares, with the prospects of liquidation hanging over them, were "offered for nothing, or with a bonus for taking them".[79]

The Scots were certainly great gamblers and their excursions into the mining industry aptly fitted the comments of *The Statist* in 1885; "Money was raised by the millions on shares and debentures . . . and shipped abroad without any systematic inquiry into the field of investment it was lavished on". A Scottish investor "thought his money as secure in Colorado as in the Bank of England" and under such misapprehensions stock markets "subsided into a lower depth of speculation until there is now hardly 10 per cent of what the people buy and sell as 'securities' that a prudent banker would lend money on at any price".[80]

The first major outburst of mining share speculation in Glasgow occurred during the Indian gold mining mania of 1879–1881. During the period from April 1879 to June 1881 thirty-three companies were formed involving a nominal capital of £4.3 million and a paid up capital of £2.8 million, the bulk of which went into the pockets of vendors and promoters.[81] All sorts were affected by the mania

v

"the hard headed folk in the north, especially at Glasgow coming more particularly under its influence". Even when the companies found gold it cost more to produce than it was worth and when the bubble burst many companies quickly disappeared. By 1883 nineteen were in liquidation and the shares of most became unmarketable, "a few pence or at the best one or two shillings, being their prices when a purchaser could be found". Glasgow also participated in the 1885 mining share speculation which arose out of the success of the Indian Mysore Co. but it was very shortlived.[82] The Glasgow market at this period also provided a congenial home for several copper mining shares among them the Tharsis, Glasgow Caradon and Huntingdon companies, and a few tin shares as well.

The Scots had also shown an interest in American gold mining for many years but on the whole it had been rather lukewarm. They had participated through acquiring shares brought out by London financial houses during and after the 1849 Californian gold rush, but no Scottish company was organized for gold mining in the next two decades. During the period of frenzied speculation in London 1870–73 the Scots only formed three small gold mining companies all of which failed. They did however hold shares in several large English promotions, notably the Flagstaff, the Richmond Consolidated and the Emma. The fraud associated with the latter company undoubtedly shyed off the Scots from such mining ventures. Anyway, at the time they were involved in supporting less risky domestic promotions.

The first major Scottish excursion into the formation of mining companies came in 1881 when the highly enterprising directors of the Scottish American Investment Co. sponsored the Scottish Pacific Coast Mining Co. Ltd. with a nominal capital of £100,000, £85,000 of which was called up immediately. Within four years it had been wound up and the accompanying swindle was such that Edinburgh never again provided a home for mining ventures.[83] The only major mining concern with Edinburgh headquarters was the Arizona Copper Co., in which the Scottish American Mortgage Co. had a hand, formed in 1882 with a large capital of £875,000. It had a difficult and discouraging start but ultimately the company yielded considerable profits to its Scottish originators.[84]

Future Scottish sponsorship of mining ventures was thus left to be undertaken by the lesser men of capital and reputation of Glasgow. In the late eighties and nineties American proprietors went there to seek funds to keep their declining enterprises going and local solicitors and accountants had no difficulty in enlisting the interest of investors. Little money was however lost since the "wily Scots deliberately refrained from following the London investment pattern after their initial participation in the mania of 1881–82"[85] Scotland plodded along with a few mining promotions every year and it was only during the 1895–96 boom that mining registrations in Glasgow rose above the double figure mark.

The "Kaffir" boom of 1895 certainly had its repercussions north of the border. The state of the Glasgow market was not far behind that of London, where, in the early months of that year "speculation grew as quotations advanced until it became the wildest and most indiscriminate gamble the Stock Exchange had witnessed for many years".[86] The valuation of Transvaal companies alone rose from £50 million to £215 million. In order to ease the settlement problem associated with the large increase in the volume of dealing the Glasgow Stock Exchange extended the settlement to a fourth day so that more time was allowed for the passing of names thus avoiding the need to resort to frequent buying in and selling out.[87] The voluminous and excited dealings in mining shares, few of which were quoted in the official list, greatly disrupted the general business of the market, and in May 1895 when the "noise and confusion became unendurable" the mining market was separated from the general market and held in what had previously been the Reading Room adjoining the general market. The mining market had no call over but buyers and sellers dealt as they liked and transactions were notified on slips handed to the official in charge.[88]

Glasgow's last speculative fling in the pre-1914 era, and Edinburgh's also, came with the 1909–10 rubber boom which transformed the local rubber market from a select and somewhat sleepy preserve with very wide margins into an active and competitive one. Dealings were such in Glasgow that it proved necessary to move rubber dealings from the general market to the mining market. On the London market there were nearly a hundred jobbers engaged chiefly in rubber dealings, having abandoned less active markets. One effect of this was to drive a good deal of business in other securities to the provinces; jobbers involved in the rubber rush found greater profits in rubber dealing than in thinly veiled shunting activity, and London brokers were thus drawn to the provincial exchanges for dealing in textiles, iron and steels, tobacco and motor shares, etc., which greatly strengthened their hold on such markets.[89] The boom itself was associated with the introduction of plantation production and the steep rise in rubber prices arising from a shortage of natural rubber. In the promotional activity both Glasgow and Edinburgh played a prominent part with nine companies formed in the former, and fifteen in the latter centre during 1907–10. The paid up capital of thirty-eight rubber companies registered in Scotland in 1912 amounted to £2.2 million;

v*

capitalizations varied from £20,000 to £150,000, mostly with shares of £1, although some were 2s. shares.[90] Edinburgh's lead over Glasgow in this area is not surprising since it had a long standing link with the industry dating from 1856 when Charles Goodyear, the inventor of the process of vulcanization, formed the North British Rubber Co.

Scottish interest in American railway shares was not of course the monopoly of the Dundee and Edinburgh investment companies and trusts. During the early 1870s Scottish investors acquired securities brought to this country by arbitrage dealers and which were then offered for sale by the larger London houses.[91] Interest during this period was largely concentrated in about twenty companies, fifteen of which gave little or no return. Not only was the return low but the method of dealing in them was also distinctly dubious. They were usually in certificates of ten shares each in the names of large arbitrage dealers and they were passed from hand to hand without transfers being made and registered so that the dangers of fraudulent circulation were very great. The number of stock shares and bonds quoted on the Glasgow list rose from about a dozen in 1873 to well over 50 in 1883. Glasgow at this time had the main Scottish market in American rails and on occasions it even rivalled London; in 1884 there was "much business transacted in London representing adjustments with Glasgow", while the northern market "frequently aspires to 'pull the wires' in certain American railway issues".[92] Canadian rails also attracted Scottish investors and at the turn of the century Glasgow did a large amount of business in the shares of the Canadian Pacific and the Grand Trunk Railway of Canada.

The Scottish stock exchanges were of course not without some special markets in domestic industries. Glasgow and Edinburgh had active markets in shale oil shares, Dundee in jute companies, and both Aberdeen and Dundee in fishing companies. Also there were the markets in the shares of numerous miscellaneous companies which greatly increased in number during the mid-nineties boom. The origins of the shale oil industry date back to 1853 when James Young developed a process for distilling oil from shale. In 1866 the private company was converted into a joint stock company; Young's Paraffin Light and Mineral Oil Co. Ltd. The lapse of the patent brought a minor boom in mineral oil companies with five new companies appearing between 1869–72.[93] Oil shares soon became a "pet fancy of Scottish speculators especially in Glasgow where the trade had its quarters". The biggest upsurge of investment interest however occurred in the early eighties under the stimulus of a shortage of United States oil supplies. "A 'boom' was started in oil shares. Old workings were taken up again and reorganized; new companies were started, and promoters pocketed liberal bonuses, either in shares or cash. But nothing could check the rush into 'oils'. Every new venture was over-applied for, and most of the shares ran up to high premiums before a retort had been erected, and it takes twelve months at least to start a well-equipped refinery".[94] In the ensuing reaction the shares (usually £10 with £8. 10s. 0d paid up) of both the paying companies and the speculative ventures all showed losses which were estimated by *The Statist* at £0.5 million for 1884. Over-production during the next few years caused further sharp falls in the prices of oil products, but for a few years at least the leading companies managed to scrape together the time honoured dividends which ranged from eight to twenty-five per cent. At this time seventeen issues were quoted on the Glasgow Stock Exchange with a paid up value of nearly £2.0 million. The continued decline in oil prices and increasing foreign competition, notably from the United States, brought in 1887 a drop in dividends and a "downright thorough-going scare" in oil shares.[95] The relatively thin market could offer little "resistance to such a panic stricken crowd of sellers and the attacks of adverse speculators". Daily share prices dropped "until most of them had little left between them and zero". Shares in the leading companies were well below half the prices of the prosperous days but these were mild reversals compared to what befell Young's which slumped from £10 to £2.[96] About a dozen oil companies survived into the nineties but oil share prices never recovered from the 1887 collapse, while the long-term survivors were restructured with shares of lower value. In the years just before the First World War Scottish mineral oil interests were involved in promoting oil exploration overseas, for example, the Burmah Oil Co., and the Anglo Persian Oil Co. which was largely financed by Burmah Oil. In fact, in 1919 the Anglo Persian Oil Co. took over the Scottish Oil Co. which was an amalgamation of the main shale oil companies.[97]

Although jute was successfully established as part of the Dundee coarse spinning industry by the 1840s, the fortunes of the noted "Juteocracy" were not made until the Crimean and American Civil Wars when Dundee became the world centre of the jute cloth trade. Part of the profits then made were later used to finance plants in the Hooghly district of Bengal and thereby build up a dangerous rivalry to the local factories.[98] Following the success of plants set up in 1855 and 1859, Thomas Duff, who managed one of them, floated with the help of Dundee interests, the Samnugger Jute Co. Ltd. in 1874. Its success led to the formation of the Victoria Jute Co. Ltd. in 1883, and the Titaghar Jute Co. Ltd. in 1884.

The three had a combined capital of £1.3 million and were dealt in on the Dundee Stock Exchange; the latter company is still quoted.[99]

Dundee also witnessed in the early 1880s a "large and on the whole healthy extension" of its shipping interests. *The Dundee Yearbook* of 1882 listed ten shipping companies, but only the Dundee Perth and London Shipping Co. dated back to the first half of the century; its paid up capital in 1882 was £120,000. The total nominal capital of the shipping section of the Dundee list in 1882 was £752,440 with £670,657 paid up. Some of the smaller companies in the list represented the local whaling activity which had been given a new lease of life by the demand for whale oil from the jute industry. By 1914 only three shipping concerns were listed in Dundee.

An interesting feature of the Aberdeen share list in the late nineties was the inclusion of several trawling companies following the introduction of steam trawling in the eighties.[100] The prosperous state of the industry and the promise of a bright future led to sales of groups of trawlers to limited companies. It was not difficult to float such concerns since it was "well known that similar undertakings working from the port of Aberdeen are earning and distributing dividends of from 10 per cent to 40 per cent".[101] All had £1 shares with, in most cases, 10s. paid. In 1903 the trawling and fishing section of the Aberdeen list numbered thirteen companies.

In the area of general industry company formation the Scottish experience in the 1890s followed very much the trend displayed south of the border. Over the period 1890–94 the number of limited companies registered annually in Scotland increased from 150 to just over two hundred. The boom in company formation during the next few years took the figure to well over 300, reaching a peak of nearly 400 in 1898.[102] The pace fell off sharply with the passing of the Companies Act of 1900 which imposed much more stringent provisions as to disclosure of contracts and information, and during the years 1901–04 it was down to between 200–250 per year. Thereafter it settled at about 200, except for an increase to over 400 in 1909, until the immediate pre-war period when it rose to just over 400.

The 1890s boom of course witnessed the formation of many new concerns but a significant element in it was the conversion to limited status of several well established Scottish companies, no doubt, attracted by the ease of going public on a rapidly rising market. The way was shown by the registration as a limited company in 1890 of the Paisley thread enterprise of J. P. Coats, which soon established itself as a leading Scottish 'blue chip'. Other well known companies converted at this time were David Colville & Sons

(1895), Redpath Brown & Co. (1896), United Collieries (1898), and in 1900 Babcock and Wilcox. The boom also brought additional work to brokers acting as agents for companies seeking a stock exchange quotation. In Edinburgh the bulk of this work was undertaken by Laurie & Kerr, Bell, Cowan and Co., and Gilmour and Shaw. On the basis of a rough count of the companies granted a quotation on the Edinburgh Stock Exchange between 1899 and 1906 it would seem that some 40% were below £100,000, nominal capital, that about 40% of them were between £100,000 and £300,000, and that only a fifth of them were larger than £300,000. Nominal values of course overstate the actual amount of capital raised. One estimate for a later period, 1911–13, put the actual capital raised in Scotland at well below £5.0 million and perhaps no more than £2.3 million.[103] However, it seems reasonabe to assume that during periods of very active company formation that the amount of money raised would have been well above this lower figure.

Scottish firms seeking a quotation on the Stock Exchanges had to conform to the same sort of requirements as had already been noted for their counterparts in England. The main reasons for refusing a quotation were also similar, namely, that an insufficient amount of a company's capital had been issued, that it was not "sufficient held locally" to justify a quotation, that the prospectus did not contain provisions refraining directors from using the funds of a company to purchase its own shares, and that there were provisions which imposed a lien on fully paid shares.

E. The First World War, 1914–1918

On July 31, 1914 the Scottish stock exchanges closed following the closure of the London Stock Exchange. Dealing continued unofficially but very few transactions took place with the markets running along "very narrow lines". In Glasgow transactions were negotiated between offices, or on the pavement in St George's Place where members met for an hour or two each day until September when they were given access to various rooms in the Stock Exchange.[104] Similar arrangements prevailed in Edinburgh. On the whole Scottish brokers were critical of the emergency arrangements arrived at in the south, but they went along with them for the sake of unity.[105] In particular they felt that the rates of interest charged under the provisions of the moratorium were too low and that higher ones would have induced more open positions to be closed. Scottish markets, particularly Glasgow, had always been speculative; it was said "that in normal times three-fourths of the transactions recorded are of a more or less speculative character". Despite this it was maintained that there was never any need for any of the exceptional measures since northern markets conducted their speculation on conservative lines; "Advances against securities have always been freely conceded by Scotch banks, but the managements have invariably insisted on margins of from 20 per cent to 25 per cent – a precaution which proved very fortunate when the crash came".[106] The extent and nature of the open position of the Glasgow market in the Autumn of 1914 was as follows; loans with margin outstanding to London clearing banks and branches, £63,000; to all other banks, £3,178,097; to other institutions, firms and individuals not members of the Stock Exchange, £275,111; a total of £3,516,208. There were no loans without margin.[107] It was also felt that there would have been little difficulty in keeping markets open and settling the account in the middle of August at the usual date. However, the Scottish markets accepted the emergency regulations as laid down as conditions for reopening on January 4, 1915, and they operated within such restrictions until they were released from them by the Treasury in 1922.

F. Scottish Share Markets since 1918

For several decades before the first World War railway stocks were regarded as one of the safest of investments and the market in them was among the best on the stock exchanges. In the Scottish share lists local railways featured prominently, particularly so in the case of Glasgow which had a very good market in Scottish railway ordinaries. However, the Railways Act of 1921 brought in an amalgamation scheme which resulted in the grouping into two companies of the five major Scottish companies. The Caledonian Railway Co. (capital £58.8 million), The Glasgow and South Western Railway Co. (£19.8 million), and the Highland Railway Co. (£7.9 million) were put into the North Western, Midland and West Scottish group (L.M.S.), while the Great North of Scotland Railway Co. (£7.0 million), and the North British Railway Co. (£68.6 million) went into the North Eastern, Eastern and East Scottish group (L.N.E.R.).[108] Thus at one stroke the local rail market was decimated; the number of home rails in the Glasgow list fell from 51 to 21, the four large companies and some very minor lines. Admittedly shareholders obtained more stable prices and readier marketability for their new holdings, but it meant that the main railway market centred increasingly on London. Even these larger groups disappeared with vesting day January 1, 1948 when the railway network was nationalized.

Another market which shrank greatly was that in foreign securities, especially United States and Canadian stocks. Sales of United States stocks during the First World War to help the war effort certainly affected the Glasgow market; the bulk of the securities listed were classified as requisitioned by the Treasury. By 1939 only a dozen or so American stocks remained in the Glasgow list. The same pattern of events occurred during the Second World War with a large selling drive leading to a further reduction in the foreign securities market. Virtually all that remains of a foreign nature in the Scottish Stock Exchange list are shares in tea and rubber estates, many of which are of Scottish parentage.

Even the share markets in indigenous companies were not immune from reduced activity. As companies grew in size and share ownership became geographically more diffuse markets tended to drift to London. In the case of such highly indigenous activities involving banks, insurance, and investment trust companies this trend was accelerated during the inter-war years by the policy of non-division of commission with agents relentlessly pursued by the stock exchanges. For this reason Edinburgh in the early twenties lost its excellent market in insurance shares, while in the thirties the same pressures operated on the market in local bank shares. By the outbreak of the Second World War Edinburgh had lost its claim to be a leading market in bank shares. Since 1950 a series of amalgamations reduced the number of Scottish banks from eight to the present three, two of which are quoted.[109] These are the Bank of Scotland and the National and Commercial Banking Group which owns the Royal Bank of Scotland. Also quoted are the big London clearing banks.

The investment trust share market put up somewhat greater resistance. Between 1915 and 1930, 47 new trusts were formed in Scotland, 20 in Edinburgh, 21 in Glasgow and the rest in Aberdeen and Dundee.[110] This made a total number of 79 trusts, with eight management groups and an estimated capital of £113 million. This increase in the number of trusts occurred because it was thought that the optimum size of a trust should be around £2.0 million, and that the creation of new trusts offered opportunities for further industrial and geographical diversification. An important difference between Scottish and London trusts was that the former had higher gearing ratios and made greater use of temporary debentures and loans, all of which served to cause greater fluctuations in earnings on ordinary shares. Also, they tended to hold a larger proportion of their investments in United States securities. The policy of selling U.S. securities during the Second World War thus had a major impact on Scottish trusts and many reduced their holdings from 50% to 5% of their portfolios.[111] This led to a switch to domestic securities. During the post-war period they gradually rebuilt their American portfolio to nearly a third of total investments. By 1964 the number of Scottish trusts had been reduced to 61, largely as a result of amalgamations, with an employed capital of just over £300 million. The main market in trust shares is centred in Edinburgh, while locally based trusts are also dealt in on the other Scottish markets; the total listed in the Scottish list is now 94, which includes some London based trusts.

The diminution in the size of some of the markets noted above was however compensated for by the expansion in the domestic industrial and commercial section. Between 1918 and 1939 such stocks quoted in the Glasgow list increased from 120 to over 180, and as a result the list of the mid-thirties represented "almost every one of the economic strata of Glasgow development", while they had not lost the local characteristic of being liable to greater price fluctuation than their counterparts in southern markets.[112] The late twenties was by far the most active period for new issues and during 1926–1929 Glasgow brokers were involved with 165 issues, while Edinburgh brokers handled 32, with 10 divided between Aberdeen, Dundee, Greenock and Paisley brokers. In the boom year 1928 Glasgow brokers alone handled 70 new issues. the main ones involved in this particular activity being Buchanan, Gardner and Tennant, Kidston, Geoff & Co., and Pearson, Connor & Co. Macgregor, Walker & Co. was the most active Edinburgh broker with regard to new issues in this period. During the depression period new issues fell away to very low levels but recovered after 1934 and averaged about 20 a year up to the outbreak of war.[113]

Since the war the volume of Scottish new issues has increased considerably with well over 1,000 issues during the years 1946 to 1968. From an average of 25 issues a year during the immediate post-war years the average annual figure for the 1960s has reached 60 issues. Some 28% of these issues were share exchanges and conversions (these increased greatly in number in the sixties), around 40% were issues relating to rights and capitalizations, a further 25% were placings and introductions, while 8% were public issues and offers for sale. For the most part the issues were handled jointly by a London and a provincial broker and only in the case of about a dozen issues per year was the latter the sole broker to an issue, which was usually a placing or an introduction involving sums of less than £500,000.[114] The most active brokers in this area were Parsons & Co., and Penny & Macgregor of Glasgow, and in Edinburgh, Macgregor, Walker & Co., and Bell, Lawrie, Robertson & Co.

G. The Scottish Stock Exchange
There is no need to rehearse the reasons for the regionalisation of the provincial stock exchanges. Suffice it to say that the Scottish

markets were quick to respond to the threat uttered by the Jenkins Committee on Company Law, which reported in 1962, that the Board of Trade should re-examine the list of recognised stock exchanges with a view to reducing their number and increasing their size. Indeed, proposals for some sort of amalgamation among the Scottish markets had been mooted before the appearance of the Jenkins Report, and it was eventually agreed that the exchanges should aim at a common floor which would bring dealing advantages and lower administrative costs.[115] The nudge from the Jenkins Committee gave these discussions greater urgency and they subsequently took in the desirability of an adequate compensation fund and new issue supervision.

It was found however, that the suggestion for a common floor was not practicable at that stage but that an acceptable alternative would be common membership and a unified daily list. Following lengthy discussions proposals were agreed on for the creation of the Scottish Stock Exchange, with a total membership of just over 200, consisting of Glasgow, Edinburgh, Aberdeen and Dundee, and the new arrangement came into force in January 1964. The Greenock Stock Exchange did not join since all its members were accountants and the local organisation was wound up in September 1965. The markets continued to operate as before except that clearing arrangements were computerized on a regional basis. However, in April 1971 all share dealings were centralized on the new trading floor of the reconstructed Glasgow Stock Exchange. As on the other regional exchanges the basis of the dealing system is the jobber/shunter or the emerging jobber. Three of these operate on the Scottish Stock Exchange and the arrangement has yielded considerable advantages particularly to the smaller markets. They are all Glasgow firms jobbing in a miscellaneous range of securities.[116]

NOTES

1 *Glasgow Courier*, June 25, 1844; also *Glasgow Herald*, June 28, 1844.
2 *Glasgow Stock Exchange Association Records* (1927), pp. 4-12. The Minutes of the Stock Exchange do not commence until July 1845.
3 Glasgow Stock Exchange, Minutes, September 11, 1845; *Glasgow Stock Exchange Association Records*, op. cit., pp. 32-3.
4 *Glasgow Stock Exchange Association Records*, op. cit., p. 33, Glasgow Stock Exchange, Minutes, October 1, 1845. In 1846 the members of the Stock Exchange were censured by their Committee for "employing members of the other local Exchanges to buy and sell shares on their own account". Accordingly a rule was passed confining the members to deal for clients solely on their own Exchange; Minutes, November 23, 1846. Both the rival markets issued shares lists which were very similar in content to the Stock Exchange list. The "Wee Room" however operated fortnightly settlements on the London pattern.

5   Edinburgh Stock Exchange, Minutes, December 16, 27, 1844.

6   *The Scotsman,* February 26, 1845. Some members of the Stock Exchange frequented the rival market during the first few months of 1845.

7   Edinburgh Stock Exchange, Minutes, January 7, 1846.

8   Ibid., April 9, August 25, 1854, December 8, 1854, November 10, 24, 1856.

9   Aberdeen Stock Exchange, Minutes, October 21, 25, 1845.

10 Dundee Stock Exchange, Minutes, March 25, 31, 1879. Born in 1814, the son of a solicitor, Andrew Ogilvie was educated at St Andrews and Glasgow universities. After a legal apprenticeship he entered the firm of Messrs. Brown, a firm of Dundee flax merchants. He probably entered stockbroking in 1845 and founded the firm of A. Ogilvie & Co. which is still operating. He died in 1898. *Dundee Year Book,* 1898, p. 82.

11 *Greenock Telegraph and Clyde Shipping Gazette,* September 25, 1888.

12 Glasgow Stock Exchange, Minutes, January 4, 1847.

13 *1878 Royal Commission,* op. cit., Q. 8146; evidence of Matthew Shields, Secretary of the Glasgow Stock Exchange.

14 Ibid., Q. 8117.

15 Ibid., Q. 8124, *Glasgow Stock Exchange Association Records,* op. cit., p. 15.

16 Edinburgh Stock Exchange, Minutes, March 8, 1888, March 3, May 3, 1899, January 16, 1934.

17 *Aberdeen Press and Journal,* October 24, 1945. The call over was held at 7.0 pm since by that time letters and stock lists had arrived from the south.

18 In 1845 Glasgow members refused to admit personal liability for bargains done with Edinburgh brokers. They rendered the names of their principals. It was eventually agreed between the two Stock Exchanges that members would "personally bind themselves for all their transactions"; Edinburgh Stock Exchange, Minutes, March 7 1845.

19 Ibid., September 20, 1860.

20 Glasgow Stock Exchange, Minutes, Rules and Regulations 1844, Rule 23; *Glasgow Stock Exchange Association Records,* op. cit., pp. 29–30.

21 Edinburgh Stock Exchange, Minutes, March 4, 1845.

22 Glasgow Stock Exchange, Minutes, Rules and Regulations 1844, Rule 22; October 13, 1845, March 31, April 14, 1846.

23 Edinburgh Stock Exchange, Minutes, August 26, 1846.

24 Glasgow Stock Exchange, Minutes, June 29, 1847.

25 Up until 1874 they used the rather cumbersome system of passing tickets with endless endorsements on them. From then on they adopted the method of passing tickets at making up prices, with a limited number of endorsements.

26 Edinburgh Stock Exchange, Minutes, August, 26, November 6, 1846.

27 Aberdeen Stock Exchange, Minutes, July 14, 1853.

28 Glasgow Stock Exchange, Minutes, October 17, 1848.

29 Edinburgh Stock Exchange, Minutes, December 22, 1845, January 15, 19, 1846; Glasgow Stock Exchange, Minutes, January 7, 28, 1846.

30 Towards the end of the century outside brokers were allowed a rebate. When the Scottish Stock Exchange joined the Council of Associated Stock Exchanges they were obliged to adopt Council provisions on outside brokers.

31 Edinburgh Stock Exchange, Minutes, December 1, 1876.

32 Ibid., April 3, 1931, October 8, 1937, May 4, 1938, March 10, 1941.

33 Edinburgh Stock Exchange, Minutes, January 2, 1860, June 4, 1873, June 7, 1939; *Glasgow Stock Exchange Association Records,* op. cit., pp. 16-7.

34 *Glasgow Stock Exchange Association Records,* op. cit., pp. 4-6.

35 Edinburgh Stock Exchange, Minutes; February 13, 1845, February 14, 1888.

36 Glasgow Stock Exchange, Minutes, November 2, 1847, December 21, 1847; Edinburgh Stock Exchange, Minutes, November 1, 1847, January 5, 1848.

37 *Glasgow Stock Exchange Association Records,* op. cit., Appendix.

38 John Reid, *Manual of the Scottish Stocks and British Funds* (1841), pp. 21-2.

39 Ibid., pp. 166-70.

40 Ibid., p. 27.

41 W. Turrentine Jackson, *The Enterprising Scot* (1968), p. 8.

42 P. L. Payne (Ed.), *Studies in Scottish Business History* (1967), pp. 336-39.

43 Lewin, *The Railway Mania and its Aftermath* (1936)., pp. 53-4, 205, 219.

44 *Scottish Railway Gazette,* Vol. 1, No. 1, April 1845; quoted by R. H. Campbell and J. B. A. Dow, *Source Book of Scottish Economic and Social History* (1968), pp. 272-3. In the case of the Edinburgh and Glasgow line over 40% of the shares subscribed for went to Liverpool and Manchester; for further details on the source of Scottish railway capital in this period see W. Vamplew, "Sources of Scottish Railway Share Capital before 1860", *Scottish Journal of Political Economy,* November 1970.

45 W. H. Marwick, *Economic Developments in Victorian Scotland* (1936), pp. 76-7.

46 W. R. Lawson. *The Scottish Investors Manual* (1884) p. 1.

47 W. H. Marwick, "The Limited Company in Scottish Economic Development", *Economic History,* February 1937, p. 415. For a full account of the legal aspects of joint stock companies in Scotland see R. H. Campbell, "The Law and the Joint Stock Company in Scotland", in Payne, op. cit., pp. 136-51.

48 Ibid., pp. 416-7.

49 Ibid., p. 418; *Burdett's Official Intelligence,* 1884, 1890.

50 Ibid., p. 418.

51 Ibid., p. 419. The Blochairn Iron Co. had a nominal capital of £600,000 but only ⅔ of the capital was subscribed, and it collapsed a year later despite its influential directorate.

52 Marwick, *Economic Developments in Victorian Scotland,* op. cit., p. 53.

53 Marwick, "The Limited Company in Scottish Economic Development", op. cit., p. 420.

54 *Statist,* January 10, 1885, p. 36, January 17, 1885, p. 65.

55 Jackson, op. cit. pp. 13-17.

56 Ibid., pp. 17-19.

57 It also built up a reserve fund which was heavily invested in bank shares; it took considerable losses with the City of Glasgow Bank crash of 1878.

58 *The Stock Exchange Yearbook,* 1879, p. 224.

W

59 Jackson, op. cit., pp. 30-5.
60 Ibid., pp. 67-8.
61 *Economist,* April 19, 1884, p. 480.
62 *Statist,* January 17, 1885, p. 65.
63 Jackson, op. cit., p. 23.
64 J. C. Gilbert, *A History of Investment Trusts in Dundee 1873-1938* (1939), p. 20.
65 Jackson, op. cit., p. 56. This trust introduced a new capital structure to the investment trust movement in Scotland with preferred and deferred stock, and with a proposed issue of debenture stock equal to the amount of subscribed rather than paid up capital.
66 D. C. Corner and H. Burton, *Investment and Unit Trusts in Britain and America* (1968), p. 28.
67 *Dundee Yearbook,* 1892, p. 54.
68 Corner and Burton, op. cit., p. 47.
69 Jackson, op. cit., pp. 75-6.
70 W. G. Kerr, "Scottish Investment and Enterprise in Texas", in Payne, op. cit., p. 368.
71 Jackson, op. cit., pp. 77-79.
72 Ibid., pp. 79-80.
73 Ibid., pp. 82-3. The Montana Sheep and Cattle Co. Ltd. in Leith; the Chalk Butters Ranche and Cattle Co. Ltd. in Greenock; the Deervale Ranche Co. Ltd. in Glasgow; each was capitalized at less than £10,000.
74 The procedure for forming cattle companies is excellently covered by Professor Jackson's book, pp. 83-4, See also *Statist,* January 10, 1885, p. 36.
75 *Dundee Year Book,* 1882, p. 28.
76 *Statist,* February 7, 1885, pp. 150-51, gives an account of the practice.
77 Jackson, op. cit., pp. 210-19. For details of the Canadian and Australian land companies, see *Burdett's Official Intelligence,* 1884; also *Statist,* January 17, 1885, p. 65.
78 Edinburgh Stock Exchange, Minutes, June 2, 1882. By 1884 it was in liquidation following a fall in the demand for timber.
79 *Statist,* January 17, 1885, p. 64. For details of the companies see Jackson, op. cit., pp. 220-34.
80 *Statist,* January 10, 1885, p. 36.
81 *Burdett's Official Intelligence,* 1884, p. 1, 351. One was a Glasgow Company, Indian Gold Mines, formed in 1879 with a capital of £110,000, paid up £86,825.
82 *Economist,* December 19, 1885, p. 1, 537.
83 Jackson, op. cit., p. 152.
84 Jackson, op. cit., chapter 7; The Arizona Copper Co., Scotland's Greatest Mining Venture.
85 Ibid., p. 161.
86 *Economist,* December 28, 1895, p. 1, 676.
87 *Economist,* January 12, 1895, pp. 40-41.
88 *Glasgow Stock Exchange Association Records,* op. cit., pp. 18-19.
89 *Economist,* November 25, 1909, May 28, 1910. London dealing in rubber shares was split between the Stock Exchange and the newly established Mincing Lane Tea and Rubber Share Brokers' Association who used to call over procedure adopted from the produce market; *Economist,* March 5, 1910.
90 *Stock Exchange Year Book,* 1914.

91 Issues of the securities of United States railroads were insignificant in London during 1862-70; during the early 1870s the pace quickened and they ran at between £12-14 million a year, Jenks, op. cit., p. 426. By 1883 137 American rail securities were quoted in London with a paid up value of over £300 million.

92 *Economist,* April 19, 1884, p. 48. October 2, 1886, p. 1, 223.

93 These were, Oakbank (1869), Dalmeny (1870), Uphall (1871), Western Calder, and Scottish Mineral Oil (1872). In 1871 there were over 50 firms in the industry, mostly small.

94 *Statist,* January 10, 1885, p. 37. Among these were, Burntisland (1881), Walkinshaw (1880), Clippens (started in 1878 but issued shares in 1882), Lanark (1883), Bathgate (1883), Hermand (1883), Pumpherston (1883 – later to form one of the largest combines) and Linlithgow (1884).

95 *The Statist* commented on what it regarded as the uniqueness of a provincial scare, suggesting that Capel Court might pick up some hints about such experiences; "A Scottish scare is something to remember. It is a grand combination of panic and skedaddle. There is no standing on ceremony in the general belt. Like a herd of frightened sheep, the holders of a 'scared' stock shut their eyes, hang their heads between their legs, and run for their lives without looking where they go". *Statist,* June 4, 1887, p. 598.

96 Ibid., p. 598, In 1887, £6 per share was written off Young's capital.

97 *Economist,* July 19, 1913, p. 114. Among the oil section of the Glasgow list in 1913 were, Mexican Eagle, Shell, Trinidad Oilfields, and California Oilfields.

98 Although local firms had been converted to limited companies the capital was firmly held in family hands.

99 Marwick, *Economic Developments in Victorian Scotland,* op. cit., pp. 81-2; see also D. Chapman, "The Establishment of the Jute Industry", *Review of Economic Studies,* Vol. VI, pp. 33-55.

100 In 1890 six shipping companies were included in the Aberdeen list.

101 Aberdeen Stock Exchanges, Minutes, May 1899.

102 Details of company registrations under the Companies Acts for Scotland are given in the Stock Exchange Year Books.

103 A. K. Cairncross, Home and Foreign Investment 1870-1913, (1953), p. 97.

104 *Glasgow Stock Exchange Association Records,* op. cit., pp. 44-5.

105 Glasgow was particularly dilatory in accepting the reopening conditions set by the authorities and extended the date of acceptance of new conditions until January 11; *Economist,* January 2, 1915, pp. 4-5. Glasgow also staged a minor rebellion against the Treasury during the 1931 crisis. On November 16, 1931, London decided to resume account dealings after the crisis suspension but without options and contangoes. Glasgow regarded this decision as timorous and decided to allow both activities because it maintained that the ban did not prevent continuations but merely made them inconvenient and dearer, and because it was damaging to the market to prevent them. Later, however, Glasgow reviewed its decision "at the special request of the Treasury". Presumably London in the first instance had received equally direct approaches; *Economist,* November 14, 1931, p. 922.

106 *Economist,* November 28, 1914, p. 946.

107 Glasgow Stock Exchange, Minutes, October 1914.

108 *Stock Exchange Year Book,* 1924.

109 The Clyesdale Bank is wholly owned by the Midland Bank.

110 Corner and Burton, op. cit., p. 47. English investment trusts are heavily concentrated in London.
111 Ibid., p. 72.
112 *Economist,* March 14, 1936, pp. 595-6.
113 *Issuing House Year Book,* 1926-1939.
114 Calculated from *'The Times' New Issue Year Books.*
115 Edinburgh Stock Exchange, Minutes, March 14, 1961; Aberdeen Stock Exchange, Minutes, August 7, 1961.
116 I. M. Fyfe, "The Scottish Stock Exchange" *The Three Banks Review,* June 1971, pp. 28-33. Details of transactions done on the Scottish markets appear regularly in *Financial Statistics,* (H.M.S.O.).

Postscript

In 1969 the Federation of Stock Exchanges in Great Britain and Ireland drew up a broad outline for an amalgamation of the Federated Stock Exchanges into a single organization. By November 1971 a detailed scheme to achieve that end was submitted to the members of all the Federated Stock Exchanges and in March 1972 they voted in favour of its acceptance, so that a single organization to be called *The Stock Exchange* will come into being in March 1973.

It will be governed by a council of forty-six members, eleven of which will be elected by provincial members. The present Federation will be dissolved, and it is anticipated that the Council of Associated Stock Exchanges will also be wound up. Administrative arrangements will be centred on London, assisted by local administrative units based on the present regional exchanges. Regional lists will continue to be issued, but the vetting of quotations will be cenralized in London. There will be a central Compensation Fund. As to settlements the long term plan is to work towards a single system, but in the meantime three settlement systems will be continued based on London, Midland/Northern and Scottish. The general principle to be followed until the setting up of a single system is that the payment for and delivery of stock must be in accordance with the practice of the trading floor on which the bargain was done.

There will be a single membership subscription on the basis that all facilities are for the use of all members. In general identical rules will apply, although provision will be made for variation in some practices as between regional units. In order to conform to the single status of members under the present London rules it is hoped that dual capacity will cease by the date of inception, although there are provisions for its continuation in exceptional circumstances. Under the new rules provincial brokers will have direct access to London jobbers either by having a dealer on the London floor, or by methods other than personal contact, but jobbers will be free to decide to what extent they will use such methods for provincial links.

In the long term some provincial floors will be closed down, but there is little likelihood of any sudden closures. The council will not have such powers within the first three years, and during the ensuing six it can only close down a trading floor if the action is approved by a majority of four-fifths of the votes cast. However, a floor may be closed at any time at the request of the local committee responsible for such a trading floor.

Appendix

STOCK EXCHANGE RECORDS

1. *Minutes*

	Date of Formation	Minutes of Committees for General Purposes consulted
England and Wales		
Liverpool	1836	1836 – 1960
Manchester	1836	1836 – 1939
Sheffield	1844	1850 – 1969
Leeds	1844	1845 – 1965
Bristol	1845	1845 – 1938
Hull	1845+	n. a.
Newcastle	1845	1876 – 1961
York	1845+	n. a.
Huddersfield	1845+, 1899*	1899 – 1963
Nottingham	1845+, 1909*	1909 – 1965
Halifax	1845+, 1896*	n. a.
Bradford	1845+, 1899*	1899 – 1965
Leicester	1845+	n. a.
Birmingham	1845	1845 – 1939
Oldham	1875	1881 – 1953
Cardiff	1892	n. a.
Swansea	1903	n. a.
Newport	1916	n. a.
Scotland		
Glasgow	1844	1844 – 1850
Edinburgh	1844	1844 – 1966
Aberdeen	1845	1845 – 1961
Dundee	1879	1879 – 1953
Greenock	1888	n. a.

+ lapsed within a few years; * reconstituted.
The minutes of the Council of Associated Stock Exchanges were consulted over the period 1890 – 1970.

2. *Rule Books*

The following printed rule books are available.

Liverpool	1846, 1866, 1901	Birmingham	1938
Leeds	1845, 1903	Oldham	1922
Bristol	1845	Cardiff	1925
Newcastle	1845	Edinburgh	1923
Nottingham	1942	Aberdeen	1911
Halifax	1902	Dundee	1885

3. *Share Lists*

The following lists are held by the stock exchanges.

Liverpool	from 1960 onwards	Huddersfield	from 1915 onwards
Manchester	„ 1886 „	Nottingham	„ 1910 „
Sheffield	„ 1875 „	Bradford[1]	„ 1900 „
Leeds	„ 1847 „	Oldham	„ 1919 „
Bristol	„ 1937 „	Glasgow[2]	„ 1845 „
Newcastle	„ 1850 „	Dundee	„ 1879 „

1. These are now at the Liverpool Stock Exchange.
2. Glasgow list from 1845 – 1963 are deposited at the University of Strathclyde.

The lists of the Edinburgh and Aberdeen Stock Exchanges were not kept by the respective committees.

Where lists were not available the local press was used since invariably they carried a shortened local share list. As local associations close down, and as others reduce their records for reasons of space, it is likely that some may be lost. It is to be hoped that the stock exchange authorities concerned will deposit such records as they no longer wish to keep with a local civic or university library.

Index

Aberdeen Stock Exchange: call-over,
289; commissions, 293; committees,
294; early brokers, 286; entry re-
quirements, 294; formation, 286;
membership, 287; new issues, 318;
premises, 295; settlements, 291;
share list, 290
Advertising, 109
Agents, 87–88, 217–18
American railway shares, 312
Ashton & Todd, 189
Ashton Todd McLaren, 111
Asquith, H. H., 176
Association of Provincial Stock and
Share Brokers, 212

Baines, Thomas, 7, 25n
Bank Charter Act, 1833, 13
Banking Copartnership Act, 1826, 13
Bank of England: consol transfers,
170–171, 172, 173–79, 181, 182,
183; cotton amalgamations, 161;
crisis of 1914, 228–34; local autho-
rity stocks, 184, 185, 186; Second
World War, 240; stock issues, 182–
83; stock registers, 4
Barber, Christopher & Sons, 258
Barry, J. D., 43–44
Bartlett, A. E., & Co., 249
Barton frauds, 110, 193–94
Beck, L., 54
Belfast Stock Exchange, 198, 223, 273
Bell, Cowan & Co., 315
Bell, Lawrie, Robertson & Co., 318
Bell, William, 91, 205
Birmingham Industrial Trust, 258
Birmingham Sharebrokers' Associa-
tion, 66
Birmingham Stock Exchange: adver-
tising, 109; call-over, 76, 236;
clerks, 97; commissions, 85, 86–87,

216, 218, 242; consols, 172–73;
country jobbing, 220-21, 236, 237;
crisis of 1914, 229, 231–32; defaulters, 108; dual capacity firms, 273;
early brokers, 65–66; entry requirements, 95, 96; formation, 66–
67; marketable lots, 78; membership, 72, 235; new issues, 249, 256,
258; outside brokers, 91, 199, 200;
price boards, 78; premises, 100–
101; quotations, 198; Second World
War, 240; settlements, 84; share
list, 33, 42, 66, 67, 79, 80, 132, 256;
shunting, 241; special settlements
in cycle shares, 132; telegraph facilities, 102, 104
Blount, Edward, 43
Borough Bank of Liverpool, 121
Boult, E. S., & Co., 37, 38
Boys-Stones, Simpson & Spencer, 112
Bradbury, Sir John, 178, 233
Bradford Stock Exchange: country
jobbing, 223; early brokers, 64;
formation, 64; re-constituted, 64
Bradley, Barnard & Co., 55
Braithwaite, Sir John, 222
Breweries, 127
Bristol Stock Exchange: advertising,
109; country broking, 223; country
jobbing, 237; defaulters, 108; dual
capacity firms, 273; early brokers,
54–55; formation, 55–57; hotel
shares, 248; new issues, 249, 256,
258; outside brokers, 198–99, 200;
premises, 101; railway share market in 1845, 39; settling days, 83–
84; share list, 33, 79, 257; shunting,
241; telegraph facilities, 103, 104
British Electricity Authority, 246
British Plate Glass Co., 115
British Shareholders Trust Ltd., 251–
52

British Transport Commission, 245
Broking capital, 106–107
Brooks, Samuel, 38
Brown, George Alexander, 21
Brunner, Mond & Co., 135
Bubble Act, 1720, 3, 8, 115
Buchanan, Gardner & Tennant, 318
Bunting, John, 146, 155

Cain, John N., 99
Call market system, 74–78, 234, 236, 289
Canals, 5–7, 65
Canal and dock companies, 128
Capital Issues Committee, 257
Cardiff Stock Exchange: country jobbing, 223; crisis of 1914, 232; dual capacity firms, 273; early brokers, 68; formation, 68; mining shares, 246, 257; new issues, 249, 258; quotations, 198
Carr, George, 43
Case, Leach & Co., 111
Cattle ranch companies, 305–309
Central Enquiry Bureau, 91, 206
Central Stock Payment, 278
Chadwick, David, 68, 123, 301
Chamberlain, Joseph, 104, 195
Chapman, W., & Co., 258
City of Glasgow Bank, 121
Coal companies, 68, 127–28, 246, 257, 300–301
Coal Industry Nationalization Act, 1946, 245
Coglan, T., 10, 11, 17, 79
Cohen Committee on Company Law, 1945, 215, 254
Coleman, Benjamin, 81
Collinson & Flint, 57
Collis, E. A., 237
Committee on Share Pushing, 1937, 252
Commissions, 85–87, 201–206, 216–18, 242, 284, 292–93, 317
Companies Acts: 1844, 116, 152; 1855, 117, 121; 1856, 117, 121; 1862, 117, 121
Company Clauses Consolidation Act, 1845, 42

Company promotion, 136
Consols: account dealings, 170; additional transfer facilities, 171–73; amount outstanding in 1853, 169; cash settlements, 170–71; consol holdings, 169; inscribed stock, 174–75, 177; new issues, 178; provincial dealings, 171, 180; provincial jobbers, 183; registered transfers, 174, 177, 178, 179, 181–82; War Loan, 179
Contract notes, 80–81
Cooke, Henry & Son., 237, 258
Cooke, Joshua, 98
Co-ordination Committee, 266
Copper mining companies, 310
Cotton mills: amalgamations, 161–62; capitalization, 147; capital gearing, 155–56; dealing in shares at a discount, 160–61; finance, 151–52, 155, 156, 160; foreign competition, 159; loan money, 152, 153–54, 158, 159, 160, 161; promoters, 146; promotion, 145–46, 147, 154; reconstruction boom of 1919, 156–57, 158; share denominations, 147; sources of capital, 147–48
Council of Associated Stock Exchanges: administration, 195–96; advertising, 62, 109; Clearing Guarantee Fund, 278; Code Laws, 196–97; country jobbing, 218–25, 239; commissions, 90, 201–206, 216–18; compensation funds, 268, 272; conference of 1939, 221–22; consol transfer, 173–74, 176, 177, 178, 182; constitution, 211; formation, 194; gilt edged, 225; indefeasibility of transfers, 194–95; outside brokers, 92, 198–201, 213–15; quotation requirements, 197–98, 215–16; Rule 88, 224; shunting, 201, 202, 204, 209n, 225
Country jobbing, 73–74, 77, 218–25, 236, 237, 239, 270–71, 273–77
Crichton Bros. & Townley, 249
Cropper, Edward, 38
Cunliffe, Lord, 178
Customs and Inland Revenue Act, 1878, 80
Cycle boom, 129–32

Dear, J. Arnitt & Co., 237
Daniel, H. A., 186
Davies, Henry & Co., 18, 19, 44
Dawson, Richard, 14, 17, 30
Defaulters, 106–109
Dublin Stock Exchange, 103, 130
Duff, Thomas, 313
Dundee Stock Exchange: call-over, 289; committees, 294; early brokers, 287; entry requirements, 294; formation, 287; membership, 287; new issues 318; premises, 295; settlements, 292; share list, 290
Dunlop Tyre Co., 131
Dutch-Rhenish Railway, 44, 45

Eadon, George, 36
East India Company, 3, 6
Easthope, Sir John, 43
Edinburgh Stock Exchange: call-over, 289; commissions, 292–93; committees, 294; crisis of 1914, 315–16; early brokers, 284–85; entry requirements, 293, 294; formation, 285; membership, 287; new issues, 318; premises, 295; quotations, 315; rules, 285; rival associations, 285–86; settlements, 291; share list, 290, 318; telegraph facilities, 295–96
Edwards, G., & Sons, 54
Edwards, John, 99
Electricity Act, 1947, 246
Electric Telegraph Co., 102
English, H., 8
Evans, Thomas, 108
Exchange banks, 299
Exchange Telegraph Co., 103, 105

Federation of Stock Exchanges in Great Britain and Ireland: branch offices, 268; compensation funds, 268; constitution, 267; dealing arrangements, 269–70, 274–77; emerging jobbers, 270–71; formation, 266–67; margin of solvency, 268; professional standards, 269; quotation rules, 260–61, 268; regulations, 267

Finance Acts: 1899, 61, 64; 1911, 174, 176; 1920, 221, 237; 1931, 221, 237
Fleming, Robert, 303, 304, 305, 306
Flint, T. W., & Co., 59
Forged Transfers Act, 1881, 110, 195
Freeguard & Co., 258
French railways: British participation, 43–44, 45; early companies, 43; provincial interest in, 44, 45, 46
Fyshe & Horton, 249

Gas Act, 1948, 246
Gas companies, 9, 25–26n, 129, 246, 287
George, D. Lloyd, 176
Gibbs & Viney, 237
Gilmour & Shaw, 315
Gladstone, Robert, 38
Gladstone, W. E., 173
Glasgow Stock Exchange: call-over, 289; carry-over, 292; clerks, 288; commissions, 218, 284, 292–93, 317; committees, 294; contract notes, 290; crisis of 1914, 315–16; early brokers, 283; entry requirements, 293, 294; formation, 283; jobbers, 288; membership, 284, 287, 288; new issues, 318; outside brokers, 284; premises, 295; price boards, 290; quotations, 315; rival associations, 284; settlements, 290–91, 311; share list, 290, 316, 317, 318; shunting, 241, 288; telegraph facilities, 295–96
Goodyear, Charles, 312
Greenock Stock Exchange, 287, 318, 319
Grindod, C., 172
Guild, John, 305
Gwent & West of England Enterprises Ltd., 258

Haberfield, Sir John, 55, 56
Halifax Stock Exchange: early brokers, 63–64; formation, 64; re-constituted, 64
Hatry Crash, 250
Henriques, D. Q., & Co., 237, 249, 258

Henriques, Edgar, & Co., 274
Heywood, Kennard & Co., 188
Higginson & Co., 251
Hill, Samuel & Co. Ltd., 259
Hodgson, David, 38
Hooley, E. T., 131, 136
Hornby, Joseph, 38
Hornsby & Co., 5
Huddersfield Stock Exchange: country jobbing, 223; early brokers, 61; formation, 61–62
Hudson, George, 41
Hudson's Bay Company, 3
Hull Exchange & Commercial Building Co., 58
Hull New Stock Exchange, 57, 58

Indian gold mining companies, 309–10
Inglis, Sir Robert, 202, 203
Insurance companies, 7–8, 118–20, 248, 296–97, 317
Investment companies, 297
Investment trusts, 304–305, 317–18
Ireland, W. H., & Co., 111
Irish railways, 42–43
Iron and steel companies, 122–23, 301
Irwin & Aspinall, 107

Jackman, W. T., 6
Jenkins Committee on Company Law, 1962, 267, 271–72, 278, 319
Johnson, Bradley & Walter, 107
Joint Advisory Committee on Stock Exchanges, 211–12
Joint stock banks: bank share market, 121–22; boom of 1836, 13–16; Scottish banks, 296, 317
Jones, Crewdson & Yorath, 135
Julott, Charles James, 21
Jute companies, 313–14

Kaffir boom, 189, 311
Kerr, Leather & Hollows, 237
Kidger, John, 145, 147, 152
Kidston, Geoff & Co., 318
Kleinwort Benson, 259

Land and timber companies, 309
Langston, Thomas, 21, 22, 23
Lappin, James, 194
Lawrence, Charles, 43
Lawrie & Kerr, 308, 315
Lawson, H. J., 131
Lawson, W. R., 302, 309
Lea, Nathaniel, 66, 111
Lea, N., Barham & Brooks, 111
Leeds Commercial Exchange, 53, 54
Leeds Sharebrokers' Association, 53, 54
Leeds Stock Exchange: call-over, 76–77, 236; defaulters, 108; early brokers, 51–52; entry requirements, 95, 96; formation, 52–53; new issues, 249; outside brokers, 199; overseas investments, 188; premises, 101; railway share market in 1845, 40, 48n, 53; regionalization, 272; rival associations, 53; settlements, 83; share list, 33, 51; shunting, 241; telegraph facilities, 102, 103
Leeds, Thomas, & Son, 21
Leicester Stock Exchange: early brokers, 64–65; formation, 65; share list, 65
Levyssohn, Edward H., 22
Lewis, Pitt, 194
Lings, Scott, 135
Liverpool & Manchester Railway, 10, 28, 30, 33
Liverpool New Stock Exchange, 18–20
Liverpool Party, 31–32
Liverpool Stock Exchange: account periods, 81–82; call-over, 75–76, 77; carry-over, 84–85; clerks, 97; commissions, 85, 87; committees, 97; consols, 171; crisis of 1914, 228–34; defaulters, 106–107; dual capacity firms, 273; early brokers, 17; entry requirements, 95, 96; forged transfers, 194, 195; formation, 17–18; inspector of clearing, 82–83; jobbers, 236, 237; Kaffir market, 189; marketable lots, 78; membership, 72, 235; new issues, 249, 256, 258; outside brokers, 18, 91, 200, 213; overseas investments, 188, 190; premises, 99–100; price

boards, 78; quotations, 138, **139**, 215; railway share market in 1845, 37, 39; reserve funds, 99; rival association, 18; settling days, 81–82; share list, 11, 15, 33, 42, 45, 79, 80, 247, 256; shunting, 88, 89, 90, 241; special settlements, 34, 138; telegraph facilities, 102, 104

Local authority stocks: early issues, 183–84; local quotations, 187; London jobbers, 186; tender issues, 185–86; transfers, 184–85; underwriting by provincial brokers, 187

London Stock Exchange: advertising, 109; agency rules, 217–18; agents for provincial brokers, 87–88; commissions, 85, 86, 87, 88, 201, 203, 216–18, 242; compensation fund, 268; conference of 1939, 221–22; country jobbing, 218–25, 270–71; crisis of 1914, 228–34; early railway share boom, 32–33; formation, 3, 4; gilt edged prices, 225; outside brokers, 199–200, 213–15; quotation rules, 268; Rule 88, 224; Second World War, 239–40; share list, 4, 33, 35; shunting, 89–91, 201–202, 219–20, 225, 241; single capacity, 201

Low, Joseph, 4

Lowson & Ormrod, 249

Lyddon & Thomas, 258

McEwan, Alexander, 301

MacEwan, Andrew, 283

Macgregor, Walker, & Co., 318

Mackenzie, Murdo, 309

Mackenzie, William, 303, 309

Macmillan Committee, 1931, 251

Manchester Cash Stock Exchange, 24, 27n

Manchester Commercial Exchange, 23

Mancheser Stock Exchange: call-over, 77, 234, 236; carry-over, 84; clerks, 97; commissions, 85, 87, 218, 242; consols, 171; country jobbers, 237; crisis of 1914, 228–34; defaulters, 107, 108; dual capacity firms, 273; early brokers, 21–22; entry requirements, 95; forged

transfers, 195; formation, 22–23; marketable lots, 78; membership, 72, 235; new issues, 249, 256, 258; outside brokers, 23–24, 91, 200, 201; overseas investments, 188, 190; premises, 100; quotations, 138, 139, 198, 215; reserve funds, 99; rival associations, 23, 24, 27n; settlements, 81, 83; share list, 33, 42, 79, 118, 245, 248, 256; shunting, 90, 204, 241; special settlements, 34, 138; telegraph facilities, 102, 105;

Margetts & Addenbrooke, 111, 258

Martin Hardie B., & Co., 183, 237

Mellor, S. F., 157

Mewburn & Barker, 189

Midland Industrial & General Trust, 252

Midland Trust, 252

Midland & Western Stock Exchange: clearing system, 277–78; emerging jobbers, 274; formation, 272; share list, 263

Mills, Granville, 157

Moore, William, 61

Mortgage and investment companies, 302–304

Moss, John, 38, 43

Motor car companies, 132–33, 248

Muncaster, Richard, 50

Murray & Co., 258

National Association of Shareholders, 194

National Coal board, 245–46

National Debt, 4

Nationalization, 245–46

Neilson, Hornby, Crichton & Co., 110

Neville Industrial Securities, 252, 258

Newcastle Sock Exchange: call-over, 236; country jobbing, 223; crisis of 1914, 232; early brokers, 59; formation, 59; premises, 102; share list, 59, 79; share market, 257; shunting, 241

New issue boom, 1928, 249–50

New issues, costs of, 137, 254–55, 261–62

New issues, post-war provincial, 257

Newport Stock Exchange, 69, 196

Nicholson, Cyril, & Co., 239
Nicholson, J. W., & Sons, 162, 220, 223, 225, 237–39, 258
Northern Counties Brokers' Association, 272
Northern Stock Exchange: clearing system, 277; emerging jobbers, 274; formation, 272; share list, 263
Northern Territories Trust, 252
Nottingham & Midland Stock Exchange: early brokers, 62–63; formation, 62–63; re-constituted, 63
Nuttall, William, 146, 165n

Ogilvie, Andrew, 287, 294, 308
O'Hagan, H.O., 127
Oldham Stock Exchange: dealing practices, 150, 162, 163; early brokers, 146, 148; early share markets, 149–50; formation of the Lancashire Sharebrokers' Association, 150–51n, Manchester group, 150; membership, 164; premises, 151; rival organizations, 158–59; rules, 163; share list, 158, 162, 164
One ship companies, 68, 141n, 248
Outside brokers, 18, 23–24, 91–92, 199–200, 213–15, 284
Overend, Guerney & Co., 117
Overseas investments, 187–90;
Owens, John, 107

Palgrave, Inglis, 195
Parkes, William, 116
Parsons & Co., 318
Pearson, Conner & Co., 318
Pearson, James, 66, 71n
Peel, Sir Robert, 12, 13, 121
Peet & Son, 62
Penny & Macgregor, 318
Permission to deal, 254
Phillips, John, 99
Placings and introductions, 254, 258, 259–60
Platt, Ernest, 157
Post-war boom, 1919, 246–47
Powell, T. W., 76
Price boards, 78–79
Property companies, 301–302
Provincial Brokers' Stock Exchange,

211, 212–13, 215, 222, 225, 226n, 266, 267
Public issues and offers for sale, 253, 260

Quotations, 137–39, 198, 215, 260, 315

Rae, Edward, 89, 110, 175, 195, 197, 199, 203, 204, 205
Rae, George, 110, 170, 195
Railton, J., & Son., 22, 37, 111
Railton, Sons & Leedham, 111
Railway Act, 1921, 245, 316
Railway amalgamations, 245, 316
Railway carriage and wagon companies, 124
Railways: early promotions, 28–29; formation of companies, 29–30; Liverpool shareholders, 38–39, 48n; preference shares, 42; provincial quotation requirements, 34; relief from share calls, 41; Scottish railway companies, 298–300; shareholders, 30, 31, 32, 38; share allotment, 31, 40; share dealings, 34–35, 47n; share index, 36; share price movements, 36; size of provincial markets, 36–37, 48n; speculative dealings, 37, 47n
Reading, Lord, 233
Regionalization, 272–73
Reid, John, 285, 296, 297, 298
Rensburg & Co., 183, 237
Richardson, Goodluck & Co., 4
Richmond, Horace, 99
Ridsdale, J. H., 44, 51, 53
Ritchie, W. M., 294
Roberts, J. B. & R., 51
Rubber boom, 1909–10, 311–12
Rudge, Percy, 99

Salt Union, 135
Schroeder, J. H., & Co., 251
Schuster, Leo, 38
Scott, W. R., 3
Scottish company registrations, 1863–79, 301
Scottish mining companies, 310–11

Scottish Stock Exchange: clearing system, 277; dual capacity firms, 273, 274; formation, 318–19; jobbers, 319; membership, 318–19
Scrivenor, Harry, 98
Shale oil companies, 312–13
Share auctions, 9–10
Sharp, A. E., & Co., 258
Sheffield & Hallamshire Stock Exchange, 51
Sheffield Stock Exchange: call-over, 236; country jobbing, 223; crisis of 1914, 229, 232; early brokers, 50; formation, 51; marketable lots, 78; membership, 72; new issues, 258; outside brokers, 199; overseas investments, 188; premises, 101–102; rival association, 51; share list, 33, 50–51, 79, 246, 257; shunting, 241; telegraph facilities, 103, 104
Shields, Matthew, 295
Shipping companies, 120, 297, 314
Shunting, 73–74, 77, 88–92, 201–202, 204, 219–20, 225, 241, 275, 288
Sibary, Thomas, 58
Simpson, Albert, 152
Singer & Friedlander, 259
Sohmes & Tripp, 44
Somerset House List, 212, 213
South Sea Bubble, 3
Smith, F. E. & S., 51, 237
Smith, Keen, Barnett & Co., 66, 111, 237, 258
Stamp Act, 1891, 61
Staveacre, F. W., & Co., 237, 249
Steel Act, 1949, 246
Stock, B. S., Son & Co., 111, 258
Sun Mill Co., 145
Swansea Stock Exchange, 68–69, 196

Telegraph system, 102–104
Telegraph and telephone companies, 124, 126
Tennant family, 300, 301
Textile amalgamations, 135–36

Thackeray & Sayce, 68
Thomson, Poulett, 12, 13
Tilney & Co., 109–110, 258
Tinley, T., & Co., 111
Tobacco company amalgamations, 136
Trading Companies Act, 1834, 115
Trawling Companies, 314
Treasury: consol transfers, 174, 175, 176, 177, 178; control of new issues, 234; crisis of 1914, 229–34, 316, 317; Second World War, 239–40, 257
Trustee Investment Act, 1889, 184
Tudor, Owen, 99

Underwood, Frank L., 306
Underwriting, 136–37, 253
United Alkali, 135
United Stock Exchange, 266, 273, 325–26

Wall & Lloyd, 180–81, 183, 204
Water companies, 8–9, 128–29
Watson, James, 283, 294, 296, 297
Watson, John, & Co., 51
Watson, R. B., & Co., 37, 51, 52, 53
Wever, Frank, & Son, 51
Wheelock, T., & H., 237
White, Sir George, 127, 198
Wilkie, Thomas, 5
Wilkinson, Charles, 57, 58
Wilkinson, John, 64
Winstanley, T., 10
Wise, Speak, Sherlock & Edmondson, 258
Withers, Richard, 75, 86, 108, 171, 172, 173
Woodcock, H. C., & Co., 237, 249
Wotherspoon, Matthew, 39

York Stock Exchange, 60